PYRAMID FOOTBALL

THE NON-LEAGUE FOOTBALLERS
WHO'S WHO

EDITOR: TONY WILLIAMS

**COMPILERS: STEVE WHITNEY
BRUCE SMITH**

Published by Tony Williams

ISBN No.   1 869 833 13 9

Typesetting: Kentones

Photo Reproduction: Westspring Graphics, Weston-S-Mare.
Colour Reproduction: Isca Reprographics, Exeter.
Production Control: Ken Bithell.

Printed by: Richard Clay Ltd, Bungay, Suffolk.

Distributed by: Little Red Witch Book Distribution,
Helland Cottage, Helland, North Curry, Taunton, Somerset TA3 6DU
Tel: 0823 490684   Fax: 0823 490281

It hasn't been easy!

We knew it would take time to persuade players to fill in their details on questionnaire, especially as this 'Who's Who' was the first in the series, and neither club officials or their players quite knew what was expected of them.

Our thanks go to the hundreds who have taken the time to answer our questions and we hope this book will make their efforts seem worthwhile. We know a number of senior players (indeed some clubs) are missing but hopefully each edition will become more comprehensive as more replies are received.

We have attempted to make the book both useful and amusing while also photographically stimulating and statistically interesting. At least the players within the Pyramid football leagues have received a little of the star treatment which we hope they and their supporters will appreciate.

Tony Williams

EDITOR: TONY WILLIAMS.

Editorial Assistants: Adrian Barber, Ken Bithell, George Brown, Bruce Smith, Steve Whitney, Michael Williams, James Wright.

Editorial Address: Helland Cottage, Helland, North Curry, Taunton, Somerset. TA3 6DU.

Acknowledgements

The early collection of forms was kindly undertaken by Steve Whitney and Bruce Smith and Steve went on to 'chase' some of the missing senior players and transfer the information of all those at the top of the pyramid on to computer discs.

Steve's knowledge of senior players, their clubs and their transfers is immense, and regular readers of 'The Non-League Club Directory' will be pleased to hear that his club players' lists will be back in next season's edition.

Our thanks go to Steve for all his help and enthusiasm and hopefully the groundwork put in will enable future Who's Who compilations to be even more comprehensive.

The excellent work of Ken Bithell on production control, the colour separations of Isca at Exeter and the black and white bromides of Westspring Graphics is greatly appreciated. It's a very good 'team' that seems to be going from strength to strength.

Special thanks go to all our photographers and if we have missed any from the list on Page 256 we sincerely apologise.

Abbley, Steve   (D)
(GLOUCESTER CITY)

D.O.B. 19.3.57   **Nickname:** Abbs
Profession: Accountant
Single
Hobbies: Football, Golf

PLAYING CAREER

Honours: Swindon Boys & Wilts County Rep; FA XI; Southern Lge Prem Div Winners Medal

Club	Seasons	Transfer	Apps	Goals
Swindon Town	79-84		23	
Cheltenham Town	84-85			
Witney Town	84-85			
Cheltenham Town	85-88			
Wycombe Wanderers	88-90			
Trowbridge Town	1990			

Abbott, Gary   (F)
(WELLING UNITED)

D.O.B. 7.11.64   **Nickname:** Abbo
Profession: Pipe Fitter
Married   **Wife's name:** Kay
Children: Sydnee
Hobbies: Swimming, Tennis, Snooker

PLAYING CAREER

Honours: London Youth Rep; England Semi-Pro Int; Southern Lge Premier Div Winners; Kent Senior Cup Winners; Welling P.O.Y. 85/86

Club	Seasons	Transfer	Apps	Goals
Welling United	81-87	£15,000		
Barnet	87-88	£40,000		
Enfield	88-90	£30,000		

GARY ABBOTT

Acaster, Simon   (G)
(SELBY TOWN)   **Age:** 27
Previous Clubs: None   **Honours:** None

Acklam, Paul   (F)
(GRESLEY ROVERS)   **Age:** 29
Previous Clubs: Long Eaton Utd; Hucknall R-R; Borrowash; Shepshed
Honours: Derbyshire Senior Cup winners (3); Northern Counties (East) Lge winners; Leics Senior Cup winners.

Adams, Richard   (G)
(KEYNSHAM TOWN)   **Age:** 29
Previous Clubs: Dundry Athletic; Robinsons DRG
Honours: Somerset Senior Champions 83-88 (Robinsons DRG)

Adcock, Stephen   (M)
(GRESLEY ROVERS)   **Age:** 29
Previous Clubs: Graham Street; Borrowash Victoria; Heanor Town; Shepshed
Honours: Derbyshire Senior Cup winners

Adorno, John   (F)
(WOLVERTON AFC)   **Age:** 25
Previous Clubs: Milton Keynes City; Olney Town; Leighton Town; Milton Keynes Borough; Berkhampsted Town
Honours: U16 Berks & Bucks runners up; East Anglian Cup winners; Chilton League winners; South Midlands Challenge Trophy runners up 1989/90

Ager, Grant   (M)
(EYNESBURY ROVERS)   **Age:** 22
Previous Clubs: St.Neots Town; Potton United
Honours: UCL 1989; Hinchingbrooke Cup 1988,90; N.Beds Charity Cup 1987,90

Agutter, Timothy   (D)
(RUSHDEN TOWN)

D.O.B. 27.1.61
Profession: Fencing Contractor
Married   **Wife's name:** Kerry
Children: Chloe & Natalie
Hobbies: Golf, Swimming

PLAYING CAREER

Honours: Northampton & Northants Schoolboy Rep.; Beazer Homes Midland Div R/U 89/90

Club	Seasons	Transfer	Apps	Goals
Northampton Town	80-82			
Raunds Town	83-84			
Wellingborough Town	84-88			
Irthlingborough D's	88-89			

Ainsworth, Mark   (M)
(WESTHOUGHTON TOWN)   **Age:** 22
Previous Clubs: Huddersfield Town; Horwich RMI
Honours: None

Airey, Carl (F)
(SALISBURY) Age: 25

Previous Clubs: Barnsley (38-5); Darlington (75-28); Royal Charleroi (Belg); Chesterfield (26-4); Rotherham United (32-11); Torquay United (29-11)
Honours: Sherpa Van Trophy R/U; Division Four Promotion

Akers, Lee (D/M)
(DULWICH HAMLET) Age: 24

Previous Clubs: Carshalton Athletic; Dulwich Hamlet; Bromley; Greenwich Borough; Bromley; Dulwich Hamlet; Malden Vale
Honours: None

Akin, Duncan (D)
(DROYLESDEN) Age: 31

Previous Clubs: Curzon Ashton; Droylsden
Honours: Bass North-West Counties Div 2 Winners 86/87; HFS Loans Lge Div 1 R/U 89/90; HFS Loans Div 1 Cup Winners 87/88

DUNCAN AKIN

Alged, Gordon (G)
(WESTFIELDS) Age: 31

Previous Clubs: Pegasus Juniors
Honours: None

Ali, Wayne (D)
(BRIDLINGTON TOWN) Age: 24

Previous Clubs: North Ferriby United
Honours: None

Allcock, Ian (M)
(NEWCASTLE TOWN) Age: 29

Previous Clubs: Nantwich Town; Hednesford Town; Milton Utd; Newcastle Town; Redgate Clayton; Winsford Town

Honours: British Colleges Staffs u19; British Colleges Cup; West Mids Premier League Cup; Midland Sunday Cup (2); Staffs Sunday Cup; P.P.S Premier League (2)

Allen, Andrew (F)
(BRIDGNORTH TOWN) Age: 31

Previous Clubs: Hednesford Town; Kidderminster H.; Sutton Coldfield T.; Dudley Town; Willenhall Town; Sutton Coldfield T.; Stourbridge;
Honours: West Midlands League Player of the Year; West Midlands League Cup winner; Staffs Senior Cup winner; B'ham Senior Cup runners up; Worcester Senior Cup runners up

Allen, Calvin (F)
(FARSLEY CELTIC) Age: 30

Previous Clubs: None
Honours: None

Allen, Carl (D)
(OLDSWINFORD) Age: 17

Previous Clubs: Staffs Tigers; Gornal Atrhletic
Honours: Staffs County F.A. Youth Cup

Allen, Derek (G)
(MOOR GREEN)

D.O.B. 21.3.62
Profession: Record Promoter
Married Wife's name: Jill
Hobbies: Tennis, Travel, Music
PLAYING CAREER
Honours: Birmingham Boys Rep

Club	Seasons	Transfer	Apps	Goals
Bromsgrove Rovers	80-85			
Alvechurch	85-86			
Redditch United	86-87			

Allen, Richie (F)
(BILLINGHAM SYNTHONIA) Age: 23

Previous Clubs: Stockton

Honours: Northern League Champions 1988/89, 1989/90; Northern League Cup 1987/88, 1989/90; Durham Cup Winners Trophy 1988/89

Allen, Simon (M)
(NEWMARKET TOWN) Age: 26

Previous Clubs: St.Edmunds (1965); Bury Town; Harwich & Parkstone; Stowmarket Town; Newmarket Town
Honours: None

Alleyne, Des (F)
(BANBURY UNITED) Age: 25

Previous Clubs: Kings Heath
Honours: None

Allinson, Martin (D)

(BALDOCK TOWN) **Age:** 29

Previous Clubs: Letchworth Garden City; Hitchin Town; Pirton; Stevenage Borough

Honours: Herts County Schoolboy; Youth & FA Rep

Allport, Darren (F)

(BLACKSTONES) **Age:** 18

Previous Clubs: Stamford

Honours: None

Almond, Andrew (G)

(HORWICH RMI)

D.O.B. 5.5.71
Profession: Salesman
Single
Hobbies: Sport

PLAYING CAREER

Honours:

Club	Seasons	Transfer	Apps	Goals
Charnock Richard	83-87			
Leyland Motors	87-88			
Chorley	88-90			

Anastasi, Savvas (F)

(STAFFORD RANGERS)

D.O.B. 15.12.63 **Nickname:** Savvy
Profession: Caterer
Single
Hobbies: Watching TV

PLAYING CAREER

Honours: None

Club	Seasons	Transfer	Apps	Goals
Wolverhampton United	87-88			
Rocester	88-90			

Anderson, Darren (D)

(SLOUGH TOWN)

D.O.B. 6.9.66 **Nickname:** Wingnut
Profession: Not working
Married **Wife's name:** Lisa
Children: Calum & George (twins)
Hobbies: Sport

PLAYING CAREER

Honours: England Youth Int

Club	Seasons	Transfer	Apps	Goals
Charlton Athletic	83-86		10	1
(Crewe Alexandra - loan - 6)				
Aldershot	86-89		150	6

Anderson, Gary (M)

(ALTRINCHAM)

D.O.B. 5.1.60

PLAYING CAREER

Honours: FA Trophy Winners 85/86; Cheshire Senior Cup Winners

Club	Seasons	Transfer	Apps	Goals
South Liverpool	80-84			
Altrincham	84-87			
Runcorn	87-90			

Anderson, John (D)

(RADFORD) **Age:** 18

Previous Clubs: Keyworth United (Youth); Monty Hind B.C.

Honours: Keyworth United Player of the Year u12/u13; Monty Hind Player of the Year u16, earned County Colours for Nottinghamshire Boys Club, Sportsmanship Trophy winners; Radford Reserve Team Player of the Year; First Team Player of the Year

Anderson, Mick (M)

(GODALMING TOWN) **Age:** 30

Previous Clubs: Godalming Town (Youth); Westfield.
Honours: None

Anderson, Stewart (M)

(WITTON ALBION)

D.O.B. 20.11.59
Profession: Paint Sprayer
Married **Wife's name:** Julie
Children: Mark
Hobbies: Marathon Running

PLAYING CAREER

Honours: Manchester Boys Rep; HFS Loans Div 1 & Prem Winners; NWCL Div 1 & 2 Winners; ATS Lancs Trophy Winners 89 & 90; FA Vase Winners 88

Club	Seasons	Transfer	Apps	Goals
Chadderton	81-86			
Colne Dynamoes	86-90			

Anderson, William (F)

(MEIR KA) **Age:** 31

Previous Clubs: Bucknall Y & A

Honours: Staffs Senior League Champions 1988-89; Walsall Senior Cup winners 1989-90

Andre, Gary (F)

(CROYDON) **Age:** 29

Previous Clubs: Whyteleafe; Bradford City
Honours: None

Angell, Craig (D)

(KINTBURY RANGERS) **Age:** 17

Previous Clubs:
Honours: None

Angell, Darren (M)
(CHASETOWN) Age: 24
Previous Clubs: Tamworth; Rushall; Bilston
Honours: Banks Premier League Cup winners

Archbold, John (M)
(DORKING) Age: 29
Previous Clubs: Maidstone United; Gravesend & Northfleet; Sutton United; Carshalton Athletic
Honours: Vauxhall-Opel Lge Div 2 South Winners, Surrey Senior Cup R/U

JOHN ARCHBOLD

Archer, Vincent (F)
(FARSLEY CELTIC) Age: 29
Previous Clubs: Yorkshire Amateurs; Garforth Town; York Railway Institute
Honours: Northern Counties East Div 1 Lge & Cup Winners 87/88

Arscott, Paul (M)
(LEWES) Age: 21
Previous Clubs: Lewes; Arundel
Honours: None

Arthur, Clive (M)
(STAPENHILL) Age: 31
Previous Clubs: Derby County; Shrewsbury Town; Burton Albion; Buxton Town; Gresley Rovers
Honours: Scoreline Division 1 champions 1989-90; Buxton Player of the Year; Winners of Northern Premier League Cup

Ashby, Nick (D)
(RUSHDEN TOWN)
D.O.B. 29.12.70
Profession: Salesman
Single
Hobbies: Clay Pigeon Shooting

PLAYING CAREER
Honours: Beazer Homes Midland Div R/U 89/90

Club	Seasons	Transfer	Apps	Goals
Nottingham Forest	87-89			

Ashcroft, Ian (D)
(GAINSBOROUGH TOWN) Age: 31
Previous Clubs: Worksop Town; Harworth Colliery
Honours: Central Midlands & Supreme Division winners 1988-89; Webbe Cup 1987-88, 1988-89

Ashenden, Russell (M)
(RUSHDEN TOWN)

D.O.B. 4.2.61   Nickname: Ash or Norm
Profession: Salesman
Married   Wife's name: Jacqui
Children: Alix & Charley
Hobbies: Fitness Training, Sport

PLAYING CAREER
Honours: None

Club	Seasons	Transfer	Apps	Goals
Northampton Town	79-82			
Wycombe Wanderers	82-83			
Corby Town	83-84			
AP Leamington	84-86			
Long Buckby	86-87			
Buckingham Town	87-88			
Rushden Town	88-89			
Long Buckby	89-90			

Ashford, Noel (M)
(REDBRIDGE FOREST)

D.O.B. 15.2.58

PLAYING CAREER
Honours: England Semi-Pro Int; Isthmian Lge Premier Winners 79/80; Alliance Premier Lge Winners 82/83; Gola Lge Winners 85/86; FA Trophy Winners 81/82; Football Directories XI !

Club	Seasons	Transfer	Apps	Goals
Fulham	74-76			
Barking	76-79			
Enfield	79-86	£4,000		
Wycombe Wanderers	86-87	£15,000		
Barnet	87-88	£20,000		
Maidstone United	88-89			

NOEL ASHFORD PHOTO - PAGE 10

Askey, John (F)
(MACCLESFIELD TOWN)

D.O.B. 4.11.64   Nickname: Ask
Profession: Insurance Agent
Married   Wife's name: Elizabeth
Hobbies: Playing Sport

PLAYING CAREER
Honours: England Semi-pro Int, Middx Wanderers, NPL Trophy Winners 85 & 87, Macclesfield P.O.Y. 88/89

Club	Seasons	Transfer	Apps	Goals
Port Vale	80-86			
Milton United	86-87			

JOHN ASKEY

Askins, Sonny (D)

(PENRITH) Age: 17

Previous Clubs:

Honours: None

Astley, Stephen (D)

(GRESLEY ROVERS) Age: 30

Previous Clubs: Park Rangers; Smethwick Highfield; Wolverhampton Utd; Oldbury

Honours: Derbyshire Senior Cup (twice); Banks's League Cup

Aston, Robert (G)

(GRESLEY ROVERS) Age: 30

Previous Clubs: Stoke City; Hanley Town; Eastwood Hanley; Oswestry Town; Welsh Pool; Congleton Town

Honours: Staffs Senior Cup; Derby Senior Cup (3); Mid Cheshire League & Cup (2); Welsh Inter Cup

Atkins, Anthony (M)

(TUNBRIDGE WELLS) Age: 36

Previous Clubs:

Honours: Kent League Champions 1984/85; Kent League Cup winners 1985/86, 1987/88

Atkinson, Brian (M)

(SEATON DELAVAL AMATEURS) Age: 24

Previous Clubs: Benwell Blues; Scotswood S.C

Honours: Northumberland Senior Benevolent Bowl winners; McEwans Northern Alliance Premier Division champions

Atkinson, Patrick (F)

(GATESHEAD)

D.O.B. 22.5.70   Nickname: Paddy
Profession: Sales Rep
Single
Hobbies: Golf,Eating & Drinking

PLAYING CAREER

Honours: Redheugh Boys Rep; Durham Senior Cup R/U 88/89

Club	Seasons	Transfer	Apps	Goals
Sheffield United	86-88			
Hartlepool United	88-89		21	3

Attwood, Richard (G)

(HALESOWEN HARRIERS) Age: 25

Previous Clubs: Halesowen Harriers; Bromsgrove Rovers

Honours: Birmingham Senior Cup winners

Austin, Julian (M)

(KINTBURY RANGERS) Age: 24

Previous Clubs: Great Shefford; Lambourn; New Inn; Swan

Honours: None

Auld, Jamie (D)

(WESTHOUGHTON TOWN) Age: 23

Previous Clubs: Anchor Cables

Honours: None

Aymes, Adrian (M)

(AFC LYMINGTON) Age: 26

Previous Clubs: Eastleigh; Lymington Town; Wellworthy Athletic; Gosport Borough

Honours: None

Ayton, Gary (D)

(CLACTON TOWN) Age: 18

Previous Clubs: Brightlingsea

Honours: None

NOEL ASHFORD (REDBRIDGE FOREST & ENGLAND)

Babb, Darren (D)
(SALTASH UNITED) Age: 22
Previous Clubs: Tavistock; Launceston
Honours: South Western League Rep XI

Bachra, Davinder (M)
(WILLENHALL TOWN) Age: 22
Previous Clubs: University College of Wales, Aberystwyth 1986-89; Aberystwyth Town 1989-90
Honours: None

Back, Geoff (F)
(WESTBURY UNITED) Age: 31
Previous Clubs: Westbury United; Chippenham Town
Honours: Wilts Lge Div 2 runners up; Wilts Lge Subsidary Cup Winners

Baddeley, Kevin (D)
(CHIPPENHAM TOWN) Age: 28
Previous Clubs: Bristol City; Swindon Town; Wealdstone; Cheltenham Town; Trowbridge Town
Honours: Somerset Senior Cup winners; Wilts Premier Shield Winners; Gloucester Senior Cup winners; Southern Premier League champions; Southern League Cup runners up

Bailey, Alan (D)
(BRAINTREE TOWN) Age: 32
Previous Clubs: Haverhill Rovers
Honours: Eastern Counties Lge Winners & R/U; Eastern Counties Lge Cup R/U; FA XI

Bailey, Andrew (G)
(STAPENHILL) Age: 18
Previous Clubs: Schlegal UK; Burton Albion; Moira Utd
Honours: Scoreline Comb Division 1 winners 1989-90

Bailey, Christopher (D)
(OAKWOOD) Age: 26
Previous Clubs:
Honours: Division 2 runners up; Division 2 Cup winners

Bailey, Clifford (M)
(61 FC) Age: 34
Previous Clubs: Vauxhall Motors; Walden Rangers; Shillington; Leighton Town
Honours: None

Bailey, David (M)
(SANDWELL) Age: 23
Previous Clubs: Bromsgrove Rovers; Halesowen Town
Honours: None

Bailey, Nigel (M)
(GAINSBOROUGH TOWN) Age: 28
Previous Clubs: Rochdale; Burnley; Mexborough Town; Rossington Main; Pilkington Recs
Honours: None

Bailey, Stephen (G)
(ROMSEY TOWN) Age: 32
Previous Clubs: Moneyfields; Fareham Town; Waterlooville; Pirelli General; Totton; Fareham Town
Honours: Hants Senior Representative; Wessex League Winners 1989-90

Bailley, Wayne (G)
(KINTBURY RANGERS) Age: 32
Previous Clubs: Hungerford
Honours: Berks & Bucks Representative

Bainbrick, Mark (G)
(BIGGLESWADE TOWN) Age: 28
Previous Clubs: Arlesey Town; Stotfold
Honours: N.Beds Charity Cup winners

Baines, Andrew (F)
(HYDE UNITED)

D.O.B. 21.12.62	Nickname: Chap	
Profession: Sheet Metal Worker		
Married	Wife's name: Susan	
Children: Simon		
Hobbies: Cycling		

PLAYING CAREER
Honours: NWCL Div 1 Winners; NPL Div 1 R/U; Lancs Floodlight Cup Winner & R/U

Club	Seasons	Transfer	Apps	Goals
Ashton United	82-84			
Stalybridge Celtic	84-90			

Baker, Brian (G)
(FARLEIGH ROVERS) Age: 23
Previous Clubs: Faleigh Rovers; Croydon
Honours: None

Baker, Kevin (M/F)
(WINSFORD UNITED) Age: 32
Previous Clubs: Chester City; Witton Albion; Droylsden; Winsford United; Glossop
Honours: None

Baker, Martin (D)
(ALTRINCHAM)

D.O.B. 26.2.67   **Nickname:** Bambi
Professsion: Decisions Support Analyst
Single
Hobbies: Squash

PLAYING CAREER
Honours:

Club	Seasons	Transfer	Apps	Goals
Berkhamsted	83-84			
Watford	84-85			
Rhyl	85-88			

Baker, Neil (M)
(THATCHAM TOWN)   **Age:** 25

Previous Clubs: Ecchinswell; Newbury Town; Kintbury Rangers

Honours: North Hants League winners; North Hants League Cup runners up; Graystone Cup winners & runners up; Hungerford Cup winners & runners up; Rep: Hampshire F.A. 1989/90; Runners up Wessesx League Cup 1989/90

Baker, Paul (F)
(GREAT HARWOOD TOWN)   **Age:** 26

Previous Clubs: Clitheroe

Honours: Lamot Pils Cup 1990

Baker, Sean (F)
(HENDON)

D.O.B. 7.3.62   **Nickname:** Bakes
Profession: Managing Director of Retail Carpet Outlet
Married   **Wife's name:** Julie
Hobbies: Sport

PLAYING CAREER
Honours: Herts County Youth Rep; English County FA Winners; Vauxhall-Opel Lge Div 1 & 2 R/U; Herts Senior Cup Winners & R/U; London Senior Cup R/U; Herts Charity Cup Winners & R/U

Club	Seasons	Transfer	Apps	Goals
Boreham Wood	78-83			
Tottenham Hotspur	83-84			
Maidstone United	85-86			
Finchley	86-87			
Harrow Borough	1987			
Leyton-Wingate	87-88			

Baldwin, John (D)
(FLEETWOOD TOWN)

D.O.B. 13.12.64   **Nickname:** Jez
Profession: Chef
Married   **Wife's name:** Andrea
Children: Jake
Hobbies: Squash, Cycling, Jogging

PLAYING CAREER
Honours: Lancs Schoolboy Rep; Royal Navy & Combined Services Youth Rep; Fleet Air Arm Inter Command Winners 85/86

Club	Seasons	Transfer	Apps	Goals
Leyland Celtic	87-88			
Bamber Bridge	88-89			

Baldwin, Marvin (M)
(HORWICH RMI)

D.O.B. 29.6.68
Profession: Student
Single
Hobbies: Golf,Tennis

PLAYING CAREER
Honours: Lancs Youth Rep; British Polytechnic Rep; NWCL Div 1 Winners

Club	Seasons	Transfer	Apps	Goals
Feniscowles	86-88			
Rossendale United	88-89			

Ball, Brett (M)
(WARMINSTER TOWN)   **Age:** 17

Previous Clubs: None

Honours: None

Ball, Trevor (G)
(NORTHWICH VICTORIA)

D.O.B. 14.2.64   **Nickname:** Lars Elstrup
Profession: Gardener
Single
Hobbies: Cricket

PLAYING CAREER
Honours: Chester Schoolboy Rep.; Welsh Semi-Pro Int; NPL R/U & Presidents Cup Winners; Upton,Rhyl & Bangor P.O.Y.

Club	Seasons	Transfer	Apps	Goals
Upton AA	80-82			
Wem Town	82-83			
Rhyl	83-84			
Bangor City	85-90			

Bancroft, Paul (M)
(KETTERING TOWN)

D.O.B. 10.9.64   **Nickname:** Banky
Profession: Not working
Single
Hobbies: Badminton,Music

PLAYING CAREER
Honours: England Semi-pro Int; FA Trophy R/U 87

Club	Seasons	Transfer	Apps	Goals
Derby County	81-85			
Crewe Alex	loan		21	3
Northampton Town	85-86		25	
Nuneaton Borough	86-87			
Burton Albion	86-87	£12,000		
Kidderminster Harriers	88-90	£12,000		

Banks, Chris (D)
(BATH CITY)

D.O.B. 12.11.65   **Nickname:** Banko
Profession: Not working
Single
Hobbies: All Sports

PLAYING CAREER

Honours: Staffs County Rep; Beazer Homes Lge R/U 89/90; Bath P.O.Y.89/90

Club	Seasons	Transfer	Apps	Goals
Port Vale	82-88		65	2
Exeter City	88-89		45	1

Banks, Kingsley (G)
(BARKING)

D.O.B. 6.12.68
Profession: Not working
Single
Hobbies: Golf, Snooker

PLAYING CAREER

Honours: North-East Essex; Essex & London Schoolboy Rep; Westgate Insurance Cup Winners 88/89; Kent Senior Cup Winners

Club	Seasons	Transfer	Apps	Goals
Tottenham Hotspur	85-87			
Dartford	87-89			
Basildon United	89-90			
Enfield	90-91			

Bardin, Jeffery (M)
(ATHERTON LABURNUM ROVERS) Age: 22

Previous Clubs: Atherton Town

Honours: None

Bareham, Alan (D)
(EYNESBURY ROVERS) Age: 25

Previous Clubs: St.Neots Town; Potton United

Honours: UCL Premier; Hinchgbrooke Cup (2); North Beds Charity Cup (2); Hunts Premier Cup; UCL Benevolent Cup; Beds Senior Cup

Barker, Peter (F)
(WITHAM TOWN) Age: 25

Previous Clubs: Marquis Sports; Bishop's Stortford; Boreham Wood

Honours: None

Barlow, Wayne (M)
(DARTFORD)

D.O.B. 12.2.71
Profession: Motor Insurance Agent
Single
Hobbies: Sport

PLAYING CAREER

Honours: None

Club	Seasons	Transfer	Apps	Goals
Gillingham	87-89			
Sittingbourne	89-90			

Barnes, Andy (F)
(SUTTON UNITED) Age: 23

Previous Clubs: Woodcote Rovers; Chipstead.

Honours: Dan Air League Champions; Croydon 1st Division Winners

Barnes, Gary (M)
(CHIPSTEAD) Age: 27

Previous Clubs: Redhill Youth/reserves/1st team; Hoxley Town

Honours: Surry School Boys

Barnes, Peter (F)
(RADCLIFFE BOROUGH)

D.O.B. 10.6.57   **Nickname:** Barnsey
Profession: Self-Employed
Married   **Wife's name:** Alison
Children: Eloise & Jessica
Hobbies: Tennis, Squash

PLAYING CAREER

Honours: Manchester Schoolboy Rep; England Youth Int; England Full & Under-23 Int; Football League Rep; Football League Cup Winners 74/75; Young P.O.Y.1976 Manchester City

Club	Seasons	Transfer	Apps	Goals
Manchester City	72-78	£750,000	115	15
West Bromwich Albion	79-80	£930,000	77	23
Leeds United	81-82	£115,000	31	1
Real Betis[Spain]	82-83			
Leeds United	83-84	£65,000	27	4
Coventry City	84-85	£50,000	18	2
Manchester United	85-87	£20,000	20	2
Manchester City (Bolton Wanderers - loan - 2; Port Vale - loan - 3)	87-88		8	
Hull City	1988		11	
Tampa Bay R.(USA)	88-90			
Northwich Victoria	1990			

Barnes, Phil (D)
(CHIPSTEAD) Age: 32

Previous Clubs: Loughborough University; British Universities; Carshalton Athletic

Honours: Dan Air League Champions

Barnet, Paul (D)
(EASTWOOD TOWN) Age: 25

Previous Clubs: Harworth Colliery; King's Lynn
Honours: Notts Senior Cup Winners

Barnett, Andy (M)
(SELBY TOWN) Age: 27

Previous Clubs: Selby Town; York RI; York City; Harrogate Town; Goole Town

Honours: NCE Div 1 & League Cup winners 1988; NCE Div 2 runners up 1990

Barnett, Benjamin (M)
(DARTFORD)

D.O.B. 18.12.69
Profession: Degree Student
Single
Hobbies: Tennis, Archery

PLAYING CAREER
Honours: None

Club	Seasons	Transfer	Apps	Goals
Bishop's Stortford	88-90			
Dartford	1990			

Barnett, Gary (D)
(WITHAM TOWN) Age: 25

Previous Clubs: Hertford Town; Hoddesdon Town; Brimsdown Rovers; Stansted; Kingsbury Town; St.Margaretsbury; Saffron Walden Town
Honours: Herts Senior Cup R/U

Barnett, John (F)
(SELBY TOWN) Age: 33

Previous Clubs: Selby Town; York RI
Honours: NCE Div 2 runners up 1986 & 1990

Baron, Trevor (D)
(WOKING) Age: 28

Previous Clubs: Marlow; Burnham; Chertsey; Windsor & Eton; Slough Town; Windsor & Eton.
Honours:

Barrett, Keith (D)
(REDBRIDGE FOREST)

D.O.B.
Profession: Assistant Accountant
Married Wife's name: Anne
Children: Gemma & Luan.
Hobbies:

PLAYING CAREER
Honours: England Semi Pro Int.; F.A. Trophy Winner; GMV Conference Champions; Vauxhall-Opel League Winner; Alliance Premier Winner; Berger Isthmian League Winner; London Senior Cup Winner; S.E. Counties (Junior) Champions; Football Directories XI.

Club	Seasons	Transfer	Apps	Goals
Arsenal	71-72			
Tottenham H.	72-74			
Barking	74-80			
Enfield	80-86			
Wycombe Wanderers	86-89			

Barrett, Michael (G)
(CHELTENHAM TOWN) Age:

Previous Clubs: Exeter City; Heavitree United; Exmouth Town; Crediton United; Exmouth Town.
Honours: Western League Championship Winner; Devon County

Barrett, Stephen (D)
(CLACTON TOWN) Age: 35

Previous Clubs: Brighton & HA; Ilford; Dagenham; Billericay; Hendon; Grays; Tiptree; Brantham
Honours: London F.A.

Barron, Paul (G)
(WELLING UNITED)

D.O.B. 16.9.55 **Nickname:** Barras
Profession: Fitness Consultant
Married **Wife's name:** Ceri
Children: Joe
Hobbies: Golf

PLAYING CAREER
Honours: British Students Rep; FA Xl; Charity Shield R/U; Milk Cup Final R/U; Crystal Palace P.O.Y. (2); West Bromwich Albion (2)

Club	Seasons	Transfer	Apps	Goals
Welling United	73-75			
Plymouth Argyle	75-77	£75,000	44	
Arsenal	77-79	£400,000	8	
Crystal Palace	80-81	£65,000	90	
West Bromwich Albion	81-84	£30,000	63	
Stoke City		loan	1	
Q. P. R.	84-87		32	
Reading		loan	4	
Welling United	88-89			
Cheltenham Town	89-90			

KEITH BARRETT (Redbridge Forest)

Barrow, Mark (M)

(ST.DOMINCS) Age: 27

Previous Clubs: Burscough

Honours: None

Barrow, Mark (F)

(GREAT HARWOOD TOWN) Age: 29

Previous Clubs: Chorley; Clithroe

Honours: Numerous

Barry, John (D)

(GRESLEY ROVERS) Age: 22

Previous Clubs: Slack & Parr; Kimberley; Shepshed

Honours: Derbyshire Senior Cup

Barry, Terry (D)

(BECKENHAM TOWN) Age: 20

Previous Clubs: Greenwich Borough

Honours: None

Barthorpe, Paul (M)

(RADFORD) Age: 29

Previous Clubs: Saracans Villa; Sutton Rovers; Brodsworth Miners Welfare

Honours: None

Bartlett, Peter (D)

(WEALDSTONE)

D.O.B. 12.9.58 **Nickname:** Barto
Profession: Service Engineer
Married **Wife's name:** Tracey
Children: Louise & Sam
Hobbies: Reading, Music

PLAYING CAREER

Honours: Middx & Surrey Schoolboy Rep.; Middx County Rep.; Middx Senior Cup Winner

Club	Seasons	Transfer	Apps	Goals
Hampton	72-81			
Epsom & Ewell	81-83			
Leatherhead	83-84			
Hayes	84-87			
Staines Town	87-89			

Barton, Dave (D)

(OAKWOOD) Age: 29

Previous Clubs: Whyteleaf; Redhill

Honours: None

Barton, Joey (M)

(KNOWLSEY UNITED) Age: 28

Previous Clubs: Northwich Victoria; Warrington Town

Honours: Player of the Year 1989 Knowlsey

Bashir, Naseem (M)

(SLOUGH TOWN)

D.O.B. 12.9.69
Profession: Not working
Single
Hobbies: Sport

PLAYING CAREER

Honours: None

Club	Seasons	Transfer	Apps	Goals
Reading	86-90		5	1

Batchelor, Paul (G)

(LEWES) Age: 29

Previous Clubs: Ringmer; Haywards Heath; Burgess Hill Town

Honours: None

Bateman, Mark (G)

(WELWYN GARDEN CITY) Age: 20

Previous Clubs: None **Honours:** None

Bater, Phil (D)

(GLOUCESTER CITY)

D.O.B. 26.10.55 **Nickname:** Chopper
Profession: Landscape Gardener
Married **Wife's name:** Helen
Children: Geraint & Sam
Hobbies: Fishing

PLAYING CAREER

Honours: Wales Youth Int; Wales U-21 Int; Welsh Cup Winners; Wrexham & Bristol Rovers P.O.Y.

Club	Seasons	Transfer	Apps	Goals
Bristol Rovers	73-81		212	2
Wrexham	81-83		73	1
Bristol Rovers	83-86		98	1
Brentford	86-87		19	2
Cardiff City	87-90		76	

Batey, Alan (M)

(PENRITH) Age: 26

Previous Clubs: Haltwhistle CP; Consett; Chester-Le-Street

Honours: None

Baverstock, Ray (D)

(GLOUCESTER CITY)

D.O.B. 3.12.63 **Nickname:** Baver
Profession: Company Director
Married **Wife's name:** Debbie
Children: Jack & Jade
Hobbies: Sport

PLAYING CAREER

Honours: FA XI; Southern Lge Winners 84/85; Cheltenham P.O.Y.(3)

Club	Seasons	Transfer	Apps	Goals
Swindon Town	80-84		17	
Cheltenham Town	84-90			

Beach, Trevor (D)
(TUNBRIDGE WELLS) Age: 25
Previous Clubs: None
Honours: Kent League Cup 1987/88

Beal, Craig (D)
(THATCHAM TOWN) Age: 19
Previous Clubs: None   **Honours:** None

Beard, Matthew (D)
(BOGNOR REGIS TOWN)

D.O.B. 29.1.71   **Nickname:** Ivan
Profession: Higher Clerical Officer
Single   **Hobbies:** All Sports
Honours: English Colleges Rep
Previous Clubs: None

Beardmore, Neal (M)
(NEWCASTLE TOWN) Age: 20
Previous Clubs: Port Vale; Eastwood Hanley; Rotherham United
Honours: Represented Stoke-on-Trent & Staffordshire; Youth sides age 11-19

Beare, Ian (M)
(ROMSEY) Age: 19
Previous Clubs: Portsmouth; Bath City
Honours: None

Beattie, Andy (D)
(CAMBRIDGE CITY)

D.O.B. 9.2.64

PLAYING CAREER
Honours: GMVC Winners 88/89

Club	Seasons	Transfer	Apps	Goals
Cambridge United	82-87		97	2
Maidstone United	87-89			
Barnet	89-90			

Beattie, Andy (M)
(MERTHYR TYDFIL)

D.O.B. 26.9.58

PLAYING CAREER
Honours: Welsh Semi-Pro Int; Welsh Cup Winners 86/87; Beazer Homes Premier Div Winners 88/89

Club	Seasons	Transfer	Apps	Goals
Newport County	76-78			
Bridgend Town	78-83			
Mangotsfield United	83-85			

Beavan, Philip (M)
(PEGASUS JUNIORS) Age: 23
Previous Clubs: Lads Club; Hinton
Honours: None

Beck, Malcolm (D)
(KEYNSHAM TOWN) Age: 32
Previous Clubs: Odd Down; Bath City; Welton Rovers; Yeovil Town; Forest Green; Paulton; Trowbridge Town; Frome Town
Honours: Somerset Schools and Senior

Beddad, Dean (M)
(BIGGLESWADE TOWN) Age: 28
Previous Clubs: Langford
Honours: SML Championship

Bee, Elijah (M)
(BROMLEY) Age:
Previous Clubs: Local; Leyton Wingate   **Honours:** None

Beech, Glenn (M)
(BOSTON UNITED)

D.O.B. 6.12.60   **Profession:** Painter & Decorator
Married   **Wife's name:** Linda
Children: Jay & Billy
Hobbies: Swimming, Snooker

PLAYING CAREER
Honours: Lincs County Schoolboy Rep; FA Vase Winners 83/84; Lincs Senior Cup Winners (2); GMVC R/U 88/89

Club	Seasons	Transfer	Apps	Goals
Aston Villa	76-78			
Spalding United	78-81			
Bourne Town	81-82			
Stamford	82-85			
Rushden Town	85-86			
Grantham	86-87			
Boston United	87-88	£10,000		
Kettering Town	88-90	£5,000		

GLENN BEECH

Belfon, Frank   (F)
(RUSHDEN TOWN)

D.O.B. 18.2.65
Profession: Waterboard Operator
Single
Hobbies: Sport

PLAYING CAREER

Honours: Northants County Youth Rep; Rushden P.O.Y. 88/89

Club	Seasons	Transfer	Apps	Goals
Wellingborough Town	80-81			
Northampton Town	81-84		79	15
Wellingborough Town	84-85			
Buckingham Town	85-86			
Wellingborough Town	86-87			

Belford, Dale   (G)
(SUTTON COLDFIELD TOWN)   Age: 23

Previous Clubs: Aston Villa; Sutton Coldfield Town; Notts County; V.S.Rugby; Nuneaton Borough; Tamworth
Honours: FA Vase Winners 88

Bell, Ian   (M)
(SOMERSHAM TOWN)   Age: 28

Previous Clubs: Warboys Town
Honours: None

Bell, Jimmy   (F)
(KNOWSLEY UNITED)   Age: 25

Previous Clubs: Burscough; South Liverpool; Kirkby Town; Winsford; Rhyl
Honours: None

Bell, Michael   (M)
(SEATON DELAVAL AMATEURS)   Age: 23

Previous Clubs: Dudley Welfare; Ikast (Denmark)
Honours: Northumberland Senior Benevolent Bowl winner; McEwans Northern Alliance Premier Division winner

Bell, Steve   (M)
(GAINSBOROUGH TOWN)   Age: 20

Previous Clubs: Grimsby Town; Immingham Town; Blyth Spartans; Boston; Ernst Borel (Hong Kong)
Honours: None

Bendon, Steven   (D)
(WELLINGBOROUGH)   Age: 26

Previous Clubs: Whitworths; Raunds; Rushden; Rothwell
Honours: UCL Res Div 1 League runners up

Benfield, David   (M)
(AFC LYMINGTON)   Age: 27

Previous Clubs: MMI Sports; AFC Totton; Eastleigh Town; Romsey Town

Honours: Hampshire League winner; Wessex League winner; Wessex League Cup runner up; Hants Intermediate Representative

Benham, David   (M)
(SELSEY)   Age: 27

Previous Clubs: West Ham Utd (South East Counties); Portsmouth (SEC); Chichester
Honours: County League Div 2 runners up; Div 2 Cup winners (Chichester)

Bendon, John   (D)
(NEWTOWN)   Age: 35

Previous Clubs: St.Helens; Irlam Town; South Liverpool; Bangor City; Oswestry Town
Honours: F.A.Vase winner

Benham, Lee   (M)
(FARLEIGH ROVERS)   Age: 32

Previous Clubs: Warlingham
Honours: None

Bennett, Clinton   (D)
(SANDWELL BOROUGH)   Age: 25

Previous Clubs: Oldswinford; Dudley Town; Tividale; Ashtree Highfield
Honours: None

Bennett, Colin   (D)
(WARMINSTER TOWN)   Age: 26

Previous Clubs: Heytesbury; Warminster Town; Melksham Town
Honours: None

DARREN BARNARD
(Wokingham Town)

DEREK BELL
(Gateshead)

Bennett, Greg (D)
(COLESHILL TOWN) **Age:** 27

Previous Clubs: Boldmere; Solihull Borough; Knowle; Strafford Town; Wolverhampton Casuals

Honours: None

Bennett, Martyn (D)
(WORCESTER CITY)

D.O.B. 4.8.61

PLAYING CAREER

Honours: England Schoolboy Int

Club	Seasons	Transfer	Apps	Goals
West Bromwich Albion	78-90		182	9

Benning, Terry (M)
(HAYES)

D.O.B. 27.10.61
Profession: Builder
Married **Wife's name:** Deborah
Children: Lauren & Lee
Hobbies: Sport

PLAYING CAREER

Honours: Watford Schools Rep,Herts Youth Rep; Vauxhall-Opel Div 1 Winners & Div 2 R/U

Club	Seasons	Transfer	Apps	Goals
Watford	1977			
Brentford	78-79			
Northwood	79-81			
Tring Town	81-82			
St.Albans City	82-86			
Hendon	86-87			
Chesham United	87-88			
St.Albans City	88-90			

Bensted, David (D)
(DARTFORD)

D.O.B. 14.8.63
Profession: Not working
Single
Hobbies: Collecting Foreign Coins

PLAYING CAREER

Honours: Vauxhall-Opel Lge Premier Winners 88/89

Club	Seasons	Transfer	Apps	Goals
Brimsdown Rovers	87-88			
Leytonstone & Ilford	88-89			
Redbridge Forest	89-90			

Bentley, David (D)
(FARSLEY CELTIC) **Age:** 21

Previous Clubs: Leeds United; Guiseley; Whitby Town
Honours: None

Bentley, Steve (D)
(ROSSENDALE UNITED)

D.O.B. 7.7.56 **Nickname:** Bents
Profession: Bonus Surveyor
Married **Wife's name:** Julie
Children: Paul,Natalie & Sarah
Hobbies: Driving

PLAYING CAREER

Honours: Manchester Boys Rep; FA Vase Winners; HFS Loans Premier & Div 1 Winners.

Club	Seasons	Transfer	Apps	Goals
Stalybridge Celtic	81-82			
Salford City	82-85			
Colne Dynamoes	85-90			
Mossley	1990			
Salford City	1991			

Benton, David (D)
(KIDDERMINSTER HARRIERS)

D.O.B. 8.1.71 **Nickname:** Beno
Profession: Electronics Technician
Single
Hobbies: Swimming

PLAYING CAREER

Honours: Aston Schoolboy Rep; Kidderminster Y.P.O.Y. 89/90

Club	Seasons	Transfer	Apps	Goals
Birmingham City	87-88			

Beresford, Brian (F)
(GRESLEY ROVERS) **Age:** 35

Previous Clubs: Walsall; Chesterfield; Armitage; Brereton Social; Willenhall; Worcester; Corby; Shepshed; Dudley; Stapenhill

Honours: F.A. XI, West Midlands League XI; W.Mids League Championship; S.Mids League Championship; Derbyshire Senior Cup

Bernard, Paul (F)
(CHIPPENHAM TOWN) **Age:** 27

Previous Clubs: Clandown; Frome Town
Honours: None

Berry, Gwynne (D)
(SUTTON UNITED)

D.O.B. 18.12.63
Profession: Sales Rep
Single
Hobbies: Water-skiing

PLAYING CAREER

Honours: Vauxhall-Opel Lge Div 2 R/U 88/89; Surrey Senior Cup R/U 87/88; Whyteleafe P.O.Y. 87/88

Club	Seasons	Transfer	Apps	Goals
Whyteleafe	83-86			
Banstead Athletic	86-87			
Whyteleafe	87-89	£5,000		

Best, John (F)

(SEATON DELAVAL AMATEURS) Age: 20

Previous Clubs: Bedlington Terriers; Ponteland United; Seaton Terrace

Honours: McEwans Northern Alliance League Subsidiary Cup winners

Beste, Robin (F)

(CARSHALTON ATHLETIC)

D.O.B. 16.3.66   **Nickname:** Bestey
Profession: Not working
Married

PLAYING CAREER

Honours: Surrey Senior Cup Winners 89/90

Club	Seasons	Transfer	Apps	Goals
Chelsea	82-84			
Dulwich Hamlet	85-86			
Warlingham FC	86-87			

Bicknell, Richard (M)

(GODALMING TOWN) Age: 23

Previous Clubs: Godalming Town (Youth); Cranleigh; Staines Town.

Honours: None

Biddle, Andy (F)

(SUTTON COLDFIELD TOWN) Age: 25

Previous Clubs: Boldmere St.Michael; Paget Rangers
Honours: Sutton Sports Personality of the Year 1989

Biddle, Gary (F)

(BOGNOR REGIS TOWN)

D.O.B. 9.3.69
Profession: Administrator
Single
Hobbies: Golf,Music

PLAYING CAREER

Honours: None to date.

Previous Clubs: None

Biddle, Mick (F)

(CONGLETON TOWN)

D.O.B. 17.8.61   **Nickname:** Toto
Profession: Sheet Metal Worker
Married   **Wife's name:** Barbara
Children: Adam,Matthew & Daniel

PLAYING CAREER

Honours: Staffs Youth Rep; Cheshire Lge Div 2 Winners; Staffs Senior Cup Winners 84; Congleton P.O.Y.79/80.

Club	Seasons	Transfer	Apps	Goals
Stoke City	76-78			
Port Vale	78-79			
Congleton Town	79-83			
Witton Albion	83-84			
Eastwood Hanley	84-88			

Biggins, Mark (M/F)

(WOKING) **D.O.B.** 18.4.62

Previous Clubs: Hampton; Hanwell; Feltham; Maidenhead; St. Albans; Windsor & Eton.

Honours:

MARK BIGGINS

Billows, Dave (F)

(WINSFORD UNITED) Age: 24

Previous Clubs: Marine, South Liverpool, Irlam Town
Honours: Lancs Floodlit Trophy R/U

Birch, Alan (M)

(FRICKLEY ATHLETIC) **D.O.B.** 12.8.56

PLAYING CAREER

Honours: None

Club	Seasons	Transfer	Apps	Goals
Walsall	72-78	£25,000	171	23
Chesterfield	78-80	£200,000	90	35
Wolverhampton W.	80-81	£100,000	15	
Barnsley	81-83		44	11
Chesterfield	83-84		32	5
Rotherham United	84-86		101	28
Scunthorpe United	86-87		23	2
Stockport County	87-88		20	3
Frickley Athletic	88-90			
Matlock Town	90-91			

Birch, Darren (M)

(ALFRETON TOWN) Age: 20

Previous Clubs: Brigg Town; Cambridge United
Honours: None

Birchall, Michael   (F)
(ST.DOMINICS)   **Age:** 21
Previous Clubs:
Honours: None

Bird, Alan   (M)
(CHIPPENHAM TOWN)   **Age:** 23
Previous Clubs:
Honours: None

Bird, Kevin   (M)
(STAPENHILL)   **Age:** 26
Previous Clubs: Long Eaton Utd; Ilkeston Town; Eastwood Town; Ilkeston Town; Belper Town; Alfreton Town; Derby County
Honours: Leicester Senior Cup winner; Tebbutt Brown Cup winner 1988-89

Bird, Tony   (G)
(NEWPORT AFC)   **Age:** 32
Previous Clubs: Cardiff Corriers
Honours: Hellenic League championship

Bishop, Dean   (M)
(BRAINTREE TOWN)   **Age:** 31
Previous Clubs: Clapton; Chelmsford City; Hornchurch
Honours: None

Bishop, Frank   (F)
(BRAINTREE TOWN)   **Age:** 34
Previous Clubs: Romford; Chelmsford City; Dartford; Tonbridge AFC; Chelmsford City; Wivenhoe Town; Heybridge Swifts; Witham Town
Honours: None

Bishop, John   (M)
(BRAINTREE TOWN)   **Age:** 19
Previous Clubs: Great Waltham United
Honours: None

Blackbourne, Matthew   (M)
(SPALDING UNITED)   **Age:** 17
Previous Clubs: Grimsby Town
Honours: Lincs Youth Cup winners

Blackler, Martin   (M)
(WYCOMBE WANDERERS)

D.O.B. 14.3.63

PLAYING CAREER
Honours: FA XI; Trowbridge P.O.Y. 86/87

Club	Seasons	Transfer	Apps	Goals
Swindon Town	79-83		9	
Witney Town	83-85			
Cheltenham Town	85-86			
Trowbridge Town	86-88			

MARTIN BLACKLER

Blackley, Glen   (G)
(CONGLETON TOWN)

D.O.B. 24.4.62

PLAYING CAREER
Honours: Derbyshire Senior Cup Winners (3); HFS Loans Premier Div R/U; Presidents Cup R/U

Club	Seasons	Transfer	Apps	Goals
Buxton	80-83			
Macclesfield Town	83-84			
Leek Town	84-88			
Rocester	88-90			

Blade, Paul   (D)
(DARTFORD)

D.O.B. 27.4.66
Profession: Builder
Single
Hobbies: Golf, Tennis

PLAYING CAREER
Honours: None

Club	Seasons	Transfer	Apps	Goals
Crystal Palace	84-85			
Southend United	1985			
Charlton Athletic	1985			
Erith & Belvedere	85-86			

PAUL BANCROFT (KETTERING TOWN & ENGLAND)

Blain, Colin (M)
(NORTHWICH VICTORIA)

D.O.B. 7.3.70
PLAYING CAREER
Honours: Staffs Senior Cup Winners; Mid-Cheshire Senior Cup Winners

Club	Seasons	Transfer	Apps	Goals
Halifax Town	87-89		41	1

Blakebrough, Chris (F)
(REDBRIDGE FOREST)

D.O.B. 5.6.68 Nickname: Blakey
Profession: British Telecom Engineer
Single
Hobbies: All Sports
PLAYING CAREER
Honours: Essex Senior Cup Winners 88/89, London Senior Cup R/U/ 88/89

Club	Seasons	Transfer	Apps	Goals
Hornchurch	85-86			
Clapton	86-87			
Hornchurch	87-88			
Clapton	88-89			

Blakemore, Charlie (F)
(CHASETOWN) Age: 23
Previous Clubs: Shifnal Town; Bilston Town
Honours: Banks Premier League Cup winners 1989/90

Blauche, David (M)
(BIDEFORD TOWN) Age: 42
Previous Clubs: Newport County; Tooting & Mitcham; Farnborough Town; Barnstaple Town; Ilfracombe Town
Honours: None

Blodes, Stephen (D)
(MIRRLEES BLACKSTONES) Age: 29
Previous Clubs: Derby County; Stamford Town; Rushden Town; Grotham
Honours: F.A.Vase runners up

Blow, David (D)
(HYDE UNITED)

D.O.B. 30.3.67
Profession: Not working
Single
Hobbies: Sport
PLAYING CAREER
Honours: None

Club	Seasons	Transfer	Apps	Goals
Burnley	83-84			
Glossop	84-86			
Horwich RMI	86-87			

Blythe, Andy (F)
(LEWES) Age: 23
Previous Clubs: Croydon
Honours: None

Bodley, Mick (D)
(BARNET)

D.O.B. 14.9.67 Nickname: Bodders
Profession: Laminator
Single
Hobbies: Golf, Clay Pigeon Shooting
PLAYING CAREER
Honours: South East Counties Lge Winners

Club	Seasons	Transfer	Apps	Goals
Chelsea	85-88	£55,000	10	1
Northampton Town	88-89		23	

Bolle, Jon (F)
(BARKING)

D.O.B. 18.11.64 Nickname: Bolley
Profession: Sales Manager
Married Wife's name: Alison
Hobbies: All Sports, Relaxing with family
PLAYING CAREER
Honours: London Schools Rep; Essex County Youth Rep; Essex Thameside & Essex Senior Cup Winners; Barking P.O.Y.84/85.

Club	Seasons	Transfer	Apps	Goals
Leyton Orient	80-83			
Clapton	83-84			
Barking	84-86			
Dagenham	86-88			
Leyton-Wingate	88-90			

Bolton, Jimmy (F)
(CARSHALTON ATHLETIC)

D.O.B. 17.12.62
Married
PLAYING CAREER
Honours: England Schoolboy Int; Vauxhall-Opel Lge Winners; Surrey Senior Cup Winners 89/90.

Club	Seasons	Transfer	Apps	Goals
Tottenham Hotspur	79-82			
Hillingdon Borough				
Wimbledon				
Farnborough Town				
Tooting & Mitcham United				
Farnborough Town				
Kiruna(Sweden)				
Harrow Borough				

Bon, Martin (D)
(SANDWELL BOROUGH) Age: 20
Previous Clubs: Princess End
Honours: None

Bond, Len (G)

(YEOVIL TOWN)

D.O.B. 12.2.54   **Nickname:** Bondie
Profession: Sports Salesman
Single
Hobbies: Squash, Cricket, Rugby, Snooker, Golf

PLAYING CAREER

Honours: Yeovil Schoolboy Rep; Somerset Schoolboy Rep; Brentford P.O.Y. 79/80; Weymouth P.O.Y. 85/86

Club	Seasons	Transfer	Apps	Goals
Bristol City	70-76		30	
Exeter City		loan	30	
Torquay United		loan	3	
Scunthorpe United		loan	8	
Colchester United		loan	3	
St.Louis Stars(USA)	76-77			
Brentford	77-80		122	
Exeter City	80-83		138	
Weymouth	83-87			

Bone, Jonathan (D)

(HITCHIN TOWN)   Age: 21

Previous Clubs: Luton Town
Honours: England Schoolboy Int

Boneham, Craig (D)

(NEWMARKET TOWN)   Age: 19

Previous Clubs:

Honours: None

Booker, Trevor (F)

(WELLING UNITED)   **D.O.B.** 26.2.69

Previous Clubs: Millwall

Honours: London Senior Cup Winners 89/90.

TREVOR BOOKER

Bookman, Jeff (M)

(WINGATE)   Age: 37

Previous Clubs: Ilford; Wingate; Leyton-Wingate

Honours: Herts Senior Trophy winner; S.Mids Lge Div 1990; F.A.Amateur Cup finalist

Boot, Andrew (M)

(CHASETOWN)   Age: 19

Previous Clubs: Hednesford Town

Honours: None

Booth, Derek (F)

(WESTHOUGHTON TOWN)   Age: 22

Previous Clubs: Bolton Wanderers; Wigan Athletic

Honours: Wigan A.L Prem winners (2); Laithwaite Shield winners (2); Hughes Cup winners (2); West Lancs Lge Div 1 winners

Booth, Paul (D)

(HORWICH RMI)

D.O.B. 7.12.65   **Nickname:** Boothy
Profession: Not working
Married   **Wife's name:** Elaine
Hobbies: Sport

PLAYING CAREER

Honours: None

Club	Seasons	Transfer	Apps	Goals
Bolton Wanderers	83-85		1	
Crewe Alexandra	85-86	27		
Tranmere Rovers		Loan	3	
Preston North End		Loan	3	

Bootland, Graham (D)

(SELBY TOWN)   Age: 26

Previous Clubs: York City; Hull City; York RI

Honours: North Yorkshire County Youth Team Captain; NCE Div 1 championship & Cup winners; North Riding County Cup winners; NCE Div 2 runners up

Borch, Chris (M:F)

(TOOTING & MITCHAM UNITED)   Age: 22

Previous Clubs: Carshalton Athletic

Honours: None

Botting, Terry (D)

(HORSHAM)   Age: 25

Previous Clubs: Youth team product

Honours: None

Bottomley, John (D)

(GRESLEY ROVERS)   Age: 25

Previous Clubs: Burton Albion

Honours: Derbyshire Senior Cup winners (3); Banks's Brewery League Cup winners

Bougourd, Alan   (F)
(VALE RECREATION)   Age: 35
Previous Clubs:
Honours: 12 Guernsey caps; 12 Guernsey Priaulx Championship; 4 Channel Island Champioship (Upton Park Trophy)

ALAN 'Titch' BOUGOURD

Boun, Ian   (F)
(SOMERSHAM TOWN)   Age: 27
Previous Clubs: Downham Town
Honours: None

Bourne, Brian   (M)
(CONGLETON TOWN)

D.O.B. 13.3.64
Single
Hobbies: Golf, Athletics

PLAYING CAREER
Honours: None

Club	Seasons	Transfer	Apps	Goals
Chedleton FC	87-89			

Bowden, Roger   (M)
(WARMINSTER TOWN)   Age: 37
Previous Clubs: Warminster Town; Frome Town
Honours: None

Bowden, Steven   (M)
(MEIR K.A.)   Age: 25
Previous Clubs:
Honours: None

Bower, Peter   (D)
(PICKERING TOWN)   Age: 33
Previous Clubs:
Honours: Div 2 N.E.Counties all Scarborough League & Cups

Bowering, Jon   (D)
(BRIDGWATER TOWN 84)   Age: 24
Previous Clubs: Bridgwtaer Town; Taunton Town
Honours: Runners up Somerset Senior League Div 2 & Somerset Senior Cup; Somerset Representative cap; Somerset Senior League Div 1 & Prem Div winners; Somerset Senior Cup

Bowgett Paul   (D)
(HITCHIN TOWN)   Age: 36
Previous Clubs: Letchworth Garden City; Wimbledon; Wealdstone; Baldock Town
Honours: Gola Lge Winners; FA Trophy Winners

Bowler, Paul   (F)
(MOSSLEY)

D.O.B. 8.1.67   **Nickname:** Tom
Profession: Engineer
Single   **Hobbies:** Cricket, Golf

PLAYING CAREER
Honours: Mossley P.O.Y.89/90

Club	Seasons	Transfer	Apps	Goals
Chadderton	85-88			
Chorley	1988			
Chadderton	88-89			

Bowler, Robbie   (G)
(KNOWSLEY UNITED)   Age: 26
Previous Clubs: Warrington Town; Runcorn; Kirkby Town
Honours: None

Bolster, Eric   (M)
(MIRRLEES BLACKSTONE)   Age: 30
Previous Clubs: Stamford Belvedere   **Honours:** None

Boyd, Ian   (D)
(GAINSBOROUGH TOWN)   Age: 34
Previous Clubs: Louth United; Pilkington Recs; Maltby Miners Welfare; Yorkshire Main; Harworth Colliery; Denaby United
Honours: Central Midland League and Cup

Boyd, Sean   (D)
(BIGGLESWADE TOWN)   Age: 22
Previous Clubs: Sandy Albion; Langford   **Honours:** None

Boyers, Martyn   (M)
(SPALDING UNITED)   Age: 35
Previous Clubs: Louth Utd; Gainsborough Trinity; Skegness Town; Boston; Grantham Town; Kings Lynn
Honours: Midland Lge PoY 1978; Lincs Senior Cup 78,88; UCL Championhip 1988; Lincoln County F.A. Player/Manager

Boyland, Mark (F)

(V.S.RUGBY)

D.O.B. 30.3.58
Profession: Kitchen Fitter
Married
Nickname: Boylo
Hobbies: Golf
Wife's name: Lisa

PLAYING CAREER

Honours: Southern Lge Premier Div Winners; Middx Wanderer.

Club	Seasons	Transfer	Apps	Goals
Oxford City	76-79			
Banbury United	79-83			
Witney Town	83-84			
Cheltenham Town	84-87			
Wycombe Wanderers	87-88			
Aylesbury United	88-89			
Cheltenham Town	89-90			

Boyle, Michael (G)

(SHOTTON COMRADES)   **Age:** 23

Previous Clubs: Gretna; Ashington; Durham City
Honours: None

Boyle, Terry (D)

(MERTHYR TYDFIL)   **D.O.B.** 29.10.58

PLAYING CAREER

Honours: Welsh Schoolboy Int; Welsh U-21 & Full Int

Club	Seasons	Transfer	Apps	Goals
Tottenham Hotspur	75-77			
Crystal Palace	77-81		26	1
Wimbledon		loan	5	1
Bristol City	81-82		37	
Newport County	82-86		166	11
Cardiff City	86-89		128	7
Swansea City	89-90		27	1

Bradder, Gary (M)

(ATHERSTONE UNITED)

D.O.B. 6.3.61
Profession: Skilled Sheet Metal Worker
Married
Children: Kelly, Danielle & Liam
Hobbies: Music
Nickname: Brad
Wife's name: Dawn

PLAYING CAREER

Honours: Beazer Homes Midland Div Winners 88/89 & R/U 87/88,Midland Floodlit Cup Winners

Club	Seasons	Transfer	Apps	Goals
Bedworth United	80-85			
Atherstone United	85-88			
Gloucester City	88-89			

Bradley, Andrew (F)

(CHIPPENHAM TOWN)   **Age:** 21

Previous Clubs: South Cerney; Cirencester Town; The Herd (Cirencester Utd)

Honours: Senior County Cup 1989 runner up

Brady, John (F)

(ALTRINCHAM)

D.O.B. 25.8.58
Profession: Garage Proprietor
Single
Hobbies: Golf,Tennis,Cricket
Nickname: Jabber

PLAYING CAREER

Honours: Lancs Schoolboy Rep; NWCL Winners 82/83; HFS Loans Lge Premier Winners 87/88; P.O.Y.at Burscough; Chorley & Southport.

Club	Seasons	Transfer	Apps	Goals
Preston North End	77-81			
Burscough	82-83			
Southport	83-84			
Altrincham	84-85			
Southport	1985			
Buxton	85-86			
Chorley	86-90			

JOHN BRADY

Brain, Ian (M)

(BEDWORTH UNITED)   **Age:** 24

Previous Clubs: Atherstone United   **Honours:** None

Brain, Simon (F)

(CHELTENHAM TOWN)

D.O.B. 31.3.66
Single
Profession: Toolroom Machinist
Hobbies: Golf, Snooker

PLAYING CAREER

Honours: Worcs Schoolboy Rep; Evesham P.O.Y. 88/89

Club	Seasons	Transfer	Apps	Goals
Moreton Town	85-87			
Malvern Town	87-88			
Evesham United	88-90			

Braithwaite, Rod (F)

(KINGSTONIAN) D.O.B. 19.11.65

Previous Clubs: Fulham (50 - 17); Farnborough Town.
Honours: FA XI; Vauxhall Lge Rep.

Brassington, Lee (M)

(OLDSWINFORD) Age: 25

Previous Clubs: Alvechurch; Lye Town; Halesowen Harriers; Princess End Utd

Honours: Birmingham County F.A. Youth cap

Bray, Paul (G)

(HINCKLEY ATHLETIC) Age: 25

Previous Clubs: Barwell Athletic; Earl Shilton Albion; Hinckley

Honours: None

Brazier, Colin (D)

(KIDDERMINSTER HARRIERS)

D.O.B. 6.6.57
Profession: Heating Engineer
Married **Wife's name:** Christine
Hobbies: Squash, Golf

PLAYING CAREER

Honours: Birmingham Schoolboy Rep; Warks County Schoolboy Rep; Football League Cup Winners 79/80; Football Lge Div 2 Winners 76/77; England Semi-Pro Int

Club	Seasons	Transfer	Apps	Goals
Alvechurch	74-75			
Wolverhampton W.	75-82		78	2
Jacksonville Teamen	1982			
Birmingham City	82-83		11	1
Lincoln City	1983		9	
Walsall	83-87		115	4

Brazil, Alan (F)

(CHELMSFORD CITY)

D.O.B. 15.5.59

PLAYING CAREER

Honours: Scottish Under-21 & Full Int; Football League Div 1 R/U 80/81 & 81/82; UEFA Cup Winners 80/81

Club	Seasons	Transfer	Apps	Goals
Ipswich Town	77-82		154	70
Tottenham Hotspur	82-84		31	9
Manchester United	84-86		31	8
Coventry City	1986		15	2
Queens Park Rangers	86-87		4	
Witham Town	1988			
Chelmsford City	1988			
FC Baden (Swi)	88-89			
Chelmsford City	1989			
Southend Manor	1989			
Bury Town	89-90			
Stambridge	1990			

Brennan, Andy (D)

(WALTHAMSTOW PENNANT) Age: 27

Previous Clubs: Barking; Woodford Town
Honours: Spartan League Cup winner

Brentano, Steve (D/M)

(BRIDLINGTON TOWN) Age: 28

Previous Clubs: Hull City (12)
Honours: Noth-East Counties Lge Winners,FA Vase R/U 89/90

Brereton, Carl (D)

(PRESCOT) Age: 22

Previous Clubs: Formby **Honours:** None

Brett, David (M)

(COLWYN BAY) Age: 29

Previous Clubs: Chester City
Honours: Welsh Alliancs Lge & Cup Winners; Bass NWCL Cup Winners

Brissett, Trevor (D)

(NEWCASTLE TOWN) Age: 30

Previous Clubs: Stoke City; Port Vale; Darlington; Crewe; Stafford; Witton Albion; Barrow; Macclesfield
Honours: Floodlight Cup winners; Cheshire Senior Cup winners

Bristow, David (M)

(BANBURY UNITED) Age: 26

Previous Clubs: Swindon Town; Banbury Utd; Buckingham Town; Brackley Town
Honours: S.E.Counties League winners

Britnell, Garry (M)

(ENFIELD) D.O.B. 6.9.64

Profession: Bricklayer
Married **Wife's name:** Amanda
Children: Ben **Hobbies:** Tennis

PLAYING CAREER

Honours: None

Club	Seasons	Transfer	Apps	Goals
Canvey Island	83-85			
Chelmsford City	85-86			
Dartford	86-90			

Broadhead, Steve (F)

(WINGATE) Age: 21

Previous Clubs: None
Honours: South Midlands Div 1 R/U.

Broadstock, Peter (M)

(WESTHOUGHTON TOWN) Age: 18

Previous Clubs: Atherston Colls (Youth); Ince Central
Honours: Lancs Under 18's Inter League winner & runners up; Lancs Youth team member

Brogan, Paul (D)
(CHELTENHAM TOWN)

D.O.B. 7.7.70   **Nickname:** Brogs or Shoes
Profession: Professional Footballer
Single
Hobbies: Golf, Snooker

PLAYING CAREER
Honours: None

Club	Seasons	Transfer	Apps	Goals
Moor Green	86-88			
Mansfield Town	88-90			

Brookes, Morgan (M)
(OLDSWINFORD FSC)   **Age:** 22
Previous Clubs:
Honours: Birmingham County Youth Representative

Brooks, Steve (M)
(CHELTENHAM TOWN)

D.O.B. 14.7.61   **Nickname:** Brooksy
Profession: Electrician
Married   **Wife's name:** Sue
Children: Clare & Charlotte
Hobbies: Fishing, Cricket

PLAYING CAREER
Honours: England Semi-Pro Int; FA XI.

Club	Seasons	Transfer	Apps	Goals
Clanfield	80-82			
Witney Town	81-85			

Broom, Jason (M)
(BILLERICAY TOWN)   **Age:** 21
Previous Clubs: Eton Manor
Honours: None

Broomfield, Neil (D)
(AFC LYMINGTON)   **Age:** 20
Previous Clubs: Wellworthy Athletic
Honours: Bournemouth Senior Cup winners; Wessex League Cup winners

Brotherston, Noel (F)
(CHORLEY)

D.O.B. 18.11.56

PLAYING CAREER
Honours: Northern Ireland Schoolboy & Youth Int,FA Youth Cup Winners 73/74
Northern Ireland Under-21 Int,Northern Ireland Full Int

Club	Seasons	Transfer	Apps	Goals
Tottenham Hotspur	73-76		1	
Blackburn Rovers	76-87		317	40
Bury	87-90		38	4
Scarborough		loan	5)	

Brown, George (D)
(CWMBRAN TOWN)   **Age:** 31
Previous Clubs: Cardiff Corinthians
Honours: Welsh Amateur Cup 1984-85; Cardiff and South Glamorgan Schools

Brown, John (M)
(STALYBRIDGE CELTIC)

D.O.B. 6.12.67   **Nickname:** Bobble
Profession: Not working
Single
Hobbies: Golf

PLAYING CAREER
Honours: None

Club	Seasons	Transfer	Apps	Goals
Liverpool	84-87			
Winsford United	87-88			
Witton Albion	88-91			

Brown, Keith (M)
(BATH CITY)

D.O.B. 25.9.59
Profession: M/C Engineer
Married   **Wife's name:** Christine
Children: Gemma
Hobbies: All Sports

PLAYING CAREER
Honours: None

Club	Seasons	Transfer	Apps	Goals
Bristol St.George	76-77			
Bristol Rovers	77-81		7	
Bath City	81-86	£2,000		
Cheltenham Town	86-89	£5,000		

KEITH BROWN

Brown, Linton   (F)
(BRIDLINGTON TOWN)   Age: 22
Previous Clubs: Local football
Honours: North-East Counties Lge Winners,FA Vase R/U 89/90

Brown, Mark   (D)
(CALNE TOWN)   Age: 23
Previous Clubs: Melksham Town
Honours: Wilts Ghia Cup winners 1986

Brown, Michael   (D)
(GENERAL CHEMICALS)   Age: 25
Previous Clubs: General Chemicals; Coachmans; Winninton Park
Honours: Pyke Cup winner; Cheshire Amateur winner; Runcorn Cup winner; Northwich Cup winner

Brown, Mike   (D)
(WARMINSTER TOWN)   Age: 34
Previous Clubs:
Honours: None

Brown, Paul   (D)
(SANDWELL BOROUGH)   Age: 29
Previous Clubs: Redditch; Old Rory; M & B
Honours: None

Brown, Philip   (F)
(KETTERING TOWN)

D.O.B. 16.1.66   **Nickname:** Browny
Profession: Not working
Married   **Wife's name:** Joanne
Children: John & Daniel
Hobbies: Golf,Snooker

PLAYING CAREER
Honours: Football Lge Div 4 Winners; GMVC Winners

Club	Seasons	Transfer	Apps	Goals
Chesterfield	82-87	£5,000	97	25
Stockport County	1987	£6,000	23	1
Lincoln City	87-90		43	3

Brown, Ray   (F)
(RHYL)   Age: 26
Previous Clubs: Crewe Alexandra; Wigan Athletic; Winsford United
Honours: None

Brown, Rod   (F)
(STROUD)

D.O.B. 11.11.59
Profession: Sales Manager
Married   **Wife's name:** Janice
Children: Dean
Hobbies: Sport

PLAYING CAREER
Honours: None

Club	Seasons	Transfer	Apps	Goals
Brechin City	80-82			
Brechin City	84-86			
Arbroath	86-88			
Brechin City	89-90			
Gloucester City	1990			

Brown, Ronald   (D)
(SHOTTON COMRADES)   Age: 35
Previous Clubs: Shotton Juniors; Hartlepool United; Wingate Wanderers; Wingate
Honours: Houghton District League winners; Northern League Player of the Year

Brown, Stef   (F)
(ALFRETON TOWN)   Age: 32
Previous Clubs: Berwick Rangers; Dalkeith Thistle; Newtongrange Star
Honours: None

Brown, Stephen   (M)
(PICKERING TOWN)   Age: 28
Previous Clubs: Scarborough; Bridlington Town; Pickering Town; Whitby Town
Honours: N.East Counties Div 2 Champions (Pickering); N.East Counties Div 2 champions (Scarborough Res)

Brown, Trevor   (M)
(KINTBURY RANGERS)   Age: 24
Previous Clubs: Supermarine; Lambourn
Honours: None

PHILIP BROWN (Kettering Town)

Brown, Warren (M)

(EYNESBURY ROVERS) Age: 21

Previous Clubs: Eynesbury Rovers; Peterborough United; St.Neots Town; Eynsebury Rovers; Potton United

Honours: UCL Winners & Benevolent Cup; Beds Charity Cup; Hinchingbrooke Cup; Huntingdonshire Junior & Senior Caps

Brown, Wayne (D)

(WELLING UNITED)

D.O.B. 19.1.70   **Nickname:** Brownie
Profession: Computer Installations Engineer
Single
Hobbies: Body-building, Listening to Soul Music

PLAYING CAREER

Honours: None

Club	Seasons	Transfer	Apps	Goals
No previous clubs				

Browne, Simon (D)

(WEYMOUTH)

D.O.B. 2.4.71
Profession: Building Society Clerk
Single
Hobbies: Cricket, Tennis

PLAYING CAREER

Honours: Dorset Schoolboy Rep; Dorset Combination Winner.

Club	Seasons	Transfer	Apps	Goals
No previous clubs				

Browning, Keith (M)

(OAKWOOD) Age: 26

Previous Clubs: East Grinstead; Southampton; Crawley Town

Honours: None

Bruce, Peter (G)

(BARKING)

D.O.B. 16.11.64
Nickname: Bruso
Profession: Investment Administrator
Single
Hobbies: Water-skiing

PLAYING CAREER

Honours: Essex Youth Rep; Vauxhall Lge Premier Winners 88/89

Club	Seasons	Transfer	Apps	Goals
Walthamstow Avenue	87-88			
Leytonstone & Ilford	88-89			
Redbridge Forest	1989			

Brush, Paul (D)

(ENFIELD)

D.O.B. 22.2.58   **Nickname:** Brushy
Profession: Not working
Married   **Wife's name:** Sue
Children: Peter & James
Hobbies: Golf

PLAYING CAREER

Honours: None

Club	Seasons	Transfer	Apps	Goals
West Ham United	77-85	£30,000	185	1
Crystal Palace	85-87	£12,000	53	3
Southend United	87-90		84	1

Bryant, Jonathan (D/M)

(CROYDON) Age: 22

Previous Clubs: Tooting & Mitcham United
Honours: None

Buchanan, Gary (M)

(LANGLEY SPORTS) Age: 24

Previous Clubs: Eastbourne Utd; Hastings Utd; Eastbourne Town

Honours: Sussex County League Challenge Cup winner 1989-90; Eastbourne Charity Cup winner 1989-90

Buckland, Mark (M)

(CHELTENHAM TOWN)

D.O.B. 18.8.61   **Nickname:** Buckers
Profession: Scaffolder
Married   **Wife's name:** Yvonne
Children: Rhea
Hobbies: Sport

PLAYING CAREER

Honours: Glos County Youth Rep; Southern Lge Premier Div Winners.

Club	Seasons	Transfer	Apps	Goals
AP Leamington	79-83			
Wolverhampton W.	83-85		50	5
Kidderminster Harriers	85-87			

Buckley, Mark (F)

(MORETON TOWN) Age: 28

Previous Clubs: Wolverhampton Wanderers; Worcester City; Bromsgrove Rovers; Redditch Utd; Malvern Town; Evesham Utd

Honours: Midland Div Southern League champioship

Buckley, Steve (D)

(BOSTON UNITED) D.O.B. 16.10.53

PLAYING CAREER

Honours: GMVC Winners 87/88

Club	Seasons	Transfer	Apps	Goals
Burton Albion	71-74			
Luton Town	74-77		123	9
Derby County	77-85		323	21
Lincoln City	86-88		36	2

Budinger, Gary (M)

(CROYDON) Age: 30

Previous Clubs: Tooting & Mitcham United; Feltham; Walton & Hersham
Honours: None

Bull, Gary   (F)
(BARNET)

D.O.B. 12.6.66   Nickname: Bully
Profession: Not working
Single
Hobbies: Golf, Sport

PLAYING CAREER

Honours: None

Club	Seasons	Transfer	Apps	Goals
Swindon Town	83-84			
Southampton	85-87			
Cambridge United	87-88		13	4

Bull, John   (F)
(BECKENHAM TOWN)   Age: 20
Previous Clubs:
Honours: None

Bullingham, Andrew   (D)
(OLDSWINFORD FSC)   Age: 22
Previous Clubs: Nottingham Forest; Stourbridge; Tipton;
Kidderminster Harriers

Honours: England Schoolboys Rep; W.Mids County Captain

Bullions, Ian   (D/M)
(V.S.RUGBY)

D.O.B. 27.12.63   Nickname: Bully
Profession: Self-Employed Builder
Single
Hobbies: Golf, Walking

PLAYING CAREER

Honours: Leics Schoolboy Rep.; Westgate Insurance Cup
Winners; Midland Floodlit Cup Winners; Hinckley Town P.O.Y.
87/88

Club	Seasons	Transfer	Apps	Goals
Hinckley Athletic	80-83			
Bedworth United	83-84			
Hinckley Town	84-89			

Bungay, Norman   (D)
(BECKENHAM TOWN)   Age: 36
Previous Clubs: Crockenhill; Alma Swanley; Darenth Heathside;
Thames Polytechnic

Honours: Kent Senior Trophy winner (Crockenhill)

Burden, Barry   (F)
(HORSHAM)   Age: 19
Previous Clubs: Youth team product
Honours: None

Burford, Lee   (M)
(SANDWELL BOROUGH)   Age: 21
Previous Clubs: Tipton Town
Honours: None

Burgess, Raymond   (M)
(WELLING UNITED)

D.O.B. 14.10.56   Nickname: Burge
Profession: Driver
Married   Wife's name: Sue
Children: Kevin & Michelle
Hobbies: Golf

PLAYING CAREER

Honours: London Youth Rep; Southern Lge Premier Div
Winners; London Senior Cup & Kent Senior Cup Winners;
Welling P.O.Y. (2)

Club	Seasons	Transfer	Apps	Goals
No previous clubs.				

Burgess, Steve   (D)
(WINSFORD UNITED)   Age: 27
Previous Clubs: Middlewich; Nantwich Town
Honours: None

Burke, Brendan   (F)
(MOSSLEY)

D.O.B. 13.10.70   Nickname: Friar Tuck
Profession: Bank Clerk
Single
Hobbies: Music, Reading

PLAYING CAREER

Honours: None

Club	Seasons	Transfer	Apps	Goals
Manchester United	86-88			
Oldham Town	88-89			

Burke, Mark   (D)
(HITCHIN TOWN)   Age: 23
Previous Clubs: None
Honours: Herts & Beds County Rep

Burke, Melvyn   (D)
(CLITHEROE)   Age: 22
Previous Clubs: Radcliffe Boro; Clitheroe; Salford
Honours: None

Burke, Neil   (D)
(NEWCASTLE TOWN)   Age: 28
Previous Clubs: Parkway Clayton (Sundays); Kidsgrove Athletic;
Goldenhill Wanderers

Honours: Represented Staffordshire Youth; 2 Midland Sunday
Cup wins; 2 runners up; Numerous other local trophies

Burke, Paul   (M)
(BECKENHAM TOWN)   Age: 21
Previous Clubs: Dulwich Hamlet
Honours: None

Burney, John (D)
(BRAINTREE TOWN)   Age: 33

Previous Clubs: Southend United; Chelmsford City; Tilbury; Maldon Town; Witham Town; Heybridge Swifts; Witham Town

Honours: English Schools Trophy Winners; Essex Senior Lge Winners & R/U; Essex Senior Lge Cup Winners (2) & R/U; East Anglian Cup Winners

Burns, Chris (M)
(CHELTENHAM TOWN)

D.O.B. 9.11.67   **Nickname:** Fredy or Phsycho
Profesion: Bricklayer
Married   **Wife's name:** Bev
Hobbies: Cheese Rolling

PLAYING CAREER

Honours: Bristol Schoolboy Rep

Club	Seasons	Transfer	Apps	Goals
Brockworth	84-86			
Sharpness	87-88			

Burnside, Ricky (F)
(BOGNOR REGIS TOWN)

D.O.B. 19.1.61   **Nickname:** Ricky of the Rocks
Profession: Full-time with Bognor on Commercial side
Married   **Wife's name:** Karen
Hobbies: Golf,Shooting

PLAYING CAREER

Honours: Hants & Southampton Schoolboy Rep; Bill Dellow Cup Winners 86/87; Vauxhall Lge Rep XI.

Club	Seasons	Transfer	Apps	Goals
AFC Bournemouth	82-85			
Waterlooville	85-87			
Birkirkara FC[Malta]	87-88			
Waterlooville	88-89			

Burr, Colin (D)
(SEATON DELAVAL AMATEURS)   Age: 26

Previous Clubs: Benwell Blues; Scotswood S.C

Honours: Northumberland Minor Cup winners; Northumberland Senior Benevolent Bowl runners up

Burr, Steve (F)
(MACCLESFIELD TOWN)

D.O.B. 12.1.61   **Nickname:** Burrie
Profession: HGV Driver
Married   **Wife's name:** Cheryl
Children: Ross

PLAYING CAREER

Honours: NPL Premier Div & Cup Winners; FA Trophy R/U; Macclesfield P.O.Y.

Club	Seasons	Transfer	Apps	Goals
Lichfield				
Atherstone Town				
Stafford Rangers				

Burrell, Mark (D)
(WITTON ALBION)

D.O.B. 18.6.63   **Nickname:** Buzz
Profession: Buyer
Single
Hobbies: Golf,Tennis,Squash

PLAYING CAREER

Honours: Worksop Schoolboys Rep; NCEL Div 2 Winners 84/85; HFS Loans LgE Cup Winners 88/89; Presidents Cup R/U 89/90; Witton Albion P.O.Y.89/90

Club	Seasons	Transfer	Apps	Goals
Retford Town	84-85			
Gainsborough Trinity	85-87			
Goole Town	87-89			

Burrows Malcolm (M)
(WINSFORD UNITED)   Age: 25

Previous Clubs: General Chemicals
Honours: None

Burrows, Martin (M)
(SHOTTON COMRADES)   Age: 25

Previous Clubs: None   **Honours:** None

Burrows, Paul (M)
(CLITHEROE)   Age: 24

Previous Clubs: Radcliffe Borough
Honours: None

Burton, Christopher (F)
(KIDDERMINSTER HARRIERS)

D.O.B. 9.3.70
Profession: Claims Handler
Single
Hobbies: Sport

PLAYING CAREER

Honours: Aston Schoolboy Rep; West Mids Schoolboy Rep

Club	Seasons	Transfer	Apps	Goals
Northampton Town	86-87			

Burton, Ralph (M)
(WOLVERTON AFC)   Age: 24

Previous Clubs: Milton Keynes City
Honours: None

Burton, Tom (D)
(PEGASUS JUNIORS)   Age: 31

Previous Clubs: Christleton
Honours: None

Butcher, Daryl (F)
(VALE RECREATION)   Age: 27

Previous Clubs: Guernsey Rangers; Sylvans; Guernsey Rangers
Honours: None

Butcher, Ian (F)
(CHELMSFORD CITY)

D.O.B. 28.7.72   **Nickname:** Ferret
Profession: Carpenter
Single
Hobbies: Cricket, Golf

PLAYING CAREER

Honours: None

Club	Seasons	Transfer	Apps	Goals
Braintree Town	85-86			

Butler, Craig (F)
(ALFRETON TOWN)   Age: 18

Previous Clubs: Local football
Honours: None

Butterworth, Steve (M)
(STAFFORD RANGERS)

D.O.B. 16.8.66   **Nickname:** Butty
Profession: Construction Worker
Single
Hobbies: Sport

PLAYING CAREER

Honours: None

Club	Seasons	Transfer	Apps	Goals
Northampton Town	82-84			
Buckingham Town	84-88			
V S Rugby	88-91			

TERRY BOTTING (Horsham)

Buzaglo, Timothy (F)
(WOKING)

D.O.B. 20.6.61   **Nickname:** Scuffer
Profession: Computer Operator
Married   **Wife's name:** Rita
Hobbies: Cricket, Golf, Tennis

PLAYING CAREER

Honours: None

Club	Seasons	Transfer	Apps	Goals
Weysiders FC	79-86			

Buzzard, Stephen (M)
(MORETON TOWN)   Age: 25

Previous Clubs: Easington Sports
Honours: None

Bye, Andy (D)
(FARNBOROUGH TOWN)

D.O.B. 5.6.63
Previous Clubs: Gosport Borough; Fareham Town; Basingstoke Town.
Honours: FA XI; Vauxhall League Rep.; Vauxhall-Opel Lge R/U 88/89.

ANDY BYE

Bye, Robert (D)
(TUNBRIDGE WELLS)   Age: 24

Previous Clubs: Brockley; Penhill Standard; Danson
Honours: Sunderland Shield (Spartan League)

Byrne, Damen (D)
(GAINSBOROUGH TOWN)   Age: 26

Previous Clubs: Sheffield Utd; Maltby Miners Welfare; Mexborough Town
Honours: Division One championship; Whitbread County Senior & cup

Byrne, Kevin (D)
(DESBOROUGH TOWN)   Age: 29

Previous Clubs: Corby Town; Irthlingborough Diamonds; Stewarts & Lloyds
Honours: Mansell Cup winners 1983-84

Byrne, Peter (D)
(ALTRINCHAM)

D.O.B. 24.9.67   **Nickname:** Byrnesy
Profession: Recreation & Leisure Manager
Single
Hobbies: Sports,Health & Fitness

PLAYING CAREER

Honours: Liverpool Schoolboys Rep; Merseyside County Schoolboys Rep; Central Lge Winners; Cheshire Senior Cup Winners(3)

Club	Seasons	Transfer	Apps	Goals
Everton	84-85			
Liverpool	85-86			
Runcorn	86-89			

Byron, Paul (D)
(FLEETWOOD TOWN)

D.O.B. 9.5.65   **Nickname:** Byro
Profession: Mechanic
Single
Hobbies: Golf, Socialising

PLAYING CAREER

Honours: Lancs County Schoolboy Rep; NPL Winners 85/86; NPL Challenge Shield Winners 86/87; HFS Loans Lge Presidents Cup Winners 89/90; Barrow Y.P.O.Y. 81/82 & 82/83; Southport P.P.O.Y. 88/89

Club	Seasons	Transfer	Apps	Goals
Barrow	81-85			
Blackburn Rovers	85-86			
Hartlepool United	86-88		1	
Southport	88-89			

TREVOR BARRON
(Woking)

DALE BROOKS
(Bury Town)

STEVE BOWDEN
(Meir K.A.)

GARY BULL (BARNET)

Caesar, John (F)
(MARLOW)

D.O.B. 3.4.65   Nickname: JC
Profession: Bricklayer
Single
Hobbies: Pool, Football

PLAYING CAREER

Honours: None

Club	Seasons	Transfer	Apps	Goals
Oakridge FC	82-84			
Flackwell Heath	85-87			

Cain, Alpheus (F)
(BANBURY UNITED)   Age: 22

Previous Clubs: Nuneaton Borough
Honours: None

Caley, David (M)
(CLACTON TOWN)   Age: 25

Previous Clubs:
Honours: None

Callaghan, Ian (M)
(NORTHWICH VICTORIA)

D.O.B. 5.8.69

PLAYING CAREER

Honours: Mid-Cheshire Senior Cup Winners; Staffs Senior Cup Winners

Club	Seasons	Transfer	Apps	Goals
Bolton Wanderers	87-89			1

Callingham, Paul (D)
(LANGLEY SPORTS)   Age: 21

Previous Clubs: Langley Sports; Eastbourne United; Eastbourne Town; Hailsham Town

Honours: Sussex County League Div 2 champions 1987/88; Sussex County League Challenge Cup winner 1989/90; Represented Sussex at Senior level & youth; Brighton Evening Argus County 5 a side champions 1989/90; Eastbourne Charity Cup winner 1989/90

Calvert, Carl (M)
(DENABY UNITED)   Age: 20

Previous Clubs: Rotherham United; Gisborne City (New Zealand); Stocksbridge
Honours: South Yorkshire u15 F.A. Cup winner 1989

Camden, Chris (F)
(MACCLESFIELD TOWN)

D.O.B. 28.5.63   Nickname: Cammy
Profession: Not working
Married   Wife's name: Clare
Children: Emma & Charlotte
Hobbies: Cricket, Squash

PLAYING CAREER

Honours: FA XI

Club	Seasons	Transfer	Apps	Goals
Tranmere Rovers	81-82			
Poulton Vics	82-83			
Chester City	1983		12	5
Oswestry Town	83-85			
Tranmere Rovers	86-87		3	1
Chorley	1987			
Ellesmere Port	1987			
South Liverpool	87-88	£3,000		
Stafford Rangers	88-90			

Campbell, Gary (M)
(BROMLEY)   Age: 24

Previous Clubs: Finchley; Boreham Wood; Leyton Wingate; Leyton Orient
Honours: None

Campbell, Kenton (D)
(BROMLEY)   Age: 26

Previous Clubs: Leyton Wingate
Honours: Supporters Player of the Year 1989-90 (Leyton)

Campbell, Kevin (D)
(SEATON DELAVAL AMATEURS)   Age: 28

Previous Clubs: Tow Law Town
Honours: Northern League XI; Northern League Championship runners up; Northern League Challenge Cup runners up

Campbell, Winston (M/F)
(BOSTON UNITED)

D.O.B. 9.10.62   Nickname: Winnie
Profession: Social Worker
Single

PLAYING CAREER

Honours: Sheffield Schoolboys Rep; South Yorks Schoolboys Rep; England Youth Int

Club	Seasons	Transfer	Apps	Goals
Barnsley	79-86	£40,000	128	9
Doncaster Rovers		loan	3	
Rotherham United	86-88		69	9
Stafford Rangers	89-90			

Cappuccio, Peter (F)
(CHELMSFORD CITY)

D.O.B. 6.2.63   Nickname: Cappa
Profession: Printer   Hobbies: Viniculture
Married   Wife's name: Verna

PLAYING CAREER

Honours: North West Kent & Kent Schoolboy Rep; Kent Senior Cup Winners

Club	Seasons	Transfer	Apps	Goals
Crockenhill	80-83			
Cray Wanderers	83-86			
Erith & Belvedere	86-88			
Dulwich Hamlet	88-89			

Capstick, James   (D)
(BARROW)

D.O.B. 12.4.59   **Nickname:** Capper
Profession: Not working
Married   **Wife's name:** Linda
Children: Glenn James & Graham
Hobbies: Golf, Reading

PLAYING CAREER
Honours: HFS Loans Lge Premier Winners; NPL Cup R/U; Lancs Floodlight Cup R/U; West Lancs Lge Cup Winners; Vickers P.O.Y. 81/82, 82/83 & 83/84

Club	Seasons	Transfer	Apps	Goals
Vickers SC	80-84			
Dalton United	1984			
Barrow	84-89	£800		
Morecambe	89-90			
Barrow	1990			
Morecambe	1990			

Carey, Paul   (D)
(TUNBRIDGE WELLS)   Age: 26
Previous Clubs:
Honours: None

Carmichael, John   (G)
(SANDWELL BOROUGH)   Age: 23
Previous Clubs: Northfield; Bilston; Oldbury
Honours: None

Carnell, Mark   (M)
(MELTON TOWN)   Age: 21
Previous Clubs: Petfoods; Molwell Wocks
Honours: None

Carolan, Pat   (M)
(TOOTING & MITCHAM UNITED)   Age: 30
Previous Clubs: Gillingham; Carshalton Athletic; Clapton; Dulwich Hamlet; Croydon
Honours: None

Carpenter, Dave   (D)
(WARMINSTER TOWN)   Age: 42
Previous Clubs: Heavitree United; Dawlish Town; Heavitree United; Tiverton Town; Heavitree United; Elmore; Heavitree United
Honours: Devon County; Devon Premier Cup Winners

Carpenter, Gary   (D)
(EXMOUTH TOWN)   Age:
Previous Clubs: Heavitree United; Torrington
Honours: None

Carpenter, Matthew   (M)
(WARMINSTER TOWN)   Age: 16
Previous Clubs: None
Honours: Wiltshire County u15

Carr, Michael   (F)
(SANDWELL)   Age: 27
Previous Clubs: V.S.Rugby; Boldmere St.Michael; Princess End Utd; Tividale; Evesham; Redditch
Honours: League Championship; 2 cup medals

Carre, Scott   (M)
(VALE RECREATION)   Age: 22
Previous Clubs: Vale Recreation (Youth); Belgrave Wanderers; St.Martin's
Honours: Guernsey u21 cap 1988-89

Carrick, Eddie   (F)
(BILLERICAY TOWN)   Age: 24
Previous Clubs: Colchester United; Walsall; Basildon United
Honours: None

Carrick, Finton   (M)
(WELWYN GARDEN CITY)   Age: 27
Previous Clubs: Welwyn Garden United; Stevenage Borough; Hertford Town
Honours: Herts u16's

Carroll, Dave   (M)
(WYCOMBE WANDERERS)

D.O.B. 20.9.66

PLAYING CAREER
Honours: England Youth Int; Berks & Bucks Senior Cup Winners 89/90

Club	Seasons	Transfer	Apps	Goals
Fulham	83-85			
Wembley	85-86			
Ruislip Manor	86-88	£6,000		

DAVE CARROLL

Carroll, John (M)

(EYNESBURY ROVERS) **Age:** 26

Previous Clubs: Eynesbury Rovers; St.Neots Town; Eynesbury Rovers; Potton United; Stotfold
Honours: UCL 1987; Wallspan Cup 1988; Beds, Charity Cup 1987 & 1988

Carroll, Matthew (D)

(KIDDERMINSTER HARRIERS) **D.O.B.** 15.5.72

Profession: Electrician
Single **Hobbies:** Sport

PLAYING CAREER

Honours: Birmingham County Schoolboy Rep; West Mids County Schoolboy Rep

Club	Seasons	Transfer	Apps	Goals
Wolverhampton W's	83-87			

Carroll, Robert (F)

(YEOVIL TOWN)

D.O.B. 15.2.68 **Nickname:** Smoulders
Profession: Local Government Officer
Single **Hobbies:** Golf, Water-skiing

PLAYING CAREER

Honours: Bob Lord Trophy Winners 89/90; Capital Lge Cup Winners 87/88

Club	Seasons	Transfer	Apps	Goals
Southampton	84-86			
Gosport Borough	1986			
Brentford	86-88		30	10
Fareham Town	88-89	£5,000		

ROBERT CARROLL

Carter, Mark (F)

(RUNCORN) **D.O.B.** 17.12.60

PLAYING CAREER

Honours: England Semi-Pro Int; FA Trophy R/U 83/84 & 85/86; Cheshire Senior Cup Winners

Club	Seasons	Transfer	Apps	Goals
Liverpool	78-79			
South Liverpool	79-81			
Bangor City	81-84			

Cartwright, Mark (D)

(NEWTOWN) **Age:** 25

Previous Clubs: Wrexham; Oswestry Town; Brymbo Steelworks; Lex XI; Bangor City; Colwyn Bay
Honours: European C.W.C. appearance with Bangor City

Cartwright, Steve (D)

(TAMWORTH) **Age:** 25

Previous Clubs: Tamworth; Colchester United (11)
Honours: FA Vase Winners 1989

Casey, Kim (F)

(CHELTENHAM TOWN) **D.O.B.** 3.3.61

Profession: Insurance Inspector **Nickname:** Case
Married **Wife's name:** Kim
Hobbies: Tennis, Golf

PLAYING CAREER

Honours: England Schoolboy Int; England Semi-Pro Int; Middx Wanderer; FA Trophy Winner

Club	Seasons	Transfer	Apps	Goals
Sutton Coldfield Town	78-80			
AP Leamington	80-82	£1,000		
Gloucester City	82-83	£3,000		
Kidderminster Harriers	83-90	£25,000		

Caskey, Mark (G)

(CROYDON) **Age:** 18

Previous Clubs: Local football
Honours: Croydon Schoolboy Rep; Surrey Youth Rep; Southern Youth Lge & Cup Winners

Cass, Dave (G)

(BILLERICAY TOWN) **Age:** 28

Previous Clubs: Billericay Town; Aveley; Leyton Orient
Honours: Essex Thames side Trophy winners medal

Catley, Paul (G)

(BRAINTREE TOWN) **Age:** 18

Previous Clubs: None
Honours: Essex Youth Rep

Catley, Russell (M)

(PEGASUS JUNIORS) **Age:** 25

Previous Clubs: Dales United; Westfields
Honours: None

KIM CASEY (CHELTENHAM TOWN & ENGLAND)

Catlin, Garry (M)

(STAPENHILL) Age: 28

Previous Clubs: Stapenhill; Norman Cockran; Telefusion; Burton North End

Honours: Scoreline Combination Div 1 League championship; Derby Senior League Premier Div Championship; Leicester Combination Winners 1988-90; Leicester Intermediate Shield Winners 1988-90

Caulfield, Colin (G)

(WOKING)

D.O.B. 19.12.63 **Nickname:** Corfs
Profession: Life Assurance Consultant
Single
Hobbies: Cricket, Golf

PLAYING CAREER

Honours: Surrey Youth Rep; FA Youth Rep; Addlestone P.O.Y.

Club	Seasons	Transfer	Apps	Goals
Addlestone & W.	81-85			
Wimbledon	81-85 (N.C.)			
Wokingham Town	85-89			

Caulfield, Mark (M)

(SUTTON COLDFIELD TOWN) Age: 24

Previous Clubs: Oldbury United; Paget Rangers
Honours: Birmingham County Youth & Senior Rep

Caulton, Chris (M)

(STAPENHILL) Age: 27

Previous Clubs: Newhall United; Burton Albion

Honours: Leicester Senior League winners 1988-90; Tebbutt Brown Winners 1988-90; Stapenhill Player of the Year 1989-90 & Players Player of the Year

Cawte, Malcolm (D)

(SELSEY) Age: 32

Previous Clubs: Bognor Regis Town; Portfield; Selsey; Chichester; Sidlesham

Honours: None

Cawston, Mervyn (G)

(REDBRIDGE FOREST) D.O.B. 4.2.52

PLAYING CAREER

Honours: England Schoolboy Int; Football League Div 4 Winners 80/81

Club	Seasons	Transfer	Apps	Goals
Norwich City	69-75		4	
(Southend United - loan 10; Newport County - loan 4)				
Gillingham	75-76		19	
Chicago Sting (USA)	76-78			
Southend United	78-83		189	
Stoke City	83-84			
Chelmsford City	1984			
Southend United	84-85		9	
Maidstone United	85-89		10	

Chadbourne, Steven (G)

(ALFRETON TOWN) Age: 25

Previous Clubs: Notts County; Nottingham Forest; Mansfield Town; Arnold; Oakham United
Honours: Nottingham Schoolboy Rep; England Schoolboy Int

Chadburn, Craig (D)

(DENABY UNITED) Age: 25

Previous Clubs: Parkgate; Sheffield; Ecclesfield Red Rose

Honours: Sheffield Senior Cup Winners 1987; Represented Sheffield & Hallamshire County FA u18's

Chadwick, Paul (M)

(BIGGLESWADE) Age: 30

Previous Clubs: Letchworth; Arlesey; Baldock; Arlesey; Stotfold

Honours: UCL Cup winner; North Beds Charity Cup winner; SML Championship

Chalcraft, Phil (D)

(GODALMING TOWN) Age: 27

Previous Clubs: Ockfield Social

Honours: Godalming Town P.O.Y. 88/89 & 89/90.

Chalk, Ian (F)

(SALISBURY) Age: 25

Previous Clubs: Wrexham; Peterborough United; Bemerton Athletic; Warminster
Honours: Salisbury P.O.Y.

Challis, Paul (D)

(ERITH & BELVEDERE)

D.O.B. 24.9.66 **Nickname:** Shanksy
Profession: HGV Driver
Single
Hobbies: Golf, Snooker, Weight Training

PLAYING CAREER

Honours: Greenwich Borough P.O.Y.88/89 & 89/90

Club	Seasons	Transfer	Apps	Goals
Greenwich Borough	88-90			
Dartford	90-91			

Chaloner, Mark (D)

(COLWYN BAY) Age: 28

Previous Clubs: New Broughton; Brymbo Steelworks
Honours: Bass NWCL Cup Winners

Chamberlain, Glyn (D)

(NEWCASTLE TOWN) Age: 33

Previous Clubs: Burnley; Chesterfield; Halifax Town; Kettering Town; Buxton; Hyde United; Matlock Town; Droylsden

Honours: N.P.L. Cup winners

Champ, Steve (M)

(BRAINTREE TOWN) Age: 20

Previous Clubs: Hatfield Peverel; Bramston CML; Witham Town
Honours: None

Champion, Daren (M)
(HORSHAM) Age: 23
Previous Clubs: Horsham; Arundel; Crawley Town; Steyning Town; Lancing
Honours: Sussex Senior Cup Winners 87/88

Chandler, Ricky (M)
(GLOUCESTER CITY) D.O.B. 26.9.61
Profession: Salesman
Married **Wife's name:** Rachel
Hobbies: Golf

PLAYING CAREER
Honours: Southern Lge Midland Div Winners 88/89

Club	Seasons	Transfer	Apps	Goals
Bristol City	78-83		71	16
Bath City	83-86			
Yeovil Town	86-88			

Chaplin, Mark (D)
(HORSHAM) Age: 25
Previous Clubs: Youth team product
Honours: None

Chapman, Craig (D)
(GUISBOROUGH TOWN) Age: 19
Previous Clubs: Newcastle Unitd; Guisborough Town
Honours: Northern Intermediate League Cup; Central League

Chapman, Jim (M)
(BIGGLESWADE TOWN) Age: 23
Previous Clubs: Sandy Albion
Honours: County Youth Cap

Chapman, Mark (G)
(HORSHAM) Age: 30
Previous Clubs: Grays Athletic; Aveley
Honours: None

Chapman, Robbie (M)
(M. BLACKSTONES) Age: 26
Previous Clubs: Stamford AFC; Wisbech; Holbeach
Honours: F.A. Vase runners up

Chard, Chris (F)
(THATCHAM) Age: 30
Previous Clubs: Thatcham; Hungerford
Honours: None

Charles, Roger (M)
(ABINGDON TOWN) Age: 22
Previous Clubs: Oxford United
Honours: FA XI; Hellenic Lge Winners 86/87; Spartan Lge Winners 88/89; Hellenic Lge & Cup R/U 86/87; Berks & Bucks Senior Cup R/U 88/89; Abingdon P.O.Y. 88/89

Chawner, Mick (M)
(BILSTON TOWN) Age: 25
Previous Clubs: Boldmere St.Michael; Paget Rangers; Sutton Coldfield Town
Honours: None

Clack, Raymond (D)
(CONGLETON TOWN) Age: 34
Previous Clubs: Congleton Town; Leek Town; Congleton Town; Winsford Town.
Honours: HFS Loans Lge R/U 89/90

Clark, Alan (M)
(BOOTLE) Age: 30
Previous Clubs: Maghull; Bootle; Burscough
Honours: None

Clark, Dave (D)
(BOGNOR REGIS TOWN)

D.O.B. 22.1.64
Profession: Butcher
Single
Hobbies: Sport

PLAYING CAREER
Honours: Sussex County Rep

Club	Seasons	Transfer	Apps	Goals
Wick FC	84-90			

Clark, Gavin (M)
(VALE RECREATION) Age: 18
Previous Clubs:
Honours: Guernsey Youth Cap 1989-90

Clark, Nicky (M)
(WALTHAMSTOW PENNANT) Age: 20
Previous Clubs: Leyton Orient Youth
Honours: None

Clarke, Andrew (F)
(BARNET)

D.O.B. 22.7.67 **Nickname:** Dark Shark
Profession: Not working
Single
Hobbies: Football

PLAYING CAREER
Honours: Barnet P.O.Y. 89/90

Club	Seasons	Transfer	Apps	Goals
St.Mary's FC	87-88			

Clarke, Andy (D)
(PEGASUS JUNIORS) Age: 20
Previous Clubs: Withington; Bromyard
Honours: None

Clarke, Ian (M)
(NEWTOWN) Age: 30
Previous Clubs: Oswestry Town; Caernarfon Town; Rhyl
Honours: ??

Clarke, Mark (F)
(EASTWOOD TOWN) Age: 18
Previous Clubs: Grimsby Town
Honours: None

Clarke, Nicholas (D/M)
(CROYDON) Age: 19
Previous Clubs: Charlton Athletic
Honours: None

Clarke, Paul (F)
(HAYES)

D.O.B. 11.5.62 **Nickname:** Clarkey
Profession: Groundsman
Married **Wife's name:** Chris
Children: Laura & Emily
Hobbies: Sport

PLAYING CAREER
Honours: Wilts Youth Rep; South West England Rep; Feltham P.O.Y. (3)

Club	Seasons	Transfer	Apps	Goals
Feltham	82-89			

Clarke, Steve (M)
(KEYNSHAM TOWN) Age: 27
Previous Clubs: Broad Plan; Bishop Sutton; Clevedon Town; Brislington; Keynshaw Town
Honours: None

ANDREW CLARK (Barnet)

Clarke, Steve (D)
(SANDWELL BOROUGH) Age: 30
Previous Clubs: Dudley Town; Tividale; Boldmere St.Michaels; Paget Rangers; Rushall Olympic; Harrisons; Mile Oak Rovers
Honours: None

Clarkson, Philip (M)
(FLEETWOOD TOWN)

D.O.B. 13.11.68 **Nickname:** Turtle
Profession: Mechanic
Single
Hobbies: Golf

PLAYING CAREER
Honours: Fleetwood P.O.Y. (2)

Club	Seasons	Transfer	Apps	Goals
Wyre Villa	84-87			

Claydon, Jeremy (M)
(BURNHAM RAMBLERS) Age: 27
Previous Clubs: Runwell; Billericay
Honours: None

Clayton, Darren (G)
(SUTTON COLDFIELD TOWN) Age: 24
Previous Clubs: Knowle; Paget Rangers; Sutton Coldfield Town; Midvag (Faroe Isles)
Honours: Sutton P.O.Y.87/88

Clegg, Graham (D)
(MOOR GREEN)

D.O.B. 25.1.60 **Nickname:** Cleggy
Profession: P.E.Teacher
Married **Wife's name:** Wendy
Children: Stephanie
Hobbies: Cricket, Golf

PLAYING CAREER
Honours: England Public Schools Rep; British Colleges Rep; FA XI

Club	Seasons	Transfer	Apps	Goals
Blackpool	75-81			
Sutton Coldfield Town	81-85			
Moor Green	85-86			
Burton Albion	86-87	£500		

Clemmence, Neil (M)
(WELLING UNITED)

D.O.B. 29.7.64 **Nickname:** Clemmo
Profession: Cabinet Maker
Married **Wife's name:** Nicola
Hobbies: DIY

PLAYING CAREER
Honours: Southern Lge Premier Div Winners 85/86; Kent Senior Cup & London Senior Cup Winners

Club	Seasons	Transfer	Apps	Goals
Dartford	83-85			

COLIN COWPERTHWAITE (BARROW)

Clover, Keith (D)
(CLEATOR MOOR CELTIC) Age: 29
Previous Clubs: Cleator Moor Celtic; Workington
Honours: None

Clowes, Greg (D)
(KIDSGROVE ATHLETIC)

D.O.B. 7.10.64   **Nickname:** Clowsy
Profession: Sales Director
Married   **Wife's name:** Tracey
Children: Oliver
Hobbies: Gardening, Most Sports

PLAYING CAREER
Honours: Leek P.O.Y. 88/89

Club	Seasons	Transfer	Apps	Goals
Leek Town	87-90			
Congleton Town	90-91			

Coates, John (M)
(SAWBRIDGEWORTH TOWN) Age: 23
Previous Clubs: Tottenham Hotspur Schoolboy
Honours: Essex Schoolboy Rep; London F.A. u17 & u19

Coates, Martin (M)
(BROMLEY) Age: 29
Previous Clubs: Dulwich Hamlet; Dartford; Hendon; Barking; Leytonstone Ilford
Honours: Southern League Prem winners (Dartford); Vauxhall Opel Div 1 & Premier Div

Cobb, Anthony (M)
(MARLOW)

D.O.B. 9.4.61   **Nickname:** Bobby
Profession: Scaffolder
Married   **Wife's name:** Mandy
Children: Susska

PLAYING CAREER
Honours: None

Club	Seasons	Transfer	Apps	Goals
Buckingham Town	75-76			
Aylesbury United	76-82			
Winslow United	82-83			
Chesham United	84-86			
Aylesbury United	87-88			
Thame United	1988			
Buckingham Town	88-89			

Codrington, Kenny (D)
(WELLINGBOROUGH TOWN) Age: 25
Previous Clubs: Irchester Eastfield; Rushden Town
Honours: None

Coe, Paul (M)
(NEWMARKET TOWN) Age: 22

Previous Clubs: Soham Town Rangers; Histon
Honours: Leading Goal Scorer 1989/90

Coghlan, Duncan (M)
(BRAINTREE TOWN) Age: 18
Previous Clubs: Chelmsford City
Honours: Essex Youth Rep

Colbran Simon (M)
(TUNBRIDGE WELLS) Age: 20
Previous Clubs: Ashford; Hastings
Honours: None

Coleby, Stuart (D)
(BILLINGHAM SYNTHONIA) Age: 30
Previous Clubs: Whitby Town; Scarborough
Honours: Northern League 2nd Div Trophy 1986-87; N Lge Championship 1988-89,1989-90; N Lge Cup 1987-88, 1989-90; Durham Cup winners Trophy 1988-89

Coleman, John (F)
(MORECAMBE)

D.O.B. 12.10.62   **Nickname:** Coley
Profession: Clerk
Married   **Wife's name:** Lorraine
Children: Leanne, Kayleigh & Lauren
Hobbies: Golf, Tennis, Cricket

PLAYING CAREER
Honours: Kirkby Schoolboy Rep; Liverpool County Youth Rep; Southport P.O.Y. 86/87

Club	Seasons	Transfer	Apps	Goals
Kirkby Town	79-83			
Burscough	83-85			
Marine	85-86			
Southport	86-87			
Runcorn	87-88			
Macclesfield Town	1988			
Rhyl	88-89			
Witton Albion	89-90			

Coleman, Phil (D)
(WIVENHOE TOWN)

D.O.B. 8.9.60

PLAYING CAREER
Honours: None

Club	Seasons	Transfer	Apps	Goals
Millwall	77-80	£15,000	36	1
Colchester United	80-83		86	6
Wrexham		loan	17	2
Chelmsford City	83-84			
Exeter City	1984		6	
Aldershot	84-85		45	5
Dulwich Hamlet	85-86			
Millwall	86-87		10	
Colchester United	87-88		10	

BILLY COLE (Waterlooville)

Coles, David   (G)
(GAINSBOROUGH TOWN)   Age: 20
Previous Clubs: Motherwell Hamilton; Scunthorpe United; Louth United
Honours: None

Coles, Frank   (M)
(BROMLEY)   Age: 25
Previous Clubs: Charlton (Comb); Leytonstone; Dagenham; Leytonstone; Leyton-Wingate; Enfield
Honours: Vauxhall Opel winners (Prem)- Leytonstone

Coles, Neil   (F)
(BANBURY UNITED)   Age: 24
Previous Clubs: Chipping Norton Town
Honours: None

Colfer, John   (M)
(ST ALBANS CITY)
D.O.B. 30.10.63   **Nickname:** Ears
Profession: Scaffolder
Single
Hobbies: Socialising

PLAYING CAREER
Honours: Herts County Rep; London Colney P.O.Y. 87-88

Club	Seasons	Transfer	Apps	Goals
London Colney	87-88			
Hitchin Town	88-89			

Collier, Chris   (F)
(GOOLE TOWN)   Age: 26
Previous Clubs: Selby Town; York RI; Selby York RI; Selby Town.
Honours: NCE Div 2 runners up 1990

Collier, Peter   (F)
(GOOLE TOWN)   Age: 22
Previous Clubs: Plymouth Argyle; York City; Selby Town
Honours: NCE Div 2 runners up 1990; Selby Town leading scorer 1986-1990

Collier, Russell   (D)
(CHELMSLEY TOWN)   Age: 27
Previous Clubs: Chelmsley Town; Kingsbury United; Chelmsley Town; Wythall
Honours: President Cup winners & runners up

Collings, Gary   (D)
(NEWMARKET TOWN)   Age: 38
Previous Clubs: Lowestoft Town; Gorneston; Wroxham; Watton; Sudbury
Honours: None

Collins, Jimmy   (M)
(MORECAMBE)

D.O.B.   **Nickname:** "JC"
Profession: Not working
Single
Hobbies: Snooker, Squash

PLAYING CAREER
Honours: FA Vase Winners 86/87; HFS Loans Lge Div 1 Winners 87/88, St.Helens P.O.Y. 86/87

Club	Seasons	Transfer	Apps	Goals
Derby County	81-83			
St.Helens Town	84-87			
Fleetwood Town	87-89			

Collins, John   (F)
(TOOTING & MITCHAM UNITED)   Age: 24
Previous Clubs: Cuffley; Dulwich Hamlet; Wealdstone
Honours: None

Collins, Steve (D)
(KETTERING TOWN)

D.O.B. 21.3.62
Profession: Not working
Married **Wife's name:** Yvonne
Hobbies: Cricket

PLAYING CAREER

Honours: None

Club	Seasons	Transfer	Apps	Goals
Peterborough United	78-83	£10,000	94	1
Southend United	83-84		51	
Lincoln City	84-85		24	
Peterborough United	85-87		122	2

Colvin, Darren (F)
(ROMSEY TOWN) **Age:** 18
Previous Clubs:
Honours: Wessex League Champions

Collymore, Dave (F)
(CROYDON) **Age:** 21
Previous Clubs: Fulham; Tooting & Mitcham United
Honours: Surrey Youth Rep; England Youth Int

Comber, Phil (D)
(HAILSHAM TOWN) **Age:** 31
Previous Clubs: Burgess Hill Town; Hassocks; Eastbourne United
Honours: Sussex u18; Sussex Schools; Sussex Intermediate; Full Sussex Rep

Comer, Paul (G)
(SWINDON ATHLETIC) **Age:** 33
Previous Clubs: Wootton Bassett Town; Hungerford Town; Calne Town; Lambourne
Honours: None

Compton, Paul (D)
(BASHLEY)

D.O.B. 6.6.61 **Nickname:** Compo
Profession: Carpet Cleaner
Married **Wife's name:** Elaine
Children: Lee, Jay & Jack
Hobbies: Sport

PLAYING CAREER

Honours: None

Club	Seasons	Transfer	Apps	Goals
Cardiff City	77-78			
Trowbridge Town	78-80			
AFC Bournemouth	80-82		64	
Aldershot	83-84		13	
Torquay United	84-86		95	4
Newport County	86-89		27	2
Weymouth	89-91			

Connelly, Simon (M)
(BURNHAM RAMBLERS) **Age:** 22
Previous Clubs: None **Honours:** None

Conner, Mark (D)
(KNOWSLEY UNITED) **Age:** 28
Previous Clubs: Southport; Formby; Kirkly Town
Honours: 1989/90 Knowsley Player of the Year

Conner, Steve (D)
(REDBRIDGE FOREST) **D.O.B.** 14.7.64
Profession: Assistant Bank Manager
Married **Wife's name:** Tracy
Hobbies: Golf

PLAYING CAREER

Honours: England Semi-Pro Int; Tilbury P.O.Y. 85/86; Dartford P.O.Y. 87/88

Club	Seasons	Transfer	Apps	Goals
Grays Athletic	83-84			
East Thurrock United	84-85			
Tilbury	85-86	£2,000		
Dartford	86-90	£3,500		

Conning, Peter (M)
(YEOVIL TOWN) **D.O.B.** 18.10.64
Profession: Professional Footballer
Single **Hobbies:** Reading, Kite Flying

PLAYING CAREER

Honours: England Schoolboy Int; Merseyside Schoolboy & Youth Rep; England Semi-Pro Int; FA Trophy Winners 85/86; GMAC Cup R/U 87/88; Bob Lord Trophy Winners 89/90

Club	Seasons	Transfer	Apps	Goals
Liverpool	80-83			
Wigan Athletic	1984			
South Liverpool	1984			
Altrincham	84-86			
Rochdale	86-87		40	2
Weymouth	87-89	£13,000		

Connolly, Joseph (D:M)
(MALDEN VALE) **Age:** 23
Previous Clubs: Banstead Athletic; Carshalton Athletic
Honours: Surrey Senior Cup Winners 88/89 & 89/90; Gilbert Rice Cup Winners 86/87

Connor, Joe (F)
(WITTON ALBION) **D.O.B.** 15.5.65
Profession: Recruitment Officer
Married **Wife's name:** Donna
Children: Natalie **Hobbies:** Sport

PLAYING CAREER

Honours: None

Club	Seasons	Transfer	Apps	Goals
Stockport County	80 83			
Mossley	83-87			
Hyde United	87-90	£10,000		

GLYN CREASER (WYCOMBE WANDERERS)

Connor, Tommy (D)

(BILLINGHAM SYNTHONIA) Age: 32

Previous Clubs: South Bank; East Fife; Seaham Red Star; Easington
Honours: None

Conwell, Thomas (M)

(CHESTER LE STREET) Age: 22

Previous Clubs: Murton; Dunston Fed
Honours: None

Cooke, Colin (D)

(COLESHILL) Age: 32

Previous Clubs: Coleshill Town; Sutton Town
Honours: None

Cooke, Robbie (F)

(KETTERING TOWN) D.O.B. 16.2.57

Nickname: Cookie **Profession:** Sales Rep
Married **Wife's name:** Linda
Children: Lyndsey, Adam & Gavin
Hobbies: Golf

PLAYING CAREER

Honours: England Semi-Pro Int; Brentford P.O.Y. 86/87; GMVC R/U 88/89

Club	Seasons	Transfer	Apps	Goals
Mansfield Town	73-78		20	1
Grantham	78-80	£15,000		
Peterborough United	80-83	£15,000	134	68
Cambridge United	83-85	£25,000	68	26
Brentford	85-87	£30,000	135	54
Millwall	87-88		6	1

ROBBIE COOKE

Cooke, Terry (M)

(COLWYN BAY) Age: 28

Previous Clubs: Chester City
Honours: None

Cooksley Ade (D)

(MIRRLEES BLACKSTONES) Age: 29

Previous Clubs: R.A.F.; Somersham; Victoria Goch (Germany)
Honours: Combined Services

Coombe, Mark (G)

(SALISBURY) Age: 21

Previous Clubs: AFC Bournemouth; Bristol City; Carlisle United; Colchester United (3); Torquay United (8)
Honours: FA Youth Rep

Cooper David (D)

(STAPENHILL) Age: 30

Previous Clubs: Heanor Town; Stapenhill; Heanor Town; Ilkeston Town; Mickloover RBL; Rainbow Athletic

Honours: Player of the Year with Heanor; B.E.Webb Cup with Heanor & Ilkeston Town

Cooper, Geoff (D)

(BARNET)

D.O.B. 27.12.60 **Nickname:** Coops
Profession: Not working
Married **Wife's name:** Karen
Children: Luke & Emma

PLAYING CAREER

Honours:

Club	Seasons	Transfer	Apps	Goals
Bognor Regis Town	77-87			
Brighton & H. A.	87-89		15	

GEOFF COOPER

Cooper, Graham (M)
(SHOTTON COMRADES) Age: 19
Previous Clubs: Sunderland AFC; Blackhall
Honours: Great Britain Schools (u17)

Cooper, Jim (D)
(BARKING)

D.O.B. 27.3.68   **Nickname:** Coops
Profession: Steel Fixer
Single
Hobbies: Socialising.

PLAYING CAREER
Honours: London & Essex Schoolboy Rep; Vauxhall-Opel Lge Div 1 Winners; Essex Senior Cup Winners & R/U

Club	Seasons	Transfer	Apps	Goals
Barking	86-87			
Leytonstone & Ilford	87-88	£1,000		
Dagenham	88-89			

Cooper, Lee (F)
(PICKERING TOWN) Age: 30
Previous Clubs: Hackness; Scalby; Southcliffe; Pickering; Eastfield; T.A. D Coy; Scarborough AFC
Honours: Gola League winners with Scarborough

Cooper, Michael (D)
(SHOTTON COMRADES) Age: 21
Previous Clubs: Hartlepool Utd; Blackhall
Honours: None

Cooper, Richard (M)
(YEOVIL TOWN)

D.O.B. 7.5.65   **Nickname:** Coops
Profession: Not working
Single
Hobbies: All Sports, Reading, Music
PLAYING CAREER
Honours: None

Club	Seasons	Transfer	Apps	Goals
Sheffield United	80-85		12	
Lincoln City	85-87	£10,000	107	2
Exeter City	87-89		69	2
Weymouth	89-91			

Cooper, T (D)
(CHELMSLEY TOWN) Age: 28
Previous Clubs: Coleshill Town; GEC Witton
Honours: Sutton League Premier winners (top scorer 36 goals)

Copeland, Simon (D)
(EASTWOOD TOWN) Age: 22
Previous Clubs: Rochdale; Gainsborough Trinity.
Honours: Notts Senior Cup Winners

Copley, Gary (G)
(GAINSBOROUGH TOWN) Age: 29
Previous Clubs: Barton Town; Winterton Rangers; Maltby Miners Welfare; Barnsley
Honours: None

Copping, Simon (M)
(WALTHAMSTOW PENNANT) Age: 19
Previous Clubs: Leyton Orient (Youth)
Honours: None

Coppinger, Anthony (M)
(STAPENHILL) Age: 27
Previous Clubs: Bolehall Swifts; Newhall; Gresley Rovers
Honours: Leicester Senior Div Champions 1988-89; Tebbutt Brown Cup winners 1988-89

Corbett, Jonathan (D)
(HITCHIN TOWN) Age: 22
Previous Clubs: Aylesbury United; Dunstable
Honours: None

Corbin, Carlo (M)
(MALDEN VALE) Age: 25
Previous Clubs: Carshalton Athletic; Dartford
Honours: None

Corkain Stephen (D)
(BILLINGHAM SYNTHONIA) Age: 23
Previous Clubs: Hull City
Honours: Northern Lge Championship Trophy 1989-90; Northern Lge Cup 1989-90

Corlett, Stuart (D)
(BOGNOR REGIS TOWN)

D.O.B. 9.10.71   **Nickname:** Arthur Daley
Profession: Roofer
Single
Hobbies: Sport
PLAYING CAREER
Honours: British Colleges Rep

Club	Seasons	Transfer	Apps	Goals
Crystal Palace	88-89			

Corney, Robert (M)
(PICKERING TOWN) Age: 23
Previous Clubs: Wykeham
Honours: None

Corner, Danny (D)
(WESTFIELDS) Age: 21
Previous Clubs: Hereford United; Worcester City; Abergavenny Thursdays
Honours: HFA Senior Challenge Cup winners with Westfields

IAN CRAWLEY (TELFORD UNITED)

Corns, Simon (M)

(PRESCOT)   Age: 25

Previous Clubs: St.Helens Town
Honours: None

Cosgrove, Martin (M)

(PENRITH)   Age: 22

Previous Clubs: Annan Athletic
Honours: None

Costello, Mark (D)

(SUTTON UNITED)   **D.O.B.** 1.10.71
Nickname: Cos   **Profession:** Plumber
Single
Hobbies: Squash

PLAYING CAREER

Honours: Surrey Schoolboy & Youth Rep; Sutton Youth P.O.Y. 87/88

Club	Seasons	Transfer	Apps	Goals
No previous clubs				

Cottin, Martin (G)

(AFC LYMINGTON)   Age: 27

Previous Clubs: Brockenhurst; Lymington Town; Salisbury; AFC Totton; Brockenhurst

Honours: Hants Senior Representative; Hants Senior Cup runners up.

Cottington, Brian (D)

(KINGSTONIAN)

D.O.B. 14.2.65

PLAYING CAREER

Honours: FA Trophy Winners 87/88

Club	Seasons	Transfer	Apps	Goals
Fulham	83-86		73	1
Enfield	86-89			

Coultan, Colin (D)

(RADFORD)   Age: 26

Previous Clubs: Nettleham; Lincoln United
Honours: None

Court, Jason (D/M)

(HAYES)

D.O.B. 25.1.66
Profession: Carpenter
Single
Hobbies: Golf

PLAYING CAREER

Honours: Herts Youth Rep

Club	Seasons	Transfer	Apps	Goals
St.Albans City	82-86			
Chalfont St.Peter	86-87			
Boreham Wood	87-88			

Courtney, Ian (D)

(AFC LYMINGTON)   Age: 24

Previous Clubs: Hythe & Dibden; Blackfield & Langley

Honours: Southampton Senior League champions; Hampshire Senior Cup runners up; Wessex League Rep.

Covington, Gavin (D)

(HITCHIN TOWN)   Age: 20

Previous Clubs: Dunstable; Barnet
Honours: None

Cowan, Ralph (D)

(TOOTING & MITCHAM UNITED)   Age: 29

Previous Clubs: Witney Town; Oxford City; Lewes
Honours: Sussex County Cricketer

Cowdell Andrew (D)

(BRIDGNORTH TOWN)   Age: 28

Previous Clubs: West Bromwich Albion; GKN Sankey; Broseley Athletic

Honours: None

Cowie, John (M)

(WOLVERTON AFC)   Age: 23

Previous Clubs: Partick Thistle; East Stirling
Honours: u21 Scottish Juvenile Cup 1986-87

Cowley, Duncan (M)

(NORTON & STOCKTON ANCIENTS)   Age: 21

Previous Clubs: Hartlepool United; Wolviston; Middlesborough; South Bank

Honours: Picked for England u19 while at college

Cowperthwaite, Colin (F)

(BARROW)

D.O.B. 16.4.59   **Nickname:** Cowps
Profession: Painter & Decorator
Married   **Wife's name:** Karen
Children: David
Hobbies: Golf, Horse Racing

PLAYING CAREER

Honours: NPL Winners 83/84 & 87/88; FA Trophy Winners 89/90; Barrow P.O.Y. 78/79 & 88/89

Club	Seasons	Transfer	Apps	Goals
Cartmel	70-76			
Milnthorpe Corinthians	76-77			
Netherfield	1977			
Barrow	77-Date		+500	

Cox, Andrew (D)

(ST ALBANS CITY)

D.O.B. 1.5.69   **Nickname:** Coxy
Profession: Carpenter
Single
Hobbies: Sports

PLAYING CAREER

Honours: Herts Schoolboy & Youth Rep; Chipperfield P.O.Y. 85/86; Berkhamsted P.O.Y. 87/88

Club	Seasons	Transfer	Apps	Goals
Chipperfield	85-86			
Tring Town	86-87			
Berkhamsted Town	87-88			

Cox, Jeff (D)

(KEYNSHAM TOWN) Age: 29

Previous Clubs: Mangotsfield Utd; Melksham Town

Honours: None

Cox, Neil (M)

(WELWYN GARDEN CITY) Age: 22

Previous Clubs:

Honours: Hertfordshire u18

Coxon, Mark (D)

(SELBY TOWN) Age: 25

Previous Clubs: York RI

Honours: Northen Counties East Div 1 champions + League Cup winners 1988; County u19 honours; NCE Div 2 runners up 1990

Coy, Andrew (D)

(CHASETOWN) Age: 23

Previous Clubs:

Honours: BBL Premier League Cup winners 1989-90

Coy, Bobby (D)

(MOOR GREEN)

D.O.B. 30.11.61
Profession: Technical Rep & Adviser
Married **Wife's name:** Anita
Children: Ryan Scott
Hobbies: Golf, Photography, Running, Quizzes

PLAYING CAREER

Honours: King's Norton Schoolboy Rep; West Mids County Rep; Football Lge Div 2 R/U 82/83; Div 4 R/U 85/86, Div 4 Winners 86/87, Beazer Homes Lge Premier Winners 87/88, Wolves Young P.O.Y. 81/82, Chester P.O.Y.85/86

Club	Seasons	Transfer	Apps	Goals
Wolverhampton W's	78-84		58	
Chester City	84-86		98	2
Northampton Town	86-88		17	1
Aylesbury United	88-89			

Coyne, Brian (M)

(NEWTOWN) Age: 32

Previous Clubs: Celtic; Shrewsbury Town; Oswestry; Findley

Honours: None

CHRIS COOK (Kings Lynn)

Cracknell Andrew (D)

(DENABY UNITED) Age: 28

Previous Clubs: South Kirkby Colliery; Ossett Town; Grimethorpe

Honours:

Crane, Andrew (D)

(SUDBURY TOWN) Age: 23

Previous Clubs: Ipswich Town; Shrewsbury Town; Hereford United

Honours: England Youth Int,Jewson Lge Winners 89/90

Cranfield, Mark (D)

(BRAINTREE TOWN) Age: 19

Previous Clubs: Brightlingsea United

Honours: Essex Senior Lge Winners

Cranmer, Barry (D)

(SALISBURY) Age: 28

Previous Clubs: Andover

Honours: Salisbury P.O.Y.(2)

Crawley, Ian (F)

(TELFORD UNITED) D.O.B. 18.5.60

PLAYING CAREER

Honours: FA Vase Winners 82/83; FA Trophy Winners 88/89; GMAC Cup Winners 86/87

Club	Seasons	Transfer	Apps	Goals
Nuneaton Borough	78-82			
VS Rugby	82-85	£3,000		
Kettering Town	85-88	£6,000		

Creaser, Glyn (D)
(WYCOMBE WANDERERS)   D.O.B. 1.9.59

PLAYING CAREER

Honours: FA XI

Club	Seasons	Transfer	Apps	Goals
Wolverton Town	79-82			
Northampton Town	82-83			
Wolverton Town	83-84			
Kettering Town	84-85			
Wolverton Town	1985			
Barnet	85-88	£15,000		

Crimmen, Paul (F)
(OAKWOOD)   Age: 24

Previous Clubs: Oakwood; Horsham Town; Southwick

Honours: None

Cripps, Stephen (M)
(CHIPPENHAM TOWN)   Age: 26

Previous Clubs: Melksham Town; Aveley; Avon-Bradford; Trowbridge

Honours: None

Crips, Martin (M)
(EYNESBURY ROVERS)   Age: 16

Previous Clubs: None

Honours: Scott Gatty Cup 1990

Crompton, Stephen (G)
(CHEADLE TOWN)   Age: 23

Previous Clubs: Crewe Alexandra; Stockport County; Mossley; Hyde United

Honours: Cheshire County Boys; Stockport F.A. Boys

Crossley, Matt (D)
(WYCOMBE WANDERERS)   D.O.B. 1.8.68

PLAYING CAREER

Honours: Berks & Bucks Senior Cup Winners 89/90

Club	Seasons	Transfer	Apps	Goals
Aldershot	84-85			
Basingstoke Town	85-86			
Newbury Town	86-87			
Overton United	1987			

Crotwell, Christopher (F)
(BLACKSTONES)   Age: 21

Previous Clubs: Peterborough United (Y.T.S); British Rail; Bourne Town; Kings Lynn; Stamford

Honours: Top goal scorer for Stamford 1989-90

Crouch, Steve (M)
(CHELTENHAM TOWN)   D.O.B. 15.10.69

Nickname: Crouchy   Profession: Trainee Accountant
Single   Hobbies: Rugby

PLAYING CAREER

Honours: South West Schoolboy Rep; Glos County Youth Rep

Club	Seasons	Transfer	Apps	Goals
Frampton United	85-87			

Crowley, Richard (D)
(BATH CITY)   D.O.B. 28.12.59

Nickname: Lasher   Profession: Technician
Married   Wife's name: Beverley
Children: Luke, Daniel & Nicola
Hobbies: Golf, Most Sports

PLAYING CAREER

Honours: Avon & Glos Schoolboy Rep; FA XI; Western Lge Cup Winners; Glos Senior Cup Winners (3); Somerset Premier Cup Winners (3)

Club	Seasons	Transfer	Apps	Goals
Frome Town	81-83			
Bath City	83-85			
Stroud	85-87			
Cheltenham Town	87-90	£3,000		

MATT CROSSLEY (Wycombe Wanderers)

Crown, Nick (F)
(GRAYS ATHLETIC)   D.O.B. 3.2.62

Profession: Financial Consultant
Married   Wife's name: Michelle
Hobbies: Tennis, Cricket

PLAYING CAREER

Honours: FA XI; Southern Lge Premier Div Winners 84/85; Vauxhall-Opel Div 1 Winners 86/87 & R/U 87/88; Essex Senior Cup Winners 87/88 & R/U 88/89

Club	Seasons	Transfer	Apps	Goals
Grays Athletic	79-81			
Epping Town	81-82			
Barking	82-84			
Dartford	84-86	£7,000		
Leytonstone & Ilford	86-87			

Cuddy, Paul (D)
(WITTON ALBION)

D.O.B. 21.2.59
Profession: Engineer
Married   **Wife's name:** Kate
Children: Samantha Jane
Hobbies: Golf, Tennis, Snooker

PLAYING CAREER
Honours: Manchester Schoolboys Rep; England Semi-Pro Int; FA Trophy Winners & R/U; Chorley P.O.Y. 79/80; Altrincham P.O.Y. (2); Witton Albion P.O.Y. 89/90

Club	Seasons	Transfer	Apps	Goals
Manchester City	70-72			
Bolton Wanderers	73-74			
Rochdale	75-77		1	
Huddersfield Town	1977			
Blackpool	77-78			
Chorley	79-81	£1,000		
Altrincham	81-89	£3,000		

Cuffie, Michael (M)
(DUNSTABLE)   Age: 27
Previous Clubs: Southall; Dunstable; Chelmsford City; Dunstable; Hitchin Town
Honours: None

Cumiskey, Peter (M)
(BOOTLE)   Age: 34
Previous Clubs: Bootle; Southport; Burscough
Honours: None

Cumming, Micky (G)
(THATCHAM)   Age: 20
Previous Clubs: Hungerford; Reading
Honours: None

Cunningham, Brian (D)
(SOMERSHAM TOWN)   Age: 23
Previous Clubs: Hemingford Grey; St.Ives Town; Eynesbury Rovers
Honours: None

Cunningham, Malcolm (D)
(MOSSLEY)

D.O.B. 5.12.71   **Nickname:** Cunny
Profession: Mill Worker
Single   **Hobbies:** Socialising

PLAYING CAREER
Honours: Lancs Youth Cup R/U

Club	Seasons	Transfer	Apps	Goals
Blackburn Rovers	88-90			

Currah, Michael (D)
(PENRITH)   Age: 31
Previous Clubs: Gretna; Chester Le Street
Honours: None

Curran, Paul (D)
(NORTHWOOD)   Age: 26
Previous Clubs: Kingsbury Town; Hendon; Finchley
Honours: Middx Charity Cup winners; Spartans League Cup winners & League runners up 1989-90

Curry, Ian (D)
(BRIDLINGTON TOWN)   Age: 18
Previous Clubs: Sheffield Wednesday
Honours: None

Curtis, Darren (M)
(WINGATE)   Age: 22
Previous Clubs: None
Honours: Winner Herts Senior Trophy 1988; South Midlands Lge Div 1 runners up 1990

Curtis, David (G)
(DARTFORD)

D.O.B. 20.1.64
Profession: Not working
Married   **Wife's name:** Alison
Children: Perry & Daniel

PLAYING CAREER
Honours: Essex Senior Cup Winners 89/90

Club	Seasons	Transfer	Apps	Goals
Barking	89-90			

Curtis, Gary (D)
(NEWTOWN)   Age: 19
Previous Clubs: Grimsby Town; Northwich Vics
Honours: None

Cusack, David (D)
(BOSTON UNITED)

D.O.B. 6.6.56
Profession: Player-Manager of Boston United
Divorced
Children: Lucy-Ann & Thomas David
Hobbies: All Sports

PLAYING CAREER
Honours: None

Club	Seasons	Transfer	Apps	Goals
Sheffield Wednesday	71-78	£50,000	104	1
Southend United	78-83	£50,000	260	20
Millwall	83-85	£40,000	96	15
Doncaster Rovers	85-88		112	4
Rotherham United	1988		30	

Cuthbert, Michael (F)
(SOMERSHAM TOWN)   Age: 26
Previous Clubs: St.Ives; Eynesbury Rovers
Honours: None

PAUL CUDDY (WITTON ALBION)

seen here in action for Altrincham. His Yeovil opponent in this photo is Guy Whittingham, who is now with Portsmouth

Dack, James (M)
(SUTTON UNITED)

D.O.B. 2.6.72   **Nickname:** Dacky
Profession: Heating Engineer
Single
Hobbies: Golf, Squash

PLAYING CAREER

Honours: South London Schoolboy Rep; Surrey County Youth Rep; Epsom P.O.Y. 88/89

Club	Seasons	Transfer	Apps	Goals
Epsom & Ewell	87-89			

Daly, Gerry (M)
(TELFORD UNITED)

D.O.B. 30.4.54
Profession: Player-Manager

PLAYING CAREER

Honours: Republic of Ireland U-21 & Full Int; Football League Div 2 Winners 74/75

Club	Seasons	Transfer	Apps	Goals
Bohemians	71-73			
Manchester United	73-76	£175,000	111	23
Derby County	76-79	£310,000	112	31
Coventry City (Leicester City - loan	79-83 17-1)		84	19
Birmingham City	83-85		32	1
Shrewsbury Town	85-86	£15,000	55	8
Stoke City	86-87		22	1
Doncaster Rovers	87-89		39	4

GERRY DALY

Daniel, Peter (D)
(BEDWORTH UNITED)   Age: 27

Previous Clubs: Nuneaton Borough; Atherstone United
Honours: None

Darby, Peter (G)
(SPALDING UNITED)   Age: 22

Previous Clubs: Holbrook St.Michaels; Heanor Town; Scarborough; Telford United; Eastwood Town; Crookes
Honours: F.A. Trophy Finalist 1988 (Telford); British Polytechnic National Squad

Darrell, Peter (D)
(PICKERING TOWN)   Age: 24

Previous Clubs: Thornton Dale
Honours: None

Davenport, Danny (D)
(BECKENHAM TOWN)   Age: 22

Previous Clubs: Greenwich Borough; Southwick Sports
Honours: None

Davenport, Gary (M)
(CONGLETON TOWN)

D.O.B. 22.1.63   **Nickname:** Davo
Profession: Test bay operator
Married   **Wife's name:** Debbie
Hobbies: Golf, Drinking

PLAYING CAREER

Honours: NWCL Div 1 R/U 85/86

Club	Seasons	Transfer	Apps	Goals
No previous clubs.				

Davies, Anthony (D)
(SANDWELL BORO)   Age: 23

Previous Clubs: Dudley Town; Prince's End; Gornal Athletic
Honours: None

Davies, Gareth (M)
(AFC LYMINGTON)   Age: 23

Previous Clubs: Plessey Christchurch; Mudeford Mens Club
Honours: Hants Senior Cup runners up 1989-90; Wessex League Cup winners 1988-89; George Few Cup winners 1987-88

Davies, Glyn (D)
(CLITHEROE)   Age: 28

Previous Clubs: Prestwich Heys
Honours: None

Davies, Ian (D)
(CLACTON TOWN)   Age: 27

Previous Clubs:
Honours: None

Davies, Kevin (D)

(WESTFIELDS) Age: 26

Previous Clubs: Hereford United; Gloucester City; Trowbridge

Honours: None

Davies, Paul (F)

(KIDDERMINSTER HARRIERS) D.O.B. 9.10.60

Profession: Warehouse Salesman

PLAYING CAREER

Honours: None

Club	Seasons	Transfer	Apps	Goals
Cardiff City	78-80			
Trowbridge	80-82			
S.C. Hercules	82-83			

Davies, Peter (F)

(GATESHEAD) D.O.B. 10.10.55

Profession: Self-employed electrical contractor

PLAYING CAREER

Honours: Sunderland Schoolboy Rep; Newcastle Youth Rep; Northern Lge Winners 78/79 & 79/80; Belgian Div 3 Winners 82/83; NPL Winners 85/86; NPL R/U 89/90; NPL Cup R/U 89/90.

Club	Seasons	Transfer	Apps	Goals
Hartlepool United	73-75			1
Gateshead	75-76			
Whitley Bay	76-77	£200		
Carlisle United	77-78			
Blyth Spartans	78-80			
Gateshead	80-81			
Racing Jette (Belg)	81-83	£2,000		
Gateshead	83-86			
Barrow	86-87			
Alnwick Town	87-88			
Chester-Le-Street	88-89			

Davies, Phil (F)

(MOOR GREEN) D.O.B. 29.7.66

Profession: Bank Official
Single **Hobbies:** All Sports

PLAYING CAREER

Honours: Warwicks Schoolboy Rep; Southern Lge R/U 87/88; Moor Green P.O.Y. 86/87

Club	Seasons	Transfer	Apps	Goals
84-86	Moor Green			

Davies, Philip (F)

(STAPENHILL) Age: 32

Previous Clubs: Hednesford; Rushall Olympic; Willenhall; Atherstone; Polesworth; Walsall Wood

Honours: Presidents Cup winners 1982-83 & Mid Comb Lge Challenge Cup winners (Polesworth); Runners up F.A.Vase 1981 (Willenhall); Walsall Senior Cup (Rushall)

Davies, Stuart (G)

(RADCLIFFE BOROUGH) Age: 27

Previous Clubs: Prestwich Heys; Radcliffe Borough; Atherton LR; Horwich RMI

Honours: None

Davis, Anthony (F)

(SEATON DELAVAL AMATEURS) Age: 21

Previous Clubs: Seaton Terrace

Honours: None

Davis, Ian (M)

(BRIDLINGTON TOWN) Age: 25

Previous Clubs: Hull City (28-1); Bridlington Trinity

Honours: None

Davis, Mark (F)

(GUISBOROUGH TOWN) Age: 29

Previous Clubs:

Honours: Skol Northern Lge Cup winners; Skol Northern Lge Div 2nd runners up 1985-86

Davy, Russell (G)

(CHIPSTEAD) Age: 24

Previous Clubs: Charlton Athletic; Whyteleafe

Honours: None

PHIL DAWSON (Sutton United)

Daws, Nicky (D/M)

(ALTRINCHAM)   D.O.B. 15.3.70
Nickname: Henry   Profession: Student
Single   Hobbies: Sport

PLAYING CAREER

Honours: Greater Manchester Schools Rep; Cheshire Youth Rep; Altrincham P.O.Y.89/90.

Club	Seasons	Transfer	Apps	Goals
Flixton	86-88			

Dawsen, George (D)

(HINCKLEY ATHLETIC)   Age: 22
Previous Clubs: Witherley United; Atherstone United
Honours: None

Dawson, Paul (D/M)

(HENDON)   D.O.B. 23.11.66
Nickname: Daws Profession: Production Assistant for Print co.
Married   Wife's name: Lisa
Children: James   Hobbies: DIY, Golf, Family

PLAYING CAREER

Honours: Middx County Youth Rep; FA County Youth Cup R/U; S.E.Counties Lge Winners 85/86; Vauxhall-Opel Lge Div 2 N Winners 86/87; Finchley P.O.Y. 87/88 & 89/90

Club	Seasons	Transfer	Apps	Goals
Brentford	84-86			
Harrow Borough	86-87			
Chesham United	1987			
Finchley	87-90			

Dawson, Philip (M)

(SUTTON UNITED)   D.O.B. 9.8.65
Nickname: Olly Reed   Profession: Builder
Single   Hobbies: Golf

PLAYING CAREER

Honours: Surrey Youth Rep; Vauxhall-Opel Lge Premier Winners 84/85 & 85/86; Surrey Senior Cup Winners 84/85 & 86/87

Club	Seasons	Transfer	Apps	Goals
Chipstead	81-83			

Dawson, Russell (F)

(EXMOUTH TOWN)   Age: 26
Previous Clubs: Exmouth Town; Dawlish Town
Honours: Devon County Western League Championship

Day, Colin (M)

(HAYES)   D.O.B. 2.5.68
Nickname: Daisy Profession: Assistant Production Controller
Single   Hobbies: Snooker,Golf,Tennis

Honours: None
Previous Clubs: Thorn EMI (Hayes) 86-89

Day, Paul (F)

(ST.DOMINICS)   Age: 18
Previous Clubs: None
Honours: None

Day, Steven (M)

(CORNARD UNITED)   Age: 20
Previous Clubs: Cornard United
Honours: None

Deeley, Darren (F)

(RACING CLUB WARWICK)   Age: 24
Previous Clubs: Northampton Town; Bedworth United; AP Leamington; Banbury United
Honours: Midland Combination Premier Div Winners & R/U

Delf, Barrie (G)

(GRAYS ATHLETIC)   D.O.B. 5.5.61
Nickname: Delfie   Profession: Local Government Officer
Married   Wife's name: Julie
Children: Scott & Lee
Hobbies: Golf, Cricket, Squash

PLAYING CAREER

Honours: Kent Senior Cup Winners 86/87; Essex Senior Cup Winners 87/88 & R/U 88/89; Essex & Thameside Trophy Winners 87/88; Vauxhall-Opel Lge Div 1 R/U 87/88; Grays P.O.Y. 87/88 & 89/90

Club	Seasons	Transfer	Apps	Goals
Aston Villa	78-80			
Southend United	82-83		1	
Dartford	86-87			

Dell, Paul (M)

(NEWMARKET TOWN)   Age: 31
Previous Clubs: None
Honours: England Stablelads Winner 1985

Dell, Steve (G)

(LANGNEY SPORTS)   Age: 29
Previous Clubs: None
Honours: Sussex Intermediate Cup winner 1985-86; Sussex County League Div 3 Champion & Lge Cup winner 1986-87; Sussex Co Lge Div 2 champion 1987-88; Sussex Co Lge Challenge Cup winner 1989-90; Sussex Co Lge Rep games; Eastbourne Charity Cup Winner 1989-90; Brighton Evening Argus County 5-a-side Champion 1989-90

Delvis, Kerry (D)

(BANBURY UNITED)   Age: 21
Previous Clubs: Coventry City; Nuneaton Borough
Honours: None

Dempsey, Paul (M)

(WOLVERHAMPTON AFC)   Age: 20
Previous Clubs: Northampton Town; Leighton Town
Honours: None

Denby, Richard (M)

(GRESLEY ROVERS)   Age: 26
Previous Clubs: Chesterfield; Boston United; Huthwaite; Alfreton
Honours: Derbyshire Senior Cup (2); Notts Senior Cup

Dennis, Lenny (F)
(SUTTON UNITED) D.O.B. 13.11.64
Nickname: Dr Spock **Profession:** Student
Single **Hobbies:** Visiting Physio's!

PLAYING CAREER
Honours: Jamaica International; Vauxhall-Opel Lge Premier Div Winners 85/86

Club	Seasons	Transfer	Apps	Goals
Crystal Palace	80-82			
Bromley	82-84			
Dulwich Hamlet	84-85			

LENNY DENNIS

Dennison, Pat (D)
(WINGATE) Age: 28
Previous Clubs: Wealdstone **Honours:** None

Dent, Keith (D)
(WITHAM TOWN) Age: 35
Previous Clubs: Local football
Honours: Essex Senior Lge Winners 85/86 & R/U 86/87; Essex Senior Trophy Winners 85/86

Denton, Andrew (G)
(DENABY UNITED) Age: 20
Previous Clubs: Glasshoughton; Pontefracet
Honours: None

Denton, Mark (D)
(BROMLEY) Age: 29
Previous Clubs: Croydon; Dulwich Hamlet; Charlton (A); Redbridge Forest
Honours: None

Derby, Lenny (D)
(RACING CLUB WARWICK) Age: 24
Previous Clubs: Coventry Sporting; AP Leamington; Coventry Sporting
Honours: None

Devlin, Mick (D)
(NORTHWOOD) Age: 30
Previous Clubs: Kingsbury Town; Finchley
Honours: Spartan League Cup & League runners up 1989-90

Diaper, Bob (D)
(SALISBURY) Age: 29
Previous Clubs: Oxford United; Swindon Town; Amesbury; Salisbury
Honours: Wilts County Rep

Dick, Martin (D)
(GRESLEY ROVERS) Age: 29
Previous Clubs: Long Eaton Utd; Hucknall; Borrowash
Honours: Derbys Senior Cup winners (3); N. Counties (East) Lge winners

Dickens, Chris (D)
(EASTWOOD TOWN) Age: 22
Previous Clubs: Mastinmoor Oak **Honours:** None

Dilger, Rob (F)
(LEATHERHEAD) Age: 28
Previous Clubs: Leatherhead; Epsom & Ewell; Dorking; Carshalton Athletic; Dorking
Honours: Vauxhall-Opel Lge Div 2 Winners; Surrey Senior Cup R/U

PAUL DYSON (Telford Utd.)

PAUL DAVIES
(KIDDERMINSTER HARRIERS & ENGLAND)

Dineen, Jack (F)
(BOGNOR REGIS TOWN)

D.O.B. 23.9.70
Profession: Not working
Single
Hobbies: Sport

PLAYING CAREER

Honours: Republic of Ireland U-18 Int

Club	Seasons	Transfer	Apps	Goals
Brighton & H. A.	86-89			

Dingwall, Micky (F)
(REDBRIDGE FOREST)

D.O.B. 2.1.56   **Nickname:** Dingers
Profession: Teacher
Married   **Wife's name:** Dee
Children: Ben & Jamie

PLAYING CAREER

Honours: Isthmian Lge Premier Winners 78/79, 81/82; Vauxhall Lge Premier Winners 88/89; Vauxhall Lge Div 1 Winners 86/87; Gola Lge Winners 83/84; Hitachi Cup Winners 81/82; London Senior Cup Winners 78/79 & 81/82; Essex Senior Cup Winners 81/82; FA XI; Vauxhall-Opel Lge Rep; Middx Wanderer

Club	Seasons	Transfer	Apps	Goals
Barking	77-80	£2,500		
Leytonstone & Ilford	80-83	£3,500		
Maidstone United	83-85	£3,500		
Dartford	84-86	£2,500		
Leytonstone & Ilford	86-89			

MICKY DINGWALL

Dixon, Paul (M)
(EXMOUTH TOWN)   Age: 34
Previous Clubs:
Honours: Western League Championship winner; Combined Services

Dixon, Tony (F)
(CHASETOWN)   Age: 27
Previous Clubs: Pelsall Villa
Honours: Banks's Brewery League Cup winners

Doble, Simon (D)
(CALNE)   Age: 21
Previous Clubs:
Honours: County Youth & County Senior

Dobson, Dave (F)
(WITHAM TOWN)   Age: 21
Previous Clubs: Leyton Orient; Grays Athletic; Bishop's Stortford
Honours: None

Dobson, Stephen (D)
(SHOTTON COMRADES)   Age: 29
Previous Clubs: Shotton Comrades; Pelton Fell; Burnhope WMC
Honours: None

Dodd, Steve (M)
(GODALMING TOWN)   Age: 33
Previous Clubs: Woking, Westfield.
Honours: Dan Air League Championship; Dan Air Lge Rep.

Doe, Brendan (F)
(SOMERSHAM TOWN)   Age: 22
Previous Clubs: Great Shelford; Histon
Honours: None

Doherty, Mark (M)
(CHIPSTEAD)   Age: Old
Previous Clubs: Crystal Palace; Bromley; Farleigh Rovers
Honours: None

Doherty, Neil (F)
(BARROW)

Nickname: Doc   **D.O.B.** 21.2.69
Profession: Clerk
Single
Hobbies: Golf

PLAYING CAREER

Honours: FA Trophy Winners 89/90

Club	Seasons	Transfer	Apps	Goals
Watford	85-88			

Dolman, Neil (D)
(STAPENHILL)   Age: 25
Previous Clubs: St.Mary's; Plough Athletic; Burton & District
Honours: Campbell Orr Sheild; Burton & District Premier Division winners 1987-88/1988-89; WHL Harrison Shield; Score Combination winners 1989-90

Donn, Nigel (M)

(DOVER ATHLETIC) D.O.B. 2.3.62

PLAYING CAREER

Honours: Beazer Homes Premier Div Winners 89/90

Club	Seasons	Transfer	Apps	Goals
Gillingham	80-82		3	
Leyton Orient	82-83		24	2
Maidstone United	83-87			

Donnellan, Leo (M)

(WEALDSTONE) D.O.B. 19.1.65

PLAYING CAREER

Honours: England Youth Int; Republic of Ireland U-21 Int

Club	Seasons	Transfer	Apps	Goals
Chelsea	82-84			
(Leyton Orient - Loan 6)				
Fulham	85-90		79	4

Donnelly, Brian (D)

(V.S.RUGBY) D.O.B. 14.7.66

Profession: Roofer/Cladder
Single **Hobbies:** Sport

PLAYING CAREER

Honours: Midland Floodlit Cup Winners

Club	Seasons	Transfer	Apps	Goals
No previous clubs				

Donnelly, Peter (M)

(COLWYN BAY) Age: 25

Previous Clubs: United Services (Chester); Oswestry Town; Rhyl
Honours: Bass NWCL Cup Winners

NEIL DOHERTY (Barrow)

Donohue, Michael (D)

(ST.DOMINICS) Age: 20

Previous Clubs:
Honours: None

Donovan, Neil (F)

(BANBURY UNITED) Age: 21

Previous Clubs: Buckingham Town)
Honours: None

Doody, Lee (D)

(RADCLIFFE BOROUGH) Age: 19

Previous Clubs: Manchester United; Preston North End
Honours: None

Doolan, John (M)

(KNOWSLEY UNITED) Age: 22

Previous Clubs: Mossley
Honours: None

Doolan, Paul (D/M)

(GATESHEAD)

D.O.B. 20.4.66 **Nickname:** Doola
Profession: Plumber
Married **Wife's name:** Jacqui
Hobbies: Golf,Swimming

PLAYING CAREER

Honours: NPL Winners 85/86; HFS Loans Lge Premier R/U 89/90; HFS Loans Lge Cup R/U 89/90; Gateshead P.O.Y. 84/85

Club	Seasons	Transfer	Apps	Goals
Gateshead	84-87			
Bishop Auckland	87-88			

Dorado, Mark (F)

(BURNHAM RAMBLERS) Age: 23

Previous Clubs: Runwell
Honours: None

Doran, Ian (M)

(ALTRINCHAM)

D.O.B. 26.9.69
Profession: Carpet Fitter
Single
Hobbies: Sport

PLAYING CAREER

Honours: None

Club	Seasons	Transfer	Apps	Goals
Cammell Laird	88-90			

Doran, Peter (M)

(ST.DOMINICS) Age: 24

Previous Clubs: Bootle
Honours: None

Doughty, Steve (F)
(NEWPORT AFC) **Age:** 30
Previous Clubs: Frampton United; Forest Green Rovers; Stroud
Honours: F.A. Vase winners 1982; Hellenic League winners 1981

Douglas, Adam (D)
(CHIPPENHAM TOWN) **Age:** 27
Previous Clubs: South Galmorgan Institute; North Ferriby Utd
Honours: None

Dove, Paul (D)
(CLACTON TOWN) **Age:** 27
Previous Clubs: None **Honours:** None

Dover, Scott (M)
(MARLOW) **D.O.B.** 3.4.69
Nickname: Scotty **Profession:** Builder
Single **Hobbies:** Golf, Sky Diving

PLAYING CAREER
Honours: None

Club	Seasons	Transfer	Apps	Goals
Flackwell Heath	82-83			
Chesham United	84-85			
Amersham Town	87-89			

Dowding, Martin (M)
(SALISBURY) **Age:** 29
Previous Clubs: Sholing Sports; Basingstoke Town; R-S Southampton; Fareham Town; Gosport Borough; Eastleigh
Honours: Hants County Rep

Downing, Russell (M)
(EASTWOOD TOWN) **Age:** 29
Previous Clubs: Belper Town; Alfreton Town; Heanor Town; Albany Capitals (USA); Burton Albion
Honours: Northern Counties East Lge Winners; Notts Senior Cup Winners

Drake, Steve (M)
(SELBY TOWN) **Age:** 25
Previous Clubs: York City; Rowntrees
Honours: NCE Div 1 winners 1990 runners up 1988-89; North Riding County Cup runners up

Draper, Neil (M)
(WELWYN GARDEN CITY) **Age:** 19
Previous Clubs: Welwyn Garden United
Honours: County (u16+u18); Brentford (Youth Team)

Drewe, Dave (F)
(WOLVERTON AFC) **Age:** 27
Previous Clubs: Buckingham Town; Milton Keynes City; Milton Keynes Borough; Leighton Town
Honours: None

Drewe, Steve (F)
(WOLVERTON AFC) **Age:** 27
Previous Clubs: Buckingham Town; Milton Keynes Bororugh; Leighton Town
Honours: None

Drury, Martin (M)
(ALFRETON TOWN) **Age:** 17
Previous Clubs: Local football
Honours: None

Duckett, Peter (D)
(SANDWELL) **Age:** 23
Previous Clubs: Dudley; Stourbridge; Dudley; Princess End; Gornal
Honours: None

Duffell, Kevin (D)
(TOOTING & MITCHAM UNITED) **Age:** 26
Previous Clubs: Epsom & Ewell; Leatherhead; Epsom & Ewell
Honours: None

Duffield, Jess (F)
(OLDWINSFORD FSC) **Age:** 22
Previous Clubs: Oldwinsford (Youth); Stourport Swifts
Honours: None

Duffy, Eugene (M)
(CHEADLE TOWN) **Age:** 28
Previous Clubs: North Withington; Curzon Ashton; Droysden
Honours: Manchester Boys & North England Colleges Representative u11

Duffy, Tony (D)
(ST.DOMINICS) **Age:** 35
Previous Clubs: Vauxhall Motors; Burscough; Winsford; Chorley; Marine; Southport
Honours: None

Dummett, Ian (D)
(SEATON DELAVAL AMATEURS) **Age:** 29
Previous Clubs: Scotswood S.C.; Ponteland United
Honours: Northumberland Senior Benevolent Bowl winners; McEwans Northen Alliance Premier Division championship

Dunbar, Robert (F)
(SHOTTON COMRADES) **Age:** 28
Previous Clubs: Ashington Town; Durham City
Honours: None

Duncan, Paul (M)
(ST.DOMINICS) **Age:** 21
Previous Clubs: Bootle **Honours:** None

Dunne, John (M)

(GODALMING TOWN) **Age:** 25

Previous Clubs: None

Honours: None

Dunne, Sean (F)

(SUTTON COLDFIELD TOWN) **Age:** 30

Previous Clubs: Paget Rangers; Sutton Coldfield Town; Paget Rangers

Honours: None

Dunning, C (F)

(SHOTTON COMRADES) **Age:** 24

Previous Clubs: Hartlepool Res; Shotton Comrades; Hartlepool Boys Welfare; Greatham; Wingate

Honours: None

Durham, Kevin (M)

(BARNET)

D.O.B. 6.4.62 **Nickname:** Durrers
Profession: Sales Rep
Married **Wife's name:** Jackie
Children: Matthew, Jack
Hobbies: Football

PLAYING CAREER

Honours: Vauxhall-Opel Lge Rep

Club	Seasons	Transfer	Apps	Goals
Abingdon Town	80-82			
Oxford City	82-86			
Wycombe Wanderers	86-90	£15,000		

Durkan, John (M)

(SEATON DELAVAL AMATEURS) **Age:** 24

Previous Clubs: Westerhope Excelsior; Ponteland United

Honours: Northumberland Senior Benevolent Bowl winners; McEwans Northern Alliance Premier Division championship

Durrant, Peter (M)

(HORSHAM) **Age:** 23

Previous Clubs: Horsham; Steyning Town; Peacehaven & Telscombe; Lancing

Honours: Sussex Senior Cup Winners 87/88

Dutton, Dave (M)

(CROYDON) **Age:** 22

Previous Clubs: West Ham United; Croydon; Banstead Athletic; Molesey

Honours: Southern Youth Lge & Cup Winners

Dutton, Neil (M)

(CONGLETON TOWN)

D.O.B. 7.6.66 **Nickname:** Stupot
Profession: Form-maker
Single
Hobbies: Cricket,Reading

PLAYING CAREER

Honours: Staffs Youth Rep

Club	Seasons	Transfer	Apps	Goals
Knypersley Vics	84-86			
Algager	86-87			
Eastwood Hanley	87-88			
Leek Town	1989			

Dwyer, Simon (F)

(DENABY UNITED) **Age:** 24

Previous Clubs: Sheffield Wednesday (App); Mexboro' Town; Jomala (Finland); Nelson (N Zealand); Matlock Town; Gainsborough Trinity

Honours: Derbyshire Senior Cup Winners '84

Dyer, Chris (M)

(VALE RECREATION) **Age:** 31

Previous Clubs: Belgrave Wanderers

Honours: 14 Guernsey caps; Current Guernsey & Vale Rec captain; 8 Guernsey Priaulx championships; 2 Channel Island Championships

TONY DENNIS (Slough Town)

NICKY DAWS (ALTRINCHAM)

Eades, Steve (M)

(AFC LYMINGTON) Age: 29

Previous Clubs: Old Tauntonians; Warsash; Hamble; Brockenhurst

Honours: Hants Senior Cup runners up; Wessex League Cup winners

Eales, Darren (F)

(NEWMARKET TOWN) Age: 18

Previous Clubs:

Honours: u18 Cambs County; Cambs u19 schools; Cambs County Senior; East Midland Combination winners 1990

Earnshaw, Joe (F)

(PICKERING) Age: 28

Previous Clubs: South Cliff; Eastfield; Scarborough

Honours: Scarborough District Div 1 Harbour Cup; League Cup 2nd Div North East Counties

Eastoe, Peter (F)

(BRIDGNORTH TOWN) Age: 37

Previous Clubs: Wolves; Swindon; Q.P.R.; Everton; West Bromwich Albion; Sporting Clube Farense

Honours: England Youth Cap

Eatough, Martin (M)

(GREAT HARWOOD TOWN) Age: 31

Previous Clubs: Great Harwood; Morecambe; Barrow; Southport; Clitheroe; Accrington Stanley; Fleetwood; Morecambe

Honours: B.N.W.C. 1st & 2nd Div Championship; N.P.L. Cup runners up; A.T.S. Challenge Trophy winners (2); Lamot Pils Cup 1990; Player of the Year with Fleetwood, Southport & Gt. Harwood)

Eccles, Des (D)

(BECKENHAM TOWN) Age: 22

Previous Clubs: Fisher Athletic; Greenwich Borough

Honours: None

Edet, Ian (F)

(HITCHIN TOWN) Age: 25

Previous Clubs: Barking

Honours: None

Edgar, Darron (G)

(BILLERICAY TOWN) Age: 20

Previous Clubs: Canvey Island

Honours: None

Edmonds, Gary (D)

(SUTTON COLDFIELD TOWN) Age: 28

Previous Clubs: Paget Rangers; Coleshill Town; Paget Rangers; Gresley Rovers

Honours: None

Edmunds, James (D)

(PEGASUS JUNIORS) Age: 25

Previous Clubs: Ross United; Westfields

Honours: None

Edwards, Andy (F)

(NEWTOWN) Age: 25

Previous Clubs: Wrexham; George Cross (Austrailia); Western Suburbs (Aust); Morecambe; Colne Dynamoes; Caernarfon Town

Honours: Welsh u18; Welsh Cup winners (Wrexham)

Edwards, Duncan (D)

(ROSSENDALE UNITED) Age: 23

Previous Clubs: Radcliffe Borough; Clitheroe.

Honours: None

Edwards, Elfyn (D)

(MACCLESFIELD TOWN)

D.O.B. 4.5.60

Profession: Fireman
Married **Wife's name:** Carole
Children: Scott, Lorna & Carrie-Anne

PLAYING CAREER

Honours: Wales Youth Int; Wales Semi-pro Int; Alliance Premier Lge Winners 81/82; NPL Cup & Lge Winners; FA Trophy R/U 88/89; Welsh Cup R/U 78/79; Runcorn P.O.Y. 81/82

Club	Seasons	Transfer	Apps	Goals
Wrexham	77-79			
Tranmere Rovers	79-81		62	1
Runcorn	81-84			
Altrincham	84-86			

Edwards, Mark (F)

(WITTON ALBION)

D.O.B. 6.12.61 **Nickname:** Eddie

Profession: Shopkeeper
Married **Wife's name:** Gill
Children: Gareth
Hobbies: Fishing, Golf

PLAYING CAREER

Honours: NPL Winners 87/88; NPL Rep; Chorley P.O.Y. 87/88

Club	Seasons	Transfer	Apps	Goals
St.Helens Town	82-83			
Horwich RMI	83-84			
Chorley	84-88	£2,000		

Edwards, Mick (F)

(NEWMARKET TOWN) Age: 29

Previous Clubs: None

Honours: None

Edwards, Paul (D)

(BROMLEY) Age: 32

Previous Clubs: Dulwich Hamlet
Honours: None

Edwards, Sean (M)

(WESTFIELDS) Age: 21

Previous Clubs: Hereford United; Bridgenorth Town
Honours: None

Edwards, Steve (M)

(WALTLL WOOD) Age: 27

Previous Clubs: Boldmere St.Michael; Knowle; Streetly; Tamworth; Welywn; B'ham Municipal Officers
Honours: None

Edwards, St.Clair (D)

(EASTWOOD TOWN) Age: 32

Previous Clubs: Basford United; Arnold Town; Grantham Town
Honours: None

Edwards, Trevor (M)

(EASTWOOD TOWN) Age: 19

Previous Clubs: Grimsby Town
Honours: None

Eggleston, Howard (D)

(MELTON TOWN) Age: 28

Previous Clubs: Holwell Works; Wigston Fields
Honours: Leicester Senior League Champions 1983/84; Senior Cup Finalist 1986-87/1988-89

Elder, Shaun (M)

(WINSFORD UNITED) Age: 25

Previous Clubs: Eastwood Hanley
Honours: None

Eley, Kevin (M/F)

(GAINSBOROUGH TRINITY)

D.O.B. 4.3.68
Profession: Not working
Single
Hobbies: Football, Golf, Tennis

PLAYING CAREER

Honours: England Youth Rep

Club	Seasons	Transfer	Apps	Goals
Rotherham United	84-87		22	
Chesterfield	87-90		100	5

Elkington, Justin (M)

(SPALDING UNITED) Age: 18

Previous Clubs: Mansfield Town; Lincoln City; Sheffield Wed; Spurs; Ipswich; Notts County (All as School Boy)
Honours: None

Ellans, Terry (M)

(GENERAL CHEMICALS) Age: 21

Previous Clubs: Frodsham United
Honours: Cheshire Cup; Runcorn Cup

Elliott, Gaff (F)

(MELTON TOWN) Age: 34

Previous Clubs: Barnsley; Newquay; Thetford; Arnold; Lincoln Utd
Honours: Derby's Senior Cup; Notts Intermediate Cup

Elliott, Scott (M)

(GRESLEY ROVERS) Age: 23

Previous Clubs: Keyworth; Long Eaton United
Honours: None

Ellis, Andrew (M)

(NEWPORT AFC) Age: 23

Previous Clubs: Clydach Utd; Swansea University; Cardiff Corries; Bridgend Town
Honours: Welsh & British Universities

Ellis, Ronnie (M)

(MACCLESFIELD TOWN) D.O.B. 15.3.58

Previous Clubs: Burscough; Winsford United; Runcorn; Altrincham.
Honours: F.A. Trophy Winners 1986

RONNIE ELLIS

Ellis, Stephen (D)
(WITTON ALBION)

D.O.B. 4.8.65
Profession: Bank Officer
Single
Hobbies: Sport

PLAYING CAREER
Honours: None

Club	Seasons	Transfer	Apps	Goals
Winsford United	85-88			

Ellis, Steve (G)
(MARLOW)

D.O.B. 8.10.67   Nickname: Stevey
Profession: Insurance Manager
Single
Hobbies: Reading, Swimming

PLAYING CAREER
Honours: Vauxhall-Opel Div 1 & 2 Winners; Marlow P.O.Y.

Club	Seasons	Transfer	Apps	Goals
No previous clubs				

Emmerson, Neil (D/M)
(GATESHEAD)

D.O.B. 29.4.69   Nickname: Emmers
Profession: FA Coach
Single
Hobbies: Golf, Snooker

PLAYING CAREER
Honours: Gateshead Schoolboy Rep; Durham County Youth Rep; South East Counties Lge R/U 84/85; Southern Junior Floodlit Cup Winners 86/87.

Club	Seasons	Transfer	Apps	Goals
Ipswich Town	85-87			
Whitley Bay	87-88			
Spennymoor United	88-89			

Emms, Roger (D)
(NEWBURY TOWN)   Age: 23

Previous Clubs: Devizes Town; Swindon Athletic
Honours: Wiltshire County Youths; South West Counties Youth; Wiltshire County Seniors

Emslie, David (D)
(BEDWORTH UNITED)   Age: 28

Previous Clubs: Local football
Honours: None

English, Gordon (G)
(BURNHAM RAMBLERS)   Age: 26

Previous Clubs: Southminster
Honours: League Representative

Engwell, Michael (M)
(CHELMSFORD CITY)

D.O.B. 27.9.66   Nickname: Pinhead
Profession: Hod Carrier
Married   Wife's name: Sharon
Hobbies: Golf, Cricket

PLAYING CAREER
Honours: None

Club	Seasons	Transfer	Apps	Goals
Southend United	84-86		9	3
Crewe Alexandra		loan	2	
Chelmsford City	86-87			
Barking	87-89			

Entwistle, Mark (D)
(BILLERICAY TOWN)   Age: 27

Previous Clubs: Basildon United; Dartford; Chelmsford City; St.Albans City
Honours: None

Errington, Anthony (D)
(SHOTTON ALBION)   Age: 25

Previous Clubs: Tyne Tees Television; Neerc
Honours: None

Erskine, Kenny (D)
(WARMINSTER TOWN)   Age: 27

Previous Clubs: Warminster Town; Frome Town
Honours: None

Espley, Chris (D)
(RHYL)   Age: 26

Previous Clubs: Rhyl; Pilkingtons; Rhyl Victory Club
Honours: Clwyd Premier Lge & Cup Winners; Presidents Cup Winners

Esquilant, Danny (M)
(CROYDON)   Age: 21

Previous Clubs: Arsenal; Charlton Athletic; Double Flower (H.K.); Fisher Athletic
Honours: England Youth Int; FA Youth Cup Winners

Esser, David (F)
(ASHTON UNITED)   Age: 33

Previous Clubs: Everton; Rochdale (180-24); Apoel (Cyprus); Karlskrona (Swe); Altrincham; Witton Albion; Macclesfield Town; Witton Albion; Hyde United; Northwich Victoria; Witton Albion; Stalybridge Celtic; Winsford United
Honours: Northern Premier Lge & Cup Winners; Presidents Cup Winners; Mid-Cheshire Cup Winners

Essex, Steve (D)
(STAFFORD RANGERS)

D.O.B. 2.10.60   **Nickname:** Esso
Profession: Industrial Chemist
Married   **Wife's name:** Jane
Children: Thomas
Hobbies: Golf, Snooker

PLAYING CAREER
Honours: Wolverhampton Schoolboy Rep; FA XI

Club	Seasons	Transfer	Apps	Goals
Gresley Rovers	83-84			
Burton Albion	84-87	£6,000		
Aylesbury United	88-89	£7,000		

Evans, Glyn (D)
(WITHAM TOWN)   **Age:** 29

Previous Clubs: Braintree Town; Essex Police
Honours: English & British Police Rep; Braintree P.O.Y.

Evans, Nicky (F)
(BARNET)

D.O.B. 6.7.58

PLAYING CAREER
Honours: FA Trophy R/U 78/79; Herts Senior Cup Winners 85/86; GMVC R/U 86/87

Club	Seasons	Transfer	Apps	Goals
Queens Park Rangers	74-76			
Peterborough United	76-77			
Kettering Town	77-83			
Barnet	83-88	£32,000		
Wycombe Wanderers	88-91	£25,000		

Evans, Peter (M)
(SUTTON UNITED)

D.O.B. 21.1.70
Profession: Student
Single
Hobbies: Music, Tennis, Basketball

PLAYING CAREER
Honours: England Schoolboy Int; FA Youth Cup R/U 86/87

Club	Seasons	Transfer	Apps	Goals
Charlton Athletic	86-89		4	
Croydon	89-90			

Eves, Gary (D)
(BURNHAM RAMBLERS)   **Age:** 24

Previous Clubs: Burnham Ramblers; Tillingham
Honours: None

Ewens, David (D)
(YATE TOWN)   **Age:** 24

Previous Clubs: Shepton Mallett Town; Clandown
Honours: Somerset County Rep; Hellenic Lge Winners 87/88 & 88/89

NICKY EVANS

IAN EISENTRALER
(Weston super Mare)

Fagan, Michael (M)

(KNOWSLEY UNITED) **Age:** 30

Previous Clubs: Liverpool; Macclesfield; Bootle; Precot; Burscough; Kirkby Town
Honours: None

Fahy, Allen (F)

(ST.DOMINICS) **Age:** 18

Previous Clubs: None
Honours: Liverpool County FA Youth XI

Fallon, Steve (D)

(CAMBRIDGE CITY)

D.O.B. 3.8.56
Married

PLAYING CAREER

Honours: None

Club	Seasons	Transfer	Apps	Goals
Kettering Town	73-74			
Cambridge United	74-86		410	27
Histon	86-87			

Fanner, Jeff (G)

(WEMBLEY) **Age:** 28

Previous Clubs: Harrow Borough; Hillingdon Borough; Hounslow
Honours: None

Farmer, Mark (F)

(BRAINTREE TOWN) **Age:** 18

Previous Clubs: None
Honours: Essex Youth Rep

Farrelly, Mike (D)

(MACCLESFIELD TOWN)

D.O.B. 1.11.62 **Nickname:** Fazmo
Profession: Factory Manager
Married **Wife's name:** Kath
Children: Matthew & Emily

PLAYING CAREER

Honours: England Schoolboy Int; England Semi-pro Int; FA Trophy Winners

Club	Seasons	Transfer	Apps	Goals
Preston North End	81-84		82	4
Altrincham	84-89			

Farrington, Richard (G)

(NEWCASTLE TOWN) **Age:** 21

Previous Clubs: Whitchurch Alport; Leek Town
Honours: None

Fay, Gary (M)

(CHIPSTEAD) **Age:** 23

Previous Clubs: Carshalton; Tooting & Mitcham; Whyteleafe; Sutton United
Honours: None

Fay, Shaun (D:M)

(TOOTING & MITCHAM UNITED) **Age:** 20

Previous Clubs: Tooting & Mitcham United; Dulwich Hamlet; Carshalton Athletic; Whyteleafe
Honours: Surrey Youth Rep

Fear, David (D)

(ROMSEY TOWN) **Age:** 24

Previous Clubs: Warsash; AFC Totton; Fareham Town
Honours: South East England u18 Representative 1983-84; Hants Youth; Wessex League Champions; Hants Intermediate Cup winners; Hants Senior Representative; Associate Schoolboy with Southampton

Fell, Simon (M)

(FARSLEY CELTIC) **Age:** 23

Previous Clubs: Farsley Celtic; Guiseley
Honours: West Riding County Cup R/U 87/88

Fennessy, Christopher (M)

(CUMBRAN TOWN) **Age:** 28

Previous Clubs: Cardiff Corinthians
Honours: Welsh Amateur Cup 1984-85

Fenton, Spencer (D)

(WINGATE) **Age:** 22

Previous Clubs: None
Honours: Herts Senior Trophy winners 1988; South Mid Lge Div 1 runners up 1990

Ferguson, Jamie (D)

(THATCHAM) **Age:** 24

Previous Clubs: Thatcham; Marlow; Maidenhead; Chertsey
Honours: Vauxhall Opel Div 2 runners up; Vauxhall Opel Div 1 winners

Ferns, Phil (D)

(POOLE TOWN) **D.O.B.** 12.9.61

PLAYING CAREER

Honours: Vauxhall-Opel Lge Premier Winners 87/88 & R/U 86/87

Club	Seasons	Transfer	Apps	Goals
AFC Bournemouth	78-80		95	6
Charlton Athletic	80-83		38	1
Wimbledon		loan	7	
Blackpool	83-84		47	
Aldershot	84-85		24	2
Yeovil Town	85-89			

Ferris, Paul (M)

(WESTBURY) Age: 30

Previous Clubs: Chippenham Town; Devizes Town
Honours: None

Fielding, Pete (M)

(CHIPPENHAM TOWN) Age: 30

Previous Clubs: Trowbridge Town; Melksham Town
Honours: Wilts Prof Shield (3)

PETE FIELDING ANDY FISHER
(Chippenham Town) (Dorking)

Findlay, Andy (M)

(THATCHAM TOWN) Age: 24

Previous Clubs: Reading; Wokingham Town; Bracknell Town
Honours: None

Finn, Derek (F)

(CHIPSTEAD) Age: 28

Previous Clubs: Corinthian Casuals; Malden Vale; Cobham; Bath Tavern
Honours: Surry Senior Cup winner

Fisher, Ian (F)

(MELTON TOWN) Age: 22

Previous Clubs: None **Honours:** None

Fisher, Martin (F)

(GAINSBOROUGH TOWN) Age: 28

Previous Clubs: Skegness Town; Winterton Rangers; Barton Town; Maslethorpe Athletic
Honours: Lincs League Premier Division

Fisher, Richard (M)

(HITCHIN TOWN) Age: 18

Previous Clubs: Arlesey Town; Stevenage Borough
Honours: None

Fishlock, Russell (D)

(SALISBURY) Age: 20

Previous Clubs: Chippenham Town; Pewsey Vale; Swindon
Honours: Wiltshire Senior Premier Shield 1988-89

Fitzgerald, Paul (D)

(WEMBLEY) Age: 27

Previous Clubs: Willesden; Harrow Borough; Southall; Wembley; Kingsbury Town; Chalfont St.Peter
Honours: Middx County Rep

Flaherty, Charlie (M)

(WEMBLEY) Age: 27

Previous Clubs: Harrow Borough; Slough Town; Burnham; Wembley; Chalfont St.Peter
Honours: None

Flanagan, Zane (M)

(Wolverton AFC) Age: 25

Previous Clubs: Milton Keynes City; Leighton Town; Dunstable; Banbury United; Barton Rovers
Honours: Bucks Youth; Beds Senior

Flannagan, Tony (D)

(ST ALBANS CITY)

D.O.B. 28.10.69 **Nickname:** Flan or Midge
Profession: Sales Rep

PLAYING CAREER

Honours: Republic of Ireland Youth Int

Club	Seasons	Transfer	Apps	Goals
Norwich City	85-89			
Farnborough Town	89-90			

Flashman, Mark (G)

(BARNET)

D.O.B. 25.6.71 **Nickname:** Tub of Lard
Profession: Theatre Broker
Single
Hobbies: Tennis, Snooker

PLAYING CAREER

Honours: Herts County Youth Rep; FA County Youth Cup R/U.

Club	Seasons	Transfer	Apps	Goals
No previous clubs				

Fletcher, Mike (D)

(WESTHOUGHTON TOWN) Age: 27

Previous Clubs: Wigan (Youth); B.A.C. Bolton; Southport; Leyland Motors; Wigan College

Honours: Wigan Amateur League Prem Champions (5); Laithwaite Shield winners (6); Hughes Cup winners (6); L.F.A. Shield runner up; Bolton Combination winner; West Lancs Div 1 runners up; Wigan Cup winner (2)

Fletcher, Noel (M)
(LEATHERHEAD) **Age:** 34
Previous Clubs: Woking; Addlestone; Hayes; St.Albans City; Hendon
Honours: None

Flowerden, John (G)
(WOLVERTON AFC) **Age:**
Previous Clubs: Olney Town **Honours:** None

Flynn, David (D)
(HORNCHURCH) **Age:** 24
Previous Clubs: West Ham United; Beckton United; Rainham Town; Clapton; Billericay Town
Honours: Essex & London Schoolboy Rep

Flynn, Tony (M/F)
(BARKING) **D.O.B.** 12.8.58
Profession: Telephone Engineer
Married **Wife's name:** Julia
Children: Toni & Alexander
Hobbies: Golf, Music, Sports Injuries
PLAYING CAREER
Honours: Essex Senior Cup Winners; Clapton P.O.Y.79/80

Club	Seasons	Transfer	Apps	Goals
Clapton	77-81			
Aveley	81-84			
Chelmsford City	84-85			
Dagenham	85-86			
Bishop's Stortford	1986			
Chelmsford City	86-87			
Dagenham	87-88			
Gravesend & N'fleet	88-89			

BILLY FERRIS (Taunton Town)
Photo: Somerset County Gazette

Ford, Malcolm (M)
(CALNE TOWN) **Age:** 22
Previous Clubs: Marlborough Town
Honours: None

Forsyth, Richard (M)
(KIDDERMINSTER HARRIERS)

D.O.B. 3.10.70 **Nickname:** Fozzy
Profession: Not working
Single
Hobbies: Sport
PLAYING CAREER
Honours: Dudley & Brierley Hill Schoolboy Rep; West Midland County Schoolboy Rep

Club	Seasons	Transfer	Apps	Goals
Stourbridge	86-87			

Fosbury, Dean (F)
(BOGNOR REGIS TOWN)

D.O.B. 28.9.69
Profession: Salesman
Single
Hobbies: Poetry
PLAYING CAREER
Honours: England Schoolboy Int

Club	Seasons	Transfer	Apps	Goals
Portsmouth	85-87			
Waterlooville	87-88			

Foster, Danny (M)
(CHASETOWN) **Age:** 22
Previous Clubs: Hednesford (Youth); Armitage
Honours: League Champions (Hednesford Youth)

Fowler, James (F)
(CHESTER LE STREET) **Age:** 32
Previous Clubs: Evenwood; Consett; Spennymoor
Honours: Dryborough's Northern League; 5-a-side & 6-a-side County Colours; Northern League top goal scorer 1987-88

Fowler, Steven (M:F)
(TOOTING & MITCHAM UNITED) **Age:** 21
Previous Clubs: Sutton United
Honours: Surrey Schoolboy & Youth Rep

Fox, Barry (D)
(GRAYS ATHLETIC)

D.O.B. 20.5.66 **Nickname:** Foxy
Profession: Money Broker
Single
Hobbies: Golf, Crashing Cars, Holidaying, Train Spotting
Previous Clubs: Millwall (80-83)
Honours: Essex Schoolboy Rep; Essex Senior Cup Winners & R/U; Grays Young P.O.Y. 86/87 & 87/88 & P.O.Y.88/89

Foyster, Steve (G)

(BRAINTREE TOWN)   **Age:** 7.8.61

Previous Clubs: Oxford United; Banbury United; Waterlooville; Wimbledon; Gorleston
Honours: England Schoolboy & Youth Int; Norfolk County Rep; FA XI; Essex Senior Trophy Winners; Norfolk Senior Cup Winners; Eastern Counties Lge R/U (3); Eastern Counties Lge Cup Winners

Frake, Peter (M)

(OAKWOOD)   **Age:** 24

Previous Clubs: Horsham Y.M.C.A.; Three Bridges; Redhill
Honours: RUR winners; Div 2 & Cup winners; Div 1 runners up

France, Chris (F)

(DENABY UNITED)   **Age:** 21

Previous Clubs: Sheffield United
Honours: None

Francis, Nick (F)

(ENFIELD)

D.O.B. 1.7.66
Profession: Money Dealer
Single
Hobbies: Sport

PLAYING CAREER

Honours: Public Schools Rep; FA Trophy Winners 87/88; Enfield P.O.Y. 87/88

Club	Seasons	Transfer	Apps	Goals
Charlton Athletic	85-86			
Blockhouse Bay (N.Z.)	86-87			

PETER FARRELL (Barrow)

Franklin, Paul (D)

(WYCOMBE WANDERERS)

D.O.B. 5.10.63

PLAYING CAREER

Honours: FA Youth Cup Winners; Berks & Bucks Senior Cup Winners 89/90

Club	Seasons	Transfer	Apps	Goals
Watford	81-87		32	
Shrewsbury Town		loan	6	
Swindon Town		loan	5	1
Reading	87-89			

Franks, Mark (M)

(WOKING)

D.O.B. 8.5.61   **Nickname:** Frill
Profession: Electrician
Married   **Wife's name:** Claire
Children: Chloe
Hobbies: Golf, Tennis

PLAYING CAREER

Honours: Vauxhall Lge Div 1 R/U 89/90; Berks & Bucks Cup Winners 87/88 & 88/89; Maidenhead P.O.Y. 81/82

Club	Seasons	Transfer	Apps	Goals
Windsor & Eton	79-80			
Woking	80-81			
Maidenhead United	81-82			
Windsor & Eton	82-89			

Fraser, Bobby (D)

(WINSFORD UNITED)   **Age:** 37

Previous Clubs: Liverpool; Tranmere Rovers; Portmadog; Skelmersdale United; Marine; Holyhead United; Winsford United; Runcorn; Altrincham; Rhyl; Northwich Victoria
Honours: Alliance Premier Lge Winners; Welsh Lge Winners; Northern Premier Lge Winners; Cheshire Lge Winners; Welsh Cup Winners; Cheshire Senior Cup Winners; Northern Premier Lge Cup Winners; FA Trophy R/U

Fraser, Neil (F)

(HAYES)

D.O.B. 14.3.67   **Nickname:** Fraz
Profession: Litho Planner
Single
Hobbies: Golf

PLAYING CAREER

Honours: Watford Schoolboy Rep; Herts County Youth Rep; Vauxhall Lge Rep; Middx Premier Cup Winners (2)

Club	Seasons	Transfer	Apps	Goals
No previous clubs				

Freegard, John (F)

(GLOUCESTER CITY)

D.O.B. 17.3.61   **Nickname:** Friggy
Profession: Higher Technician (Enviromental Health)
Single
Hobbies: Swimming, Most Sports

PLAYING CAREER
Honours: FA XI; Wilts County Rep.

Club	Seasons	Transfer	Apps	Goals
Bath City	79-81			
Chippenham Town	81-85			
Trowbridge Town	85-87			
Bath City	87-91			

French, Jimmy   (F)
(SELSEY)   Age: 27

Previous Clubs: Selsey; Littlehampton
Honours: None

Friar, Paul   (D)
                                   Age: 27

Previous Clubs: Leicester City; Rotherham Utd; Motherwell (Loan); Charlton Athletic; Aldershot; Enfield; Fisher Athletic
Honours: Scottish Youth International

Froggatt, Allan   (D)
(RADCLIFFE BOROUGH)   Age: 30

Previous Clubs: Preston North End; Bolton Wanderers; Horwich RMI; Chorley
Honours: Cheshire League Winners

Fullbrook, Gary   (D)
(WEYMOUTH)   D.O.B. 4.5.66
Nickname: Shadow   Profession: Salesman
Married   Wife's name: Andrea
Hobbies: Work!

PLAYING CAREER
Honours: None

Club	Seasons	Transfer	Apps	Goals
Swindon Town	82-85		2	
Bath City	85-87	£3,000		
Carlisle United	87-88	£3,000	15	
Bath City	88-89	£1,500		
Gloucester City	89-90			

Furlong, John   (M)
(WELYWN GARDEN CITY)   Age: 33

Previous Clubs: Sudbury Court; Barnet; Wealdstone
Honours: South Midlands Representative side

Furlong, Paul   (F)
(ENFIELD)   D.O.B. 1.10.68
Nickname: Black Box   Profession: Van Driver
Single   Hobbies: Nights Out,
Snooker

PLAYING CAREER
Honours: FA Trophy Winners 87/88; England Semi-Pro Int.

Club	Seasons	Transfer	Apps	Goals
No previous clubs				

Furneaux, Mark   (D)
(HENDON)

D.O.B. 23.9.65   Nickname: Furns
Profession: Bricklayer
Single
Hobbies: Golf, Socialising

PLAYING CAREER
Honours: Enfield & Middx Schoolboy Rep

Club	Seasons	Transfer	Apps	Goals
Tottenham Hotspur	80-83			
Watford	83-84			
Enfield	84-87			

Furnell, Paul   (M)
(AFC LYMINGTON)   Age: 28

Previous Clubs: None

Honours: Bournemouth Senior Cup winners; Hants Senior Cup runners up; Wessex Lge Cup winners

STEVE FOSTER
(Braintree)

73

NICKY FRANCIS (ENFIELD)

Gabriel, David (M)

(TOOTING & MITCHAM UNITED) Age: 27
Previous Clubs: Corinthian Casuals
Honours: None

Gaffney, Lawrence (D)

(CHEADLE TOWN) Age: 28
Previous Clubs: Manchester Y.M.C.A; Massey Fergusson; Grasmere Rovers
Honours: None

Gale, Tim (M)

(MIRRLESS BLACKSTONES) Age: 27
Previous Clubs: Peterborough United; Grantham; Bralanda (Sweden); Kings Lynn; Corby Town; Stamford Town
Honours: Southern Prem runners up (Kings Lynn)

Gallagher, Nicky (M)

(LOUTH UNITED) Age: 19
Previous Clubs: Doncaster Rovers (1); Bridlington Town.
Honours: England Schoolboy & Youth Int

Galloway, David (M)

(ACCRINGTON STANLEY) Age: 25
Previous Clubs: Runcorn; Irlam Town; Newtown.
Honours: None

Gamble, David (M)

(ALTRINCHAM)

D.O.B. 23.3.71 **Nickname:** Gambo
Profession: Scaffolder
Single
Hobbies: Swimming, Golf
PLAYING CAREER
Honours: None

Club	Seasons	Transfer	Apps	Goals
Grimsby Town	78-89			

Gamble, Frank (F)

(ST.DOMINICS) Age: 28
Previous Clubs: Derby County; Rochdale; Morecambe; Rhyl
Honours: None

Gamble, Willie (F)

(SHEPSHED CHARTERHOUSE)

D.O.B. 5.3.68
PLAYING CAREER
Honours: GMVC Winners 87/88

Club	Seasons	Transfer	Apps	Goals
Lincoln City	85-89		42	9
Boston United	89-90			

Gammons, Robert (M)

(CHELMSFORD CITY)

D.O.B. 21.6.71 **Nickname:** Julian
Profession: Postman
Single
Hobbies: Watching West Ham!
PLAYING CAREER
Honours: Redbridge Schoolboy Rep; Essex County Schoolboy & Youth Rep.

Club	Seasons	Transfer	Apps	Goals
Arsenal	87-88			
Barking	88-90			

Gardiner, Aaron (M)

(CORNARD UNITED) Age: 20
Previous Clubs: Ipswich Town; Diss
Honours: None

Gardiner, Paul (D)

(YATE TOWN) Age: 34
Previous Clubs: Yate Town; Swindon Town; Frome Town; Taunton Town
Honours: Western Lge Winners & R/U; Western Lge Cup Winners; Hellenic League Winners 87/88 & 88/89; Gloucs Trophy Winners; Somerset Professional Cup Winners; Western Lge Rep

Gardner, Mark (D)

(PENRITH) Age: 19
Previous Clubs: Greystoke **Honours:** None

Garner, Mark (D)

(MIRRLEES BLACKSTONES) Age: 27
Previous Clubs: Stamford Y.M.C.A
Honours: None

Garrard, Ali (D)

(MELTON TOWN) Age: 25
Previous Clubs: **Honours:** None

Garratt, Mick (D)

(RUSHDEN TOWN)

D.O.B. 5.5.58 **Nickname:** Big Man
Profession: Sales Director
Single
Hobbies: Golf
PLAYING CAREER
Honours: FA XI; Irthlingborough P.O.Y. 86/87

Club	Seasons	Transfer	Apps	Goals
Irthlingborough D's	76-88			

Gate, Simon (F)

(PENRITH) Age: 21
Previous Clubs: Appleby **Honours:** None

Gates, Paul (D/M)
(SUTTON UNITED)

D.O.B. 23.11.66   Nickname: Madeley
Profession: Carpenter
Single
Hobbies: Golf

PLAYING CAREER
Honours: Surrey Youth Rep; Middx Wanderer; Chipstead P.O.Y. (4)

Club	Seasons	Transfer	Apps	Goals
Whyteleafe	83-84			
Chipstead	84-89			

Gauden, Bob (F)
(BRIDLINGTON TOWN)   Age: 31

Previous Clubs: Doncaster Rovers; Buxton; Scarborough; Burton Albion; Gainsborough Trinity; Burton Albion; Goole Town
Honours: FA XI; Northern Premier League Rep; FA Trophy R/U; FA Vase R/U 89/90; Northern Counties East League Winners

Gautrey, Jonathan (D/M)
(MARINE)

D.O.B. 19.1.66   Nickname: Sibbo
Profession: Cold Storage Manager
Married   Wife's name: Lorraine
Children: Alexandra & Alice
Hobbies: All Sports, Watching Videos

PLAYING CAREER
Honours: Southport & Sefton Boys Rep; NPL R/U; Liverpool Senior Cup Winners (2); Liverpool Junior Cup Winners.

Club	Seasons	Transfer	Apps	Goals
Bolton Wanderers	78-82			1
Southport	82-85			

Gayle, Mark (G)
(WORCESTER CITY)

D.O.B. 21.10.69

PLAYING CAREER
Honours: None

Club	Seasons	Transfer	Apps	Goals
Leicester City	85-88			
Blackpool	88-90			

Gazzard, Jason (M)
(KEYNSHAM TOWN)   Age: 18

Previous Clubs:

Honours: Somerset Floodlit Champions

Geddes, Andy (M)
(V.S.RUGBY)

D.O.B. 27.10.59   Nickname: Ged
Profession: Insurance Agent
Married   Wife's name: Sandy
Children: Natalie & Casey
Hobbies: Snooker, Music

PLAYING CAREER
Honours: Scottish League Div 1 Winners 80/81; Scottish Lge Cup R/U 80/81; Westgate Insurance Cup Winners; Birmingham Senior Cup Winners; Midland Floodlit Cup Winners

Club	Seasons	Transfer	Apps	Goals
Leicester City	77-79			
Dundee	79-82			
Wits University (S.A.)	82-84			
V.S.Rugby	84-86			
Leicester United	86-87			

Gemmell, James (F)
(CHEADLE TOWN)   Age: 29

Previous Clubs: Maine Road

Honours: Manchester League Championship & Gilgryst Cup winners

Gennard, Mark (M)
(CHELTENHAM TOWN)   Age:

Previous Clubs: Torquay United; Exmouth Town.

Honours: Western League Championship winner; England u19's Devon County

George, John (D)
(CLEATOR MOOR CELTIC)   Age: 24

Previous Clubs: Workington

Honours: None

George, Phil (M)
(MARLOW)

D.O.B. 18.3.63   Nickname: Parrot
Profession: Electrician
Single
Hobbies: All Sports

PLAYING CAREER
Honours: Middx Schoolboy Rep; Middx Charity Cup R/U.

Club	Seasons	Transfer	Apps	Goals
Southampton	79-81			
A'stone & Weybridge	83-84			
Hasselt FC (Belg)	84-85			
Feltham	1985			
Staines Town	85-86			
Kingstonian	86-87			
Leatherhead	1987			
Walton & Hersham	87-88			
Worthing	88-90			
Hayes	1990			

George, Steve (G)
(EYNESBURY ROVERS)   Age:

Previous Clubs: Eynesbury Rovers; Peterborough United

Honours: None

Gerrard, Kevin   (F)
(FLEETWOOD TOWN)

D.O.B. 6.4.62   **Nickname:** Class
Profession: Engineer
Married   **Wife's name:** Deb
Children: Hollie
Hobbies: Sport

PLAYING CAREER

Honours: None

Club	Seasons	Transfer	Apps	Goals
Blackburn Rovers	78-79			
North America	79-81			
South Africa	81-88			
Blackpool Rovers	88-89			

Gibbs, Dave   (D)
(AFC LYMINGTON)   **Age:** 32
Previous Clubs: AFC Bournemouth; New Milton; AFC Totton; Sway; Wellworthy Athletic; Blackfield & Langley
Honours: Hants League Div 1 winners

Gibbs, Donald   (M)
(GLOSSOP)   **Age:** 23
Previous Clubs:
Honours: None

Gibiliru, Joe   (M)
(KNOWSLEY UNITED)   **Age:** 28
Previous Clubs: Prescot Cable; St.Helens Town; Mosseley
Honours: English Schoolboy International

Gibson, Thomas   (D/M)
(MALDEN VALE)   **Age:** 27
Previous Clubs: Merstham; Banstead Athletic; Merstham
Honours: None

CRAIG GILL HUNGERFORD TOWN & WALES

GARRY GILL EASTBOURNE

PAUL GANT LOWESTOFT

Gibson, William   (D)
(WEYMOUTH)

D.O.B. 24.6.59
Profession: Turner
Married   **Wife's name:** Laura
Children: Heather & William John
Hobbies: Fishing, Sport

PLAYING CAREER

Honours: FA XI; Nuneaton P.O.Y.

Club	Seasons	Transfer	Apps	Goals
Leicester City	79-82		28	
Nuneaton Borough	82-86			

Giddens, Sean   (F)
(WELYWN GARDEN CITY)   **Age:** 20
Previous Clubs: Woolmer Green Rangers
Honours: None

Gill, Martyn   (M)
(SUTTON UNITED)

D.O.B. 11.5.60   **Nickname:** Gilly
Profession: Bank Manager
Divorced
Children: Janine & Laura
Hobbies: Music

PLAYING CAREER

Honours: England Semi-Pro Int; FA XI; Frickley, Boston & Stafford P.O.Y

Club	Seasons	Transfer	Apps	Goals
Frickley Athletic	79-82	£1,000		
Mossley	82-83			
Stafford Rangers	83-86			
Boston United	86-88			
Worcester City	88-89			
Stafford Rangers	89-90	£4,500		

MICKY GILLAM

Gillam, Michael (D)
(WHYTELEAFE) Age: 26
Previous Clubs: Croydon; Whyteleafe; Leatherhead; Molesey; Banstead Athletic
Honours: None

Gillings, Martin (M)
(DULWICH HAMLET) Age: 31
Previous Clubs: Chessington United; Dorking; Carshalton Athletic; Epsom & Ewell; Leatherhead
Honours: None

Gilliver, Andy (M)
(ALFRETON TOWN) Age: 7.6.71
Previous Clubs: Doncaster Rovers; Goole Town
Honours: None

Gilmore, Anthony (D)
(SEATON DELAVAL AMATEURS) Age: 29
Previous Clubs: Durham City; Eppleton C.W.; Bedlington Terriers; Whitley Bay; Chester-Le-Street Town; Ashington
Honours: Northumberland Senior Cup winners; Northumberland Senior Benevolent Bowl winners; McEwans Northern Alliance Premier Division championship

Gilmore, Phil (G)
(FARLEIGH ROVERS) Age: 28
Previous Clubs: Cobham; Farleigh Rovers; Dulwich Hamlet
Honours: None

Glasgow, Kenny (M)
(MARLOW)

D.O.B. 17.7.64
Profession: Painter & Decorator
Single
Hobbies: Football

PLAYING CAREER
Honours: Vauxhall Lge Div 1 & 2 Winners; Marlow P.O.Y. 86/87

Club	Seasons	Transfer	Apps	Goals
Flackwell Heath	83-86			
Marlow	86-88			
Flackwell Heath	88-89			

Gleane, Paul (M)
(WOLVERTON AFC) Age: 27
Previous Clubs: Wolverton MK; Bradwell St.Peters
Honours: None

Gleave, Tim (D)
(NEWMARKET TOWN) Age: 23
Previous Clubs: Cambridge City; Thetford Town; Newmarket Town
Honours: None

Glendinning, Ian (M)
(CHESTER-LE-STREET) Age: 24
Previous Clubs: Washington
Honours: None

Glover, Carl (D)
(LEWES) Age: 25
Previous Clubs: Eastbourne United
Honours: Welsh Schoolboy Int

Glover, John (D)
(WELLING UNITED)

D.O.B. 15.5.55 **Nickname:** Glovsie
Profession: Self-Employed
Separated
Children: Simon, Sarah & James

PLAYING CAREER
Honours: Merseyside Schoolboy Rep; England Semi-Pro Int; London Senior Cup Winners 88/89; Bedford P.O.Y. 79/80; Nuneaton P.O.Y. 80/81; Maidstone P.O.Y. 84/85

Club	Seasons	Transfer	Apps	Goals
Bedford Town	78-80	£3,000		
Nuneaton Borough	80-84	£2,500		
Maidstone United	84-88	£2,500		

Glynn, Sean (D)
(WELWYN GARDEN CITY) **Age:** 22
Previous Clubs:
Honours: None

Gocan, Peter (F)
(STOURBRIDGE)

D.O.B. 9.5.62 **Nickname:** Jinksey
Profession: British Telecom Clerical Officer
Married **Wife's name:** Marcia
Children: Lauren & Jade
Hobbies: Pool

PLAYING CAREER
Honours: Staffs Schoolboy Rep; Worcs Senior Cup Winners; Somerset Senior Cup Winners

Club	Seasons	Transfer	Apps	Goals
Walsall	82-85			
Oldbury United	85-86			
Stourbridge	86-87			
Worcester City	87-89			
Alvechurch	1989			
Bath City	89-90			

Godbold John (D)
(MALDEN VALE) **Age:** 24
Previous Clubs: Kingstonian; Tooting & Mitcham United; Leatherhead; Wimbledon
Honours: None

Godden, Tony (G)
(WIVENHOE TOWN)

D.O.B. 2.8.55

PLAYING CAREER
Honours: None

Club	Seasons	Transfer	Apps	Goals
Ashford Town	74-76			
West Bromwich Albion (Luton Town - loan 12 Walsall - loan 19)	76-85	£35,000	267	
Chelsea	85-86		34	
Birmingham City (Bury - loan 1)	86-88		29	
Peterborough United	88-90		24	

Godwin, Danny (D)
(TOOTING & MITCHAM UNITED) **Age:** 32
Previous Clubs: Chelsea; Wimbledon; Dulwich Hamlet; Tooting & Mitcham United; Leatherhead
Honours: Vauxhall Lge Rep

Goff, Neil (M)
(CWMBRAN TOWN) **Age:** 26
Previous Clubs: Cardiff City; Newport County; Cheltenham Town; Gloucester City
Honours: Welsh Schoolboy International

Goguel, Malcolm (D)
(ROMSEY TOWN) **Age:** 21
Previous Clubs: Bashley; Fareham Town
Honours: Wessex League Champions

Goldstraw, Stephen (D)
(CONGLETON TOWN)

D.O.B. 8.4.64
Profession: Not working
Single
Hobbies: Sport

PLAYING CAREER
Honours: HFS Loans Lge Div 1 Winners 89/90

Club	Seasons	Transfer	Apps	Goals
Leek Town	84-86			
Buxton	86-88			
Leek Town	88-90			

NIGEL GOLLEY

Golley, Nigel (D)
(SUTTON UNITED)

D.O.B. 19.5.61
Profession: Admin Officer In A Bank
Married **Wife's name:** Mandy
Children: Emma
Hobbies: Golf, Sport

PLAYING CAREER
Honours: Sutton Schoolboy Rep; FA XI; Vauxhall-Opel Lge Premier Winners 84/85 & 85/86; AC Delco Cup Winners 82/83, 83/84 & 85/86; London Senior Cup Winners 82/83; Surrey Senior Cup Winners 82/83, 83/84, 84/85, 85/86, 86/87 & 87/88; Sutton P.O.Y. 88/89

Club	Seasons	Transfer	Apps	Goals
Whyteleafe	78-81			

Gooday, Ivan (F)

(BRAINTREE TOWN) **Age:** 12.3.61

Previous Clubs: Chelmsford City; Braintree Town
Honours: Eastern Lge Winners(2) & R/U,Braintree P.O.Y.

Goodman, Steve (F)

(WALTHAMSTOW PENNANT) **Age:** 28

Previous Clubs: Tate & Lyle; Willesden
Honours: Represented London F.A.; Spartan League Cup winners 1988-89

Goodwill, Bob (G)

(PICKERING TOWN) **Age:** 34

Previous Clubs: Scarborough; Bridlington Town; Eastfield
Honours: None

MARK GOODWIN

Goodwin, Mark (M)

(KETTERING TOWN)

D.O.B. 23.2.60
Profession: Sales Rep
Married **Wife's name:** Lynda
Children: Katie & David

PLAYING CAREER

Honours: None

Club	Seasons	Transfer	Apps	Goals
Leicester City	76-80	£60,000	91	8
Notts County	80-87		237	24
Walsall	87-90		97	5

Goodwin, Peter (M)

(FARLEIGH ROVERS) **Age:** 32

Previous Clubs: Banstead
Honours: None

Gordon, Pat (F)

(BROMLEY) **Age:** 24

Previous Clubs: Millwall; Leyton Wingate
Honours: None

Gordon, Russell (F)

(TAMWORTH) **Age:** 26

Previous Clubs: Coventry City; Brighton & Hove Albion; Banbury United; Dudley Town; Stafford Rangers; Cheltenham Town
Honours: FA Vase Winners 1989

KEVIN GORMAN

Gorman, Kevin (M)

(MOSSLEY)

D.O.B. 26.10.52
Profession: Personnel Manager
Married **Wife's name:** Margaret
Children: Liam & Suzanne

PLAYING CAREER

Honours: NPL Winners (2); NPL R/U (3); NPL Shield R/U (4); FA Trophy R/U; Non-League Champion of Champions R/U; Manchester Senior Cup R/U; NPL Rep

Club	Seasons	Transfer	Apps	Goals
Bacup Borough	75-77			
Barrow	77-78			
Droylsden	78-79			
Mossley	79-83	£500		
Hyde United	83-84			
Southport	84-85			
Buxton	85-87			
Chadderton	87-89	(Player-Manager)		

Grabner, Ronald (M)

(CHEADLE TOWN) **Age:** 43

Previous Clubs: Shrewsbury Town; Hyde United; Winsford United; Macclesfield Town; Stalybridge Celtic; Curzon Ashton
Honours: English Colleges Representative; Shropshire Senior Cup winners; Cheshire Senior Cup winners

Graham, David (M)
(DULWICH HAMLET) **Age:** 25

Previous Clubs: Whyteleafe

Honours: None

JON GRAHAM

Graham, Jonathan (F)
(KETTERING TOWN)

D.O.B. 24.11.66 **Nickname:** J.G.

Profession: Painter & Decorator

Single

Hobbies: Any Sports, TV, Reading

PLAYING CAREER

Honours: None

Club

No previous clubs - from local football.

Graham, Mark (D)
(RHYL) **Age:** 25

Previous Clubs: Wrexham; Greenfield; Holywell Town; Flint Town United

Honours: Welsh Alliance Lge Winners; Cookson Cup Winners

Grainger, Paul (M)
(TELFORD UNITED) **Age:** 23

Previous Clubs: Aston Villa, Mile Oak Rovers, Wolverhampton Wanderers

Honours: FA.XI

Grant, Robert (D)
(MELTON TOWN) **Age:** 17

Previous Clubs:

Honours: None

JOHN GRANVILLE

Granville, John (G)
(WYCOMBE WANDERERS)

D.O.B. 6.5.56

PLAYING CAREER

Honours: Trinidad & Tobago Int.

Club	Seasons	Transfer	Apps	Goals
L. A. Lazers (USA)	77-80			
Cleveland Cobras (USA)	80-84			
Slough Town	84-85			
Millwall	85-86		6	
Slough Town	86-87			

Granycome, Neal (M)
(GATESHEAD) **Age:** 30

Previous Clubs: Whitby Town; Billingham Town; Billingham Synthonia.

Honours: Northern Lge 2nd Div Trophy 1986-87; N.Lge Championship 1988-89, 1989-90; N.Lge Cup 1987-88, 1989-90; Durham Cup Winners Trophy 1988-89

Gray, Andy (G)
(CLITHEROE) **Age:** 27

Previous Clubs: Bury Youth; Curzon Ashton; Wigan Athletic; Mossley; Radcliffe Borough; Morecombe

Honours: Manchester Premier runners up

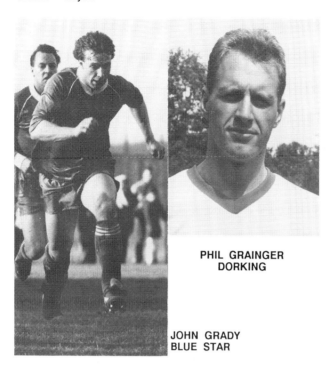

PHIL GRAINGER
DORKING

JOHN GRADY
BLUE STAR

Gray, Jason (M)

(GAINSBOROUGH TOWN) Age: 24

Previous Clubs: Worksop Boys; Babworth Rovers; Spicers; Retford Town; British Railway; East Hall United

Honours: Notts County Cup (British Railway); Nursing Cup (Retford); Retford Division 1 (Spicers)

Grears, Douglas (D)

(CLEATOR MOOR CELTIC) Age: 28

Previous Clubs:

Honours: None

Greaves, Phil (D)

(MELTON TOWN) Age: 25

Previous Clubs: Petfoods

Honours: None

Green, Bobby (D)

(CARSHALTON ATHLETIC)

D.O.B. 17.8.53
Profession: British Telecom Engineer
Married

PLAYING CAREER

Honours: FA Amateur Cup R/U; Isthmian Lge Winners; Surrey Senior Cup Winners 88/89 & 89/90; Middlesex Wanderer

Club	Seasons	Transfer	Apps	Goals
Tooting & Mitcham Utd				
Sutton United				
Corinthian Casuals				
Dulwich Hamlet				

Green, David (M)

(SALISBURY) Age: 2

Previous Clubs: Swanage & Herston; Poole Town; Swanage & Herston

Honours: None

Green, Duncan (G)

(HORSHAM) Age: 2

Previous Clubs: Steyning Town; Worthing; Lancing

Honours: None

Green Eddie (G)

(HEANOR TOWN) Age: 30

Previous Clubs: Grantham Town; Stamford AFC; Retford Town Worksop Town; Ilkeston Town

Honours: England Schools u18 International

Green, Matt (M)

(WORCESTER CITY)

D.O.B. 6.11.70

PLAYING CAREER

Honours: None

Club	Seasons	Transfer	Apps	Goals
Wolverhampton W.	87-90			

Green, Michael (M)

(LANGLEY SPORTS) Age: 28

Previous Clubs: EIB Utd; Hasting United; EIB Town

Honours: Sussex County League Div 2 Champions 1987-88 S.Lge Challenge Cup winner 1989-90; Represented Sussex a Senior & Youth; Eastbourne Charity Cup winner 1989-90 Brighton Evening Argus County 5-a-side Champions 1989-90

Green, Paul (F)

(OAKWOOD) Age: 24

Previous Clubs: Redhill

Honours: S.C.League Div 2 runners up & Cup winners

Green, Paul (M)

(BANBURY UNITED) Age: 26

Previous Clubs: Highgate United; Coleshill Town

Honours: None

Green, Paul (G)

(WARMINSTER TOWN) Age: 29

Previous Clubs: Newton Abbot Spurs; Watts Blake & Bearne Warminster Town

Honours: Wiltshire County B

Green, Russell (F)

(BROMLEY) Age: 18

Previous Clubs: Brighton & H A (A)
Honours: None

Green, Terry (M)
(FLEETWOOD TOWN)

D.O.B. 23.7.72   Nickname: Rushy
Profession: Not working
Single
Hobbies: Cricket, Snooker, Going To Night Clubs

PLAYING CAREER

Honours: Blackpool Schoolboy Rep; Lancs Youth Cup Winners; HFS Loans Lge Presidents Cup Winners; Fleetwood Y.P.O.Y. 89/90.

Club	Seasons	Transfer	Apps	Goals
Preston North End	86-88			
Wren Rovers	88-89			

Greenaway, Brian (M)
(STAINES TOWN)

D.O.B. 26.9.57

PLAYING CAREER

Honours: FA Trophy Winners 84/85; Gola Lge Winners 84/85

Club	Seasons	Transfer	Apps	Goals
Fulham	75-80		85	8
Apoel (Cyprus)	80-82			
Wealdstone	82-85			
Dagenham	85-86			
Wycombe Wanderers	86-88			
Slough Town	88-89			

Greene, Robert (F)
(SOLIHULL BOROUGH)

D.O.B. 25.10.69
Profession: Plumber
Single
Hobbies: Reading

PLAYING CAREER

Honours: England Schoolboy Int.; Westgate Insurance Cup Winner; Midland Floodlit Cup Winner.

Club	Seasons	Transfer	Apps	Goals
Aston Villa	85-87			
Oskarsham AIK (Swe)	1987			
Willenhall Town	87-89			
Burton Albion	89-90			
V.S. Rugby	1990			

Greenfield, Craig (D)
(DENABY UNITED)   Age: 21

Previous Clubs: Sheffield Wednesday; Matlock
Honours: None

Greenland, Terry (M)
(GENERAL CHEMICALS)   Age: 25

Previous Clubs: Grenadeir; Dista; Arncliffe
Honours: Liverpool Sunday League 2nd Div champions; I Zingari League 1st Div Champions

Greenough, Ricky (D)
(BRIDLINGTON TOWN)   Age: 29

Previous Clubs: Alfreton Town; Chester City (132-15); Scarborough; York City (29-1)
Honours: None

Greenway, Julian (D/M)
(FLEETWOOD TOWN)

D.O.B. 24.8.71
Profession: Work Study Officer
Single
Hobbies: Golf, Driving

PLAYING CAREER

Honours:

Club	Seasons	Transfer	Apps	Goals
Preston North End	87-89			
Colne Dynamoes	89-90			

KIM GREEN   DAVE GREENING
ELMORE   ATHERTON UTD

Gregoriou, Mike (D)
(CLITHEROE)   Age: 23

Previous Clubs: Radcliffe Borough; Clitheroe; Apoel (Nicosia)
Honours: None

Gregory, John (D)
(ST.DOMINICS)   Age: 29

Previous Clubs: None
Honours: None

Griffiths, Anthony (M)
(STAFFORD RANGERS)

D.O.B. 1.4.63　　　　　　**Nickname:** Twangy
Profession: Sales Manager
Single
Hobbies: Cricket, Golf

PLAYING CAREER
Honours: Stoke Schoolboy Rep; FA Trophy Winners & R/U; Leek P.O.Y.

Club	Seasons	Transfer	Apps	Goals
Port Vale	78-81			
Leek Town	81-85	£3,000		
Telford United	85-90	Player Exchange		

Griffiths, Neil (G)
(RHYL)　　　　　　　　　　　　　**Age:** 23

Previous Clubs: Vauxhall GM; Warrington Town
Honours: None

Griffiths, Steven (G)
(PEGASUS JUNIORS)　　　　　　**Age:** 26

Previous Clubs: Wellington
Honours: None

Grimshaw, Andrew (M)
(WITTON ALBION)

D.O.B.
Profession: Not working　　　**Nickname:** Grimmy
Married　　　　　　　　　　**Wife's name:** Wendy
Children: Zak Andrew
Hobbies: Any Sports

PLAYING CAREER
Honours: Rossendale Schoolboy Rep; Lancs Schoolboy Rep; NWCL Div 1 Winners, NWCL Div 1 R/U; HFS Loans Lge Div 1 & Premier Winners; ATS Cup Winners.

Club	Seasons	Transfer	Apps	Goals
Colne Dynamoes	84-85			
Rossendale United	85-87			
Colne Dynamoes	87-90			

Grogan, Robert (M)
(BECKENHAM TOWN)　　　　　　**Age:** 21

Previous Clubs: Dulwich Hamlet
Honours: None

Grosse, David (D)
(PICKERING)　　　　　　　　　　**Age:** 27

Previous Clubs: Bridlington Town; Bridlington Trinity; Gastfield; Brid Labour Social; Flamborough; Bempton

Honours: N.E.Counties 2nd Div winners; East Riding Senior Cup runners up twice

Grubb, Shaun (D)
(LANGNEY SPORTS)　　　　　　**Age:** 29

Previous Clubs: Eastbourne Rangers

Honours: Sussex County Lge Div 2 champions 1987-88; S.Co Lge Challenge Cup winner 1989-90; Eastbourne Charity Cup winner 1989-90

Guest, Michael (M)
(HALESOWEN HARRIERS)　　　　**Age:** 26

Previous Clubs: Halesowen Town; Gresley Rovers
Honours: Worcester Senior; Bass Vase; West Mids runners up; Derby Senior

Gumbs, David (D)
(MARLOW)

D.O.B. 22.6.67　　　　　　**Nickname:** Gummy
Profession: Not working
Single
Hobbies: Football

PLAYING CAREER
Honours: Vauxhall-Opel Lge Div 2 Winners

Club	Seasons	Transfer	Apps	Goals
Chesham United	84-87			
Flackwell Heath	87-88			
Wycombe Wanderers	1989			
Chalfont St.Peter	89-90			

Gummer, Steve (M)
(BRIDGWATER TOWN 84)　　　　**Age:** 24

Previous Clubs: None

Honours: Somerset Senior Div 1 winners; runners up in Div 2

Gunn Trevor (D)
(BRAINTREE TOWN)　　　　　　**Age:** 26

Previous Clubs: Bishop's Stortford; Brantham Athletic
Honours: Herts Senior Cup Winners; East Anglian Cup Winners

Gunner, Mark (M)
(WESTBURY)　　　　　　　　　　**Age:** 23

Previous Clubs: Avon Bradford; Warminster
Honours: Warminster Player of the Year 1989-90

Guppy, Steve (F)
(WYCOMBE WANDERERS)

D.O.B. 29.3.69

PLAYING CAREER
Honours: Berks & Bucks Senior Cup Winners 89/90

Club	Seasons	Transfer	Apps	Goals
Southampton	86-89			

Guyon, Nick (M)
(CORNARD UNITED)　　　　　　**Age:** 24

Previous Clubs: Colchester United; Clacton Town; Sudbury Town; Hatfield; Wivenhoe; Cornard Utd　　**Honours:** None

CHRIS GUY (BRAINTREE)

GARY GROGAN (CAMBRIDGE CITY)

STEVE GUPPY (WYCOMBE W.)

BILLY GOLDSTONE (BARKING)

PAUL GRAINGER (TELFORD)

Haddon, Graham (M)
(RADCLIFFE BOROUGH) Age: 25
Previous Clubs: Horwich RMI; Leyland Motors
Honours: None

Haines, Jeff (F)
(FARLEIGH ROVERS) Age: 22
Previous Clubs: Whyteleafe
Honours: None

Haines, Tony (F)
(FARLEIGH ROVERS) Age: 29
Previous Clubs: None
Honours: None

Hall, David (M)
(BRIDLINGTON TRINITY) Age: 29
Previous Clubs: North Ferriby United; Bridlington Trinity
Honours: North-East Counties Lge Winners; FA Vase R/U 89/90

Hall, John (D)
(SHOTTON COMRADES) Age: 25
Previous Clubs: Wallsend Town; Percy Main Amateurs
Honours: Benevolent Bowl winners 1985-86

Hall, Lee (D)
(GODALMING TOWN) Age: 31
Previous Clubs: Milford.
Honours: None

Hall, Mark (F)
(WESTHOUGHTON TOWN) Age:
Previous Clubs: Standish Lower Ground; Wigan Youth; Ashton Town; Wigan College; Poolstock
Honours: Wigan A.L. Prem Champs (2); Laithwaite Shield winners (2); Hughes Cup winners (2); Wigan Cup winners; West Lancs Div 1 runners up; L.F.A. Inter League winners; S.W.L Cup winners

Hall, Richard (D)
(NEWMARKET TOWN) Age: 34
Previous Clubs: Histon; SDaffron Walden; Histon
Honours: Cambs Schoolboy/Youth/Senior levels; E.C.L. Cup Runners up

Hall, Toby (F)
(HALESOWEN HARRIERS) Age: 26
Previous Clubs: Romsley AFC; Grange Athletic
Honours: None

Hall, Tony (F)
(CORNARD UNITED) Age: 30
Previous Clubs: Ipswich Town; Bury Town; Harwich; Chelmsford; Brantham
Honours: None

Hallam, Craig (F)
(WESTHOUGHTON TOWN) Age: 18
Previous Clubs: New Springs; Wigan College; Horwich R.M.I.
Honours: L.F.A. u18 Inter Lge winners & runners up; Lancs Youth Team member

Halliday, Bruce (D)
(GATESHEAD)

D.O.B. 3.1.61 **Nickname:** Doc
Profession: Not working
Married **Wife's name:** Debbie
PLAYING CAREER
Honours: None

Club	Seasons	Transfer	Apps	Goals
Newcastle United	77-82		38	1
Darlington		loan	7	
Bury	82-83		30	
Bristol City	83-85		66	
Hereford United	85-87		65	6
Bath City	87-89			
Apia (Australia)	89-90			

JEFF HAMLET
(Wembley)

Hamberger, Steve (D)
(BROMLEY) Age: 31
Previous Clubs: Millwall (Comb); Barking; Walthamstow Ave; Orient; Portsmouth; Maidstone; Leyton Wingate
Honours: Vauxhall Opel 2nd Div North

Hambels, Andrew (F)
(BANBURY UNITED) Age: 24
Previous Clubs: None
Honours: None

Hamer, Julian (G)

(MELTON TOWN) **Age:** 20

Previous Clubs: Melton Town; Grantham Town

Honours: None

Hamilton, Calvin (D)

(BEDWORTH UNITED) **Age:** 27

Previous Clubs: Aston Villa; Halesowen Town; Sandwell Borough

Honours: England Schoolboy Int

Hamilton, Mark (F)

(HARROGATE TOWN) **Age:** 29

Previous Clubs: Farsley Celtic; Leeds Ashley Road; Goole Town; Harrogate Railway; Farsley Celtic; Harrogate Town; Guisley; Harrogate Town

Honours: Yorkshire League 1st Div winners; West Riding County Cup winners (2); West Riding Co Cup runners up (3); President Cup (Northern Prem League) runners up; HFS Loans Lge 1st Div Cup winners

Hammond, Lawrence (F)

(SHOTTON COMRADES) **Age:** 27

Previous Clubs: Shotton Comrades; Thornley; Winterton Hospital

Honours: None

Hammond, Phil (G)

(LEWES) **Age:** 21

Previous Clubs: Southwick

Honours: None

Hamon, Chris (G)

(VALE RECREATION) **Age:** 31

Previous Clubs: Belgrave Wanderers

Honours: 13 Guernsey Caps; 9 Guernsey Prialulx championships; 2 Channel Island championships

Hampson, Stephen (D)

(HARROGATE TOWN) **Age:** 17

Previous Clubs: None

Honours: None

Hanchard, Martin (F)

(NORTHWICH VICTORIA)

D.O.B. 23.9.62

PLAYING CAREER

Honours: NPL Winners; Bob Lord Trophy Winners; Mid-Cheshire Senior Cup Winners; FA XI

Club	Seasons	Transfer	Apps	Goals
Stoke City	78-80			
Stafford Rangers	80-83			
Altrincham	83-85			
Telford United	85-89			

Hancock, Mark (D)

(NORTHWICH VICTORIA) **D.O.B.** 30.9.60

PLAYING CAREER

Honours: FA Trophy Winners 88/89 & R/U 87/88; Staffs Senior Cup Winners; Shropshire Senior Cup Winners

Club	Seasons	Transfer	Apps	Goals
Van Leer	80-85			
Telford United	85-89			

Hancocks, Geoff (D)

(GLOUCESTER CITY)

D.O.B. 11.7.59 **Nickname:** Basher
Profession: Fireman
Married **Wife's name:** Sally
Children: Scott
Hobbies: Motor Cars

PLAYING CAREER

Honours: FA XI; RAF Rep & Combined Services Rep

Club	Seasons	Transfer	Apps	Goals
Southam United	76-80			
RAF (Abroad)	80-81			
Cambridge City	83-88			
RAF (Abroad)	88-90			

Hancox, Richard (F)

(CHELTENHAM TOWN)

D.O.B. 4.10.68 **Nickname:** Bobble Hat
Profession: Hay Stacker
Single
Hobbies: Playing Guitar

PLAYING CAREER

Honours: Birmingham Schoolboy Rep

Club	Seasons	Transfer	Apps	Goals
Exeter City	85-87		2	
Halesowen Town	87-89			
Hednesford Town	1989			
Dudley Town	89-90			

Handford, Philip (M)

(WELLING UNITED)

D.O.B. 18.7.64 **Nickname:** Barney
Profession: Not working
Single **Hobbies:** All Sport

PLAYING CAREER

Honours: London Senior Cup Winners 88/89

Club	Seasons	Transfer	Apps	Goals
Gillingham	80-84		32	1
Wimbledon	84-86		7	
Crewe Alexandra		loan	9	
Maidstone United	86-87	£2,000		

Hankins, Gary (F)

(CHELMSLEY TOWN) **Age:** 26

Previous Clubs: Knowle; Chelmsley; Knowle

Honours: None

Hanlan, Matthew (M)
(WYCOMBE WANDERERS)

D.O.B. 5.11.66

PLAYING CAREER
Honours: Surrey Senior Cup Winners

Club	Seasons	Transfer	Apps	Goals
Sutton United	83-90			

Hanlon, Stephen (M)
(MACCLESFIELD TOWN)

D.O.B. 18.7.63 Nickname: Hano
Profession: Postman
Married Wife's name: Jayne
Hobbies: Golf, Squash, Coaching local football team

PLAYING CAREER
Honours: NPL & Cup Winners; FA Trophy R/U; Macclesfield P.O.Y.; England Semi Pro International.

Club	Seasons	Transfer	Apps	Goals
Crewe Alexandra	79-83		27	
Nantwich Town	1983			
Ekenas IF (Finland)	1983			
Oswestry Town	83-84			

BARRIE HUGHES (Accrington Stanley)

Hann, Nigel (M)
(HITCHIN TOWN) Age: 26
Previous Clubs: Boreham Wood; St.Albans City
Honours: None

Hanson, Tony (F)
(CHELMSLEY TOWN) Age: 36
Previous Clubs: Oldbury; Boldmere; Tamworth; Solihull Boro; Sutton Town

Honours: Midland Cup finalist

Harbottle, Mark (M)
(BURTON ALBION) D.O.B. 26.9.68

PLAYING CAREER
Honours: England Youth Int

Club	Seasons	Transfer	Apps	Goals
Notts County	85-87		4	1
Doncaster Rovers		loan	4	
Scarborough	1987			
Oakham United	87-88			
Shepshed C'house	88-90			

Harbron, Andy (D)
(BILLINGHAM SYNTHONIA) Age: 34
Previous Clubs: None
Honours: Northern Lge 2nd Div Trophy; N.Lge Championship (2); N.Lge Cup (2); Durham Cup winners trophy.

Hardiman, Stephen (D)
(MORETON TOWN) Age: 26
Previous Clubs: None
Honours: Gloucester Senior Cup (2); Oxford Benevolent Cup Cup; Hellenic League Championship & League Cup

Harding, Bobby (F)
(WITHAM TOWN) Age: 35
Previous Clubs: Arsenal; Ilford; Enfield; Harlow; B.Stortford; Hendon; Tiptree.
Honours: None

Harding, Mick (M/F)
(LEATHERHEAD) Age: 22
Previous Clubs: Woking; Chobham; Bracknell Town; Westfields
Honours: None

Harding, Simon (M)
(BURNHAM RAMBLERS) Age: 17
Previous Clubs: None Honours: None

Hardman, Michael (D)
(DROYLESDEN) Age: 27
Previous Clubs: Warrington Town; Runcorn; Altrincham; Macclesfield Town
Honours: Multipart Lge Winners; Multipart Lge Cup Winners; Presidents Cup Winners; Cheshire Senior Cup Winners (3); FA Trophy R/U

MICHAEL HARDMAN

Hardy, Stanley   (D)
(BLACKSTONES)   **Age:** 22

Previous Clubs: Peterborough United; Ramsey Town; Stamford Town

Honours: County Youth; UCL Cup winner

Hardwick, Gary   (F)
(BEDWORTH UNITED)   **Age:** 23

Previous Clubs: Coventry City; Stratford Town; Atherstone United £500

Honours: None

Hare, Stuart   (M)
(ROMSEY TOWN)   **Age:** 19

Previous Clubs: None

Honours: Wessex League winners

Harewood, Sherland   (F)
(CHELMSLEY TOWN)   **Age:** 26

Previous Clubs: Acton Sports

Honours: Scoreline Division One Champions 1986-87; Invitation Cup winners 1987-88

Harman, Mark   (F)
(TUNBRIDGE WELLS)   **Age:** 26

Previous Clubs: None

Honours: None

Harman, Syd   (M)
(LEWES)   **Age:** 16

Previous Clubs: Brighton & Hove Albion
Honours: Sussex Schoolboy & Youth Rep

Harmsworth, Mark   (M)
(HAYES)

D.O.B. 2.4.64
Profession: Roofer
Married   **Wife's name:** Janice
Children: Harry
Hobbies: Sport

PLAYING CAREER

Honours: London Senior Cup Winners

Club	Seasons	Transfer	Apps	Goals
Epsom & Ewell	83-85			
Hampton	85-86			
Kingstonian	86-87			
Hampton	87-88			
Fisher Athletic	88-90			

Harper, Andrew   (M)
(NEWTOWN)   **Age:** 28

Previous Clubs: Rhos Aelwld; Brymbo Steelworks
Honours: None

Harris, Alan   (D)
(SELSEY)   **Age:** 31

Previous Clubs: Selsey; Siplesham

Honours: Sussex County Div 2 (1975-76); Sussex Junior Cup (1976-77)

Harris, Carl   (M)
(MORETON TOWN)   **Age:** 22

Previous Clubs: Mid-Oxon; Oxford United Youth; Witney Town
Honours: None

Harris, Ian   (G)
(WESTBURY UNITED)   **Age:** 30

Previous Clubs: Trowbridge Town; Melksham Town; Chippenham Town; Melksham Town; Trowbridge Town; Sailsbury

Honours: Wilstshire Pro Shield (3); Great Mills Western Lge Rep side; Player of the Year awards at Melksham Town

Harris, Kevin   (D)
(BRIDGNORTH TOWN)   **Age:** 30

Previous Clubs: Madeley United; Oakengates; Stafford Rangers; Shifnal Town

Honours: Shropshire Senior Cup; WML winners (2); Midland Combination winners (1); Shropshire Senior Cup runners up (1)

Harris, Martin   (M)
(CLEATOR MOOR CELTIC)   **Age:** 34

Previous Clubs: Grimsby Town; Workington Reds; Hartlepool; Scarborough
Honours: None

KEVIN HALL (Hampton)

Harrison, Graham (M)

(CONGLETON TOWN)

D.O.B. 21.2.63 Nickname: Adge
Profession: Sheet Metal Worker
Single
Hobbies: Golf,Cricket

PLAYING CAREER

Honours: Congleton P.O.Y. 85/86

Club	Seasons	Transfer	Apps	Goals
Rolls Royce FC	79-83			

Harrison, Keith (M)

(CHASETOWN) Age: 24
Previous Clubs: Stourbridge
Honours: Banks's League Premier Cup

Harrison, Peter (D)

(GATESHEAD)

D.O.B. 14.8.59 Nickname: Harra
Profession: Self-Employed Sportswear Salesman
Married Wife's name: Julia
Children: Nathalie
Hobbies: Golf

PLAYING CAREER

Honours: Gateshead Schoolboy Rep; County Durham Schoolboy Rep; HFS Loans Lge Premier Winners

Club	Seasons	Transfer	Apps	Goals
Gateshead	79-82	£10,000		
Royal Chaleroi S C (Belg)	82-87	£2,000		
Barrow	87-89			

Harrison, Wayne (M)

(CLEATOR MOOR CELTIC) Age: 32
Previous Clubs: Workington; Sheffield Wednesday; Blackpool; Oulu Palloseura; Baltimore Blast

Honours: Great Britian Students (World student games mexico 1979); Presidents Cup winners (Workington); County honours

Hart, Adam (M)

(WINGATE) Age: 24
Previous Clubs: None

Honours: Herts Senior Trophy 1988 winners; South Midlands Lge Div 1 1990 runners up

Hart, Brian (D)

(HORWICH RMI)

D.O.B. 14.7.59 Nickname: Harty
Profession: Clerk
Married Wife's name: Ruth
Children: Gemma Louise & Leah Marie

PLAYING CAREER

Honours: GMAC Cup Winners; Lancs Floodlight Winners & R/U; Presidents Cup R/U; Glossop P.O.Y.81/82; Horwich P.O.Y.86/87

Club	Seasons	Transfer	Apps	Goals
Bolton Wanderers	75-77			
Rochdale	77-79		98	2
Bangor City	79-81			
Glossop	81-82			
Hyde United	82-83			
Mossley	83-84			
Horwich RMI	84-89			
Westhoughton Town	89-90			

Hart, Neil (M)

(RADCLIFFE BOROUGH) Age: 19
Previous Clubs: Chorley Honours: None

Hartley, Andy (M/D)

(LEWES) Age: 22
Previous Clubs: Leeds University Honours: None

Hartley, Mark (F)

(PICKERING TOWN) Age: 23
Previous Clubs: Edgehill
Honours: Scarborough District Div 1 winners; League Cup winners

Harvey, Gary (M)

(CLACTON TOWN) Age: 30
Previous Clubs: Colchester United(8); Kongsvinger (Nor); Haverhill Rovers; Wivenhoe Town; Harwich & Parkeston; Chelmsford City; Braintree Town; Harwich & Parkeston
Honours: Southern Lge Southern Div Winners

Harvey, Gary (D)

(CLACTON TOWN) Age: 24
Previous Clubs: Clacton Town; Wivenhoe Town; Harwich & Parkeston
Honours: Essex Senior Trophy winner 1989

Harvey, Tim (D)

(GAINSBOROUGH TOWN) Age: 22
Previous Clubs: Grimsby Town; Brigg Town; Bridlington Town
Honours: None

Haslem, Gary (M)

(FLEETWOOD TOWN) D.O.B. 14.5.68
Nickname: Snapper Profession: Driver/Salesman
Single Hobbies: Badminton

PLAYING CAREER

Honours: Blackpool Youth P.O.Y.

Club	Seasons	Transfer	Apps	Goals
Blackpool	83-84			
Wyre Villa	84-97			

Hatcher, Martin (D)

(BURNHAM RAMBLERS) Age: 23
Previous Clubs: None   Honours: None

Hathaway, Thomas (F)

(RACING CLUB WARWICK) Age: 22
Previous Clubs: AP Leamington; Stratford Town
Honours: None

De la Have, Michael (D)

(VALE RECREATION) Age: 19
Previous Clubs: Belgrave Wanderers
Honours: Guernsey u21 cap 1989-90

Haw, Stephen (F)

(MARINE) D.O.B. 9.11.62
Nickname: Chivers   Profession: Not working
Married   Wife's name: Lesley
Children: Christopher, Jennifer & Jack
Hobbies: Golf (Handicap 5!)

PLAYING CAREER

Honours: Liverpool Schoolboy Rep; Merseyside Youth Rep; FA XI; NPL XI; Liverpool County FA XI; Manchester County FA XI; NPL R/U; Bob Lord Trophy Winners; Cheshire Senior Cup Winners; Lancs Challenge Trophy Winners; Liverpool Senior Cup Winners (2)

Club	Seasons	Transfer	Apps	Goals
Wigan Athletic	80-81			
Runcorn	81-83			
Kirkby Town	83-84			
Marine	84-89			
Altrincham	89-90			

Hawkins, John (G)

(BALDOCK TOWN) Age: 28
Previous Clubs: Hitchin T.; Vauxhall Motors; Buckingham T.
Honours: None

Hawkins, John (F)

(SUTTON UNITED) D.O.B. 17.8.70
Nickname: Hawkeye   Profession: Groundsman
Single   Hobbies: Snooker, Boxing

Previous Clubs: None

Honours: Surrey Youth Rep; Southern Youth Lge Winners 87/88 & 88/89; John Ullman Cup Winners 88/89

Hawkins, John (D)

(NEWPORT AFC) Age: 19
Previous Clubs: Exeter City   Honours: None

Hawkins, Nick (F)

(BRIDGWATER TOWN 84) Age: 24
Previous Clubs: Bridgwater Town; Taunton Town; Minehead
Honours: Senior League Champions; League Cup winners (2); Full County Honours & Youth

Hayes, Andrew (F)

(WALTHAMSTOW PENNANT) Age: 21
Previous Clubs: None   Honours: None

Hayes, Curtis (G)

(BROMLEY) Age: 25
Previous Clubs: Metrogas
Honours: Supporters Club Player of the Year 1989-90 (Bromley)

Hayes, Terry (F)

(WELWYN GARDEN CITY) Age: 33
Previous Clubs: Hoddesdon Town; Whitwell
Honours: South Midlands Representative side

Hayes, Wayne (F)

(RADCLIFFE BOROUGH) Age: 21
Previous Clubs: None   Honours: None

Haynes, Mark (F)

(61 FC) Age: 29
Previous Clubs: Barton Rovers
Honours: S.M.L. 1st Div winners; Beds Senior Cup

Hayton, Ian (F)

(SHOTTON COMRADES) Age: 20
Previous Clubs: Chester Le Street
Honours: None

Hayward, Adrian (M)

(SOMERSHAM TOWN) Age: 26
Previous Clubs: Hemingford; Earith; St.Ives Town; Alconbury
Honours: None

Hayzelden, Keith (D)

(DARTFORD)

D.O.B. 13.12.54   Nickname: Hazel or Humble
Profession: Agency Consultant
Married   Wife's name: Denise
Children: Danny & Leah
Hobbies: Golf, Badminton, All Sports

PLAYING CAREER

Honours: Newham Schoolboy Rep; London Schoolboy Rep; Alliance Premier Lge Winners,Isthmian Lge Premier Winners; FA Trophy Winners; Hitachi Cup Winners; Essex Senior Cup Winners; FA XI; Middx Wanderer; Enfield P.O.Y.

Club	Seasons	Transfer	Apps	Goals
Leytonstone	75-83			
Leytonstone & Ilford	1983			
Enfield	83-89			
Dartford	1989			
Redbridge Forest	89-90			
Enfield	1990			

Hazell, Dave (D)

(WELWYN GARDEN CITY)   Age: 23

Previous Clubs: None

Honours: Hertfordshire u18 National Cup winners

Head Richard (M)

(HARLOW TOWN)   Age: 30

Previous Clubs: Harlow Town; Dagenham; Leytonstone & Ilford; Basildon United

Honours:

Headen, Matthew (M)

(SELSEY)   Age: 18

Previous Clubs: Bracklesham

Honours: West Sussex League Champions Div 1; Malcolm Simmond Cup winners

Healy, Antony (F)

(GLOSSOP)   Age: 23

Previous Clubs: Haslingden Youth Club; Rochdale (Youth & Reserves); Mossley; Bacup Borough; Rossendale United

Honours: League & Cup with Rossendale Reserves 1989-90)

Healey, Brendan (F)

(61 FC)   Age: 23

Previous Clubs: None   **Honours:** None

Healey, Scott (G)

(RUNCORN)   D.O.B. 22.4.70

Profession: Not working

Single   **Hobbies:** Tennis, Watching TV

PLAYING CAREER

Honours: Manchester Premier Cup R/U 89/90

Club	Seasons	Transfer	Apps	Goals
York City	86-88			
Salford City	88-89			
Colne Dynamoes	89-90			
Mossley	90-91			

SCOTT HEALEY

Heaney, Clive (M)

(CLEATOR MOOR CELTIC)   Age: 29

Previous Clubs: Workington Reds; Carlisle United; Gretna; Penrith

Honours: None

Heasman, Frank (G)

(BECKENHAM TOWN)   Age: 24

Previous Clubs: None

Honours: None

Hedgecock, Andrew (F)

(HINCKLEY ATHLETIC)   Age: 27

Previous Clubs: Ventora; Thurlaston United; Hinckley Town; Earl Shilton Albion; Hinckley; Downes

Honours: None

Heesom, Darren (D)

(MACCLESFIELD TOWN)

D.O.B. 8.5.68   **Nickname:** Himie Patel

Profession: Warehouseman

Single

Hobbies: Pool

PLAYING CAREER

Honours: None

Club	Seasons	Transfer	Apps	Goals
Burnley	85-89		46	1
Altrincham	89-90			

Hembury, Chris (M)

(BRIDGWATER TOWN (1984))   Age: 31

Previous Clubs: Burnham United; Bridgwater Town; Burnham United

Honours: Somerset Senior Lge Champions & Cup winners; Somerset County; Somerse Senior Lge Rep

Hemsley, Stuart (D)

(SUTTON UNITED)

D.O.B. 18.11.64

Nickname: Spu (from unfortunate first training session!)

Profession: Data Security Assistant

Single

Hobbies: Water-skiing, Golf, Music, Driving, Socialising

PLAYING CAREER

Honours: Surrey Youth Rep; FA XI; Middx Wanderer; Surrey Senior Cup Winners (3) & R/U; Vauxhall-Opel Lge Rep; Sutton P.O.Y. 88/89

Club	Seasons	Transfer	Apps	Goals
Croydon	81-86	£3,000		

Henderson, Martin (D)

(SPALDING UNITED)   Age: 34

Previous Clubs: Rangers; Philadelphia Jury; Leicester; Chesterfield; Port Vale

Honours: Scottish League & Cup; 2nd Division Championship (Leicester)

Henderson, Paul (D)
(CHESTER-LE-STREET) Age: 23
Previous Clubs: Richmond; Bedale; Newton Aycliffe Boys Club; North Allerton Town; Harrogate Town; Harrogate Railway
Honours: North Yorkshire County Team

Hendrie, Paul (M)
(CHELMSLEY TOWN) Age: 34
Previous Clubs: Birmingham City; Tampa Bay; Halifax Town; Stockport County; Nuneaton Borough
Honours: None

Hendy, Dale (M)
(LANGNEY SPORTS) Age: 18
Previous Clubs: E/B United; Hailsham
Honours: None

Hendy, Mark (D)
(LANGLEY SPORTS) Age: 22
Previous Clubs: E/B Town; Hailsham
Honours: Sussex County League Div 2 Champion 1987-88; Sussex County League Challenge Cup winner 1989-90; Eastbourne CHarity Cup winner 1989-90

Heneghan Martin (F)
(RADCLIFFE BOROUGH) Age: 27
Previous Clubs: Northwich Victoria
Honours:

Henley, Nick (M)
(HALESOWEN HARRIERS) Age: 18
Previous Clubs: Oldswinford
Honours: None

Heryet, Andy (D)
(HORSHAM) Age: 23
Previous Clubs: Worthing; Steyning Town; Southwick
Honours: Sussex Senior Cup Winners 88/89

Hessenthaler, Andy (M)
(REDBRIDGE FOREST)

D.O.B. 17.8.65 **Nickname:** Busy
profession: Builder
Single
Hobbies: Golf, Squash, Running
PLAYING CAREER
Honours: Kent Schoolboy Rep; England Semi-pro Int; Westgate Insurance Cup Winners 87/88 & 88/89; Kent Senior Cup Winners; Dartford P.O.Y. 89/90

Club	Seasons	Transfer	Apps	Goals
Dartford	81-82			
Charlton Athletic	84-85			
Corinthian	85-87			
Dartford	87-90			

Hewitt, Martin (F)
(BILLINGHAM SYNTHONIA) Age: 25
Previous Clubs: Hartlepool United; Billingham Synthonia; North Perth Croatia (Australia); Seaham Red Star
Honours: Northern League Cup winners Trophy 1987-88; Northern League Championship Trophy 1989-90

Hewitt, Peter (D)
(BECKENHAM TOWN) Age: 33
Previous Clubs: Walton & Hersham; Bromley; Croydon; Dulwich Hamlet; Thames Polytechnic; Southwark Sports
Honours: None

Hewlett Gary (M)
(YATE TOWN) Age: 24
Previous Clubs: Clandown; Forest Green Rovers; Cheltenham Town
Honours: Gloucs County Rep; Hellenic Lge Rep; Hellenic Lge Winners (2); Gloucs Senior Trophy Winners

Heys, Mark (F)
(CLITHEROE) Age: 26
Previous Clubs: Preston North End; Accrington Stanley; Launceston Juventus; Great Harwood
Honours: PLayers of the Year Accrington Stanley 1986-87

Higgs, Mark (M)
(TUNBRIDGE WELLS) Age: 35
Previous Clubs: Croydon; Bromley; Carshalton; Whyteleafe; Bromley
Honours: None

KEITH HILL
(Gresley Rovers)

STEVE HANLON (MACCLESFIELD TOWN)

Higgins, Mark (D)

(DENABY UNITED)   Age: 27

Previous Clubs: Ecclesfield Red Rose; Worksop Town; Sheffield
Honours: None

Higgins, Tony (F)

(BRIDLINGTON TOWN)   Age: 24

Previous Clubs: Doncaster Rovers   **Honours:** None

Highmore, Kelvin (D)

(CHIPPENHAM TOWN)   Age: 30

Previous Clubs: Chippenham Town; Corsham Town; Avon Bradford
Honours: None

Hill, Graham (D/M)

(LEATHERHEAD)   Age: 28

Previous Clubs: Saltash United; Launceston Town; Royal Navy
Honours: South Western Lge Winners

Hill, Kevin (D)

(TUNBRIDGE WELLS)   Age: 18

Previous Clubs: None   **Honours:** None

Hill, Mark (D)

(SLOUGH TOWN)   D.O.B. 21.1.61
Profession: Spare Parts Manager
Married   **Hobbies:** Golf, Tennis, Music, Photography

PLAYING CAREER

Honours: Middx Schoolboy Rep; London Schoolboy Rep; South East Counties Lge & Cup Winners; Vauxhall-Opel Lge Premier Winners 82/83; GMVC Winners 88/89; Vauxhall Lge Premier Winners 89/90; Kent Senior Cup Winners 88/89; Bob Lord Trophy R/U 84/85; Hitachi Cup R/U 82/83 & 83/84.

Club	Seasons	Transfer	Apps	Goals
Queens Park Rangers	77-80			
Brentford	80-82		56	5
Wycombe Wanderers	82-84			
Maidstone United	84-89			

Hills, Andrew (G)

(CLITHEROE)   Age: 29

Previous Clubs: Bury; Radcliffe Borough; Clitheroe
Honours: N.W.C.L. 2nd Div winners 1982-83; N.W.C.L. 1st Div winners 1984-85; N.W.C.L. Cup Finalist 1984-85; N.W.C.L. Reserve Div winners 1986-87; PLayer of the year (all with Rad Borough)

Hills, Chris (M)

(CHIPSTEAD)   Age: 25

Previous Clubs: Walton & Hersham; Epsom & Ewell; Carshalton; Leatherhead; Hampton; Merton

Honours: Surry Cup; England International

Hilton, Jeff (D)

(SAWBRIDGEWORTH TOWN)   Age: 30

Previous Clubs: Great Parndon; Solent; Sawbridgeworth Town; Stansted; Harlow Town
Honours: F.A. Vase winner 1984-85; Essex Junior Cup 1979-80,1980-81; Floodlit Cup; Essex Senior League Cup; East Anglia Cup; Charity Shield Cup

Hilton, Mark (D)

(ASHTON UNITED)   D.O.B. 15.1.60
Nickname: Hilty   **Profession:** Electronics Assembler
Single   **Hobbies:** Snooker, Cricket, Squash

PLAYING CAREER

Honours: None

Club	Seasons	Transfer	Apps	Goals
Stoke City	75-76			
Oldham Athletic	76-81		50	2
Bury	81-87		32	3
Witton Albion	87-88			
Ashton United	88-89			
Mossley	89-91	Player-Manager		

Hinchley, Gary (M)

(GUISBOROUGH TOWN)   Age: 21

Previous Clubs: Middlesborough; Brentford; Darlington; Whitby; Stockton
Honours: None

Hinshelwood, Paul (D)

(WHYTELEAFE)   D.O.B. 14.8.56

Previous Clubs: Crystal Palace, Oxford Utd., Millwall, Colchester Utd., Southend Utd., Basildon Utd., Dartford, Chelmsford.
Honours: England U21 Int., FA Youth Cup Winners, Football Lge Div 2 Winner & Division 3 Winner.

Hirons, Paul (F)

(YEOVIL TOWN)   D.O.B. 6.3.71
Nickname: Snake   **Profession:** Not working
Single   **Hobbies:** Sport

PLAYING CAREER

Honours: None

Club	Seasons	Transfer	Apps	Goals
Bristol City	87-88			
Torquay United	88-90		15	2
Bath City	1990			

Hobbs, Micky (D)

(BECKENHAM TOWN)   Age: 21

Previous Clubs: Charlton Athletic   **Honours:** None

Hockenhull, Andrew (D)

(CONGLETON TOWN)   D.O.B. 2.12.69
Nickname: Hocky   **Profession:** Painter
Single   **Hobbies:** Sport

Previous Clubs: Sandbach Town (87-89)
Honours: Sandbach P.O.Y. (2)

Hockley, Steve (D)
(NEWMARKET TOWN)   Age: 37
Previous Clubs: Soham Town Rangers
Honours: Cambs County Colours

Hodgert, Carl (D)
(HYDE UNITED)

D.O.B. 10.3.65   Nickname: Hodgy
Profession: Design Engineer
Single
Hobbies: Watching Rugby League
PLAYING CAREER
Honours: Salford Schoolboy Rep; Greater Manchester Youth Rep; NWCL Div 3 Winners; HFS Loans Lge Premier Div R/U (2); HFS Loans Lge Cup Winners; Cheshire Senior Cup Winners; Clubcall Cup R/U (2)

Club	Seasons	Transfer	Apps	Goals
Salford City	80-85			
Atherton LR	85-86			
Altrincham	86-87			

Hodgson, Niel (M)
(GUISBOROUGH TOWN)   Age: 27
Previous Clubs: None
Northern League Cup winners 1988-89; Northern League 2nd Div R.U. 1985-86

Holden, Lee (M)
(WESTHOUGHTON TOWN)   Age: 24
Previous Clubs: None
Honours: None

Holden, William (D)
(GREAT HARWOOD TOWN)   Age: 38
Previous Clubs: NOrthwich Victoria; Freemantle Town (Australia); Rishton; Glossop; Great Harwood United
Honours: None

Holder, Colin (M)
(BANBURY)   Age: 46
Previous Clubs: Coventry City; Chelmsford City; Margate; Cheltenham; Gloucester; Kidderminster H
Honours: England Youth

Holdgate, Paul (D)
(SOMERSHAM TOWN)   Age: 20
Previous Clubs: Histon; Cambridge Utd; Saffron Walden
Honours: None

Holgate, Tony (D/M)
(BRIDLINGTON TRINITY)   Age: 23
Previous Clubs: Sheffield Wednesday; Doncaster Rovers; Armthorpe
Honours: None

Hole, Nigel (F)
(LANGNEY SPORTS)   Age: 26
Previous Clubs: Q.P.R. (Youth); Lewes; Little Common; Eastbourne Town
Honours: Sussex County League Challenge Cup winner 1989-90; Eastbourne Charity Cup winner 1989-90

Holland Steve (M)
(NORTHWICH VICTORIA)   Age: 20
Previous Clubs: Derby County; Bury; Husqvarna FF (Fin); Winsford United
Honours:

Hollis, Kenny (M)
(WOLVERTON AFC)   Age: 27
Previous Clubs: Wolverton Town; Milton Keynes Borough; Haringey Borough
Honours: None

Holmans, Keith (F)
(PEGASUS JUNIORS)   Age: 19
Previous Clubs: Hereford United
Honours: None

Holmes, Mark (M)
(TUNBRIDGE WELLS)   Age: 15
Previous Clubs: None
Honours: None

Holmes, Steven (D)
(GUISBOROUGH TOWN)   Age: 19
Previous Clubs: Lincoln City; Gainsborough Trinity
Honours: GMVC Shield winners

Holmshaw, Richard (M)
(DENABY UNITED)   Age: 18
Previous Clubs: Sheffield Wednesday
Honours: None

Holt, Richard (D)
(STRATFORD TOWN)   Age: 21
Previous Clubs: Strafford Town Res; Henley Forest; Stoke City (Youth)
Honours: Mld Comb Div 2 winners 1985-86; Challenge Cup winners 1988-89

Hone, Mark (D)
(WELLING UNITED)   D.O.B. 31.3.68
Nickname: Dennis   Profession: Sales Assistant
Married   Wife's name: Julia
Children: David & Daniel
PLAYING CAREER
Honours: Surrey Schoolboy Rep; England Semi-Pro Int; FA XI
Previous Clubs: Crystal Palace, (84-89), £5,000, 11 Apps.

Hook, Robbie　　　　　　(M)
(EXMOUTH TOWN)　　　　　　Age:
Previous Clubs: Torquay United
Honours: Western League Championship winner; Devon County

Hooman, Ricky　　　　　　(M)
(MORETON TOWN)　　　　　　Age: 25
Previous Clubs: Malvern Town; Gresley Rovers; Redditch Utd
Honours: Worcester Senior BRN winners; W.Mids Banks League runners up

Hooton, Russell　　　　　　(D)
(HYDE UNITED)

D.O.B. 13.3.58　　　　**Nickname:** Hoots
Profession: Postal Assistant
Single
Hobbies: Swimming, Tennis, Running
PLAYING CAREER
Honours: Altrincham & Sale Schoolboy Rep; Manchester Schoolboy Rep; Manchester County FA XI Rep; HFS Loans Lge Premier Div R/U 87/88 & 88/89; HFS Loans Lge Cup Winners 89/90; Cheshire Senior Cup Winners 89/90; Clubcall Cup R/U 88/89 & 89/90; Hyde P.O.Y.88/89

Club	Seasons	Transfer	Apps	Goals
South Liverpool	82-85			
Witton Albion	84-86	£750		
Northwich Victoria	86-87			
Oswestry Town	87-88			

Hope, Alan　　　　　　(M)
(MEIR K A)　　　　　　Age: 24
Previous Clubs: Trader Jacks
Honours: Walsall Senior Cup winners 1989-90; Burslem & Turnstall; League & Cup 1989-90

Horn, Andrew　　　　　　(G)
(CLEATOR MOOR CELTIC)　　　　　　Age: 24
Previous Clubs: Workington; Penrith; Carlisle City
Honours: None

Horn, Michael　　　　　　(M)
(SEATON DELAVAL AMATEURS)　　　　　　Age: 24
Previous Clubs: Whitley Bay; Seaton Terrace; Morpeth Town; Shankhouse
Honours: Northunmberland Senior Cup runners up

Horne, Adrian　　　　　　(M)
(BANBURY UNITED)　　　　　　Age: 22
Previous Clubs: Lichfield　　　　**Honours:** None

Horne Darren　　　　　　(M)
(RHYL)　　　　　　Age: 24
Previous Clubs: Holywell Town; Flint Town United
Honours: Welsh Alliance Winners; North-Wales Challenge Cup Winners; Cookson Cup Winners

Horne John　　　　　　(D)
(STOURBRIDGE)　　　　　　Age: 28
Previous Clubs: Walsall; Kidderminster Harriers; Oldbury United; Ashtree Highfield
Honours: Birmingham Senior Cup Winners; Worcs Senior Cup Winners

Horrocks, Robert　　　　　　(M)
(FARLEIGH ROVERS)　　　　　　Age: 25
Previous Clubs: Whyteleafe
Honours: None

Horscroft Grant　　　　　　(D)
(LEWES)　　　　　　Age: 29
Previous Clubs: Ringmer; Lewes; Brighton & Hove Albion (2)
Honours: Sussex County Rep

Horscroft Mark　　　　　　(D:M)
(LEWES)　　　　　　Age: 30
Previous Clubs: Ringmer
Honours: Sussex County Rep

Horton, Duncan　　　　　　(D)
(WELLING UNITED)

D.O.B. 18.2.67　　　　**Nickname:** Toto
Profession: Builders Labourer
Married　　　　**Wife's name:** Debbie
Hobbies: All Sports
PLAYING CAREER
Honours: Kent Schoolboy Rep; FA XI; London Senior Cup Winners 88/89; Welling P.O.Y. 88/89

Club	Seasons	Transfer	Apps	Goals
Charlton Athletic	82-85		3	
Maidstone United	85-87			

Horton, Jamie　　　　　　(M)
(FARNBOROUGH TOWN)　　　　　　D.O.B. 20.4.62
Previous Clubs: Ash United; Godalming Town.
Honours: F.A. XI; Vauxhall-Opel Lge R/U 88/89.

Horwat, Pete　　　　　　(F)
(CALNE)　　　　　　Age: 25
Previous Clubs: Park; Supermarine; Calne; Forest Green
Honours: County Cap; County League winners

Houghton, Peter　　　　　　(F)
(GENERAL CHEMICALS)　　　　　　Age: 26
Previous Clubs: Mond Rangers; Runcorn Reserves; FC Coachman
Honours: West Cheshire League R/U 1987-88; Player of the Year (Gen Chem) 1988-89; Cheshire Amateur Cup Winners 1988-89 Pyke Cup: Winners 1986-87 R/U 1988-89; Runcorn F.A. Cup Winners 1983-1990

Houghton, Phil (D)

(BANBURY UNITED) **Age:** 32

Previous Clubs: Brackley Town; Banbury United; Buckingham Town

Honours: Oxon Senior Cup winners; Northants Senior Cup runners up

Houghton, Scott (M)

(SUTTON COLDFIELD TOWN) **Age:** 19

Previous Clubs: Kidderminster Harriers

Honours: None

Howard, Andy (F)

(BILLERICAY TOWN) **Age:** 25

Previous Clubs: Basildon United

Honours: None

Howard, Chris (D)

(WOLVERTON AFC) **Age:** 21

Previous Clubs: None

Honours: None

Howard, Lee (M)

(EASTWOOD TOWN) **Age:** 23

Previous Clubs: Mansfield Town(1); Harworth Colliery; King's Lynn

Honours: Central Midland Lge & Cup Winners 87/88

Howard, Matthew (D)

(ST ALBANS CITY)

D.O.B. 5.12.70
Profession: Not working
Single
Hobbies: Sport

PLAYING CAREER

Honours: Herts Schoolboy Rep

Club	Seasons	Transfer	Apps	Goals
Boreham Wood	80-86			
Brentford	86-89		1	

Howard, Paul (M)

(GENERAL CHEMICALS) **Age:** 24

Previous Clubs: Frodsham United; Kydds FC; FC Coachman; Helsby B.I.C.C.; Greenbank; Robin Hood

Honours: Cheshire u19's

Howarth, Frank (M)

(EXMOUTH TOWN) **Age:**

Previous Clubs: Exeter City; Torrington

Honours: Devon County

Howat, Ian (F)

(NEWTON) **Age:** 29

Previous Clubs: Chester City; Crewe Alexandra; Bangor City; Oswestry Town; Caernarfon Town

Honours: F.A. Trophy finalists with Bangor City

Howells, David (D)

(BARNET) **D.O.B.** 10.10.58

Previous Clubs: Fulham; Hillingdon Borough; Hounslow; Harrow Borough; Enfield (£12,000)

Honours: England Semi Pro Int.; F.A. Trophy Winners 1988; Gola Lge Winners 85/86; Middlesex Senior Cup Winners.

DUNCAN HORTON
(Welling United)

DAVE HOWELL
(Barnet)

Howell, Peter (M)

(KIDDERMINSTER HARRIERS)

D.O.B. 5.6.67
Profession: Professional Footballer
Single
Hobbies: Sport

PLAYING CAREER

Honours: None

Club	Seasons	Transfer	Apps	Goals
Aston Villa	83-87			

Howells, Syhon (D)

(CWMBRAN TOWN) **Age:** 23

Previous Clubs: None

Honours: Gwent Schools

Howey, Peter (M)

(FRICKLEY ATHLETIC) D.O.B. 23.1.58

PLAYING CAREER

Honours: Sheffield Senior Cup Winners 89/90; Gola Lge R/U 85/86

Club	Seasons	Transfer	Apps	Goals
Huddersfield Town	76-78		22	3
Leeds United	78-79			
Newport County	79-80			
Frickley Athletic	80-84			
Scarborough	84-85			

Hoyte, Roger (M)

(CHIPSTEAD) Age: 28

Previous Clubs: Croydon; Corinthian Casuals; Whyteleafe; Farleigh Rovers

Honours: Berger Youth Cup winners 1979-80

Hubbick, David (F)

(CORNARD UNITED) Age: 30

Previous Clubs: Ipswich Town; Wimbledon (26-6); Dagenham; Colchester United (15-1); Sudbury Town; Braintree Town

Honours: FA Vase R/U; Suffolk Senior Cup Winners; East Anglian Cup Winners

Hudson, Alan (F)

(RADCLIFFE BOROUGH) Age: 25

Previous Clubs: None Honours: None

Hudson, Gary (D)

(CLACTON TOWN) Age: 21

Previous Clubs: None Honours: None

Hughes, Alan (F)

(FLEETWOOD TOWN) D.O.B. 1.11.69

Nickname: Besty Profession: Not working
Single Hobbies: Snooker, Watching TV

PLAYING CAREER

Honours: Lancs Youth Cup Winners 85/86

Club	Seasons	Transfer	Apps	Goals
Watford	82-85			
Blackpool	85-90			

Hughes, Bernie (F)

(ACCRINGTON STANLEY) Age: 27

Previous Clubs: Glossop; Stalybridge Celtic; Droylsden

Honours: HFS Loans Lge First Div R/U 89/90

Hughes, Brian (M)

(GLOUCESTER CITY) D.O.B. 20.8.62

Profession: Glazier
Married Wife's name: Alison
Children: Katie, Kirsty & Victoria
Hobbies: Sport

PLAYING CAREER

Honours: Southern Lge Premier Div Winners 84/85; Southern Lge Midland Div Winners 88/89

Club	Seasons	Transfer	Apps	Goals
Swindon Town	80-83		80	5
Torquay United	83-84		39	6
Cheltenham Town	84-88			

Hughes, Colin (M)

(CALNE TOWN) Age: 27

Previous Clubs: Vickers; Fairford Town; Wantage Town; Highworth

Honours: None

Hughes, Gareth (M)

(MELTON TOWN) Age: 18

Previous Clubs: Pedigree Petfoods

Honours: None

Hughes, Gareth (D)

(BASHLEY) Age: 22

Previous Clubs: Newton; South Glamorgan; Newton.

Honours: Central Wales Youth XI; Welsh Colleges XI; British Colleges XI in World Student Games

Hughes, Mark (F)

(ALTRINCHAM)

D.O.B. 30.6.69 Nickname: Yosser
Profession: Not working
Single
Hobbies: Swimming, Football

PLAYING CAREER

Honours: Cheshire Schoolboy Rep

Club	Seasons	Transfer	Apps	Goals
Everton	87-88			
Irlam Town	89-90			

Hughton, Henry (D/M)

(BARKING)

D.O.B. 18.11.59 Nickname: "H"
Profession: Sports & Leisure
Single
Hobbies: DIY, Reading, Driving

PLAYING CAREER

Honours: Republic of Ireland Under-21 Int

Club	Seasons	Transfer	Apps	Goals
Leyton Orient	76-82		135	3
Crystal Palace	82-86		141	1
Brentford	86-87		10	
Leyton Orient	87-88		18	
Trollhatten (Swe)	1988			
Enfield	89-90			

Hugman, Kevin (D)
(SEATON DELAVAL AMATEURS) Age: 22
Previous Clubs: New Hartley Juniors; Blyth Spartans
Honours: Northumberland Senior Benevolent Bowl winners; McEwans Northern Alliance Premier Division championship

Hull, Colin (D)
(BALDOCK TOWN) Age: 26
Previous Clubs: Watford; Bishop's Stortford
Honours: Herts County Schoolboy; Youth & FA Rep

COLIN HULL

Hulse, Bobby (D)
(GATESHEAD) D.O.B. 5.1.57
Profession: Company Director Married
Wife's name: Maxine Children: Natalie & Bobbie James
PLAYING CAREER
Honours: None

Club	Seasons	Transfer	Apps	Goals
Middlesbrough	70-73			
Gateshead	73-82			
Stade Quimperoise	82-83	(Fra)		
Darlington	83-84		4	
Newcastle Blue Star	84-86			
Barrow	86-89			

Humberstone, Tony (M)
(CHIPSTEAD) Age: 20
Previous Clubs: Croydon; Whyteleafe; Crystal Palace (Schoolboy)
Honours: S.E.England; Croydon, Surry & London schools

Hume, Dave (M)
(BUCKINGHAM TOWN) Age: 22
Previous Clubs: Aylesbury United; Chesham United
Honours:

Humes, John (G)
(OLDSWINFORD) Age: 31
Previous Clubs: West Ham; Dartford; Bromsgrove Rovers
Honours: None

Humphrey, Delwyn (F)
(KIDDERMINSTER HARRIERS) Age: 25
Previous Clubs: Newtown; Bridgnorth Town.
Honours: Shropshire Senior Cup winners

Humphrey, John (F)
(LEATHERHEAD) Age: 21
Previous Clubs: None
Honours: None

Humphrey, Mark (M)
(EYNESBURY ROVERS) Age: 25
Previous Clubs: Eynesbury Rovers; St.Neots Town; Potton United
Honours: UCL Premier (2); Hinchingbrooke Cup (2); North Beds Charity Cup (2); Beds Senior Cup; Hunts Premier Cup; UCL Benevolent Cup; Huntingdonshire Junior & Senior caps

Humphries, Steve (G)
(TELFORD UNITED)

D.O.B. 29.5.61
PLAYING CAREER
Honours: England Semi-pro Int; Clubcall Cup Winners 88/89; Herts Senior Cup Winners; GMVC R/U 87/88

Club	Seasons	Transfer	Apps	Goals
Leicester City	78-81			
Doncaster Rovers	81-82		13	
Cardiff City	1982		1	
Wrexham	1982		2	
Oldham Athletic	82-83			
Leicester City	83-84			
Kettering Town	84-86			
Barnet	86-90	£4,000		

Hunt, Alan (M)
(SUTTON COLDFIELD TOWN) Age: 21
Previous Clubs: Youth Team
Honours:

Hunt, Andrew (D)
(WESTBURY) Age: 20
Previous Clubs: Melksham Town; Trowbridge Town
Honours: None

Hunt, John (F)

(SUTTON COLDFIELD TOWN) Age: 24

Previous Clubs: Paget Rangers
Honours: Sutton P.O.Y. 89/90

Hunt, Richard (D)

(HAYES) D.O.B. 5.1.71
Professsion: Not working
Single
Hobbies: Squash

PLAYING CAREER

Honours: None

Club	Seasons	Transfer	Apps	Goals
Queens Park Rangers	87-89			
Aldershot	89-90		7	

Hunter, Les (D)

(MATLOCK TOWN) D.O.B. 15.1.58

PLAYING CAREER

Honours: Football League Div 4 Winners 84/85

Club	Seasons	Transfer	Apps	Goals
Chesterfield	75-81		165	8
Scunthorpe United	81-83		61	8
Chesterfield	83-85		99	9
Scunthorpe United	85-87		49	5
Lincoln City	1987			
Chesterfield	87-88		25	3

Hurd, Kevin (G)

(BRIDGWATER TOWN 1984) Age: 22

Previous Clubs: None

Honours: Somerset Senior Lge champions & cup winners; Somerset Senior Cup finalists

Hurdwell, Mick (M)

(THATCHAM TOWN) Age: 25

Previous Clubs: Wokingham Town; Brackwell Town; Woking; Thatcham; Salisbury City

Honours: None

Hurford, Alan (D)

(BRIDGWATER TOWN 1984) Age: 42

Previous Clubs: Bridgwater Town; Taunton Town; Frome Town

Honours: FA XI, Rothmans National; Somerset County; South West Counties Rep; Western Lge Rep; Western Lge Champions & Cup winners; Somerset Senior Lge champions & Cup winners (2); South West County Champions; Somerset Premier Cup & Senior Cup finalists

Hurren, Keith (D)

(OAKWOOD) Age: 31

Previous Clubs: Gossop Green; Horsham Y.M.C.A.; Lingfield; Three Bridges

Honours: Sussex County 1st Div runners up (2); RUR Cup winners

Hutchinson, Mark (M)

(SUTTON COLDFIELD TOWN) Age: 2

Previous Clubs: Aston Villa; Leicester City (Carlisle United (L)) Northampton Town(2); Nuneaton Borough; Willenhall Town
Honours: England Schoolboy Int; FA Youth Cup Winners

Hutchinson, Peter (D)

(GREAT HARWOOD TOWN) Age: 3

Previous Clubs: Great Harwood Town; Clitheroe; Accrington Stanley; Great Harwood United

Honours: Lancs Combination 1979; Lancs Junior Cup 1980 George Watson Cup 1981; Bass N.W.C.L winners 3rd Div 1982-83, 2nd Div 1983-84, 1st Div 1984-85

Hutchinson, Robert (F)

(WEMBLEY) Age: 2

Previous Clubs: Tottenham Hotspur; Wembley; Harrow Borough; Kingsbury Town; Egham Town
Honours:

Hutchinson, Simon (F)
(WYCOMBE WANDERERS)

D.O.B. 24.9.69

PLAYING CAREER

Honours: England Schoolboy Int; FA School of Excellence

Club	Seasons	Transfer	Apps	Goals
Manchester United	85-88			
Eastwood Town	88-90	£7,000		

RICHARD HUXFORD (Kettering Town)

SIMON HUTCHINSON (Wycombe Wanderers)

PETER HUTTER (Aylesbury United)

Hutchinson, Tobi (F)

(LANGLEY SPORTS) **Age:** 19

Previous Clubs: Eastbourne Town

Honours: Sussex County League Challenge Cup winner 1989-90; Brighton Evening Argus County 5-a-side Champions 1989-90; Eastbourne Charity Cup winners 1989-90

Hutter, Peter (D)

(AYLESBURY UNITED) **D.O.B.** 14.10.62

Previous Clubs: Witney Town.

Honours: Vauxhall League Winners 87/88; Berks & Bucks Senior Cup Winners 85/86; FA XI.

Huxford, Richard (M)

(KETTERING TOWN)

D.O.B. 25.7.69 **Nickname:** Hodgy
Profession: Financial Adviser
Single
Hobbies: All Sports

PLAYING CAREER

Honours: None

Club	Seasons	Transfer	Apps	Goals
Scunthorpe United	85-87			
Matlock Town	87-88			
Burton Albion	88-89			
Gainsborough Trinity	89-90			

Hyde, Paul (G)

(HAYES)

D.O.B. 7.4.63 **Nickname:** Hydie
Professiuon: Management Of Colour Technician
Married **Wife's name:** Sue
Children: James & Christopher

PLAYING CAREER

Honours: Middx County Schoolboy Rep; Vauxhall Lge Rep; AC Delco Cup R/U; Middx Senior Cup R/U.

Club	Seasons	Transfer	Apps	Goals
Hillingdon Borough	81-84			

Hynds, Ian (F)

(EXMOUTH TOWN) **Age:** 25

Previous Clubs: None

Honours: None

Hynds, Steve (M)

(EXMOUTH TOWN) **Age:**

Previous Clubs: Heavitree United

Honours: Western League Championship; Devon County

Hyner, David (D)

(CHIPSTEAD) **Age:** 24

Previous Clubs: Croydon; Leatherhead; Whyteleafe

Honours: Dan Air League winners 1989-90

JAMIE HORTON
(FARNBOROUGH TOWN)

Ibbs, Damon (G)
(TUNBRIDGE WELLS) Age: 17
Previous Clubs: None
Honours: None

Iddles, Danny (F)
(YATE TOWN) Age: 25
Previous Clubs: Sharpness; Yate Town; Forest Green Rovers
Honours: None

Illey, Steve (F)
(WESTHOUGHTON TOWN) Age: 25
Previous Clubs: Tempest United
Honours: None

Ingham, Gary (G)
(BRIDLINGTON TOWN) Age: 25
Previous Clubs: Rotherham United; Gainsborough Trinity; Heanor Town; Frecheville Community; Shepshed Charterhouse; Goole Town
Honours: None

Inglis, Kenny (M)
(MELTON TOWN) Age: 29
Previous Clubs: Stamford; Bourne
Honours: None

DAVE INGRAM (Kintbury Rangers)

Ingram, Dave (M)
(KINTBURY RANGERS) Age: 35
Previous Clubs: Lambourn Sports; Hungerford Town; Newbury Town; Wokingham Town; Swindon Town; Hungerford Town
Honours: FA Rep XI, Rothmans Rep XI

Inker, Mark (M)
(HORSHAM) Age: 26
Previous Clubs: Horley Town
Honours: None

Inns, David (M)
(NEWTON) Age: 24
Previous Clubs: Newton; Caersws
Honours: None

Irani, Graham (M)
(FARLEIGH ROVERS) Age: 27
Previous Clubs: Malden Town
Honours: None

Irving, James (D)
(CLEATOR MOOR CELTIC) Age: 31
Previous Clubs: Workington
Honours: None

KEITH IRVINE (Dorking F.C.)

ANTONE JOSEPH
(KIDDERMINSTER HARRIERS)

TERRY ROBINS
(WELLING UNITED)

Jack, Raymond (F)
(MARLOW)

D.O.B. 27.7.66
Profession: Artexer
Single
Hobbies: Swimming, Pool, Music, Chess
PLAYING CAREER
Honours: English Schools FA Winners

Club	Seasons	Transfer	Apps	Goals
Flackwell Heath	86-87			
Maidenhead United	87-88			
Southall	88-89			

Jackson, Dave (D)
(EYNSEBURY ROVERS) Age: 26

Previous Clubs: St.Neots Town; Eynesbury Rovers; Potton United

Honours: Hinchingbrooke Cup (2); Hunts Premier Cup; North Beds Charity Cup; Scott Gatty Cup; Huntingdonshire Caps

Jackson, Kevin (M)
(HEANOR TOWN) Age: 31

Previous Clubs: Ilkeston Town; Eastwood Town; Alfreton Town; Belper Town; Heanor Town; Belper Town

Honours: North East Counties League champions with Belper 1984-85 & Alfreton Town 1986-87

Jackson, Steve (D)
(KNOWSLEY UNITED) Age: 28

Previous Clubs: Ellesmere Port; Prescot; Southport; Buxton; South Liverpool; Southport

Honours: None

Jackson, Tony (M)
(DROYLSDEN)

D.O.B. 3.5.71 **Nickname:** Jacko
Profession: Not working
Single
Hobbies: Snooker, Golf
PLAYING CAREER
Honours: None

Club	Seasons	Transfer	Apps	Goals
Manchester United	86-89			
Mossley	89-91			

Jacques, David (D)
(REDBRIDGE FOREST)

D.O.B. 7.10.58

PLAYING CAREER
Honours: FA XI; Southern Lge Premier Winners 83/84; GMVC Winners 88/89

Club	Seasons	Transfer	Apps	Goals
Leytonstone & Ilford	77-83			
Dartford	83-87			
Enfield	87-88	£1,000		
Maidstone United	88-89			

Jacques, Kevin (M)
(GENERAL CHEMICALS) Age: 25

Previous Clubs: Palacefields u17; Halton Sports; Vauxhall GM; Runcorn; FC Coachman

Honours: Cheshire Sat Cup; Pyke Cup; Mid Cheshire Premier (3)

James, John (F)
(GAINSBOROUGH TOWN) Age: 21

Previous Clubs: Harworth Colliery

Honours: None

James, John (F)
(OLDSWINFORD FSC) Age: 22

Previous Clubs: Newton Albion; Wolves (YTS); Tamworth

Honours: None

RICKY JEWELL (BRIANTREE)

James, Paul (F)
(NEWCASTLE TOWN) Age: 22

Previous Clubs: Eastwood Hanley; Kidsgrove Athletic; Leek Town

Honours: None

Jardine, Gary (F)
(SEATON DELAVAL AMATEURS) Age: 26

Previous Clubs: New Hartley Juniors; Annitsford Welfare

Honours: Northumberland Senior Benevolent Bowl winners; McEwans Northern Alliance Premier Division championship

Jarvis, David (F)
(NEWPORT AFC) Age: 25

Previous Clubs: Newport County; Caerleon; Mangotsfield; Brecon

Honours: Hellenic League Champions

Jarvis, Paul (M)
(BANBURY UNITED) **Age:** 27
Previous Clubs: Brackley Town
Honours: None

Jarvis, Robert (M)
(BRIDGNORTH TOWN) **Age:** 18
Previous Clubs: Shrewsbury Town
Honours: None

Jarvis, Tony (F)
(WITTON ALBION)

D.O.B. 19.3.64 **Nickname:** Jarvo
Profession: Postman
Single
Hobbies: Badminton, Snooker, Swimming

PLAYING CAREER
Honours: Bury Schoolboy Rep

Club	Seasons	Transfer	Apps	Goals
Irlam Town	83-85	£1,000		
Oldham Athletic	85-86	£1,000		
Crewe Alexandra	86-88		20	5
Colne Dynamoes	1988			

PAUL JANAWAY (WEMBLEY)

Jay, Danny (F)
(TIPTREE UNITED) **D.O.B:** 6.10.64

Previous Clubs: Hatfield Peverel; Heybridge Swifts; Tiptree United; Brantham Athletic; Clacton Town; Braintree Town
Honours: Essex & Suffolk Border Lge Rep; Essex & Suffolk Border Lge & Cup Winners; Eastern Floodlight Cup Winners

Jefferies, Michael (M)
(CHIPPENHAM TOWN) **Age:** 25
Previous Clubs:
Honours: None

Jeffrey, Billy (M)
(RUSHDEN TOWN)

D.O.B. 25.10.56 **Nickname:** Dizzy
Profession: Wholesale Manager
Married **Wife's name:** Anne
Children: Lauren
Hobbies: Golf

PLAYING CAREER
Honours: Scottish Youth Int; Oxford P.O.Y. 75/76; Kettering P.O.Y. 85/86; Rushden P.O.Y. 88/89

Club	Seasons	Transfer	Apps	Goals
Oxford United	73-81		314	24
Blackpool	82-83		14	1
Northampton Town	83-85		54	6
Kettering Town	85-87			
Blacktown City (Aust.)	1987			
Rushden Town	87-88			
Irthlingborough D's	88-89 (Player-Manager)			

Jeffreys, Paul (M)
(VALE RECREATION) **Age:** 18
Previous Clubs: Guernsey Rovers (Youth); Northerners (Youth)
Honours: Guernsey Youth Caps 1988-89 & 1989-90

Jemison, Graham (M)
(PICKERING TOWN) **Age:** 23
Previous Clubs: Pickering Town; Scarborough
Honours: None

Jenkins, Darren (G)
(ST.DOMINICS) **Age:** 28
Previous Clubs:
Honours: None

Jenkins, Gary (F)
(HAYES)

D.O.B. 5.1.63
Profession: Plasterer
Married **Wife's name:** Dee
Children: Luke & Jake
Hobbies: Sport

PLAYING CAREER
Honours: Surrey Senior Cup Winners 88/89

Club	Seasons	Transfer	Apps	Goals
Feltham	84-87			
Hounslow	1987			
Hampton	1988			
Walton & Hersham	89-90			

Jenkins, Mark   (M)
(BILLERICAY TOWN)   Age: 26
Previous Clubs: Basildon United; Southend Manor
Honours: None

Jenkins, Mel   (D)
(FARLEIGH ROVERS)   Age: 32
Previous Clubs:
Honours: None

Jenkinson, Kevin   (G)
(MEIR K.A.)   Age: 25
Previous Clubs: Meir K.A.; Miners (Sanford Hill)
Honours: None

Jenkinson, Terry   (D)
(PICKERING TOWN)   Age: 29
Previous Clubs: Tennyson; West Piper
Honours: None

Jepson, Andrew   (D)
(DULWICH HAMLET)   Age: 25
Previous Clubs: Shrewsbury Town; Oldbury United; Malden Vale
Honours: None

Jerome, Benjamin   (M)
(HINCKLEY ATHLETIC)   Age: 26
Previous Clubs: Leicester Y.M.C.A.; Hillcroft
Honours: None

Jobson, Christopher   (M)
(SHOTTON COMRADES)   Age: 27
Previous Clubs: Stockton; Durham City
Honours: None

Johnson, Billy   (D)
(WARMINSTER TOWN)   Age: 27
Previous Clubs: Warminster Town; Calne Town
Honours: None

Johnson, Brian   (M)
(MELTON TOWN)   Age: 27
Previous Clubs: Eastwood; Arnold
Honours: None

Johnson, Craig   (D)
(WITHAM TOWN)   Age: 27
Previous Clubs: Grays Athletic; Hornchurch; Aveley; Tilbury
Honours: Essex County Rep; Vauxhall-Opel Lge Div 2 South Winners 84/85; Essex Thameside Trophy R/U 84/85; East Anglian Cup Winners 88/89

Johnson, Gary   (D)
(RACING CLUB WARWICK)   Age: 24
Previous Clubs: Nuneaton Borough
Honours: None

Johnson, Ian   (M)
(DROYLSDEN)   Age: 29
Previous Clubs: Chadderton; Curzon Ashton; Rochdale(81-1); Altrincham
Honours: None

Johnson, Ian   (D)
(WEYMOUTH)

D.O.B. 14.2.69   **Nickname:** Johnno
Profession: Not working
Single
Hobbies: All Sports

PLAYING CAREER
Honours: None

Club	Seasons	Transfer	Apps	Goals
Whitley Bay	86-87			
Gateshead	1987			
Northampton Town	87-88		7	

Johnson, Kevin   (F)
(HINCKLEY)   Age: 34
Previous Clubs: Racing Club Warwick; Meadway Rovers; Hinckley Athletic
Honours: West Mldlands Premier League Runners up 1982-83; Leics Senior Cup winners 1982-83 runners up 1983-84; Leading Goalscorer 1986-87 (Hinckley); Player of the Year 1989-90 (Hinckley); Memorial Trophy 1986

PAUL JOHNSON (MACCLESFIELD TOWN)

Johnson, Mark (G)

(SEATON DELAVAL AMATEURS) Age: 24

Previous Clubs: New Hartley Juniors

Honours: Northumberland Senior Benevolent Bowl winners; McEwans Northern Alliance Premier Division championship

Johnson, Martin (D)

(RADFORD) Age: 26

Previous Clubs: British Gypsum (Newark); Winthorpe Wanderers; Newark Squires; Coddington

Honours: Newark Alliance Premier Div winners 1988-89; Div 2 winners 1984-85; Div 3 winners 1983-84

Johnson, Martin (D)

(CHELMSFORD CITY)

D.O.B. 12.4.63
Profession: Building Contractor
Married   **Wife's name:** Sue
Children: Sam
Hobbies: Sport

PLAYING CAREER

Honours: Erith P.O.Y. 85/86

Club	Seasons	Transfer	Apps	Goals
Welling United	83-84			
Erith & Belvedere	84-86			
Dulwich Hamlet	86-87			
Bromley	87-88			
Dulwich Hamlet	88-89			

Johnson, Paul (D)

(MACCLESFIELD TOWN)

D.O.B. 25.5.59   **Nickname:** Johno
Profession: Not working
Single
Hobbies: Golf, Cycling, Driving

PLAYING CAREER

Honours: None

Club	Seasons	Transfer	Apps	Goals
Stoke City	77-81	£20,000	35	
Shrewsbury Town	81-87		200	7
York City	87-89		83	3

Johnson, Paul (M)

(CHESTER-LE-STREET) Age: 22

Previous Clubs: Southampton; Gateshead; Durham City

Honours: None

Johnson, Steve (F)

(NORTHWICH VICTORIA)

D.O.B. 23.6.57
Profession: French Polisher
Married   **Wife's name:** Angela
Children: Jamie-Leigh
Hobbies: Snooker, Fishing

PLAYING CAREER

Honours: None

Club	Seasons	Transfer	Apps	Goals
Altrincham	75-77			
Bury	77-83		154	52
Rochdale	83-84	£15,000	19	7
Wigan Athletic	84-85	£40,000	51	18
Bristol City	85-86	£40,000	21	3
		(Rochdale - loan - 6-1; Chester City - loan - 10-6)		
Scunthorpe United	87-89		80	25
Chester City	89-90		38	10
Rochdale	1990		24	4

Johnstone, Paul (D)

(CLEATOR MOOR CELTIC) Age: 29

Previous Clubs: Workington; Gretna; Penrith

Honours: None

Joinson, Ian (M)

(BOOTLE) Age: 26

Previous Clubs: Hornhouse; A.C. Delco; Bootle; Melling Victoria

Honours: None

Jones, Brian (F)

(NEWTOWN) Age: 26

Previous Clubs: Abervale; Newtown; Carno

Honours: Member of NFC; Central Welsh League Championship 1987-88

Jones, Bryn.A. (D)

(COLWYN BAY) Age: 36

Previous Clubs: Denbigh Town

Honours: Portmadoc; Winsford United; Oswestry Town; Colwyn Bay; Rhyl
Welsh Semi-Pro Int; Bass NWCL Cup Winners

Jones, Colin (M)

(NEWTOWN) Age: 20

Previous Clubs: Berview; Loughborough College

Honours: Welsh Schools u16 International; Central Welsh Youth XI

Jones, David (D)

(PEGASUS JUNIORS) Age: 37

Previous Clubs: Telford United; Hereford United; Kidderminster H; Ledbury Town

Honours: None

Jones, Dean (M)

(CLITHEROE) Age: 28

Previous Clubs: Bury; Horwich R.M.I.

Honours: None

GARY JONES

Jones, Gary (F)

(KETTERING TOWN)

D.O.B. 6.4.69
Profession: Not working
Single
Hobbies: Snooker, Tennis

PLAYING CAREER

Honours: None

Club	Seasons	Transfer	Apps	Goals
Huddersfield Town	86-87			
Rossington Main	87-88			
Doncaster Rovers	88-89		20	2
Grantham Town	89-90	£17,500		

GEOFF JONES

Jones, Geoff (M)

(MOSSLEY)

D.O.B. 16.3.68   **Nickname:** Jonesy
Profession: Plumber
Married   **Wife's name:** Kirsty
Hobbies: DIY

PLAYING CAREER

Honours: None

Club	Seasons	Transfer	Apps	Goals
Chamber Colliery	87-90			

Jones, Ian (D)

(NEWTOWN)   **Age:** 26

Previous Clubs: G.K.N. Sports; Montgomery
Honours: Barritt Cup winners; Player of the Year 1989-90;
Central Welsh Championship 1987-88

Jones, Jason (M)

(ST.DOMINICS)   **Age:** 20

Previous Clubs: None   **Honours:** None

Jones, Lenny (F)

(EXMOUTH TOWN)   **Age:**

Previous Clubs: Exmouth Town; Dawlish Town; Bideford; Clyst
Rovers

Honours: Western League Championship winner

Jones, Mark (D)

(NORTHWICH VICTORIA)

D.O.B. 16.9.60

PLAYING CAREER

Honours: Mid-Cheshire Senior Cup Winners (2); Staffs Senior
Cup Winners

Club	Seasons	Transfer	Apps	Goals
Runcorn	80-83			
Preston North End	83-85		76	3
Southport	85-87			

Jones, Matthew (F)

(CHELMSFORD CITY)

D.O.B. 10.9.70
Profession: Not working
Single
Hobbies: Sport

PLAYING CAREER

Honours: England Schoolboy Int,Middx Schoolboy Rep

Club	Seasons	Transfer	Apps	Goals
Southend United	87-90		5	

Jones, Neil (D)

(SOMERSHAM TOWN)   **Age:** 26

Previous Clubs: St.Ives Town   **Honours:** None

Jones, Nigel (M)

(LANGLEY SPORTS)   **Age:** 21

Previous Clubs: Eastbourne United; Langley Sports; Eastbourne
Town

Honours: Sussex County League Challenge Cup winner 1989-
90; Eastbourne Charity Cup winners 1989-90

Jones, Paul (F)

(ROMSEY TOWN)   **Age:** 19

Previous Clubs: Romsey; Basingstoke   **Honours:** None

Jones, Paul (G)

(KIDDERMINSTER HARRIERS)

D.O.B. 18.4.67   **Nickname:** Jonah
Profession: Flour Mill Manager
Married   **Wife's name:** Louise
Children: Donna & Steven
Hobbies: Squash, DIY

PLAYING CAREER

Honours: Shropshire Youth Rep; FA XI; Kidderminster P.O.Y. 89/90

Club	Seasons	Transfer	Apps	Goals
Shrewsbury Town	83-84			
Bridgnorth Town	84-86			

Jones, Robert (F)

(BURTON ALBION)

D.O.B. 17.11.64

PLAYING CAREER

Honours: None

Club	Seasons	Transfer	Apps	Goals
Manchester City	80-82			
Leicester City	82-85		15	3
Walsall	85-86		5	
Kidderminster Harriers	87-89			

Jones, Stephen (M)

(ROMSEY TOWN)   **Age:** 31

Previous Clubs: Sholing; Totton; Brockenhurst
Honours: Hants Div 1; Wessex League

Jones, Steven (F)

(COLWYN BAY)   **Age:** 25

Previous Clubs: Pilkingtons FC; Bethesda United
Honours: Bass NWCL Cup Winners

Jones, Trevor (D)

(CHASETOWN)   **Age:** 29

Previous Clubs: Shrewsbury Town; Northwich Victoria; Oswestry; Rhaydar; Shifnal; Bridgnorth

Honours: Border Counties runners up; Intermediate Cup runners up; Banks League Cup winners; Banks Rep; Player of the Year (3)

Jordan, Nicholas (M)

(CHELTENHAM TOWN)

D.O.B. 4.12.58   **Nickname:** Cliff
Profession: Builder
Married   **Wife's name:** Zena
Children: Lauren & Joseph
Hobbies: Golf, Racing

PLAYING CAREER

Honours: Glos County Youth Rep

Club	Seasons	Transfer	Apps	Goals
Moreton Town	79-83			

ANTONE JOSEPH

Joseph, Antone (M)

(KIDDERMINSTER HARRIERS)

D.O.B. 30.9.59
Profession: Warehouseman
Married
Hobbies: Sport

PLAYING CAREER

Honours: England Semi-Pro Int

Club	Seasons	Transfer	Apps	Goals
West Bromwich Albion	75-77			
Cardiff City	77-79			
Weymouth	79-82			
Telford United	82-89			

Joslin, Gareth (D)

(CUMBRAN TOWN)   **Age:** 30

Previous Clubs: Bridgend Town; Maesteg Park
Honours: Cardiff Schools

Joyce, Kevin (F)

(STAPENHILL)   **Age:** 27

Previous Clubs: Burton Albion; Gresley; Edingale; Newhall United

Honours: Leicester Combination winners 1988-89; Leicester Intermediate Shield 1988-89; Scoreline Combination Division winners 1989-90

WAYNE JOYNES

Joynes, Wayne (M)
(MOSSLEY)

D.O.B. 1.1.64   **Nickname:** Tiny
Hobbies: Landscape Gardener
Married   **Wife's name:** Kay
Hobbies: Stamp Collecting

PLAYING CAREER

Honours: None

Club	Seasons	Transfer Apps	Goals
Maine Road	82-87		
Chadderton	87-89		

Judd Stephen (G)
(SELSEY)   **Age:** 21

Previous Clubs: Siddlesham
Honours: County League College Cup runners up; Div 4, Div 3 Sunday Selsey

Jukes, Stuart (F)
(BILLERICAY TOWN)   **Age:** 22

Previous Clubs: Fulham (App); Basildon United; Aveley; Hornchurch
Honours: None

Julian, Colin (D)
(ALFRETON TOWN)   **Age:** 25

Previous Clubs: Belper Town; Eastwood Town; Alfreton Town; Heanor Town
Honours: None

IAN GORRIE (ATHERSTONE U)

PETER HOWELL (KIDDERMINSTER H)
Photo: Kappa Sports Pictures.

STEVE HANLEY (MACCLESFIELD & ENGLAND)

DOUGIE KEAST (KETTERING TOWN)

Kandekore, Maurice (F)

(EYNESBURY ROVERS) **Age:** 22

Previous Clubs: St.Neots Town; Eynesbury Rovers; Potton United

Honours: Hinchingbrooke Cup 1990; North Beds Charity Cup 1990; Hunts Premier Cup 1990

Kane, Conrad (F)

(CARSHALTON ATHLETIC)

D.O.B. 25.7.63
Profession: Civil Servant
Single
Hobbies: Sport

PLAYING CAREER

Honours: Vauxhall-Opel Lge Rep; Middx Wanderer

Club	Seasons	Transfer	Apps	Goals
Merstham	81-83			
Dulwich Hamlet	83-84			
Bromley	84-86			

Kane, Kevan (D)

(BEDWORTH UNITED) **Age:** 25

Previous Clubs: Wolverhampton Wanderers; AP Leamington; Coventry Sporting; V.S.Rugby; Atherstone United

Honours: None

Kane, Mark (M)

(ENFIELD)

D.O.B. 31.12.61 **Nickname:** Kipper
Profession: Roofer
Single
Hobbies: Squash

PLAYING CAREER

Honours: None

Club	Seasons	Transfer	Apps	Goals
Leyton Orient	77-82			
Woodford Town	82-84			
Barking	84-88			
Tampa Bay Rowdies	1988			
Barking	88-89			
Chelmsford City	89-91			

Kavanagh, Ian (D)

(EYNESBURY ROVERS) **Age:** 29

Previous Clubs: Bedford Town; Eynesbury Rovers; Hitchin Town; Barton Rovers; Hendon

Honours: Herts Senior Cup

Keane, Liam (M/F)

(GODALMING TOWN) **Age:** 20

Previous Clubs: From youth team

Honours: None

Kearns, Ollie (F)

(RUSHDEN TOWN) **D.O.B.** 12.6.56
Profession: Property Dealer
Married **Wife's name:** Marilena
Children: Serena & Alysia **Hobbies:** Golf

PLAYING CAREER

Honours: None

Club	Seasons	Transfer	Apps	Goals
Banbury United	73-76			
Reading	77-79		86	40
Oxford United	81-82		18	4
Walsall	82-83		38	11
Hereford United	83-87		170	58
Wrexham	87-90		47	16
Kettering Town	90-91			

OLLIE KEARNS

Kearns, Steve (F)

(NEWMARKET TOWN) **Age:** 30

Previous Clubs: Newmarket Town; Cambridge City; Soham Town; Histon Town

Honours: Suffolk Cambs County FA Schools XI

Kearns, Steve (D)

(RHYL) **Age:** 19

Previous Clubs: Tranmere Rovers **Honours:** None

Kearvell, Peter (F)

(CHICHESTER CITY) **Age:** 18

Previous Clubs: Aldingbourne; East Dean

Honours: Top golascorer 1980-88 & Player of the Year 1988-89

Keast, Dougie (M)
(KETTERING TOWN)

D.O.B.   **Nickname:** Keastie
Profession: P.E.Teacher
Married   **Wife's name:** Joyce
Children: Natalie & Cameron
Hobbies: All Sports, Running, Reading

PLAYING CAREER

Honours: GMVC R/U 88/89; GMAC Cup Winners 86/87

Club	Seasons	Transfer	Apps	Goals
Shepshed C'house	82-83			

Keeley, Glenn (D)
(CHORLEY)

D.O.B. 1.9.54

PLAYING CAREER

Honours: England Youth Int

Club	Seasons	Transfer	Apps	Goals
Ipswich Town	71-74	£70,000	4	
Newcastle United	74-75		44	2
Blackburn Rovers	75-86		370	23
Everton		loan	1	
Oldham Athletic	86-88		27	1
Colchester United		loan	4	

Keen, David (F)
(CHELMSLEY TOWN)   **Age:** 29

Previous Clubs: Sutton Town; Paget Rangers; Moor Green

Honours: Scoreline Comb Div 1 winners; Presidents Cup winners; Top Goalscorer 1986-87,87-88,88-89

GARY KEEN
(Hayes)

Keen, Gary (M)
(HAYES)

D.O.B. 25.1.62   **Nickname:** Keeny
Profession: Self-Employed Industrial Cleaner
Single
Hobbies: Golf, All Sports

PLAYING CAREER

Honours: Vauxhall-Opel Lge Div 1 & 2 Winners; St.Albans P.O.Y. 86/87

Club	Seasons	Transfer	Apps	Goals
Chesham United	81-83			
St.Albans City	83-87			
Hendon	87-88			
St.Albans City	1988			
Hendon	88-90			

Keen, Mark (D)
(ENFIELD)

D.O.B. 23.7.64
Profession: Bank Clerk
Married   **Wife's name:** Mandy
Hobbies: Reading, watching films

PLAYING CAREER

Honours: Essex Senior Lge Winners 85/86; Essex Senior Trophy Winners 85/86; Kent Senior Cup Winners 86/87 & 87/88; Westgate Insurance Cup Winners 87/88 & 88/89; Dartford P.O.Y. 89/90

Club	Seasons	Transfer	Apps	Goals
Witham Town	83-86			
Dartford	86-90			

Keen, Nigel (D)
(ENFIELD)   **D.O.B.** 23.10.61

Profession: Quantity Surveyor
Married   **Wife's name:** Mandy
Hobbies: Sport, Reading

PLAYING CAREER

Honours: FA Youth Cup Winners; FA Trophy Winners; NPL Winners

Club	Seasons	Transfer	Apps	Goals
Manchester United	78-82			
Arcadia S'herds (S.A)	82-83			
Barrow	83-84			
Preston North End	84-86		24	

Keenan, Gary (D)
(SELBY TOWN)   **Age:** 25

Previous Clubs: Tadcaster Albion; York RI; Rowntrees

Honours: NCE Div 1 winners 1990 + runners up 1989

Kefford, Guy (M)
(WOLVERTON AFC)   **Age:** 24

Previous Clubs: Barton Rovers; Letchworth Garden City; Arlesey; Shillington; Leighton Town

Honours: South Mids winners & runners up; Challenge Cup; Beds Youth; Senior Team; South Mids Rep

Kelly, Abbey (M/F)

(RACING CLUB WARWICK)   Age: 27

Previous Clubs: Coventry Sporting; Stratford Town; Racing Club Warwick; St.Albans City
Honours: Midland Combination Premier Div Winners

Kelly, Neil (D)

(ALTRINCHAM)   D.O.B 31.10.70

Profession: Not working
Single   **Hobbies:** Sport
Honours: None

Previous Clubs: Stockport County (87-89)

Kelly, Omelle (F)

(HARROW BOROUGH)   Age: 24

Previous Clubs: Dulwich Hamlet; Corinthian Casuals; Dulwich Hamlet.
Honours: None

Kelly, Warren (D)

(HAYES)   D.O.B. 18.4.68

Profession: Carpenter
Single   **Hobbies:** Golf, Tennis

PLAYING CAREER

Honours: Herts County Youth Rep; FA County Youth Cup Winners; Herts Charity Cup Winners & R/U; Vauxhall-Opel Lge Rep.

Club	Seasons	Transfer	Apps	Goals
Hemel Hempstead	83-85			
St.Albans City	85-87			

KEVIN KETLEY
(Braintree)

Kelsey, Raymond (D)

(MEIR K.A.)   Age: 31

Previous Clubs: None
Honours: Staffs Senior League Champions 1988-89; Walsall Senior Cup 1989-90

Kemp, John (F)

(CLACTON TOWN)   Age: 24

Previous Clubs: Colchester Utd; Brightlingsea Utd; Wivenhoe Town; Harwich & Parkestone
Honours: Essex Senior League; Essex Senior Trophy; Essex County Cap

Kempin, Scott (F)

(HINCKLEY)   Age: 21

Previous Clubs: K.R.R. WMC; Kingsway; Whetstone Athletic
Honours: Top scorer for Hinckley 1989-90

Kendall, Paul (D)

(MACCLESFIELD TOWN)

D.O.B. 19.10.64   **Nickname:** Kenno
Profession: Commercial Manager at Halifax Town FC
Married   **Wife's name:** Julie
Hobbies: Golf, Tennis, Squash

PLAYING CAREER

Honours: GMVC Winners 86/87; FA Trophy R/U 88/89

Club	Seasons	Transfer	Apps	Goals
Halifax Town	81-86		106	6
Scarborough	86-88		35	2
Halifax Town	1988		12	

Kendrick, Carl (F)

(DENABY UTD)   Age: 27

Previous Clubs: Athersly Soc; Wolley; North Ferriby; Worsborough; Woollery
Honours: Hosp Cup winners; N.E.C. Div 2; Senior Cup runners up

Kennedy, Kevin (D)

(ST.DOMINICS)   Age: 29

Previous Clubs: None
Honours: None

Kennedy, James (M)

(61 FC)   Age: 28

Previous Clubs: None
Honours: None

Kerr, Andy (F)

(KEYNSHAM TOWN)   Age: 28

Previous Clubs: Almondsbury Greenway; Mangotsfield; Bristol M Farm; Clevedon Town
Honours: F.A.Vase Final Almondsbury; Glos County Honours

Kerr, Andy (D)
(WYCOMBE WANDERERS)

D.O.B. 7.4.66

PLAYING CAREER
Honours: Berks & Bucks Senior Cup Winners 89/90; Wycombe P.O.Y.89/90

Club	Seasons	Transfer	Apps	Goals
Shrewsbury Town	84-85		10	
Cardiff City	85-86		31	1
Telford United	86-88			

ANDY KERR

Kerrins, Wayne (D)
(DULWICH HAMLET)   Age: 25
Previous Clubs: Fulham; Chesham United; Farnborough Town; Woking
Honours: None

Kershaw, David (F)
(DROYLESDEN)   Age: 25
Previous Clubs: Whitworth Valley; Oldham Town
Honours: Bass North-West Counties P.O.Y.89/90

Kessler, Bobby (D)
(WINGATE)   Age: 31
Previous Clubs: None
Honours: South Midlands Lge Div 1 1990 runners up

Kester, Steve (M)
(EYNESBURY ROVERS)   Age: 28
Previous Clubs: St.Neots Town
Honours: Hinchingbrooke Cup 1988; Scott Gatty Cup (3)

Keys, Paul (M)
(BURY TOWN)   Age: 27
Previous Clubs: Westerfield United; Luton Town; Halifax (on loan)
Honours: None

Khan, Changez (F)
(STAFFORD RANGERS)

D.O.B. 23.3.71   Nickname: Chaka
Profession: Not working
Single
Hobbies: Sport

PLAYING CAREER
Honours: South Birmingham Schoolboy Rep

Club	Seasons	Transfer	Apps	Goals
Alloa Athletic	89-90			

Kind, David (D)
(ALFRETON TOWN)   Age: 19
Previous Clubs: Local football
Honours:

King, Brendan (M)
(WEYMOUTH)

D.O.B. 25.11.69   Nickname: Kinger
Profession: Assistant Manager For Hire Company
Single
Hobbies: Sport

PLAYING CAREER
Honours: Dorset County Youth Rep; Dorset Combination Lge Winners

Club	Seasons	Transfer	Apps	Goals
No previous clubs				

King, Julian (D)
(MALDEN VALE)   Age: 27
Previous Clubs: Dorking; Banstead Athletic; Molesey; Corinthian Casuals; Hampton
Honours: None

King, Phil (G)
(OAKWOOD)   Age: 18
Previous Clubs: None   Honours: None

King, Simon (D)
(CUMBRAN TOWN)   Age: 26
Previous Clubs: Newport County; Forest Green Rovers
Honours: Gwent Youth

Kingston, Peter (D:M)

(TOOTING & MITCHAM UNITED) **Age:** 35

Previous Clubs: Dulwich Hamlet; Fisher Athletic; Tooting & Mitcham United; Dulwich Hamlet; Croydon; Dulwich Hamlet

Honours: None

Kinnard, John (D)

(ROMSEY TOWN) **Age:** 24

Previous Clubs: Sutton United; Fareham Town; Sholing Sports; Eastleigh; Andover

Honours: England Universities Rep

Kinsella, Tony (M)

(WIVENHOE TOWN)

D.O.B. 30.10.61

PLAYING CAREER

Honours: Republic of Ireland Under-21 Int

Club	Seasons	Transfer	Apps	Goals
Millwall	77-80		61	1
Tampa Bay Rowdies	80-82	£60,000		
Ipswich Town	82-83		9	
Millwall	84-85		22	1
Enfield	85-86			
Doncaster Rovers	86-87		30	4
Chelmsford City	1987			
Bury Town	87-88			
Braintree Town	88-89			
Bury Town	89-90			

Kirk, Andy (M)

(EASTWOOD TOWN) **Age:** 27

Previous Clubs: Sutton Town; Belper Town; Heanor Town; Sutton Town; Worksop Town

Honours: Notts Senior Cup Winners

DAVE KERSHAW

Kirkham, Paul (F)

(HYDE UNITED) **D.O.B.** 5.7.69

Nickname: Kirky **Profession:** Postman
Single **Hobbies:** Sport

PLAYING CAREER

Honours: HFS Loans Lge Premier Div R/U; HFS Loans Lge Cup Winners; Cheshire Senior Cup Winners; Clubcall Cup R/U (2).

Club	Seasons	Transfer	Apps	Goals
East Manchester FC	83-86			
Manchester United	86-87			
Huddersfield Town	87-89		2	

Kirkup, Andy (M)

(RUSHDEN TOWN)

D.O.B. 17.10.64
Profession: Warehouse Manager
Married **Wife's name:** Nichola
Hobbies: Squash

PLAYING CAREER

Honours: Beazer Homes Lge Midland Div R/U 89/90

Club	Seasons	Transfer	Apps	Goals
Rushden Town	79-86			
Wellingborough Town	86-87			

Kirwan, Terry (M)

(ST.DOMINICS) **Age:** 31

Previous Clubs: None

Honours: Liverpool County FA Rep XI

Kitchener, Dave (F)

(BRIDGWATER 1984) **Age:** 19

Previous Clubs: None

Honours: Somerset Senior League & Cup winners; County Senior Cup Finalist

Kitchin, Brian (M)

(EYNESBURY ROVERS) **Age:** 24

Previous Clubs: Erith

Honours: Scott Gatty Cup winner 1990

Knapper, John (F)

(EASTWOOD TOWN) **Age:** 21

Previous Clubs: Local football

Honours: Notts Senior Cup Winners

Knee, Simon (D)

(CHIPPENHAM) **Age:** 22

Previous Clubs: Blunsdon Utd; Sanford

Honours: None

Knight, Carl (D)

(ALFRETON TOWN) **Age:** 24

Previous Clubs: Arnold Kingswell **Honours:** None

Knight, Christopher (M)

(CHIPSTEAD)   **Age:** 23

Previous Clubs: Godstone; Whyteleafe   **Honours:** None

Knight, Tony (D/M)

(SLOUGH TOWN)   **D.O.B.** 22.10.61

Profession: Self-Employed Builder   **Married**
Wife's name: Tracey   **Hobbies:** Sport

PLAYING CAREER

Honours: Hillingdon Schoolboy Rep; Middx Schoolboy Rep; Vauxhall Lge Premier Winners 89/90; Middx Senior Cup Winners; Berks & Bucks Senior Cup Winners; Vauxhall-Opel Lge Rep.

Club	Seasons	Transfer	Apps	Goals
Arsenal	77-78			
Southampton	78-81			
Hillingdon Borough	81-83			
Wembley	83-84			
Harrow Borough	84-85			

Knowles, Barry (D)

(FLEETWOOD TOWN)   **D.O.B.** 25.4.59
Nickname: B.J.   **Profession:** Self-Employed
Married   **Wife's name:** Debbie
Children: Ashley   **Hobbies:** Making Money

PLAYING CAREER

Honours: Freight Rover Trophy R/U; Wigan P.O.Y. 87/88

Club	Seasons	Transfer	Apps	Goals
Chorley	78-80			
Southport	80-82			
Runcorn	82-83			
Barrow	83-85			
Wigan Athletic	85-88		180	9
Colne Dynamoes	1988			
Altrincham	1988			

Knowles, Darren (M)

(CHASETOWN)   **Age:** 18

Previous Clubs: Bilston Town; Wolverhampton Utd
Honours: None

Kowalski, Andy (M)

(SPALDING)   **Age:** 35

Previous Clubs: Alfreton T.; Chesterfield; Doncaster R.; Peterborough Utd; Chesterfield; Boston Utd; Gainsboro Trin; Matlock T.; Shep Charterhouse

Honours: None

Kurila, Alan (D)

(KIDDERMINSTER HARRIERS)

D.O.B. 16.9.61
Profession: Wire Drawer (Jewellery Trade)
Married   **Wife's name:** Patricia Caroline
Children: Alan & Alana Patricia
Hobbies: Tennis, Swimming

PLAYING CAREER

Honours: Northants Schoolboy Rep; FA XI; Southern Lge Premier Div Winners; Southern Lge Cup Winners & R/U (2); Worcs Senior Cup Winners & R/U; Bromsgrove P.O.Y. 85/86

Club	Seasons	Transfer	Apps	Goals
Birmingham City	78-81			
Bedford Town	81-82			
Bromsgrove Rovers	82-88			
Burton Albion	88-89	£7,000		
Stafford Rangers	89-90	£11,000		

Kurzyk, Steve (M)

(PENRITH)   **Age:** 31

Previous Clubs: Penzance Town; Carlisle City
Honours: None

BARRY KNOWLES

DOMINIC KEARNS
(Boldmere St Michaels) Photo: Sutton Observer

Ladley, Ian (G)

(MIRLEES BLACKSTONE) Age: 27

Previous Clubs: Frickley Athletic; Cambridge City; Saffron Walden; Bury Town; Potton United

Honours: Southern League Southern Division Winners 1985-86

Lacy, John (D)

(WIVENHOE TOWN)

D.O.B. 14.8.51

PLAYING CAREER

Honours: None

Club	Seasons	Transfer	Apps	Goals
Kingstonian	70-71			
Fulham	71-77		168	7
Tottenham Hotspur	77-82		104	2
Crystal Palace	82-83		27	
Stanungsund (Nor)				
Barnet	84-85			
St.Albans City	85-88			

Lahiff, Sean (G)

(SLOUGH TOWN)

D.O.B. 21.1.69 **Nickname:** Aussie or Skippy
Profession: Greenkeeper
Single
Hobbies: Surfing

PLAYING CAREER

Honours: None

Club	Seasons	Transfer	Apps	Goals
Sydney City (Aust)	87-89			
Reading	1989			
Koparif (Fin)	89-90			

NICKY LEE (BRAINTREE)

Laine, Neil (M)

(VALE RECREATION) Age: 27

Previous Clubs: None

Honours: 4 Guernsey Caps (1983-89); 7 Guernsey Priaulx Championship Medals: 1980-81, 1981-82, 1982-83, 1983-84, 1986-87, 1987-88, 1988-89; 2 Channel Islands Championship Medals 1981 & 1988

Laird, Craig (M)

(BRIDGWATER TOWN 1984) Age: 26

Previous Clubs: Bridgwater Town; Minehead; Taunton Town; Weston-super-Mare

Honours: Somerset Senior League Champions/Cup Winners; County Cup Finalists; Somerset County Rep.

Lambert, Colin (M)

(MACCLESFIELD TOWN)

D.O.B. 21.9.63 **Nickname:** Lambo
Profession: Car Mechanic
Single
Hobbies: Keeping Fit

PLAYING CAREER

Honours: None

Club	Seasons	Transfer	Apps	Goals
Flixton	86-87			
Winsford United	87-90			

Lambert, Martin (F)

(WYCOMBE WANDERERS)

D.O.B. 24.9.65

PLAYING CAREER

Honours: England Schoolboy & Youth Int; Berks & Bucks Senior Cup Winners 89/90

Club	Seasons	Transfer	Apps	Goals
Brighton & H. A.	83-85		3	
Torquay United	1985		6	2
Union (Belg)	85-86			
Volendam (Hol)	86-87			
Sedan (Fra)	87-88			
Brighton & H. A.	88-89	£15,000		

Lamond, James (G)

(DESBOROUGH TOWN) Age: 30

Previous Clubs: Corby Town; Hamlet S & L; Rushden Town; Desborough Town; Cottingham

Honours: Nene Group United Counties League Runners-up 1985-86; Junior Cup Winners 1983; Nene Group UCL Knockout Cup Winners 1986-87

Land, Gil (D)

(GRESLEY ROVERS) Age: 31

Previous Clubs: Nottingham Forest Reserves; Burton Albion; Worksop Town; Heanor Town

Honours: F.A. Trophy Runners-Up; N.P.F.L. Cup Finalists; Derbyshire Cup Winners

Lander, Martin (D)
(GLOUCESTER CITY)

D.O.B. 7.8.60
Profession: British Telecom Engineer
Married   **Wife's name:** Sylvia
Children: Emma & Andrew
Hobbies: Swimming, Squash, Family Life

PLAYING CAREER
Honours: Worcs County Youth Rep; Southern League Midland Div Winners 88/89; Worcs Senior Cup Winners (2); Campion Cup Winners; P.O.Y. Kidderminster (2), Stourbridge (2) and Gloucester

Club	Seasons	Transfer	Apps	Goals
Aston Villa	70-71			
Wolverhampton W.	71-72			
Kidderminster Harriers	72-78			
Stourbridge	78-85			

Lane, Ian (D)
(BRIDGWATER TOWN 1984)   **Age:** 23
Previous Clubs:

Honours: Somerset Senior League Champions/Cup Winners; County Senior Cup Finalists

Lane, Graham (F)
(DULWICH HAMLET)   **Age:** 22
Previous Clubs: Enfield; Bromley
Honours: None

Langan, Dave (M)
(MIRLEES BLACKSTONE)   **Age:** 34
Previous Clubs: Derby County; Birmingham City; Oxford United; Walsall; Peterborough United
Honours: Milk Cup Winners; Irish International Caps

TONY LIVENS (BANGOR CITY)

Langley, Freddie (D)
(DULWICH HAMLET)   **Age:** 23
Previous Clubs: Corinthian Casuals; Tooting & Mitcham United
Honours: London Schoolboy Rep

Langley, Neil (D)
(RHYL)   **Age:** 29
Previous Clubs: Prestatyn; Rhyl; Pilkingtons
Honours: Clwyd Premier Lge & Cup Winners; Presidents Cup Winners

Langley, Tommy (F)
(SLOUGH TOWN)

D.O.B. 8.2.58

PLAYING CAREER
Honours: None

Club	Seasons	Transfer	Apps	Goals
Chelsea	74-79		142	40
Queens Park Rangers	79-80		25	8
Crystal Palace	80-82		59	9
AEK Athens(Greece)	82-84			
Coventry City	83-84		2	
Wolverhampton W. (Aldershot - loan 16-4)	84-85		23	4
Hong Kong Rangers	85-86			
Aldershot	86-87		81	21
Exeter City	87-88		21	2

Langston, David (M)
(CHASETOWN F.C.)   **Age:** 22
Previous Clubs: Brereton Social; Wolves; Armitage; Mile Oak
Honours: Banks's Brewery Cup Winners 1989-90

Lapham, Kevin (M)
(WARMINSTER TOWN)   **Age:** 33
Previous Clubs: Warminster Town; Chippenham Town
Honours: Wiltshire County; Wilts Premier Shield Winners medal

Lardner, Rob (F)
(CHIPPENHAM TOWN)   **Age:** 27
Previous Clubs: Melksham Town
Honours: Wiltshire Premier Shield

Larkin, Richard (M)
(TUNBRIDGE WELLS)   **Age:** 22
Previous Clubs: Tonbridge; Lewes
Honours: Kent League Cup

Lavender, Wayne (F)
(NEWTOWN)   **Age:** 26
Previous Clubs: Chester Res.; 'Sapa' (Finland); 'Papatoetoe' (New Zealand); Caernavon F.C.; Connatts Quay Nomads
Honours: Franklin Area Rep. (NZ); Flintshire Schools Area Rep.

Lawrence, Andy (M)

(WELWYN GARDEN CITY)   Age: 30

Previous Clubs: Hatfield Town; Bishops Stortford; Hertford; Baldock; Selby

Honours: None

Lawrence, David (D)

(SAWBRIDGEWORTH TOWN)   Age: 23

Previous Clubs:

Honours: None

Lawrence, Mark (M)

(GUISBOROUGH TOWN)   Age: 31

Previous Clubs: Hartlepool F.C.; Port Vale F.C.; Whitby Town; Bishop Auckland

Honours: Northern League Winners medal; Northern League Cup; Durham Cup

Lawrence, Mick (D)

(SELSEY F.C.)   Age: 28

Previous Clubs: Selsey; Wittering

Honours: None

Lawson, Ronald (M)

(BALDOCK TOWN)   Age: 30

Previous Clubs: Barton Rovers; Stevenage Borough; Hitchin Town; Letchworth Garden City; Harlow Town

Honours: Herts County Schoolboy; Youth & FA Rep

KENNY LAWTON

Lawton, Kenny (M)

(DROYLESDEN)   Age: 25

Previous Clubs: Port Vale; Kidsgrove Athletic; Droylsden; Leek Town

Honours: HFS Loans Lge Div 1 R/U 89/90

Lay, David (F)

(MARLOW)

D.O.B. 13.10.65
Profession: Courier
Single
Hobbies: Golf, Football

PLAYING CAREER

Honours: Wycombe Schoolboy Rep; Vauxhall-Opel Lge Div 1 Winners 87/88

Club	Seasons	Transfer	Apps	Goals
Reading	82-84			
Chesham United	84-86			
Dunstable	86-88			

Lazarus, Jeremy (G)

(WINGATE)   Age: 30

Previous Clubs: Collier Row; Woodford; Finchley

Honours: None

Lea, Mark (D)

(CALNE TOWN)   Age: 18

Previous Clubs: Swindon Town

Honours: Wiltshire Premier (Senior) Cup Winners 1989-90; Midland Youth Cup Runners-up 1988-89, 1989-90

Leaburn, Glen (M)

(CROYDON)   Age: 23

Previous Clubs: Catford Wanderers
Honours: Spartan Lge Winners 87/88; Croydon P.O.Y. 89/90

Leacock, Livingston (F)

(CHEADLE TOWN)   Age: 24

Previous Clubs: Maine Road

Honours: Manchester League Championship; Gilgryst Cup Winners

Leary, Darren (D)

(ST. DOMINICS)   Age: 18
Previous Clubs: None   **Honours:** None

Leather, Reg (D)

(HAYES)

D.O.B. 21.11.53
Profession: Builder
Married   **Wife's name:** Helen
Hobbies: Sport

PLAYING CAREER

Honours: None

Club	Seasons	Transfer	Apps	Goals
Hayes	76-78	£1,500		
Hillingdon Borough	78-80	£3,500		
Woking	80-81			
Hayes	81-83			
Southall	83-85			

Ledden, Gerard (M)

(PICKERING TOWN)   **Age:** 20

Previous Clubs: Scarborough F.C. Youth Team
Honours: North Yorkshire U-19; N.E. England

Ledwidge, Sean (D)

(61 F.C. LUTON)   **Age:** 31

Previous Clubs: Dunstable
Honours: S.M.L. Challenge Trophy Winners; Cove Windows Trophy Winners

Lee, Andrew (D)

(WITTON ALBION)

D.O.B. 14.9.62
Profession: Not working
Married   **Wife's name:** Catherine
Children: Georgia
Hobbies: Sport

PLAYING CAREER

Honours: Liverpool Schoolboy Rep; Merseyside Schoolboy Rep; England Schoolboy Int; England Semi-Pro Int; NPL Winners (2); FA Trophy Winners & R/U (2); Lancs Floodlight Trophy Winners.

Club	Seasons	Transfer	Apps	Goals
Liverpool	78-80			
Wrexham	80-81			
Bangor City	81-83			
Stafford Rangers	83-84	£1,000		
Tranmere Rovers	84-85		18	
Cambridge United	1985		9	
Runcorn	85-86			
Altrincham	86-87	£2,000		
Telford United	87-89	£20,000		
Colne Dynamoes	89-90			

Lee, Gary (D)

(GOOLE TOWN)

D.O.B. 30.4.66
Profession: Not working
Married   **Wife's name:** Cheryl
Children: Jessica Samantha
Hobbies: Sport

PLAYING CAREER

Honours: Armthorpe P.O.Y. 88/89

Club	Seasons	Transfer	Apps	Goals
Doncaster Rovers	82-85		5	
Gainsborough Trinity	85-86			
Armthorpe Welfare	86-89			

Lee, Lennie (F)

(DOVER ATHLETIC)

Previous Clubs: Ramsgate; Margate; Herne Bay; Margate; Folkestone; Ramsgate; Thanet Utd; Dover Ath.; Dover Athletic; Thanet Utd.
Honours: Beazer Homes Lge. Premier Div. Winners 1989/90, Southern Lge Southern Div. Winners 1987/88

Lee, Nigel (F)

(KEYNSHAM TOWN)   **Age:** 28

Previous Clubs: Hengrove Athletic; Odd Down; Welton Rovers; Frome Town
Honours: None

DAVID LEES

Lees, David (D)

(OLDHAM TOWN)

D.O.B. 24.8.58   **Nickname:** Spike
Profession: Catering Equipment Installer
Married   **Wife's name:** Lynn
Children: Jennifer
Hobbies: Going For A Pint

PLAYING CAREER

Honours: None

Club	Seasons	Transfer	Apps	Goals
Stoke City	74-76			
Hyde United	76-81			
Chorley	81-86			
Ashton United	86-88			
Mossley	88-89			
Curzon Ashton	1989			
Mossley	89-91			

Legg, Stuart (D)

(DARTFORD)

D.O.B. 15.6.66   **Nickname:** Leggy
Profession: Not working
Single
Hobbies: Golf

PLAYING CAREER

Honours: Hunts County Youth Rep

Club	Seasons	Transfer	Apps	Goals
Eynesbury Rovers	80-83			
(incl. spell with Norwich City Youth 81-82)				
Kettering Town	83-84			
St.Neots Town	84-85			
Chatham Town	87-88			

Lemoine, Adrian (D)
(CHELMSFORD CITY)

D.O.B. 9.10.63   **Nickname:** Asda's
Profession: Sales Engineer
Married   **Wife's name:** Lin
Hobbies: Golf, Cricket

PLAYING CAREER

Honours: Kent Schoolboy Rep; Southern Lge Premier Div Winners 85/86; Kent Senior Cup Winners 82/83 & 85/86

Club	Seasons	Transfer	Apps	Goals
Maidstone United	81-84			
Welling United	84-87			
Barking	87-90			

Lennard, Mark (F)
(WINGATE)   Age: 25

Previous Clubs: Wingate

Honours: Herts Senior Trophy Winner 1988; Runners-Up South Midlands League 1990; Leading Goalscorer South Midlands League 1990

Leonard, Carlton (D)
(NEWTOWN F.C.)   Age: 36

Previous Clubs: Shrewsbury Town; Hereford United; Cardiff City; Oswestry; Rhyle

Honours: Over 200 appearances in Football League

Leonard, Gary (M)
(GATESHEAD)

D.O.B. 28.11.65
Profession: Newsagent
Married   **Wife's name:** Allison
Children: Christina
Hobbies: Golf

PLAYING CAREER

Honours: None

Club	Seasons	Transfer	Apps	Goals
West Bromwich Albion	82-85			
Shrewsbury Town (Hereford Utd - loan 11-1)	85-88		67	3
Bury	88-89		9	1
Stockport County	89-90		18	1

Leonard, Paul Bryan (D)
(CLACTON TOWN)   Age: 21

Previous Clubs: Clacton Town; Brightlingsea United; Harwich & Parkeston

Honours: Senior League Winners 1988

Leslie, John (D/F)
(DARTFORD)

D.O.B. 25.10.55
Profession: Fitters Mate
Married
Children: Two
Hobbies: Golf, Cars

PLAYING CAREER

Honours: None

Club	Seasons	Transfer	Apps	Goals
Dulwich Hamlet	73-75			
Wimbledon	75-83		253	85
Gillingham	83-85		65	12
Millwall	85-87		20	2
Fisher Athletic	87-88			
Grays Athletic	1988			

Lewington, Colin (G)
(CHELMSFORD CITY)

D.O.B. 23.2.61   **Nickname:** Lewie
Profession: Computer Operations Supervisor
Married   **Wife's name:** Cheryl
Children: Christopher
Hobbies: Golf, Squash

PLAYING CAREER

Honours: Alliance Premier Lge Winners 82/83; Kent Senior Cup Winners 81/82; Erith P.O.Y. 76/77

Club	Seasons	Transfer	Apps	Goals
Erith & Belvedere	76-79			
Gravesend & N'fleet	79-82			
Chelmsford City	82-83			
Maidstone United	83-84			
Gravesend & N'fleet	84-85			
Chatham Town	85-86			
Corinthian	86-89			
Dulwich Hamlet	1989			

LENNIE LEE (DOVER)

Lewis, Gary (F)
(WARMINSTER TOWN)   Age: 18

Previous Clubs: Heytesbury

Honours: None

Lewis, Graham (M)
(CONGLETON TOWN)

D.O.B. 20.9.69   Nickname: Sid
Profession: Not working
Single
Hobbies: Sun Bathing, Golf, Socialising

PLAYING CAREER

Honours: None

Club	Seasons	Transfer	Apps	Goals
Crewe Alexandra	85-87			

Lewis, Martin (D)
(ALTRINCHAM)

D.O.B. 10.9.68
Profession: Hod Carrier
Single
Hobbies: Sport

PLAYING CAREER

Honours: Cheshire & Wirral Schoolboy Rep

Club	Seasons	Transfer	Apps	Goals
Heswall	87-89			

Lewis, Ray (D)
(CHIPSTEAD)   Age: 28

Previous Clubs: Sentry; Merstham; Coney Hall; Horley Town
Honours: None

ROBIN LEWIS

Lewis, Robin (F)
(KINGSTONIAN)   Age: 30

Previous Clubs: Wimbledon; Epsom & Ewell; Leatherhead; Hampton; Epsom & Ewell; Tooting & Mitcham; Kingstonian; Enfield; Kingstonian
Honours: FA Trophy Winners 1988

Lewis, Russell (D)
(MERTHYR TYDFIL)

D.O.B. 15.9.56

PLAYING CAREER

Honours: Welsh Semi-Pro Int; GMAC Cup Winners 86/87; GMVC R/U 88/89; Northampton P.O.Y. 84/85; Kettering P.O.Y. 88/89

Club	Seasons	Transfer	Apps	Goals
Bridgend Town	74-76			
Swindon Town	76-83		181	7
Northampton Town	83-85		132	6
Kettering Town	85-90			

Liddle, Tony (F)
(SAWBRIDGEWORTH TOWN)   Age: 29

Previous Clubs: Charlton Athletic; Bishops Stortford; Harlow Town

Honours: Essex Junior Cup; Southeast County Championship; Vauxhall League Winners Div 2 North 1988-89 (Harlow Town)

Lilley, Christopher (D)
(RADCLIFFE BOROUGH)   Age: 33

Previous Clubs: Rossendale United; Winsford United
Honours: None

Lilley, Simon (D/M)
(KIDDERMINSTER HARRIERS)

D.O.B. 15.10.72
Profession: Student
Single
Hobbies: Golf, Cricket

PLAYING CAREER

Honours: Hereford & Worcs Schoolboy & Youth Rep

Club	Seasons	Transfer	Apps	Goals
No previous clubs				

Lilwall, Steve (M)
(KIDDERMINSTER HARRIERS)

D.O.B. 15.2.70
Profession: Stores Supervisor
Single
Hobbies: Videos, Tennis, Table Tennis

PLAYING CAREER

Honours: Solihull, Birmingham & Central Warks Schoolboy Rep; Midland Floodlit Youth Lge R/U; Scoreline Combination Lge Winners 88/89 & 89/90; Worcs Senior Urn Winners 88/89 & 89/90

Club	Seasons	Transfer	Apps	Goals
Moor Green	87-88			

Lilygreen, Chris (F)
(NEWPORT A.F.C.)   Age: 25

Previous Clubs: Newport County; Yeovil Town; Stroud; Bath; Mangotsfield; Ebbw Vale
Honours: Hellenic League Champions

Limburn, Glen (D)

(AFC Lymington) **Age:** 28

Previous Clubs: Lymington Town; Wellworthy Athletic; Brockenhurst

Honours: Hants Senior Representative; Wessex League Cup Winners; Hants Senior Cup Finalist

Lindsay Ian (F)

(HITCHIN TOWN) **Age:** 33

Previous Clubs: Kempston Rovers; Wellingborough Town; Rushden Town

Honours: Herts County Rep

Ling, Andy (D)

(SUTTON COLDFIELD TOWN) **Age:** 21

Previous Clubs: Leicester City; Wolverhampton Wanderers

Honours: None

Liston, Tyrone (F)

(FARLEIGH ROVERS) **Age:** 30

Previous Clubs: Merstham; Malden Vale; Leatherhead

Honours: None

Little, Barry (M)

(FISHER ATHLETIC)

D.O.B. 25.8.64
Profession: Furniture Fitter
Married **Wife's name:** Angela
Hobbies: Golf, Music

PLAYING CAREER

Honours: England Youth Int

Club	Seasons	Transfer	Apps	Goals
Charlton Athletic	80-83		2	1
Dagenham	83-85			
Barnet	85-87			

Llewellyn, Nigel (D)

(KINTBURY RANGERS) **Age:** 30

Previous Clubs: None

Honours: None

Lloyd, Ian (D)

(MOSSLEY)

D.O.B. 13.6.69 **Nickname:** Lloydy
Profession: Window Cleaner
Single
Hobbies: Golf

PLAYING CAREER

Honours: NPL Winners 87/88

Club	Seasons	Transfer	Apps	Goals
Bolton Wanderers	84-86			
Chorley	86-89			

Lloyd, Martin (D)

(RADFORD F.C.) **Age:** 29

Previous Clubs: Valley Park

Honours: East Midlands League Champions

Lloyd, Nikky (M)

(DULWICH HAMLET) **Age:** 24

Previous Clubs: Sutton United; Whyteleafe; Bromley; Dulwich Hamlet

Honours: None

Lloyd, Thomas (F)

(STAFFORD RANGERS) **Age:** 26

Previous Clubs: Malpas; Witton Albion; Telford United; Rhyl

Honours: FA Trophy Winners 1989

Lockhart, Keith (M)

(CAMBRIDGE CITY)

D.O.B. 19.7.64
Married

PLAYING CAREER

Honours: None

Club	Seasons	Transfer	Apps	Goals
Cambridge United	81-85		58	8
Wolverhampton W.	85-86		25	4
Hartlepool United	86-87		2	

Lodge, Grant (D)

(BILLERICAY TOWN) **Age:** 25

Previous Clubs: Canvey Island

Honours: F.A. Vase Q-Finals 1990; Essex Senior League Champions (C. Island)

CHRIS LILYGREEN (AFC NEWPORT)

London, Paul (D)

(RACING CLUB WARWICK) Age: 27

Previous Clubs: Hurley Daw Mill; Hinckley Athletic; Coventry Sporting; Leicester United
Honours: Birmingham Junior Cup Winners 82/83

Long, Ian (M)

(SEATON DELAVAL AMATEURS) Age: 27

Previous Clubs: Shilbottle C.W.; Ponteland United

Honours: Northumberland Senior Benevolent Bowl Winners medal; McEwans Northern Alliance Premier Division Champions medal

Loveday, Martin (D)

(BECKENHAM TOWN) Age: 26

Previous Clubs: Beckenham Town; Sheppey United

Honours: None

Lovegrove, Stuart (M)

(OAKWOOD) Age: 26

Previous Clubs: Thomas Bennett

Honours: Crawley Senior Cup/Crawley Charity Shield; Crawley Jubilee Cup

Lovell, Alastair (D)

(HARROGATE TOWN) Age: 21

Previous Clubs:

Honours: None

Lovell, Neil (M)

(GRESLEY ROVERS) Age: 34

Previous Clubs: Stavely Works; Matlock Town; Eastwood Town; Sutton Town

Honours: Notts Senior cup 5 times; Derby Senior Cup 3 times; Player of the Year at 3 clubs; Won National under-21 Youth Cup Final medal with Sheffield

Lovell, Steve (D)

(Bromley) Age: 21

Previous Clubs: Brighton; Leyton Wingate; Wycombe Wanderers; Leyton Wingate

Honours: None

Lovelock, Mark (D)

(LEATHERHEAD) Age: 29

Previous Clubs: Chertsey Town; Bracknell Town
Honours: None

Lowe, Jason (D)

(KIDDERMINSTER HARRIERS)

D.O.B. 12.8.70
Profession: Production Controller
Single
Hobbies: Golf

PLAYING CAREER

Honours: Birmingham Schoolboy Rep

Club	Seasons	Transfer	Apps	Goals
Birmingham City	87-88			

Lowe, Simon (F)

(FRICKLEY ATHLETIC)

D.O.B. 26.12.62

PLAYING CAREER

Honours: Sheffield Senior Cup Winners 89/90

Club	Seasons	Transfer	Apps	Goals
Ossett Town	80-83			
Barnsley	83-84		2	
Halifax Town	84-86		77	19
Hartlepool United	1986		14	1
Colchester United	86-87			
			36	8
Scarborough	87-88		16	3
Goole Town	88-89			

Lowe, Thomas (D)

(BATH CITY)

D.O.B. 22.4.57 **Nickname:** Tiv
Profession: Not working
Married **Wife's name:** Dorothy
Children: Nicola, Abigail & Thomas

PLAYING CAREER

Honours: None

Club	Seasons	Transfer	Apps	Goals
Saltash United	82-84			
Dorchester Town	84-85			
Wimborne Town	85-86			
Saltash United	86-88			
Yeovil Town	88-91			

Luby, Sean (D)

(CHELMSLEY TOWN) Age: 25

Previous Clubs: Coleshill Town 1986-88

Honours: Player of the Year 1989-90

Lucas, Brian (F)

(BASINGSTOKE TOWN)

D.O.B. 31.1.61

PLAYING CAREER

Honours: None

Club	Seasons	Transfer	Apps	Goals
Aldershot	78-83		125	19
Farnborough Town	83-85			
Basingstoke Town	85-87			
Wokingham Town	87-90	£2,000		

RODDY BRAITHWAITE
(Kingstonian)
Photo: Dennis Nicholson.

TIM BUZAGLO (Woking)

LES BENHAM (Farleigh Rovers)
Photo: John Vass.

ANDY BLYTHE (Lewes)

ROBIN BESTE (Carshalton)
Photo: John Hutton.

PATRICK ATKINSON
(Gateshead)

TERRY BURNS (Harlow Town)
Photo: Dave West.

GARY BULL (Bull)
Photo: David Williams.

PAUL BENNETT (Littlehampton Town)
Photo: Dennis Nicholson.

PHOTO FILE

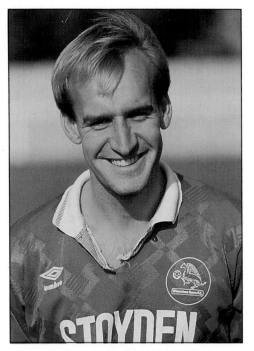

STEVE CLARK (Wivehoe Town)

ADIE COWLER (Woking)
Photo: Eric Marsh

TONY DOHERTY (Marlow)
Photo: John Hutton.

PAUL CARLTON (Ashford Town)
Photo: Edward Roffey.

TONY DIXON (Dover)
Photo: Edward Roffey.

STEVE DUNGEY (Whyteleafe)
Photo: Dave West.

RICHARD DURHAM (Newport I.O.W.)
Photo: Edward Roffey.

MARK DOBIE (Gretna)
Photo: Alan Watson.

JOHN DENTON (Yeading)
Photo: Dave West.

JOHN GAUTREY (Marine)
Photo: Dave Rannard.

MARK GOODWIN & ANDY HUNT
(Kettering Town)
Photo: Mick Cheney.

UCHE EGBE (Hendon)
Photo: John Hutton.

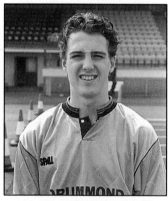

DANNY ESQUILANT (Croydon)
Photo: Dave West.

RUSSELL GORDON (Tamworth)

RONNIE ELLIS (Macclesfield Town)

PAUL GILES (Merthyr Tydfil)

JULIAN GRAY (Farnborough Town)
Photo: Dave West.

STUART EDWARDS (Halesowen
Town)

PHOTO FILE

JOHN HUMPHRIES (Leatherhead)
Photo: Tim Edwards.

TONY KELLY (Harrow Borough)
Photo: John Hutton.

ANDY HESSENTHALER
(Redbridge Forest)
Photo: D. Nicholson.

JOHN LESLIE (Dartford)

NICKY LANE (Clapton)
Photo: Gavin Ellis.

STEVE LESTER (Trowbridge Town)
Photo: Edward Roffey.

STEVE McGAVIN (Sudbury Town)

PAUL HYDE (Hayes)
Photo: John Hutton.

PAUL LOUGHLIN (Bromley)
Photo: John Hutton.

JOHN O'LEARY (Malden Vale)

JOHN McINNES (South Liverpool)

SEAN McFADDEN (Erith & Belvedere)

DEAN MANN (Leyton-Wingate)
Photo: V Robertson.

STEVE NELSON (Telford United)
Photo: John Vass.

JOHN NEAL (Bishops Stortford)
Photo: Gavin Ellis.

GARY PUGH (Ramsgate)
Photo: Francis Short.

STUART MACKENZIE (Yeading)
Photo: Dave West.

PHOTO FILE

CHRIS VIDAL (Molesey)
Photo: Dennis Nicholson.

JOHN TIMMONS (Macclesfield Town)
Photo: Keith Wilson.

COLIN TATE (Hendon)
Photo: John Hutton.

ALAN ZELEM (Macclesfield Town)

MARK WEST (Wycombe Wanderers)

KEVIN WEDDERBURN
(Leatherhead)
Photo: Edward Roffey.

GEORGE TORRANCE (Falmouth
Town)

JOHN VINCENT (Ruislip)

IAN YOUNG (Margate)
Photo: Francis Short.

Luff Tony (G)
(HITCHIN TOWN) **Age:** 28
Previous Clubs: Bedford T   **Honours:** Herts & Beds Rep

Lunt, Ian (F)
(DROYLESDEN) **Age:** 26
Previous Clubs: Altrincham; Witton Albion; Winsford United; Curzon Ashton
Honours: Manchester Premier Cup Winners 89/90

Lutkevitch, Michael (F)
(HYDE UNITED)

D.O.B. 15.4.62   **Nickname:** Luckie
Profession: Service Engineer
Married   **Wife's name:** Jackie
Children: Matthew
Hobbies: Golf

PLAYING CAREER

Honours: HFS Loans Lge Premier Div R/U (2); HFS Loans Lge Cup Winners; Clubcall Cup R/U (2); Cheshire Senior Cup Winners; Lancs Floodlit Cup Winners (2)

Club	Seasons	Transfer	Apps	Goals
Curzon Ashton	80-81			
Stalybridge Celtic	81-85			

Lynch, Adrian (F)
(PEGASUS) **Age:** 22
Previous Clubs: Bromyard Town
Honours: None

Lynch, Anthony (D)
(CHEADLE TOWN) **Age:** 30
Previous Clubs: Droylsden; Wanneroo City (Australia)
Honours: Derbyshire Cup Winners

Lynch, D (M)
(PEGASUS) **Age:** 18
Previous Clubs: Bromyard Town   **Honours:** None

Lynch, Tony (F)
(BARNET)
D.O.B. 20.1.66

PLAYING CAREER

Honours: London Schoolboy Rep

Club	Seasons	Transfer	Apps	Goals
Brentford	83-86		45	6
Maidstone United	86-88			
Wealdstone	88-90	£15,000		

Lynch, Tony (D)
(BILLINGHAM SYNTHONIA) **Age:** 32
Previous Clubs: South Bank; Bishop Auckland
Honours: Northern Lge Champions 1988-89, 1989-90; Northern Lge Cup 1989-90; Durham Cup Winners Trophy 1988-89

Lynn, Ray (M)
(BECKENHAM TOWN) **Age:** 21
Previous Clubs: None
Honours: None

Lyon, Bob (D)
(SELBY TOWN) **Age:** 28
Previous Clubs:
Honours: NCE Div 2 Runners-Up 1990

GLEN LEABURN

JOHN LACY

**JASON LOVELL
(BASHLEY)**

McAllister, Mark (D)

(SELSEY)
Age: 26
Previous Clubs: None
Honours: None

McAleese, Steven (M)

(PICKERING F.C.)
Age: 26
Previous Clubs: Eastfield; Bridlington Town
Honours: None

McAughtrie, David (D)

(NORTHWICH VICTORIA)
D.O.B. 31.1.63

PLAYING CAREER

Honours: Staffs Senior Cup Winners; Mid-Cheshire Senior Cup Winners

Club	Seasons	Transfer	Apps	Goals
Stoke City	80-83		51	1
Carlisle United	83-85		28	1
York City	85-86		64	1
Darlington	86-88		51	

McBride, Darren (F)

(WEYMOUTH)
D.O.B. 24.6.71
Nickname: Macker
Profession: Engineer
Single
Hobbies: Cricket, Golf, Table Tennis

PLAYING CAREER

Honours: Dorset County Youth Rep; Dorset Combination Lge Winners

Previous Clubs: None

McCabe, Andy (D)

(GUISBOROUGH TOWN)
Age: 27
Previous Clubs: Shildon; Gateshead
Honours: None

McCabe, J. (G)

(WESTHOUGHTON TOWN)
Age: 24
Previous Clubs: Garswood F.C.; Ashton Town; Wigan College
Honours: West Lancs Runners-Up (1st Div); Wigan Cup Winners

McCann, Gary (G)

(SUTTON UNITED)
D.O.B. 25.7.72
Nickname: Macca
Profession: Sales Assistant
Single
Hobbies: Driving, Sport

PLAYING CAREER

Honours: West London Schoolboy Rep; Surrey County Youth Rep.

Club	Seasons	Transfer	Apps	Goals
Fulham	85-90			

McCartney, S. (D)

(THATCHAM TOWN)
Age: 26
Previous Clubs: Gt. Sheppard; Kintbury; Lambourn
Honours: Hungerford Cup Winners; North Berks Div 2 Winners; Runners-Up League Cup 1989-90

McCarty, Darrell (F)

(HORWICH RMI)

D.O.B. 28.7.64
Nickname: Daz
Profession: Sports Retailer
Single
Hobbies: Skiing, Squash

PLAYING CAREER

Honours: Lancs Youth Cup Winners

Club	Seasons	Transfer	Apps	Goals
Chorley	82-84			
Leyland Motors	84-85			
Bolton Wanderers	85-86			
Marine	86-87			
Leyland Motors	1988			
Morecambe	88-89			
Leyland Motors	1989			

McClaren, Derek (D)

(BECKENHAM TOWN)
Age: 22
Previous Clubs: None
Honours: None

McClure, Douglas (D)

(HENDON)

D.O.B. 6.9.64
Profession: Sales Manager
Married
Wife's name: Michelle
Children: Lucy
Hobbies: Swimming, Cycling

PLAYING CAREER

Honours: England Schoolboy Int (Captain); England Youth Int.

Club	Seasons	Transfer	Apps	Goals
Queens Park Rangers	80-84			
Exeter City	1984			1
Torquay United	1984			4
Wimbledon	1985			2
Peterborough United	1985			4
Crewe Alexandra	1986			3
Wealdstone	86-87			
Enfield	87-88			
Fisher Athletic	88-89			
St.Albans City	89-90			

McCluskey, Paul (D)

(HERTFORD TOWN)

D.O.B. 4.1.66
Nickname: Macka
Profession: Builder
Married
Wife's name: Donna
Children: Carl
Hobbies: Sport

PLAYING CAREER

Honours: Middx Schoolboy Rep

Club	Seasons	Transfer	Apps	Goals
Yeading	88-89			
St. Albans City	89-91			

McConville, Peter (F)

(KNOWSLEY UNITED) Age: 28

Previous Clubs: Oldham Athletic; Kirkby Town

Honours: League top scorer 1988-89

McCormick, Keith (M)

(HEANOR TOWN) Age: 25

Previous Clubs: Derby County; New Haven (USA); Brooklyn (USA); Thamesmead Town; Mickleover RBL

Honours: None

McCreanor, Mick (D)

(EYNESBURY ROVERS) Age: 23

Previous Clubs: St. Neots Town; Eynesbury Rovers; Stotfold

Honours: Hinchingbrooke Cup; Scott Gatty Cup; Hunts Junior & Senior Caps

GARY McCANN
(Sutton United)

JIM McDONOUGH
(Telford United)

McCutcheon, Mark (G)

(ENFIELD)

D.O.B. 10.7.62
Profession: Stockbroker
Married Wife's name: Elaine
Hobbies: Cricket, Golf

PLAYING CAREER

Honours: Essex Schoolboy Rep; England Schoolboy Int; Vauxhall-Opel Lge Div 2 Winners 79/80 & Div 1 R/U 80/81; Beazer Homes Lge Premier R/U 87/88 & 88/89; Westgate Insurance Cup Winners 87/88 & 88/89; Middx Wanderer; Essex & Isthmian Lge Rep; Billericay P.O.Y. (2).

Club	Seasons	Transfer	Apps	Goals
Leyton-Wingate	78-79			
Billericay Town	79-86			
Dartford	86-90			

McDonagh, Jim (G)

(TELFORD UNITED) D.O.B. 6.10.52

Profession: Reserve Team Manager (Telford Utd.)

PLAYING CAREER

Honours: Republic of Ireland Int.; England Youth Int.; Football League Div 2 Winner 77/78.

Club	Seasons	Transfer	Apps	Goals
Rotherham United	70-75	£10,000	121	
Bolton Wanderers	75-79	£250,000	161	
Everton	79-80	£90,000	40	
Bolton Wanderers	80-82	£50,000	81	
Notts County	83-85		35	
Birmingham City		loan	1	
Gillingham		loan	10	
Sunderland		loan	7	
Scarborough	86-87		9	
Hudderfield Town		loan	6	
Charlton Athletic	87-88			
Galway Rovers	88-89			
Spalding United	89-90			
Grantham Town	1990			

MacDonald, Alex (M/F)

(MIRRLEES BLACKSTONES) Age: 28

Previous Clubs: Corby Town; Saffron Walden

Honours: Combined Services/R.A.F. XI

MacDonald, Andrew (D)

(BANBURY UNITED) Age: 28

Previous Clubs: Pelsall Villa

Honours: None

McDonald, Andy (F)

(BILLERICAY TOWN) Age: 28

Previous Clubs: Enfield; Aveley; Hornchurch; Heybridge Swifts

Honours: None

McDonald, Jamie (M/F)

(LEATHERHEAD) Age: 20

Previous Clubs: Local football

Honours: None

McDonald, Tony (F)

(RADCLIFFE BOROUGH) Age: 23

Previous Clubs: None

Honours: None

McDonnell, Peter (G)

(BARROW) D.O.B. 11.6.53

Profession: Not currently working
Married Wife's name: Pauline
Children: Neil & Andrew

Honours: NPL Winners 83/84; HFS Loans Lge Premier Winners 88/89; FA Trophy Winners 89/90; Lancs Cup Winners 85/86 & 86/87; FA XI; NPL Rep XI.

PLAYING CAREER

Club	Seasons	Transfer	Apps	Goals
Netherfield	71-73			
Bury	73-74	£20,000	1	
Liverpool	74-78			
Dallas Tornadoes (USA)	1978	£20,000		
Oldham Athletic	78-82		137	
Hong Kong Rangers	82-83			
Barrow	83-85			
Morecambe	85-88			

McDougall, Frank   (F)

(CLITHEROE)   Age: 32

Previous Clubs: Hearts; Hereford; Partick Thistle; Clydebank; St Mirren; Aberdeen

Honours: 2 Scottish Full Caps; European Golden Boot Award; Scottish Cup Winners medal & Scottish Premier League Medal; League Cup Winners Medal; Anglo Scottish Cup Winners Medal

McDowell, Wayne   (F)

(BANBURY UNITED)   Age: 29

Previous Clubs: Brackley Town; Long Buckby
Honours: Oxon Senior Cup, Daventry Charity Cup

McFerran, Andrew   (F)

(WARMINSTER TOWN)   Age: 23

Previous Clubs: None
Honours: None

McGee, Stephen   (D)

(CHESTER-LE-STREET)   Age: 27

Previous Clubs: Shildon; Murton; Dunston Federation
Honours: Shipowners Cup Winner; Wearside League Winners

McGettrick, Mick   (G)

(CHELMSLEY TOWN)   Age: 36

Previous Clubs: Bromsgrove Rovers 1973-75; Tamworth 1975-78; Bromsgrove Brookfield 1978-83; Chelmsley Town 1984-

Honours: Scoreline Division One Championship & Invitation Cup Winners 1986-87, 1987-88

McGinley, John   (F)

(BOSTON UNITED)   **D.O.B.** 11.6.59

PLAYING CAREER

Honours: None

Club	Seasons	Transfer	Apps	Goals
Gateshead	79-81			
Sunderland	81-82		3	
Royal Charleroi (Belg)	82-84			
Lincoln City	84-86		71	11
Rotherham United	86-87		3	
Lincoln City	87-88		41	7
Hartlepool United		loan	2	
Doncaster Rovers	89-90		10	

McGinty, Tom   (D)

(VS RUGBY)

D.O.B. 11.2.68   **Nickname:** Gint
Profession: Carpenter
Single
Hobbies: Golf

PLAYING CAREER

Honours: Coventry Schoolboy Rep; FA XI; British Colleges Rep; Westgate Insurance Cup Winners; Midland Floodlit Cup Winners.

Club	Seasons	Transfer	Apps	Goals
Coventry Sporting	86-88			
Moor Green	88-89			

McGorry, Brian   (M)

(WEYMOUTH)

D.O.B. 16.4.70
Profession: Civil Servant
Single
Hobbies: Sport, Fishing, Martial Arts

PLAYING CAREER

Honours: England Schoolboy Int; Dorset Combination Winners

Club	Seasons	Transfer	Apps	Goals
Liverpool	86-88			
Preston North End	1988			
Chorley	88-89			

McGrath, John   (D)

(KIDDERMINSTER HARRIERS)

D.O.B. 20.12.63
Profession: Fork Lift Truck Driver
Single
Hobbies: Sport

PLAYING CAREER

Honours: None

Club	Seasons	Transfer	Apps	Goals
Shrewsbury Town	79-83			
Worcester City	83-89			

McGrory, Shaun   (D/M)

(VS RUGBY)

D.O.B. 29.2.68
Profession: Not working
Single
Hobbies: Golf, Snooker

PLAYING CAREER

Honours: None

Club	Seasons	Transfer	Apps	Goals
Coventry City	84-87			
Burnley	87-90		46	2

McGurk, Shaun   (F/M)

(VALE RECREATION)   Age: 20

Previous Clubs: None
Honours: None

McIlwain, Steve (D)

(HORSHAM) **Age:** 24

Previous Clubs: Ferring; Steyning Town
Honours: Sussex Senior Cup Winners 88/89

Mackay, Scott (M)

(HINCKLEY ATHLETIC) **Age:** 20

Previous Clubs: Luton Town; Narborough & Littlethorpe

Honours: None

McKenna, John (G)
(BOSTON UNITED)

D.O.B. 21.3.62 **Nickname:** Macka Tacklebury
Profession: Not working
Single
Hobbies: Golf, Sport

PLAYING CAREER

Honours: Bootle Schoolboy Rep; Merseyside Youth Rep; England Semi-Pro Int; FA XI; NPL Rep XI; P.O.Y.at Morecambe 82/83, Durban City 85/86 & 86/87 and Boston 87/88 & 89/90

Club	Seasons	Transfer	Apps	Goals
Everton	77-79			
Formby	79-80			
Morecambe	81-84			
Durban City (S.A.)	84-86	20,000R		
Mamelodi S. (S.A.)	86-87			
Nuneaton Borough	1987			

JOHN McKENNA (Boston United)

McKenna, Ken (F)
(ALTRINCHAM)

D.O.B. 2.7.60
Profession: Financial Consultant
Married **Wife's name:** Moira
Children: Michelle & Kate
Hobbies: Gardening, Reading

PLAYING CAREER

Honours: FA Trophy Winners 88/89; Cheshire & Shropshire Senior Cup Winners; Midland Senior Lge & Cup Winners; Cheshire Amateur Cup Winners

Club	Seasons	Transfer	Apps	Goals
Tranmere Rovers	82-83		4	
Telford United	83-87			
Tranmere Rovers	87-88		14	3
Telford United	89-90	£7,500		

MacKenzie, Iain (M)

(GENERAL CHEMICALS) **Age:** 22

Previous Clubs: None

Honours: Halton District & Cheshire County Youth Teams; Pyke Cup

McKevitt, Keith (D)

(OADBY TOWN) **Age:** 30

Previous Clubs: Blaby '74; Packhorse; Wigston Town; Houghton Rangers

Honours: Rolleston Cup; Harborough Cup

KEN McKENNA (Altrincham)

McKinney, Mark (M)
(RACING CLUB WARWICK) Age: 22
Previous Clubs: Stratford Town
Honours: None

McKinnon, Paul (F)
(SUTTON UNITED)

D.O.B. 1.8.58　　　　Nickname: Macca
Profession: Sheet Metal Engineer
Married　　　　Wife's name: Inger
Hobbies: Snooker, Golf

PLAYING CAREER

Honours: Surrey Schoolboy & Youth Rep; Vauxhall-Opel Lge Premier Winners 84/85 & 85/86; AC Delco Cup Winners 83/84 & 85/86; Surrey Senior Cup Winners (6) & R/U (2); London Senior Cup Winners 82/83; Anglo Italian Cup Winners & R/U (2); Swedish Div 1 Winners; Swedish Cup R/U; Middx Wanderer; Sutton P.O.Y. 85/86 & 89/90

Club	Seasons	Transfer	Apps	Goals
Woking	74-77			
Sutton United	77-80	£15,000		
Malmo FF (Swe)	80-82			
Sutton United	1982			
Ryoden Sports (H.K.)	82-83			
Sutton United	1983			
Trelleborg FF(Sweden)	1983			
Sutton United	83-86			
Teg SK (Swe)	1986			
Sutton United	1986	£8,000		
Blackburn Rovers	86-87		6	
Orebro SK (Swe)	1987			
Sutton United	87-88			
Orebro SK (Swe)	1988			

Mackreath, Richard (D/M/F)
(BRIDGNORTH TOWN) Age: 21
Previous Clubs: G.K.N. Sankey
Honours: None

McLachlan, Brian (D)
(ST. DOMINICS) Age: 25
Previous Clubs: None　　Honours: None

McLachlan, Neil (F)
(HORWICH RMI)

D.O.B. 4.3.56
Profession: Teacher
Single
Hobbies: Any Sport, Foreign Holidays

PLAYING CAREER

Honours: None

Club	Seasons	Transfer	Apps	Goals
Wrexham	75-77			
Morecambe	77-80			
Horwich RMI	80-85			
Chorley	85-86			

McLaughlin, Andrew (D)
(CORNARD UNITED) Age: 22
Previous Clubs: None
Honours: None

Maclewd, John (D)
(SOMERSHAM TOWN) Age: 29
Previous Clubs: St. Neots Town; Warboys Town; Somersham Town
Honours: None

MacMahon, Des (M)
(THATCHAM TOWN - Player/Manager) Age: 34
Previous Clubs: Hungerford Town; Reading; Wokingham Town; Wycombe Wanderers; Windsor & Eton; Slough Town

Honours: Professional games for Reading 1984-85; England Semi-Pro Squad 1985-86; 2 County Cup Winners medals (Berks & Bucks); Anglo Italian 1979-80 (Hungerford); F.A. XI at Vauxhall Opel level 5 times

McMahon, John (M)
(MORECAMBE)

D.O.B. 19.5.64　　　　Nickname: Maccer
Profession: Assistant Sports Centre Manager
Married　　　　Wife's name: Nicola
Children: Stacey
Hobbies: Golf, Driving, DIY, Gardening

PLAYING CAREER

Honours: None

Club	Seasons	Transfer	Apps	Goals
Everton	80-82			
Southport	82-83			
South Liverpool	83-84			
Altrincham	85-86			
Witton Albion	86-87			
Runcorn	86-89			
Altrincham	89-90			

McMenemy, Paul (F)
(BROMLEY) Age: 23
Previous Clubs: West Ham; Aldershot; Northampton; Bromley; Margate

Honours: Football Combination Winners Medal 1985-86 (West Ham)

Macmillan, Robert (M)
(LEWES) Age: 18
Previous Clubs: Youth team
Honours: Sussex Youth Rep

McMullen, Michael (G)
(CLEATOR MOOR CELTIC) Age: 29
Previous Clubs: Birmingham City; Penrith; Workington Red; Newcastle Blue Star
Honours: None

McMullen, Peter (F)

(BILLINGHAM SYNTHONIA) Age: 28

Previous Clubs: Sunderland

Honours: Northern League Div 2 Trophy 1986-87; Northern League Championship 1988-89, 1989-90; Northern League Cup 1987-88, 1989-90; Durham Cup Winners Trophy 1988-89

McNall, Keith (F)

(GATESHEAD)

D.O.B. 8.5.62   **Nickname:** Maca
Profession: Mortgage Supervisor
Married   **Wife's name:** Anne
Hobbies: Golf, Snooker

PLAYING CAREER

Honours: NPL Rep XI; FA XI; NPL XI; Crook Town POY 80-81, 81-82; Gateshead POY 89-90; Multipart League Champions 85-86; HFS Loans R-U 89-90.

Club	Seasons	Transfer	Apps	Goals
Crook Town	80-84			
Gateshead	83-88			
Bishop Auckland	87-89			

McNally, David (F)

(MORETON TOWN) Age: 28

Previous Clubs: Bromsgrove Youth Centre; Oldswinford; Fairfield Villa; Bromsgrove Athletic; Eastwood Bank; Bromsgrove Rovers

Honours: None

McNamara, Ronnie (D)

(DORKING) Age: 30

Previous Clubs: Carshalton Athletic

Honours: Vauxhall-Opel Lge Div 2 South Winners; Surrey Senior Cup R/U

COLIN McCRORY (Droylesden)

McNeil Bobby (D)

(BRIDLINGTON TOWN) Age: 27

Previous Clubs: Hull City (138-3); Lincoln City (4); Preston North End (43); Carlisle United (19)

Honours: FA Vase R/U 89/90; Northern Counties East Lge Winners

McNeilis, Stephen (D)

(WITTON ALBION)

D.O.B. 8.11.63   **Nickname:** Macker
Profession: Not Working
Married   **Wife's name:** Lynn
Children: Stephen, Anthony, Nichola
Hobbies: Pool, Fishing

PLAYING CAREER

Honours: Formby P.O.Y. 84; Colne P.O.Y. 90

Club	Seasons	Transfer	Apps	Goals
Formby	80-84			
Burscough	84-87			
Northwich Victoria	87-89			
Colne Dynamoes	89-90			

RONNIE McNAMARA

McShane, Gary (M)

(ST ALBANS)

D.O.B. 4.10.67   **Nickname:** Gazza
Profession: Printer

PLAYING CAREER

Honours: Rep.Arsenal Schoolboys

Club	Seasons	Transfer	Apps	Goals
St Albans	87-90			

McQuade, Martin (M)

(NORTON & STOCKTON ANCIENTS) Age: 28

Previous Clubs: Stockton F.C.; South Bank; Wingate; West Auckland; Norton

Honours: North Riding Senior Cup Winners; Monkwearmouth Cup Runners-Up

Mable, Paul (F/M)

(HEANOR TOWN)   Age: 24

Previous Clubs: Scunthorpe United; Alfreton Town; Borrowash Victoria; Gresley Rovers

Honours: Derbyshire Senior Cup

Macauley, Steve (D)

(FLEETWOOD TOWN)

D.O.B. 4.3.69   **Nickname:** Macca
Profession: Student
Single
Hobbies: Golf, Socialising

PLAYING CAREER

Honours: Blackpool & Lancs Schoolboy Rep; North-West England Rep; FA Youth Cup Winners 86/87

Club	Seasons	Transfer	Apps	Goals
Manchester City	85-89			

Madden, Craig (F)

(FLEETWOOD TOWN)

D.O.B. 25.9.58
Profession: Not working
Married   **Wife's name:** Kathryn
Children: Thomas
Hobbies: Snooker, Golf

PLAYING CAREER

Honours: Stockport & East Cheshire Youth Rep; Bury P.O.Y. 82/83

Club	Seasons	Transfer	Apps	Goals
Bury	77-87	£50,000	297	129
West Bromwich Albion	87-88	£50,000	12	3
Blackpool	88-90	(Wrexham 91loan - 8)	24	
York City	1990		4	

ANDY MADDOCKS Photo: John Denton

Maddocks, Andy (F)

(GRESLEY ROVERS)   Age: 27

Previous Clubs: Tamworth; Atherstone; VS Rugby; Hinckley Town

Honours: West Midland League Winners twice; West Midlands League Cup Winners twice

Maddox, Danny (D/M)

(FLEETWOOD TOWN)

D.O.B. 29.12.71
Profession: Not working
Single
Hobbies: Snooker

PLAYING CAREER

Honours: None

Club	Seasons	Transfer	Apps	Goals
Wigan Athletic	88-90			

Maguire, Paul (M)

(NORTHWICH VICTORIA)

D.O.B. 21.8.56

PLAYING CAREER

Honours: Football League Div 3 Winners; Welsh Cup Winners; Mid-Cheshire Senior Cup Winners; Staffs Senior Cup Winners

Club	Seasons	Transfer	Apps	Goals
Kilbirnie Ladeside	74-76			
Shrewsbury Town	76-79		151	35
Stoke City	79-83		107	24
Tacoma (USA)	83-85			
Port Vale	85-88		115	22

Mahon David (M)

(RADCLIFFE BOROUGH)   Age: 27

Previous Clubs: Accrington Stanley; Radcliffe Borough; Rossendale United; Accrington Stanley

Honours: North-West Counties Lge Winners

Mahone, Darren (F)

(CLEATOR MOOR CELTIC)   Age: 21

Previous Clubs:

Honours: None

Mahone, Martin (D)

(CLEATOR MOOR CELTIC)   Age: 28

Previous Clubs: Cleator Moor; Penrith

Honours: None

Mahoney, Jim (M)

(FARLEIGH ROVERS)   Age: 23

Previous Clubs: Whyteleafe

Honours: None

Mahy, Paul (G)
(VALE RECREATION) **Age:** 23
Previous Clubs: None
Honours: Jereme Cup Winners 1988-89 (C.I. Knock-Out Cup)

Mailey Kevin (G)
(WINSFORD UNITED) **Age:** 22
Previous Clubs: Bolton Wanderers
Honours: None

BOB MAKIN

Makin, Bob (D)
(DARTFORD - Player-Manager)

D.O.B. 6.12.53
Profession: Accountant
Married **Wife's name:** June
Children: Carly & Lucy

PLAYING CAREER
Honours: Isthmian Lge Premier Div Winners 78/79; Vauxhall-Opel Lge Premier Div Winners 88/89; Southern Lge Premier Div Winners 83/84; FA XI; Southern & Isthmian Lge Rep XI; Barking P.O.Y. (3)

Club	Seasons	Transfer	Apps	Goals
Barking	71-82			
Dagenham	82-83			
Dartford	83-85			
Chelmsford City	85-87			
Dartford	87-88			
Leytonstone & Ilford	88-89			
Redbridge Forest	89-90			
Barking	1990			

Main, Graham (G)
(BURNHAM RAMBLERS) **Age:** 34
Previous Clubs: Basildon United; Dagenham; Tilbury; Averley; Barking; Witham
Honours: F.A. Trophy

Malban, Danial (F)
(MEIR K.A.) **Age:** 30
Previous Clubs: Redgate Clayton
Honours: Staffs Senior League Champions 1986-87; Walsall Senior Cup Winner 1986-87 (Redgate Clayton)

Malban, Gary (F)
(Meir K.A.) **Age:** 27
Previous Clubs: Foley F.C.
Honours: Staffs Alliances Champions 1989-90; Staffs Alliances Runners-Up; Walsall Senior Cup 1989-90

Malcolm Duncan (D)
(SALISBURY) **Age:** 18
Previous Clubs: Exeter City
Honours: None

Mallender, Gary (M)
(GAINSBOROUGH TRINITY)

D.O.B. 12.3.59 **Nickname:** Mally
Profession: Machine Operator
Married **Wife's name:** Cheryl
Hobbies: Golf, Walking

PLAYING CAREER
Honours: Rep Barnsley Boys; Rep Yorkshire Boys; Won Northern Intermediate League + Cup with Barnsley Juniors; FA Trophy R-U Medal 84-85; Gola League R-U 85-86; Rep Lincs FA XI; Rep FA XI; Rep HFS Loans XI.

Club	Seasons	Transfer	Apps	Goals
Barnsley	75-79		0+2	
Boston United	79-85			
Frickley Athletic	85-89			

Malone, Barney (M)
(BILLINGHAM SYNTHONIA) **Age:** 29
Previous Clubs: South Bank]
Honours: Northern League Championship 1988-89, 1989-90; Northern League Cup 1987-88, 1989-90; Durham Cup Winners Trophy 1988-89

Malpas, Mike (D)
(GLOUCESTER CITY)

D.O.B. 12.9.60 **Nickname:** Malps
Profession: Sales Executive
Married **Wife's name:** Detty
Children: Ashley, Jessica, Lewis
Hobbies: All Sports

PLAYING CAREER

Honours: WL Cup Winners Medal; Somerset Prem. Cup 83-84; SL Midland Div. Championship 88-89.

Club	Seasons	Transfer	Apps	Goals
Bristol City	75-77			
Minehead	77-78			
Bristol Rovers	78-80			
Bath City	80-81	£3000		
Frome Town	81-84	£1500		
Forest Green Rovers	84-88			

Mancini, Carlo   (M)

(KEYNSHAM TOWN)   Age: 27

Previous Clubs: Keynsham Town; East Worle; Keynsham Town; Welton Rovers

Honours: None

Manley, Shaun   (D)

(LEWES)   Age: 19

Previous Clubs: Youth team

Honours: Sussex Youth Rep

Mann, Neil   (M)

(SPALDING UNITED)   Age: 17

Previous Clubs: Notts County; Nottingham Forest; Grimsby Town

Honours: None

Manning, Lee   (M)

(VALE RECREATION)   Age: 22

Previous Clubs: None

Honours: Guernsey under-21 Cap 1988; Stranger Charity Cup Winners 1989-90; Jereme Cup Winners 1988-89

Mansbridge, Gary   (F)

(BOGNOR REGIS TOWN)

D.O.B. 1.2.71
Profession: Not Working
Single

PLAYING CAREER

Honours: Rep British Colleges 88-89

Club	Seasons	Transfer	Apps	Goals
No previous clubs.				

Mantle, Barry   (D)

(NEWTOWN)   Age: 24

Previous Clubs:

Honours Central Wales Youth Rep. XI

Mardenborough, Keith   (M)

(RACING CLUB WARWICK)   Age: 33

Previous Clubs: Fairfield Villa; Shirley Town; Stratford Town

Honours: Midland Combination Div 1 R/U

Margerrison, John   (M)

(ST ALBANS CITY)

D.O.B. 20.10.55
Profession: Not working
Married   Wife's name: Susan
Children: Sam & Faye

PLAYING CAREER

Honours: None

Club	Seasons	Transfer	Apps	Goals
Tottenham Hotspur	72-75			
Fulham	75-78		71	9
Leyton Orient	79-81		80	6
Kansas City (USA)	81-82			
Boreham Wood	82-83			
Wealdstone	83-86			
Barnet	86-88			
Wealdstone	88-90			

Markham, David   (M)

(OADBY TOWN)   Age: 25

Previous Clubs: YMCA; Anstey Nomads; Lutterworth Town

Honours: Leicester City Youth; Nottingham Forest Youth

Marley, Mick   (D/M)

(VALE RECREATION)   Age: 27

Previous Clubs: None

Honours: 7 Guernsey Caps 1986-90; 7 Guernsey Priaulx Championship medals 1981-82, 1982-83, 1983-84, 1985-86, 1986-87, 1987-88, 1988-89; 1 Channel Islands Championship medal (Upton Park Trophy) 1988

Marriner, Graham   (D)

(BOGNOR REGIS TOWN)

D.O.B. 18.12.60
Profession: Roof Tiler
Married   Wife's name: Judith
Children: Two

PLAYING CAREER

Honours: AC Delco Cup Winner 86-87; Gravesend & N. POY 87-88, 88-89; Rep Vauxhall League; Sussex Senior Cup 79-80,80-81,81-82,82-83,83-84,86-87.

Club	Seasons	Transfer	Apps	Goals
Portsmouth	76-78			
Gravesend & Northfleet	78-79			

Marris, Martin   (D)

(NEWMARKET TOWN)   Age: 29

Previous Clubs: Soham Town Rangers

Honours: Suffolk County Youth/Cambs County Youth

Marsh, Darren   (M)

(OLDSWINFORD)   Age: 18

Previous Clubs:

Honours: Worcestershire County F.A. Youth Cap

Marsh, Darren (F)

(ROCESTER)   Age: 21

Previous Clubs: Mile Oak; Burton Albion Res; Stapenhill.

Honours: Leicester Combination Winners 1988-89; Leicestershire Intermediate Shield 1988-89; Scoreline Combination Division 1 Winners 1989-90 (Leading Scorer)

Marsh, Simon (M/F)

(HALESOWEN HARRIERS)   Age: 19

Previous Clubs: Kidderminster Harriers; Stourport Swifts

Honours: Midland Floodlight Youth League Winners 1987 & Cup Winners; League Runners-Up 1988; Scoreline Reserve League Winners 1988

Marshall, Chris (M)

(LANGNEY SPORTS)   Age: 28

Previous Clubs: Eastbourne Working Mens Club; Manhattan

Honours: Sussex Intermediate Cup Winners 1985-86; Sussex County League Div 3 & Lge Cup Winners 1986-87; Sussex County League Div 2 Champions 1987-88; Sussex County League Challenge Cup Winner 1989-90; Represented Sussex at Senior level & Rep. games; Eastbourne Charity Cup Winner 1989-90; Brighton Evening Argus County Five-a-Side Champions 1989-90

GARRY MANSON   DEAN MARTIN
(POOLE TOWN)   (FISHER ATH)

Marshall, Paul (D/M)

(HARROGATE TOWN)   Age: 27

Previous Clubs: Pickering Town; Frickley Athletic; Harrogate Town

Honours: County Cup Winners

Martin Darren (D)

(COLWYN BAY)   Age: 23

Previous Clubs: Flint Town
Honours: Bass NWCL Cup Winners

Martin, Duane (M/F)

(HINCKLEY F.C.)   Age: 24

Previous Clubs: Anstey Nomads; Friar Lane OB; Earl Shilton Albion

Honours: Senior League Div 1 Winners (Earl Shilton) 1988-89

Martin, Ian (D/M)

(SELSEY)   Age: 23

Previous Clubs: Arundel; Chichester; Selsey
Honours: Division 1 Champions 1986-87 (Arundel)

Martin, Mick (G)

(VS RUGBY)

D.O.B. 24.3.58
Profession: Haulier
Married   **Wife's name:** Jayne
Children: Kerry, Claire, Stacey
Hobbies: Chess, Fishing

PLAYING CAREER

Honours: VS Rugby P.O.Y. 89/90; Birmingham Senior Cup; Westgate Insurance Cup; Midland Floodlit Cup.

Club	Seasons	Transfer	Apps	Goals
Hinckley Athletic	76-79			
Bedworth United	79-87			
Shepshed Charterhouse	87-88 (Part Season)			
Nuneaton Borough	87-88 (Part Season)			

Martin, Paul (D)

(BRIDGWATER TOWN 1984)   Age: 28

Previous Clubs: Bridgwater Town; Frome Town
Honours: Somerset Senior League Champions/Cup Winners

Marquand, Richard (D)

(VALE RECREATION)   Age: 17

Previous Clubs: None
Honours: Guernsey Youth Cup 1988-89

Maskell, Alan (G)

(SHOTTON COMRADES)   Age: 21

Previous Clubs:
Honours: None

Mason, Bob (F)

(SELBY TOWN)   Age: 27

Previous Clubs: Tadcaster Albion; York R.I.; North Ferriby United; Bridlington Town

Honours: NCE Div 1 Champions & League Cup Winners 1988; F.A. Vase Semi-Finalist 1989; F.A. Vase Finalist 1990

Mason, Chris (M)

(HALESOWEN HARRIERS)   Age: 28

Previous Clubs: Smethwick Highfield (Sandwell Borough); Oldbury United

Honours: West Midland Player of the Year; F.A. Non-League XI

Mason, Keith (G)
(WITTON ALBION)

D.O.B. 19.7.58 **Nickname:** Mace
Profession: Sales Rep For Plumbers Merchant
Married **Wife's name:** Brigid
Children: Daniel Joseph & Louise Rebecca
Hobbies: Golf, Music, Reading

PLAYING CAREER

Honours: Leics County Rep; FA Vase Winners 87/88; ATS Cup Winners; HFS Loans Lge Premier & Div 1 Winners.

Club	Seasons	Transfer	Apps	Goals
Lutterworth Town	77-78			
Wigston Fields	78-81			
Leicester City	81-82			
Huddersfield Town	82-86		30	
Colne Dynamoes	87-90			

Mason, Tommy (D)
(ENFIELD) Age: 31

Previous Clubs: Fulham (6), Brighton & Hove Albion, Dulwich Hamlet, North Shore (NZ), Farnborough Town

Honours: New Zealand International, Vauxhall-Opel Lge Runners Up 88/89

Massey, Kevin ( )
(NEWMARKET TOWN) Age:

Previous Clubs: Cambridge United **Honours:** None

Massey, Stuart (M)
(SUTTON UNITED)

D.O.B. 17.11.64 **Nickname:** Beaker
Profession: Self-Employed Electrician
Single
Hobbies: Golf, Squash, Tropical Fish

PLAYING CAREER

Honours: Surrey County Youth Rep; FA XI; Chipstead P.O.Y.86/87; Walton & Hersham P.O.Y. 88/89

Club	Seasons	Transfer	Apps	Goals
Chipstead	84-86			
Sutton United	86-87			
Carshalton Athletic	1987			
Walton & Hersham	87-89			

Matthews, Steve (M)
(ST ALBANS CITY)

D.O.B. 29.8.61 **Nickname:** Matty
Profession: Assistant Manager
Married **Wife's name:** Shirley
Children: Hayley Louise & Simon Lee
Hobbies: Running, Football

PLAYING CAREER

Honours: FA XI; FA Vase Winner 89/90; Vauxhall Lge Div 2 Winners; Middx FA Rep.

Club	Seasons	Transfer	Apps	Goals
Hounslow	88-89			
Yeading	89-90			

Matthias Tony (M)
(MALDEN VALE) Age: 22

Previous Clubs: Dulwich Hamlet; Croydon
Honours: None

Mawhinney, John (M)
(61 F.C. LUTON) Age: 29

Previous Clubs: Luton; Tottenham; Watford; St. Albans; Letchworth; Hitchin

Honours: F.A. Youth Cup Winner 1979; National N.A.B. Boys Club Winners 1978

Maybury, Jason (D)
(WORKSOP TOWN) Age: 21

Previous Clubs: Sheffield Wednesday; Sheffield United; Hull City; Goole Town; **Honours:** None

Maynard Dave (M)
(WINSFORD UNITED) Age: 25

Previous Clubs: Army; British Forces Hong Kong
Honours: Hong Kong Div 3 Winners 88/89

JEFF MEACHAM

Meacham, Jeff (F)
(GLOUCESTER CITY)

D.O.B. 6.2.62 **Nickname:** Meach
Profession: Electrician
Married **Wife's name:** Helen
Children: Ryan
Hobbies: All Sport and Sports Quizzes

PLAYING CAREER

Honours: Rep. Avon Boys; Rep. FA XI

Club	Seasons	Transfer	Apps	Goals
Glastonbury	79-80			
Forest Green Rovers	80-82			
Trowbridge Town	82-85			
Bristol Rovers	84-86		26	9
Weymouth	86-87	£15000		
Bath City	86-88	£10000		
Trowbridge Town	88-90			

Meachin, Paul (F)
(MARINE)

D.O.B. 17.7.56   **Nickname:** Meach
Profession: Pipefitter
Married   **Wife's name:** Fiona
Children: Sam
Hobbies: Winemaking, Cricket

PLAYING CAREER

Honours: Rep Wirral Youth; Rep NPL XI and FA XI; Won 5 Liverpool Sen Cups; Won 2 Lancs. Trophies; Won 1 League Cup

Club	Seasons	Transfer	Apps	Goals
Southport	74-75		3	0
New Brighton	75-77			
Marine		£250		

Meads, Ray (D)
(TUNBRIDGE WELLS)   **Age:** 33

Previous Clubs: Bromley

Honours: Kent League Champions 1984-85; Kent League Cup Winners 1985-86; 1987-88

Meagan, David (M)
(CLEATOR MOOR CELTIC)   **Age:** 18

Previous Clubs: None   **Honours:** None

Meakes, John (D)
(WELWYN GARDEN CITY)   **Age:** 24

Previous Clubs: None   **Honours:** None

Meeds, Jason (F)
(EYNESBURY ROVERS)   **Age:** 19

Previous Clubs: Eynesbury Rovers; Cambridge City; Potton United

Honours: Hunts Premier Cup; Beds Charity Cup; Hunts Junior & Senior Caps

Megson, John (D)
(DENABY UNITED)   **Age:** 25

Previous Clubs: Sheffield Wednesday; Chesterfield; Denaby; Gainsborough

Honours: None

Mellish, Stuart (M)
(WITTON ALBION)

D.O.B. 19.11.69   **Nickname:** Melly
Single

PLAYING CAREER

Honours: Rochdale Young P.O.Y.

Club	Seasons	Transfer	Apps	Goals
Blackpool	June-Oct 86			
Rochdale	86-89		42 + 19	1
Altrincham	June-Oct 89			
Witton Albion	89-Present			
Wrexham	89-90	(Loan)	5	1

Mellor, Steve (D)
(NEWBURY TOWN - Player Manager)   **Age:** 38

Previous Clubs: Frickley Athletic; Bridlington Town; Heanor Town; Mexborough Town; Basingstoke Town; Salisbury

Honours: Sheffield & Hampshire Senior Cup Winners; Derbyshire Senior Cup Winners; Hampshire Senior Cup Runners-Up

Merchant, Nigel (D)
(CHIPPENHAM TOWN)   **Age:** 29

Previous Clubs:

Honours: None

Meredith, Alan (F)
(PEGASUS)   **Age:** 24

Previous Clubs:

Honours: None

Meredith, Neil (M)
(BRIDGNORTH TOWN)   **Age:** 22

Previous Clubs: Shrewsbury Town; Poole Town; Telford United

Honours: Macbar Reserves League Winners (twice); Midland League Cup (twice); Midland Youth Cup Finalists; Dorset Senior Cup Winners; F.A. Trophy Winners

Messenger, Gary (F)
(BARROW)

D.O.B. 3.5.62   **Nickname:** Messa
Profession: Process Worker
Married   **Wife's name:** Janice
Children: Kristian
Hobbies: Golf

PLAYING CAREER

Honours: NPL Pres. Cup 83-84; FA Trophy Winners 1990

Club	Seasons	Transfer	Apps	Goals
Workington	84-87			
Newcastle Blue Star	87-88			
Workington	88-89			

Mikurenda, Richard (M)
(MARLOW)

D.O.B. 27.10.63   **Nickname:** Micky
Single
Hobbies: Football

PLAYING CAREER

Honours: Vauxhall Prem Championship

Club	Seasons	Transfer	Apps	Goals
Wycombe Wanderers	83-85			

Milburn, Ian (D)
(PENRITH)   **Age:** 19

Previous Clubs: Carlisle United

Honours: None

PAUL McKINNON

(SUTTON UNITED)

Miles, Colin (M)

(CHIPSTEAD) **Age:** 29

Previous Clubs: Carshalton Athletic; Epsom & Ewell; Croydon; Bridgwater Town

Honours: Vauxhall Opel League Rep. XI; South Wales Schoolboys Rep.; Dan Air League Rep.

Millen, Derek (D)

(WEYMOUTH)

D.O.B. 27.5.71 **Nickname:** Plank
Profession: Service Engineer
Single
Hobbies: Anything with Sport

PLAYING CAREER

Honours: Dorset Comb.League No previous clubs.

Miller, Peter (D)

(WOLVERTON A.F.C.) **Age:**

Previous Clubs: Olney Town

Honours: Stantonbury Charity Cup Runners-Up

Miller, Tommy (D)

(ALTRINCHAM)

D.O.B. 3.5.58

PLAYING CAREER

Honours: Cheshire Senior Cup Winners

Club	Seasons	Transfer	Apps	Goals
Liverpool	76-77			
Earle	77-86			
Runcorn	86-90			

Millett, Kevin (D)

(DUNSTABLE) **Age:** 36

Previous Clubs: Dunstable; Luton Town; Hillingdon Borough; Barnet; Maidstone United; Barnet; Enfield; Dunstable; Hitchin Town
Honours: GM Vauxhall Conference R/U (2)

Millinchip, Mark (F)

(OLDWINSFORD) **Age:** 23

Previous Clubs: None

Honours: Worcestershire County F.A. Youth Cup

Mills, David (G)

(A.F.C. LYMINGTON) **Age:** 18

Previous Clubs: Wellworthy Athletic

Honours: Hants Youth Representative

Milroy, Chris (F)

(RHYL) **Age:** 22

Previous Clubs: Wrexham; Holywell Town; Flint Town
Honours: Welsh Lge Winners; North-Wales Challenge Cup Winners; Cookson Cup Winners

DEAN MURPHY (WORKINGHAM TOWN)

Milton, Nick (M)

(EYNESBURY ROVERS) **Age:** 17
Previous Clubs: None
Honours: None

Mintram, Spencer (M)

(LEWES) **Age:** 17
Previous Clubs: Brighton & Hove Albion
Honours: Sussex Schoolboy Rep

Mings, Adrian (F)

(BATH CITY) **Age:** 21
Previous Clubs: Melksham Town; Chippenham Town.
Honours: None

Minikin, Mark (D)

(BRIDGNORTH TOWN) **Age:** 28
Previous Clubs: G.K.N. Sankey; Broseley Athletic
Honours: None

Mitchell, Stewart (D)

(WOKING)

D.O.B. 3.1.61 **Nickname:** Mitch
Profession: Not working
Married **Wife's name:** Katie
Hobbies: Golf, Lazing Around

PLAYING CAREER

Honours: FA XI; Vauxhall Lge Div 1 R/U 89/90; Berks & Bucks Cup Winners 87/88 & 88/89, Windsor P.O.Y. 86/87 & Woking P.O.Y. 89/90

Club	Seasons	Transfer	Apps	Goals
Gateshead	78-80			
Hayes	80-83			
Hendon	83-84			
Slough Town	1985			
Maidenhead United	85-86			
Windsor & Eton	86-89	£2,500		

Moffatt, Greg　(D)

(NEWTOWN)　Age: 26

Previous Clubs: Chester City; Oylimpiakos; TP55 Senjoha (Finland); Naxxar Lions (Malta); Sparta Rotterdam; Bangor; Caernarvon

Honours: League Championship & U.E.F.A. Cup place (Olyimpiakos)

Mogg, David　(G)

(GLOUCESTER CITY)

D.O.B. 11.2.62　**Nickname:** Moggy
Profession: Storekeeper
Married　**Wife's name:** Nicola
Children: Robyn & Shannon　**Hobbies:** Sport

PLAYING CAREER

Honours: England Schoolboy Int.; England Youth Int.; Somerset Cup Winners (4); Bath P.O.Y. (2)

Club	Seasons	Transfer	Apps	Goals
Bristol City	78-81			
Atvidaberg (Swe)	81-82			
Bath City	82-88	£10,000		
Cheltenham Town	88-90			

Mogg, Joe　(D)

(MELTON TOWN)　Age: 24

Previous Clubs: Leicester United; Shepshed Charterhouse; Holwell Works　**Honours:** None

Molloy, Chris　(D)

(ST HELENS TOWN)

D.O.B. 7.12.70
Profession: Painter
Single
Hobbies: Any Sport

PLAYING CAREER

Honours: None

Club	Seasons	Transfer	Apps	Goals
York City	87-89			
Witton Albion	89-90			

Monaghan, John　(D)

(KINTBURY RANGERS)　Age: 29

Previous Clubs: Wantage Town
Honours: Berks & Bucks Jnr

Monger, Paul　(D)

(GODALMING TOWN)　Age: 22

Previous Clubs: Godalming Town; Molesey; Leatherhead

Honours: None

Monsby, Lee　(F)

(OAKWOOD)　Age: 28

Previous Clubs: Horsham; Horsham YMCA; Steyning; Three Bridges; Chipstead; Oakwood

Honours: Dan Air Championship; Sussex County Div 1 Runners-Up (twice); Sussex County Div 2 Championship

Mooney, David　(M)

(KINTBURY RANGERS　Age: 29

Previous Clubs: Hungerford Town; Newbury Town; Thatcham Town; Lambourn; Didcot Town

Honours: Winning League with Newbury Town

Mooney Simon　(D)

(RADCLIFFE BOROUGH)　Age: 20

Previous Clubs: Oldham Athletic

Honours: Lancashire Lge Div 2 Winners

Moore, Andy　(M)

(BILSTON TOWN)　Age: 29

Previous Clubs: Wednesfield; Blakenall; Gresley Rovers.

Honours: Staffs County League Winners; Derbyshire Senior Cup Winners; Midland Combination Div 1 Winners

Moore, Bill　(D)

(HINKLEY ATHLETIC Player Manager)　Age: 36

Previous Clubs: Coventry City; Barwell Athletic; Hinckley Athletic; Bedworth United; Shepshed Charterhouse; Mile Oak Rovers; Leicester United; Melton Town; Sileby Town; Hinckley Town; Hinckley F.C.

Honours: Southern Junior Floodlight Cup; Birmingham Senior Cup; Leicestershire Senior Cup; West Midlands League Runners-Up; Leics County F.A. Caps (30+)

Moore, Bobby　(M)

(HINCKLEY)　Age: 28

Previous Clubs: Hinckley T; Downess Sports; Earl Shilton Albion; Hinckley　**Honours:** Florentine Bowl (Hinckley)

Moore, J　(D/M)

(GENERAL CHEMICALS)　Age: 39

Previous Clubs: Weston British Legion; Runcorn Albion; Runcorn

Honours: Chester Lge; Central Cheshire R/Up; Northwich Cup

Moore, Mark　(M)

(TUNBRIDGE WELLS)　Age: 28

Previous Clubs: Crowborough

Honours: Kent League Champions 1984-85; Kent League Cup Winners 1985-86, 1987-88

Moore, Martin (M/F)
(GUISBOROUGH TOWN) Age: 24

Previous Clubs: Peterlee; Shildon; Stockton; Peterborough United

Honours: Div 2 Champions (twice); North Riding Senior League Runners-Up; League Cup Winners

Moore, Neil (M)
(PRESCOT A.F.C.) Age: 22

Previous Clubs: Bolton Wanderers; Southport F.C.; Loyola College (USA)

Honours: Lancashire County F.A. Youth Team; Named in all-south USA team (1987)

Moore, Peter (M)
(CHELMSLEY TOWN) Age: 23

Previous Clubs: Mile Oak Rovers; Bolehall Swifts; Chelmsley

Honours: Schoolboy honours

Moore, Stephen (G)
(GUISBOROUGH TOWN) Age: 26

Previous Clubs: Whitby Town; Billingham Synthonia

Honours: None

Moore, Tony (Asst. Man./D)
(GAINSBOROUGH TOWN) Age: 32

Previous Clubs: Rochdale; Crewe Alexandra; Sheffield United; Grantham Town; Gainsborough Trinity; York City

Honours: None

Moran, Ed (M)
(MELTON TOWN) Age: 25

Previous Clubs: Willington; Spennymoor **Honours:** None

Moran, Richie (F)
(KETTERING TOWN) Age: 25

Previous Clubs: Fareham T; Gosport Boro; Fujita (Japan); Birmingham C 1990/91 (3-1); Kettering **Honours:** None

Moreland Andy (M)
(LEWES) Age: 20

Previous Clubs: Eastbourne United
Honours: Sussex County Rep

Morey, Alun (M)
(SELSEY) Age: 19

Previous Clubs: Chichester Youth U-18

Honours: Young Player for Selsey 1989; Sussex U-18 Rep.

Morey, Bernard (D)
(SELSEY F.C.) Age: 39

Previous Clubs: None

Honours: Sussex Div 2 Winners (twice); Player of the Year (3)

Morgan, Gareth (F)
(CWMBRAN TOWN) Age: 23

Previous Clubs: Cardiff City **Honours:** Cardiff Schools

Morgan, Ian (D)
(BANBURY UNITED) Age: 22

Previous Clubs: Walsall; Pelsall Villa
Honours: None

Morgan, Martin (D/M)
(BROMLEY) Age: 29

Previous Clubs: Tooting & Mitcham; Hendon; Tooting & Mitcham; Gravesend; Dulwich Hamlet; Carshalton; Dulwich Hamlet

Honours: None

Morgan, Robert (M)
(KEYNSHAM TOWN) Age: 22

Previous Clubs: West Town Harriers; St Pancras; Crosscourt United; Stockwood Green; Broad Plain House

Honours: Somerset League Winners; Somerset Cup Winners; General Portfolio Cup Winners

Morris, Carl (M)
(MOOR GREEN)

D.O.B. 10.11.69
Profession: Quantity Surveyor
Single
Hobbies: Sport

PLAYING CAREER

Honours: Rep Birmingham Boys League

Club	Seasons	Transfer	Apps	Goals
Aston Villa	86-89			
Atherstone	89-90			

MILNER (NETHERFIELD)

Morris, David (M)
(DENABY UNITED) **Age:** 27

Previous Clubs: Spalding United; Eastwood Town

Honours: None

Morris, Marc (F)
(WINGATE) **Age:** 31

Previous Clubs: Wingate; Borehamwood

Honours: Winners Herts Senior Trophy 1988; South Midlands League Div 1 Runners-Up 1990; Scored 492 goals in 16 seasons with Wingate

Morrison, Andy (M)
(PEGASUS JNRS) **Age:** 24

Previous Clubs: Lads Club; Hinton; Llandrindod Wells

Honours: None

Morton, Paul (M)
(SANDWELL BOROUGH) **Age:** 24

Previous Clubs: W.B.A; Dudley Town; Solihull Borough; Wingate

Morwood, Colin (M)
(GAINSBOROUGH TOWN) **Age:** 27

Previous Clubs: Brigg Town; Winterton Rangers; Scunthorpe United **Honours:** None

Moryan, Richard (M)
(CALNE TOWN) **Age:** 19

Previous Clubs: Swindon Town; Devizes Town

Honours: Midland Youth Cup Runners-Up with Swindon (twice)

Mosely, Steve (M)
(ENFIELD)

D.O.B. 26.11.62 **Nickname:** Mose
Profession: Insurance Administrator
Married **Wife's name:** Sally Ann
Hobbies: Golf

PLAYING CAREER

Honours: Essex County Rep; Billericay P.O.Y. 86/87; Barking P.O.Y 88/89

Club	Seasons	Transfer	Apps	Goals
Stambridge	83-85			
Billericay Town	85-87			
Barking	87-89	£6,000		
Dartford	89-91			

Moses, James (F)
(SEATON DELAVEL AMATEURS) **Age:** 27

Previous Clubs: Alnwick Town; Percy Main; Benwell Blues; Washington

Honours: Northumberland Minor Cup Winners Medal; Northumberland Senior Benevolent Bowl Winners Medal; McEwans Northern Alliance Premier Division Championship Winners Medal

Moss, Ernie (F)
(KETTERING TOWN) **D.O.B.** 19.10.49

PLAYING CAREER

Honours: Football League Div 4 Winners 69/70 & 84/85; GMVC R/U 88/89

Club	Seasons	Transfer	Apps	Goals
Chesterfield	68-75	£16,000	271	95
Peterborough United	75-76	£20,000	35	9
Mansfield Town	76-78	£16,000	57	21
Chesterfield	78-80	£15,000	107	33
Port Vale	80-82		74	23
Lincoln City	82-83		11	2
Doncaster Rovers	83-84		44	15
Chesterfield	84-86		91	33
Stockport County	86-87		26	7
Scarborough	87-88		23	4
		(Rochdale - loan 10-2)		
Kettering Town	88-90			
Matlock Town	90-91			
Shepshed C/house	1991			

Mossman, David (M)
(BOSTON UNITED)

D.O.B. 27.7.64 **Nickname:** Mossy
Profession: Sales Manager at Kellogs
Married **Wife's name:** Alison
Hobbies: Golf, DIY

PLAYING CAREER

Honours: England Schoolboy Int; GMVC Winners 87/88

Club	Seasons	Transfer	Apps	Goals
Sheffield Wednesday	82-86			
(Bradford City loan 3-1),				
(Stockport County loan 10-4)				
Rochdale	85-86	£10,000	10	
Stockport County	86-87	£7,000	27	2
Lincoln City	87-88			
Boston United	88-89			
Stafford Rangers	89-90			

Moteane, Dave (D)
(ROMSEY TOWN) **Age:** 20

Previous Clubs: Hedge End Rangers; Portsmouth; Basingstoke Town; Salisbury Town

Honours: Hampshire Senior Cup; Wessex League Champions

Mountford, Dave (D/M)
(EYNESBURY ROVERS) **Age:** 38

Previous Clubs: Northwich Victoria; Stafford Rangers; Milton Utd; Eastwood Hanley; Irchester Eastfield **Honours:** None

Mountford Keith (F)
(LEEK TOWN) **Age:** 28

Previous Clubs: Port Vale; Milton Utd; Eastwood Hanley; Macclesfield; Altrincham

Honours: Northern Premier Lge Winners 85/86, NPL Challenge & Presidents Cup winners 85/86

KEITH MOUNTFIELD

Mountford, Mick (D)
(WELWYN GARDEN CITY) Age: 22
Previous Clubs: Welwyn Garden Utd
Honours: Park Street

Moussaddik, Chokri (G)
(WYCOMBE WANDERERS)

D.O.B. 23.2.70 Nickname: Chuck
PLAYING CAREER
Honours: None

Club	Seasons	Transfer	Apps	Goals
Wimbledon	87-89			

Muldoon, John (Utility)
(NEWTOWN) Age: 25
Previous Clubs: Wrexham; HIK (Finland); Morecambe; Colne Dynamoes; Oswestry; Bangor
Honours: Welsh Cup Winners (Wrexham)

Mulhearn, Terry (F)
(MORETON TOWN) Age: 25
Previous Clubs: Worcester City
Honours: Midland Combination Challenge Trophy Winners Medal 1989-90; Midland Combination Runners-Up League Medal (Res. Div) 1989-90

Mullen, Mark (G)
(BILLINGHAM SYNTHONIA) Age: 24
Previous Clubs: Norton & Stockton Ancients
Honours: Northern League Championship 1988-89, 1989-90; Northern League Cup 1989-90, 1987-88; Durham Cup Winners Trophy 1988-89

Mullen, Richard (G)
(MERTHYR TYDFIL) D.O.B. 4.6.64
PLAYING CAREER
Honours: Welsh Schoolboy Int; Welsh Semi-Pro Int

Club	Seasons	Transfer	Apps	Goals
Ton Pentre	84-88			

Mullineux, Ian (D)
(HORWICH RMI)

D.O.B. 10.11.68 Nickname: Mully
Profession: Not working
Single
Hobbies: Swimming
PLAYING CAREER
Honours: None

Club	Seasons	Transfer	Apps	Goals
Bolton Wanderers	85-87			

Mumford, Rod (D)
(CORNARD UNITED) Age: 36
Previous Clubs: Haverhill Rovers; Sudbury Town; Long Melford
Honours: None

Murcott, Lee (M)
(WALTHAMSTOW PENNANT) Age: 28
Previous Clubs: Barking; Maidstone United
Honours: None

Murgatroyd, Andrew (F)
(CALNE) Age: 26
Previous Clubs: Wills F.C.; Supermarine; Devizes
Honours: Wilts Senior Cup Final Winners; Hellenic Premier Runners-Up

FRANK MURPHY

Murphy Dean (D)

WOKINGHAM TOWN)
Age:

Previous Clubs: Harpenden Town; Barnet (£3,000); Wokingham

Honours: None

Murphy, Frank (F)

BARNET)

D.O.B. 1.6.59

PLAYING CAREER

Honours: Clubcall Cup Winners 88/89; GMVC R/U 87/88 & 89/90

Club	Seasons	Transfer	Apps	Goals
Corby Town	78-80			
Desborough Town	80-82	£2,000		
Kettering Town	82-84	£5,000		
Nuneaton Borough	84-86	£6,000		
Kettering Town	86-87	£10,000		

Murphy, Greg (D)

GENERAL CHEMICALS)
Age: 20

Previous Clubs: Christleton; Frodsham United; Helsby Bicc; F.C. Couchman; Greenbank; Kydds Wine Bar

Honours: Cheshire U-19

Murphy, Stephen (D)

CLITHEROE)
Age: 25

Previous Clubs: Padiham

Honours: North West Counties Division 3 Runners-Up

Murray, Paul (M)

DEAL TOWN)
Age: 20

Previous Clubs: Charlton Athletic; Dover Athletic; Erith & Belvedere; Gravesend & Northfleet; Deal Town; Croydon

Honours: Northern Ireland Youth & Under-21 Int; FA Youth Cup R/U

Murray, Stephen (D)

FARLEIGH ROVERS)
Age: 30

Previous Clubs: Banstead

Honours: None

Murtagh, Dave (D)

NEWCASTLE TOWN)
Age: 29

Previous Clubs: Kidsgrove Athletic; Buxton; Droylsden; Congleton Town

Honours: Mid-Cheshire League Winners & Cup Winners; HFS Loans Div 1 Runners-Up; Cup Runners-Up

Myers, Gary (G)

KNOWSLEY UNITED)
Age: 29

Previous Clubs: Vauxhall GM; Formby

Honours: League Player of the Month 1989 for Bass NWCL

Myles, Richard Alan (D)

(DENABY UNITED)
Age: 24

Previous Clubs: Leeds United; Kiveton Park; Mexborough Town; Sheffield Club; Gainsborough Trinity

Honours: None

PAUL MOODY (WATERLOOVILLE)

Nash, Keith (G)

(CHIPPENHAM TOWN)   Age: 33

Previous Clubs: Calne Town; Bristol City

Honours: Wiltshire County Rep. Western League Div 1 Winners 1982 (Capt); Over 500 games for Chippenham Town

Nash, Garry (F)

(FARLEIGH ROVERS)   Age: 28
Previous Clubs: Malden Town   **Honours:** None

Naylor, Lee (M)

(A.F.C. LYMINGTON)   Age: 19
Previous Clubs: Poole Town; Bashley   **Honours:** None

Nazir, Subtan (D)

(FARSLEY CELTIC)   Age: 26
Previous Clubs: Thackley   **Honours:** None

Neal, John (F)

(BISHOP'S STORTFORD)   D.O.B. 11.3.66

PLAYING CAREER

Honours: England Schoolboy Int

Club	Seasons	Transfer	Apps	Goals
Millwall	82-84		6	1
Barnet	84-85			
Walthamstow Avenue	85-86			
Basildon United	1986			
Harlow Town	86-87			
Dagenham	87-88			
Barking	88-89			

Nealon Philip (F)

(WINSFORD UNITED)   Age: 25

Previous Clubs: Blackpool; Altrincham; Flixton; Derby County; Seattle Sounders (USA)

Honours: None

Neate, Paul (M)

(WESTBURY UNITED)   Age: 24

Previous Clubs: Trowbridge Town; Odd Down

Honours: Westbury United Player of the Year 1989-90

eedham, Michael (D)

(ALFRETON TOWN)   Age: 18
Previous Clubs: Local football   **Honours:** None

Neil, Graham (M)

(WESTHOUGHTON TOWN)   Age: 28

Previous Clubs: Wigan Youth; Crown F.C.; Wigan College

Honours: Wigan A.L. Premier Champions (5); Laithwaite Shield Winners (6); Hughes Cup Winners (6); L.E.A. Shield Runners-Up; L.W.L. League Winners; L.F.A. Inter League Winners; Wigan Cup Winners

Nelson, Paul (D)

(RHYL)   Age: 22

Previous Clubs: Whitchurch Alport; Wrexham; Malpas; Telford United

Honours: FA Trophy Winners

Nethercott, Kyle (F)

(KEYNSHAM TOWN)   Age: 26

Previous Clubs: Hengrove Athletic; Robinsons DRG

Honours: Somerset Senior Cup Winners (Hengrove)

Nethercott, Stuart (D)

(KEYNSHAM TOWN)   Age: 22

Previous Clubs: Hengrove Athletic; Odd Down; Frome Town

Honours: Somerset Senior Cup (Hengrove); Somerset County Honours

Neufville, Paul (M)

(HITCHIN TOWN)   Age: 24

Previous Clubs: Vauxhall Motors; The 61 FC (Luton); Barnet; Langford

Honours: Beds County Rep

Newcombe, Giles (G)

(GAINSBOROUGH TRINITY)   D.O.B. 7.9.68

Nickname: Chucky-Chucky **Profession:** Warehouse Operative
Married   **Wife's name:** Joanne
Hobbies: Sport

PLAYING CAREER

Honours: None

Club	Seasons	Transfer	Apps	Goals
Rotherham United	84-89		7	

Newell, Andy (G)

(WITTON ALBION)   D.O.B. 18.5.62

Nickname: Juggler   **Profession:** Salesman
Married   **Wife's name:** Mel
Children: David   **Hobbies:** Fishing, Squash

PLAYING CAREER

Honours: None

Club	Seasons	Transfer	Apps	Goals
Wren Rovers	85-89			

Newland, Ray (G)

(NEWTOWN)   Age: 19
Previous Clubs: Chester City; Winsford   **Honours:** None

Newman, Andy (D)

(GODALMING TOWN)   Age: 28
Previous Clubs: Guildford & Worplesden   **Honours:** None

Newman, David (D)

(DULWICH HAMLET)   Age: 20

Previous Clubs: Crystal Palace; Whyteleafe; Bromley

Honours: None

Newman, Dick   (D)
(BIGGLESWADE TOWN)   Age: 32
Previous Clubs: Stotfold; Arlesey; Biggleswade Town; Potton United
Honours: Beds Premier Cup; UCL Champions (twice); Hinchingbrook Cup; Senior Cup; Charity Cup; UCL League Cup; Beds County Cup

Newman, Paul   (D)
(WARMINSTER TOWN)   Age: 29
Previous Clubs: Warminster Town; Calne Town
Honours: None

Newman, Paul   (D/M)
(OADBY TOWN)   Age: 19
Previous Clubs: Wigston Fields; Oadby Town; Leicester United
Honours: County Youth level; Lincoln F.C. (Apprentice)

Newton Doug   (M)
(HEDNESFORD TOWN)   Age: 31
Previous Clubs: Chesterfield; Eastwood Town; Alfreton Town; Belper Town; Burton Albion; Altrincham; Shepshed Charterhouse; Boston United; Scarborough (5); Stafford Rangers; Goole Town; Eastwood Town; Bedworth United
Honours: England Semi-Pro Int; FA Trophy Winners

Newton, Paul   (M)
(CHEADLE TOWN)   Age: 22
Previous Clubs: Manchester City; Flixton; Stockport County
Honours: Stockport Boys

Nevitt, Gary   (M)
(GUISBOROUGH TOWN)   Age: 18
Previous Clubs: Nottingham Forest
Honours: North Riding Rep. Cleveland

Niblett, Nigel   (D)
(VS RUGBY)   D.O.B. 12.8.67
Nickname: Nibbo   **Profession:** Fitter
Single   **Hobbies:** Sport
Previous Clubs: Snitterfield Sports; Stratford Town
Honours: FA XI; Westgate Insurance Cup Winners; Birmingham Senior Cup Winners; Midland Floodlit Cup Winners; Stratford P.O.Y.85/86

Nicely, Donald   (D)
(CONGLETON TOWN)   D.O.B. 29.4.64
Profession: Financial Adviser
Single   **Hobbies:** Golf, Squash
Previous Clubs: Leek Town; Droylesden
Honours: Leek P.O.Y.87/88

Nichol, Bryan   (D)
(SHOTTON COMRADES)   Age: 20
Previous Clubs: Chester-le-Street
Honours: None

Nicholas, Alan   (F)
(RHYL)   Age: 22
Previous Clubs: Malpas; Llay RBL   **Honours:** None

Nicholls, Adam   (M)
(HALESOWEN HARRIERS)   Age: 21
Previous Clubs: Wolverhampton Wanderers; Kidderminster Harriers; Willenhall Town; Halesowen Harriers
Honours: None

Nicholls, Steve   (M)
(BRIDGWATER TOWN 1984)   Age: 26
Previous Clubs: Bridgwater Town; Taunton Town
Honours: Somerset Senior League Championship 1989-90; Somerset Senior League K.O. Cup 1989-90

Nicholson, Paul   (M/F)
(GATESHEAD)   D.O.B. 13.8.68
Nickname: Nicho   **Profession:** Spray Painter
Single   **Hobbies:** Golf
Previous Clubs: Winlaton YD; Chester-le-Street; Winlaton YD
Honours: Newcastle Schoolboy Rep; Gateshead District Boys Rep.

Nicholson, Tony   (D)
(SELBY TOWN)   Age: 19
Previous Clubs: York City Intermediates
Honours: North Yorkshire & West Riding County Rep. Honours; NCE Div 2 Runners-Up 1990

Nicol, Paul   (D)
(KETTERING TOWN)   D.O.B. 31.10.67
Profession: Not working   **Single**
Hobbies: Sport   **Honours:** None

PLAYING CAREER

Club	Seasons	Transfer	Apps	Goals
Scunthorpe United	84-90		75	2

Nisbett, Walter   (M)
(ALTRINCHAM)   D.O.B. 10.2.60
Nickname: Nesser   **Profession:** Lorry Driver
Single   **Hobbies:** Cars
Previous Clubs: Wythenshawe Am.; Barrow; Mossley; Hyde United; Winsford Utd.
Honours: None

Noble, Wayne   (M)
(GLOUCESTER CITY)   D.O.B. 11.6.67
Nickname: Bunter   **Profession:** Not working
Single   **Hobbies:** Sport

PLAYING CAREER

Honours: None

Club	Seasons	Transfer	Apps	Goals
Bristol Rovers	83-87		21	1
Yeovil Town	87-88			

PAUL NICHOLSON (Gateshead)

PAUL NICHOL (Kettering)

Nock, David (G)

(BRIDGNORTH TOWN) Age: 26

Previous Clubs: G.K.N. Sankey; Newport Town
Honours: None

Norman, Sean (D)

(CHESHAM UNITED) D.O.B. 27.11.66

Previous Clubs: Lowestoft Town; Colchester Utd. (21 + 1); Wycombe Wands.; Wealdstone (£10,000)
Honours: None

Norton, Dave (D)

(WELWYN GARDEN CITY) Age: 24

Previous Clubs: Welwyn Garden United; Stevenage Borough
Honours: Herts U-16s

Norton, Paul (G)

(WORKSOP TOWN) Age: 20

Previous Clubs: Sheffield Utd; Hartlepool Utd; Bridlington Town
Honours: Northern Intermediate League Winners

Norton, Trace (F)

(EXMOUTH TOWN) Age:

Previous Clubs: Aston Villa; Gresley Rovers
Honours: None

Noteman, Wayne (M)

(BRIDLINGTON TOWN) Age: 25

Previous Clubs: Yorkshire Main; Harrogate RA; Goole Town; Farsley Celtic; Harrogate Town; Frickley Athletic
Honours: Northern Counties East Lge Winners; FA Vase R/U 89/90

Nugent, Richard (D)

(BARNET) D.O.B. 20.3.64

Nickname: Beckenbauer **Profession:** Toolmaker
Married **Wife's name:** Joanne
Hobbies: Golf, Squash **Honours:** None

PLAYING CAREER

Club	Seasons	Transfer	Apps	Goals
Royston Town	84-86			
Stevenage Borough	86-87			
Hitchin Town	1987			
St.Albans City	87-88			

Nunn, David (M)

(GAINSBOROUGH TOWN) Age: 25

Previous Clubs: East Midland United; Woodsetts Welfare; Cottam F.C.
Honours: Nursing Cup, Notts Junior Cup, Retford Div 2 (all with Cottam)

Nunn, Phil (G/D)

(GAINSBOROUGH TOWN) Age: 21

Previous Clubs: Worksop Town; Cottam F.C.
Honours: None

Nuttell, Michael (F)

(WYCOMBE WANDERERS) D.O.B. 22.11.68

Nickname: Nutty **Profession:** Not working
Single **Hobbies:** Snooker, Squash

PLAYING CAREER

Honours: None

Club	Seasons	Transfer	Apps	Goals
Peterborough United	85-88	£8,000	21	
Crewe Alexandra		loan	3	1
Carlisle United		loan	2	
Gloucester Town	88-91			
Cheltenham Town	1991	£6,000		

ERNIE MOSS (KETTERING TOWN)

O'Berg, Paul (M)

(HORWICH RMI) D.O.B. 8.5.58

Profession: Company Director
Married **Wife's name:** Helen
Children: Nikki, Ben & Laurie
Hobbies: Business & Football

PLAYING CAREER

Honours: Malta Lge Div 1 Winners 87/88; Div 2 Winners 86/87 & Div 3 Winners 85/86 & Premier Div Winners 88/89; Naxxar P.O.Y. 87/88; Sliema P.O.Y. 88/89

Club	Seasons	Transfer	Apps	Goals
Bridlington Trinity	77-79			
Scunthorpe United	79-84		165	30
Stockport County		loan	3	
Chester City		loan	6	2
Wimbledon	84-85		8	
Rotorua (N.Z.)	1985		(Player-Manager)	
Naxxar Lions (Malta)	85-88	£25,000		
Sliema Wndrs (Malta)	88-89			

O'Brien, Andrew (D)

(HENDON) D.O.B. 22.5.63

Nickname: Nob **Profession:** Accountant
Single
Hobbies: Tropical Fish, Tennis, Swimming

PLAYING CAREER

Honours: Middx Schoolboy Rep; England Schoolboy Squad Rep; Vauxhall Lge Rep XI; Middx Senior Cup Winners; Middx Charity Cup Winners; Hendon P.O.Y. (2)

Club	Seasons	Transfer	Apps	Goals
Hendon	81-87			
Kingsbury Town	87-89			

O'Brien, Christopher (D)

(HYDE UNITED) D.O.B. 21.2.70

Nickname: O'B **Profession:** Postman
Single
Hobbies: Golf, Snooker

PLAYING CAREER

Honours: Lancs Youth Cup Winners 86/87 & 87/88; HFS Loans Lge Cup Winners 89/90; Cheshire Senior Cup Winners 89/90; Clubcall Cup R/U 89/90

Club	Seasons	Transfer	Apps	Goals
Bolton Wanmderers	86-89			

O'Brien, Denis (G)

(MALDEN VALE) Age: 32

Previous Clubs: Finchley; Epping Town; Hertford Town; Croydon
Honours: None

O'Brien, John (M)

(STRATFORD TOWN) Age: 30

Previous Clubs: Army Football; RAF League Rep. Team (London & Mids)

Honours: Army Cup Runners-Up; League Challenge Cup Winners 1988-89

O'Brien, Sean (D)

(BILLINGHAM SYNTHONIA) Age: 25

Previous Clubs: Shildon; Norton & Stockton Ancients; Billingham Town

Honours: Northern League Championship Trophy 1989-90

O'Callaghan, Phil (M)

(WALTHAMSTOW PENNANT) Age: 27

Previous Clubs: Millwall Res.

Honours: Spartan League Cup Winners Medal 1988-89

O'Connor, Malcolm (F)

(NORTHWICH VICTORIA)

D.O.B. 25.4.65

PLAYING CAREER

Honours: NPL Cup Winners; Mid-Cheshire Senior Cup Winners; Staffs Senior Cup Winners

Club	Seasons	Transfer	Apps	Goals
Curzon Ashton	81-82			
Rochdale	82-83		16	3
Curzon Ashton	83-85			
Hyde United	85-88	£10,000		

O'Donovan, Anthony (D)

(SOMERSHAM TOWN) Age: 21

Previous Clubs: St Ives Town
Honours: None

O'Driscoll, Paul (M)

(SALISBURY) Age: 19

Previous Clubs: Southampton; Swindon Town; Wycombe Wanderers
Honours: None

O'Hagan, Patrick (G)

(CWMBRAN TOWN) Age: 19

Previous Clubs: Newport County; Cardiff City; Stroud
Honours: Welsh Youth Cup Winner with Cardiff City

O'Hehir, John (D)

(BROMLEY) Age: 25

Previous Clubs: Millwall; Crystal Palace; Leyton Wingate
Honours: Vauxhall Opel Div 1 (L. Wingate)

O'Kane, Paul (D)

(HEANOR TOWN) Age: 20

Previous Clubs: Matlock Town
Honours: None

O'Leary John (M)

(MALDEN VALE) Age: 26

Previous Clubs: Bromley **Honours:** None

O'Leary, Kevin   (F)
(NEWBURY TOWN)   **Age:** 24
Previous Clubs: Nutfield United; Romsey Town; Bashley
Honours: Soton League & Cup Winners; Wessex League Winners & Cup Runners-Up; Beazer Homes Southern Div Winners

O'Loughlin, Colin   (M)
(CHEADLE TOWN)   **Age:** 24
Previous Clubs: Maine Road; Flixton
Honours: Manchester League Championship & Gilgryst Cup Winners

Oliver, Lee   (M)
(DENABY UNITED)   **Age:** 21
Previous Clubs: Matlock Town; Sheffield Wednesday; Gainsborough Trinity; Worksop Town; Eastwood Town; Goole Town; Alfreton Town
Honours: Sheffield U-15 English Schools Winners; S. Yorkshire U-15 Winners; N.I.L.C. Runners-Up

Oliver, Richard   (M)
(SELBY TOWN)   **Age:** 22
Previous Clubs: None
Honours: None

Oliver, Tony   (G)
(WEYMOUTH)

D.O.B. 22.9.67   **Nickname:** T.O.
Profession: Not working
Single
Hobbies: Art, Music, Antiques

PLAYING CAREER
Honours: Dorset Schoolboy Rep; South of England Schoolboy Rep; FA XI

Club	Seasons	Transfer	Apps	Goals
Portsmouth	83-86			
Brentford	87-88		12	

O'Neill, Shaun   (D)
(ALFRETON TOWN)   **Age:** 38
Previous Clubs: Leeds United; Chesterfield(450-5); Matlock Town
Honours: Football Lge Div 4 Winners; Anglo-Scottish Cup Winners

Orton, Mark   (M)
(HINCKLEY ATHLETIC)   **Age:** 22
Previous Clubs: Nuneaton Boro'; Atherstone
Honours: None

Orr, Peter   (D)
(KNOWSLEY UNITED)   **Age:** 31
Previous Clubs: Prescot Cable; Northwich Victoria; Southport
Honours: None

Orrell, Steve   (F)
(CLITHEROE)   **Age:** 26
Previous Clubs: Ashton United; Prestwich Heys; Leek Town
Honours: Leek Town Player of the Season 1986-87

Osborne, Gary   (D)
(HORNCHURCH)   **Age:** 22
Previous Clubs: Local football
Honours: None

O'Sullivan, Willie   (M)
(CRAWLEY TOWN)   **D.O.B.** 5.10.59
PLAYING CAREER
Honours: Irish Youth Int

Club	Seasons	Transfer	Apps	Goals
Charlton Athletic	76-77		2	
Dartford	77-84			
Gravesend & N'fleet	84-85			
Fisher Athletic	85-86			
Dover Athletic	86-88			
Crawley Town	1988			
Dulwich Hamlet	1988			
Crawley Town	88-89			
Bromley	1989			

SEAN O'CONNELL
(Hampton)

Pace, Jeffrey   (M)

(GENERAL CHEMICALS)   Age: 36

Previous Clubs: Runcorn Boys Club

Honours: Runcorn F.A. Cup Winners; League Winners; Northwich F.A. Cup Winners

Packer, Tim   (M)

(AFC LYMINGTON)   Age: 27

Previous Clubs: Wellworthy Athletic

Honours: Bournemouth Senior Cup Winners; Wessex League Cup Winners; Hants Intermediate Rep.; Hants Senior Cup Runners-Up

Paige, Jason   (G)

(TUNBRIDGE WELLS)   Age: 19

Previous Clubs: Maidstone United; Corinthian

Honours: Kent Intermediate Cup

Painter, Robert   (D)

(NEWPORT AFC)   Age: 19

Previous Clubs: Cardiff City

Honours: Hellenic League Champions

Palgrave, Brian   (M)

(STAFFORD RANGERS)   D.O.B. 12.7.66

Nickname: Pally   Profession: Postman

Married   Wife's name: Rachel
Children: Christopher
Hobbies: Snooker, Swimming, Badminton

PLAYING CAREER

Honours: Nuneaton P.O.Y. 87/88

Club	Seasons	Transfer	Apps	Goals
Walsall	83-87		19	5
Kettering Town	1987			
Port Vale	1987		4	
Nuneaton Borough	87-88	£3,000		
Bromsgrove Rovers	88-90			

Palmer, David   (D)

(BATH CITY)   D.O.B. 10.4.61

Profession: Sales Rep
Married   Wife's name: Cath
Children: James
Hobbies: Golf

PLAYING CAREER

Honours: Beazer Homes Lge Premier Div R/U 89/90; Bath P.O.Y. 83/84

Club	Seasons	Transfer	Apps	Goals
Bristol Rovers	77-81		1	

Palmer, Wayne   (M)

(SANDWELL BOROUGH)   Age: 28

Previous Clubs: Bromsgrove; Lye Town
Honours: None

Pamphlett, Tony   (D)

(REDBRIDGE FOREST)

D.O.B. 13.4.60

PLAYING CAREER

Honours: Kent Schoolboy Rep; GMVC Winners 88/89

Club	Seasons	Transfer	Apps	Goals
Cray Wanderers	78-84			
Dartford	84-86			
Maidstone United	86-90		7	

Pape, Andy   (G)

(ENFIELD)   D.O.B. 22.3.62

PLAYING CAREER

Honours: England semi-Pro Int.; Gola League Winners 85/86; F.A/ Trophy Winners 1988; Middlesex senior Cup Winners.

Club	Seasons	Transfer	Apps	Goals
Q.P.R.	79-80		1	
Ikast (Den)				
Crystal Palce				
Charlton Athletic				
Feltham				
Harrow Borough				

ANDY PAPE

Pardey, Graham   (D)

(AFC LYMINGTON)   Age: 28

Previous Clubs: Lymington Town; Wellworthy Athletic; Brockenhurst
Honours: Bournemouth Senior Cup; Wessex League Cup Winners; Hants Senior Cup Runners-Up

Parker, Andrew   (M)

(SOMERSHAM TOWN)   Age: 30

Previous Clubs: Norwich City; Cambridge City; Ely City; Soham Rangers
Honours: None

Parker, Carl   (M)

(DROYLESDEN)   Age: 19

Previous Clubs: Burnley; Colne Dynamoes
Honours: None

Parker, Derrick   (F)
(FRICKLEY ATHLETIC)

D.O.B. 7.2.57

PLAYING CAREER

Honours: Football League Div 3 & 4 Winners; Mid-Cheshire Senior Cup Winners (2); Staffs Senior Cup Winners

Club	Seasons	Transfer	Apps	Goals
Burnley	74-75		6	2
Southend United	75-79		129	43
Barnsley	79-82		107	32
Oldham Athletic	82-84		57	11
Doncaster Rovers		loan	5	1
Burnley	84-86		43	10
Rochdale	86-87		7	1
North Ferriby United	1987			
Northwich Victoria	87-90			

Parker, Jeff   (D)
(NORTHWICH VICTORIA)

D.O.B. 23.1.69

PLAYING CAREER

Honours: None

Club	Seasons	Transfer	Apps	Goals
Crewe Alexandra	87-88		10	

Parker, Robert   (F)
(ALFRETON TOWN)   Age: 21

Previous Clubs: Sheffield United; Gainsborough Trinity
Honours: None

Parker, Sean   (F)
(WESTHOUGHTON TOWN)   Age: 25

Previous Clubs: Elton Fold

Honours: L.E.A. Shield Winners; Bolton Comb. Premier Winners

Parkinson, Keith   (M)
(FLEETWOOD TOWN)

D.O.B. 7.8.63
Profession: Not working
Single
Hobbies: Golf, Reading

PLAYING CAREER

Honours: None

Club	Seasons	Transfer	Apps	Goals
Manchester City	79-82			
Sligo Rovers	82-83			

Parnaby, David   (D)
(BARROW)   D.O.B. 20.11.54

Profession: P.E.Teacher
Married   **Wife's name:** Jean
Children: Ian & Stuart   **Hobbies:** Cricket, Family

PLAYING CAREER

Honours: Durham Schoolboy Rep; FA XI; NPL Winners 82/83 & 85/86; Gateshead P.O.Y. 83/84

Club	Seasons	Transfer	Apps	Goals
Spennymoor United	71-72			
Durham City	76-78			
Gateshead	78-90			

Parnham, Lawrie   (G)
(SOMERSHAM TOWN)   Age: 28

Previous Clubs: Waltham Abbey
Honours: None

Parr, Andy   (M)
(WOKING)

D.O.B. 8.10.66   **Nickname:** Parry
Profession: Sales Rep
Single
Hobbies: Golf, Sport

PLAYING CAREER

Honours: Reading Schoolboy Rep; Berks Schoolboy & Youth Rep; England Schoolboy Int.; South East Counties Lge Winners; Football Combination Winners; Southern Junior Cup R/U; Vauxhall-Opel Lge Div 1 & 2 R/U; FA XI

Club	Seasons	Transfer	Apps	Goals
West Ham United	83-86			
Farnborough Town	1986			
Marlow	86-87			
Woking	87-88			
Chertsey Town	88-89			

Parr, Iain   (D)
(EYNESBURY ROVERS)   Age: 22

Previous Clubs: St Neots Town
Honours: Scott Gatty Cup Winners 1990

Parris, Pip   (F)
(LEWES)   Age: 31

Previous Clubs: Lewes; Worthing
Honours: Sussex FA Rep; Vauxhall Lge Golden Boot Winner 87/88

Parry, David   (D)
(BILLINGHAM SYNTHONIA)   Age: 30

Previous Clubs: South Bank; Whitby Town; Billingham Synthonia; Shildon; Peterlee

Honours: Northern League 2nd Div Trophy 1986-87; Northern League Cup 1987-88, 1989-90; Northern League Championship 1988-89, 1989-90; Durham Cup Winners Trophy 1988-89

Parselle, Norman   (Utility)
(NEWPORT AFC)   Age: 20

Previous Clubs: Newport County; Stroud
Honours: Hellenic League Champions 1989-90

Pascucei, Giulio (F)
(WINGATE) Age: 26
Previous Clubs: None
Honours: None

Pask, Andrew (D)
(DARTFORD)

D.O.B. 9.11.70
Profession: Land Referencer
Single
Hobbies: Cars

PLAYING CAREER
Honours: None

Club	Seasons	Transfer	Apps	Goals
West Ham United	87-89			
Redbridge Forest	89-90			

Pask, Ray (D/M)
(SAWBRIDGEWORTH TOWN) Age: 30
Previous Clubs: Harlow Town (1977-84); Grays
Honours: Isthmian Youth Cup; Vauxhall Opel League Div 1 Runners-Up 1982-83

Pass, Stuart (D)
(CHELMSLEY TOWN) Age: 22
Previous Clubs: Moor Green (1986-87); Sutton Town (1987-88)
Honours: Goal of the Season; Player of the Year & Supporters Player

Pateman Colin (D)
(LEWES) Age: 35
Previous Clubs: None
Honours: Sussex County Rep

Paterson, Billy (F)
(CHIPSTEAD) Age: 34
Previous Clubs: Hamilton Academicals; Crystal Palace; Crawley Town; Whyteleafe
Honours: Hamilton Schoolboys U-15; Lanarkshire Schoolboys U-15; Scotland U-15 International

ayne, David (M)
(BATH CITY)

D.O.B. 22.5.62
Profession: Chef
Single
Hobbies: Manager of Bemmy Down Sunday Side (Bristol)

PLAYING CAREER
Honours: FA XI; Beazer Homes Midland Div Winners 88/89; Beazer Homes Premier Div R/U 89/90

Club	Seasons	Transfer	Apps	Goals
Bath City	85-88	£2,000		
Gloucester City	88-89			

Payne Lawrence (F)
(WINSFORD UNITED) Age: 24
Previous Clubs: Whitchurch Alport
Honours: None

Payne, Mick (M)
(CHIPPENHAM TOWN) Age: 23
Previous Clubs: Kettering Town; Rothwell Town
Honours: None

Payne, Shane (D)
(SOMERSHAM TOWN) Age: 29
Previous Clubs: Ely City; Soham; Chatteris Town
Honours: None

Peace, John (G)
(BANBURY UNITED) Age: 32
Previous Clubs: Blakenall; Pelsall C & S; Wolverhampton United; Deeley's; Pelsall Villa; Harrisons
Honours: None

Peaks, Andrew (D)
(RUSHDEN TOWN)

D.O.B. 25.11.70   Nickname: Peaksy
Profession: Warehouse Manager
Single
Hobbies: Fishing, Cricket
Previous Clubs: Northampton Town (86-89)
Honours: Northants Schoolboy Rep; Beazer Homes Midland Div R/U 89/90

RUSSELL PARMELO
(Bromsgrove Rovers)

Pearce, Graham (D)
(ENFIELD)

D.O.B. 8.7.59   **Nickname:** Franz
Profession: Football Coach
Single
Hobbies: Coaching Kids

PLAYING CAREER

Honours: None

Club	Seasons	Transfer	Apps	Goals
Hillingdon Borough	75-78			
Barnet	78-81			
Brighton & Hove A.	81-86		88	2
Gillingham	86-88		65	
Brentford	88-89		18	
Maidstone United	89-90		27	

Pearman, Alan (G)
(CORNARD UNITED)   Age: 34

Previous Clubs: Braintree; Halstead; Sudbury Town; Clacton; Cornard United

Honours: None

Pears, Carl (D/M)
(HINCKLEY)   Age: 19

Previous Clubs: Barwell Athletic; Earl Shilton Albion; Hinckley Athletic

Honours: Leicestershire Senior League Div 1 Winners 1988-89 (Earl Shilton)

Pearson, Mark (F)
(CLEATOR MOOR CELTIC)   Age: 24

Previous Clubs: Barrow; Workington
Honours: None

BENNY PHILLIPS
(Mossley)

Pearson, Richard (M)
(BURNHAM RAMBLERS)   Age: 19

Previous Clubs: None

Honours: Essex Senior League Div 1 Winners; Bill Spurgeon Cup Runners-Up; Mid-Essex Charity Cup Winners

Pearson Sean (M)
(HITCHIN TOWN)   Age: 24

Previous Clubs: Langford
Honours: None

Peel, David (D)
(CONGLETON TOWN)

D.O.B. 26.11.52
Profession: Computer Operator
Single
Hobbies: Sport

PLAYING CAREER

Honours: Cheshire Senior Cup Winners

Club	Seasons	Transfer	Apps	Goals
Whitley Bay				
Bangor City				
Altrincham				
Macclesfield Town				

Pemberton Tony (M)
(RADCLIFFE BOROUGH)   Age: 22

Previous Clubs: Preston North End; Atherton LR; Lancaster City; Colne Dynamoes
Honours: None

Penhaligon, Garry (G)
(BOGNOR REGIS TOWN)

D.O.B. 13.5.70   **Nickname:** Bingo
Profession: Football Coach
Single
Hobbies: Golf

PLAYING CAREER

Honours: Cornwall Schoolboy & Youth Rep; Cornwall County XI Rep

Club	Seasons	Transfer	Apps	Goals
Newquay	85-86			
Plymouth Argyle	86-89		2	
Newquay	89-90			

Penny, Derrick (F)
(WARMINSTER TOWN)   Age: 27

Previous Clubs: Warminster Town; Westbury United
Honours: None

Penrose, Stuart (M)
(SANDWELL BOROUGH)   Age: 24

Previous Clubs: Dudley Town; Princes End United; Gornal
Honours: None

Perrett, Dave   (F)

(AFC LYMINGTON)   Age: 22

Previous Clubs: Lymington Town; Wellworthy Athletic

Honours: Bournemouth Senior Cup; Hants Senior Cup Finalist; Herts Senior Rep.

Perry, David   (M)

(GAINSBOROUGH TRINITY)

D.O.B. 14.5.67   **Nickname:** Fred
Profession: Fitter
Single
Hobbies: Sport

PLAYING CAREER

Honours: None

Club	Seasons	Transfer	Apps	Goals
Chesterfield	87-89		17	
Sheffield FC	89-90			

Perry, Matthew   (D/M)

(CHIPSTEAD)   Age: 19

Previous Clubs: Nork Sunday F.C.

Honours: None

Pethick, Robbie   (M/D)

(SALTASH UNITED)   Age: 19

Previous Clubs: Plymouth Argyle

Honours: Plymouth Schoolboys; Devon Schoolboys; South West Counties Champions 1988-89

Petruccio, Nino   (D)

(WALTHAMSTOW PENNANT)   Age: 26

Previous Clubs: Walthamstow Avenue

Honours: Represented London F.A.; Spartan Cup Winners Medal 1988-89

Phillips Benny   (D)

(MOSSLEY)   Age: 30

Previous Clubs: Crewe Alexandra; Bury (14); Winsford United; Stalybridge Celtic; Mossley; Witton Albion; Barrow; Buxton; Witton Albion; Chorley; Stalybridge Celtic; Droylsden; Rossendale United

Honours: None

Phillips, Clifford   (D)

(KINTBURY RANGERS)   Age: 25

Previous Clubs: Wantage Town; Kintbury; Lambourn; Didcot Town

Honours: None

Phillips, Gary   (G)

(WELWYN GARDEN CITY)   Age: 20

Previous Clubs: Hertford Town; St. Albans City; Little Heath

Honours: Herts Schools U-18

Phillips, Gary   (G)

(BARNET)

D.O.B. 20.9.61   **Nickname:** Stig or Spit
Profession: Groundsman
Married   **Wife's name:** Sonia
Children: Elisha
Hobbies: Golf, Cricket, Gardening

PLAYING CAREER

Honours: South of England Schoolboy;Rep; England Semi-Pro Int; FA XI; Freight Rover Trophy R/U 84/85; Barnet P.O.Y. 82/83 & 83/84; Brentford P.O.Y. 85/86

Club	Seasons	Transfer	Apps	Goals
Brighton and Hove A.	78-79			
West Bromwich Albion	79-81			
Barnet	81-84	£5,000		
Brentford	84-88	£25,000	171	
Reading	88-89	£12,500	34	
Hereford Utd		loan	6	

Phillips, Greg   (M)

(NORTHWOOD)   Age: 24

Previous Clubs: Wembley

Honours: Spartan League Runners-Up 1989-90; Spart League Cup Winners 1989-90

Phillips, Ian   (D)

(KETTERING TOWN)

D.O.B. 23.4.59
Profession: Gas Engineer
Married   **Wife's name:** Fiona
Children: Laura & Jenna
Hobbies: Golf

PLAYING CAREER

Honours: South East Counties Lge & Cup Winners

Club	Seasons	Transfer	Apps	Goals
Ipswich Town	75-77			
Mansfield Town	77-79		23	
Peterborough United	79-82	£5,000	97	3
Northampton Town	82-83		42	1
Colchester United	83-86		150	10
Aldershot	87-90		106	2

Pickering, Neil   (D)

(WORKSOP TOWN)   Age: 29

Previous Clubs: Crookes F.C.; Sutton Town

Honours: Central Midlands Cup Winners (Crookes)

Piggon, Adrian   (D)

(BEDWORTH UNITED)   Age: 22

Previous Clubs: Nuneaton Borough

Honours: None

Piggott, Stephen (F)
(CONGLETON TOWN)

D.O.B. 25.12.62   **Nickname:** Piggy
Profession: Postman
Married   **Wife's name:** Diane
Children: Ashley & Lewis
Hobbies: Walking, Speedway

PLAYING CAREER
Honours: Crewe Schoolboy Rep; Mid-Cheshire Senior Cup R/U 86/87; Congleton P.O.Y. 88/89

Club	Seasons	Transfer	Apps	Goals
Nantwich Town	78-80			
Winsford United	80-83			
Nantwich Town	83-85			
Winsford United	86-88			

Pilkington, Anthony (M)
(CLEATOR MOOR CELTIC)   Age: 27
Previous Clubs: Cleator United
Honours: None

Pike, Richard (M)
(BRIDGNORTH TOWN)   Age: 25
Previous Clubs: Newtown   **Honours:** None

Pinkowski, Dave (M)
(NEWMARKET)   Age: 33
Previous Clubs: Kings Lynn; Mildenhall; Thetford Town
Honours: None

Plaskett, Stephen (D)
(GATESHEAD)

D.O.B. 24.4.71   **Nickname:** Placa
Profession: Not working
Single
Hobbies: Saturday Nights, Golf

PLAYING CAREER
Honours: Newcastle Schoolboy Rep; Northumberland Youth Rep

Club	Seasons	Transfer	Apps	Goals
North Shields	88-89			
Hartlepool United	89-90		20	

Pluckrose, Allan (M)
(AYLESBURY UNITED)

D.O.B. 3.7.63   **Nickname:** Breigal
Profession: Physical Training Instructor
Married   **Wife's name:** Margaret
Children: Ryan
Hobbies: Cycling, Triathlon, Music

PLAYING CAREER
Honours: Devon Youth Rep; FA XI; Combined Services Rep

Club	Seasons	Transfer	Apps	Goals
Falmouth Town	80-82			
Torquay United	82-83		3	
SV Viktoria Goch (Ger)	85-88			

Pocock, Burgess (D)
(BILLERICAY TOWN)   Age: 26
Previous Clubs: Basildon United
Honours: None

Poole, David (M)
(BOGNOR REGIS TOWN)

D.O.B. 25.11.62
Profession: Accountant
Married   **Wife's name:** Amanda
Children: Thomas
Hobbies: Football, Cricket

PLAYING CAREER
Honours: Sussex Schoolboy & Youth Rep; AC Delco Cup Winners 86/87; Sussex Senior Cup Winners (6) 79/80 - 83/84 & 86/87; Bognor P.O.Y. 83/84 & 84/85

Club	Seasons	Transfer	Apps	Goals
Wick	77-78			
Southampton	78-80			

Poole, Gary (D/M)
(BARNET)

D.O.B. 11.9.67
Profession: Not working
Single
Hobbies: Golf, Tennis, Skiing, Sky Diving

PLAYING CAREER
Honours: Essex & London Schoolboy Rep

Club	Seasons	Transfer	Apps	Goals
Tottenham Hotspur	85-87			
Cambridge United	87-88		50	4

GARY POOLE

Pope, Grenville (F)

(BIDEFORD) Age: 23

Previous Clubs: Launceston; Plymouth Argyle; South Carolina Gamecocks (1985-89); Holsworthy

Honours: N.C.A.A. Final Four Medal 1988 (USA); Runners-Up South Western League Launceston

Pope, Tony (D)

(WOLVERTON) Age: 26

Previous Clubs: Buckingham Town; Leighton Town

Honours: None

Pople, Ian (G)

(BRIDGWATER TOWN 1984) Age: 27

Previous Clubs: Burnham United

Honours: Somerset Senior League Div 2 Runners-Up; Somerset Senior League Div 1 Champions/Premier Div Champions; Somerset Senior League Cup Winners

Portman, Nigel (D)

(WINGATE) Age: 23

Previous Clubs: None

Honours: Herts Senior Trophy 1988; Runners-Up South Midlands League Div 1 1990

Portway, Steve (F)

(WITHAM TOWN) Age: 22

Previous Clubs: Dagenham; Walthamstow Avenue; Bishop's Stortford; Brentwood

Honours: None

Powell, Adrian (G)

(NEWTOWN) Age: 26

Previous Clubs: Cardiff City; Rhayder Town; Llanidloies Town

Honours: Welsh Youth Squad member

Powell, Phil (M)

(WESTFIELDS) Age: 34

Previous Clubs: Hereford United; Kington Town

Powell, Stephen (D)

(NORWICH UNITED) Age: 25

Previous Clubs: Oulton Broad Eagles (Jnr); Ashlea Boys Club; Gorleston; Lowestoft Town

Honours: School Area Rep.; Norfolk County Rep.

Powell, Steve (D)

(BURTON ALBION) D.O.B. 20.9.55

PLAYING CAREER

Honours: England Schoolboy & Youth Int; England Under-23 Int; Football League Div 1 Winners 74/75

Club	Seasons	Transfer	Apps	Goals
Derby County	71-84		352	20
Shepshed C'house	86-90			

Powell, Steven (D)

(MEIR K. A.) Age: 30

Previous Clubs: H & R Johnson

Honours: Staff Senior League Champions 1988-89; Walsall Senior Cup Winners 1989-90

Pratt, Bradley (D)

(WOKING) D.O.B. 25.7.63

Profession: Sales Rep
Single **Hobbies:** Golf, Tennis

PLAYING CAREER

Honours: Vauxhall-Opel Lge Premier R/U 88/89; Div 2 R/U 85/86 & Div 1 R/U 89/90

Club	Seasons	Transfer	Apps	Goals
Camberley Town	80-81			
Wokingham Town	81-82			
Bracknell Town	82-83			
Egham Town	83-86			
Bracknell Town	86-87			
Farnborough Town	87-89			
North Shore (N.Z.)	89-90			

BRADLEY PRATT

Pratt, Mike (D)

(NEWPORT A.F.C.) Age: 24

Previous Clubs: Newport County; Bath City; Ebbw Vale

Honours: Captain of Welsh Youth

Pratt, Ray (F)

(BIDEFORD TOWN) Age: 31

Previous Clubs: Llanelli; Swansea City; Cardiff City; Merthyr Tydfil; Exeter City

Honours: Welsh Youth International

Preece, Brian (F)

(NEWPORT A.F.C.) Age: 32

Previous Clubs: Hereford United; Newport County; Trowbridge; Minehead; Gloucester City; Bridgnorth; Barry; Westfields

Honours: Hellenic Lge Champions; England Schoolboy Int.

Preece, John (D)
(BRIDGNORTH TOWN) Age: 19
Previous Clubs: Walsall

Prendergast, Darren (F)
(CHEADLE TOWN) Age: 19
Previous Clubs: Tranmere Rovers (YTS); Bramhall
Honours: None

Preston, David (D)
(MEIR K. A.) Age: 27
Previous Clubs: Stoke City
Honours: Staffs Senior League Champions 1988-89; Walsall Senior Cup Winners 1989-90

DAVID PRESTON

Preston, Richard (Utility)
(HEANOR TOWN) Age: 23
Previous Clubs: Sandiacre Town; Stanton; Scarborough Town; Burton Albion
Honours: None

Preston, Simon (F)
(ROMSEY TOWN) Age: 29
Previous Clubs: Eastleigh; B.A.T.
Honours: Wessex League Winners; Hants Rep. XI (6 caps)

Price, Glenn (F)
(HAYES) D.O.B. 8.10.62
Nickname: Pricey Profession: Not working
Single Hobbies: Sport

PLAYING CAREER
Honours: None

Club	Seasons	Transfer	Apps	Goals
Frimley Town	80-85			
Camberley Town	85-89			
Staines Town	1989			
Chesham United	89-90			

Price, Neil (D)
(STAINES TOWN) D.O.B. 15.2.64

PLAYING CAREER
Honours: FA Cup R/U

Club	Seasons	Transfer	Apps	Goals
Watford	82-84		8	
Plymouth Argyle		loan	1	
Blackpool		loan	13	
Swansea City	84-85		3	
Wycombe W.	85-87			
Staines Town	87-89			
Wealdstone	89-90			

Price, Nigel (M)
(NEWTOWN) Age: 22
Previous Clubs: Abermule; Newtown; Carno
Honours: Youth Cup Winner; Rep. honours

Price, Paul (D/M)
(WIVENHOE TOWN) D.O.B. 23.3.54

PLAYING CAREER
Honours: Wales Under-21 Int,Wales Full Int

Club	Seasons	Transfer	Apps	Goals
Luton Town	71-80	£200,000	207	8
Tottenham Hotspur	81-83		39	
Minnesota Kicks (USA)	83-84			
Swansea City	84-85		61	1
Saltash United	85-86			
Peterborough United	86-87		86	
Chelmsford City	87-88			

Price, Ryan (G)
(STAFFORD RANGERS) D.O.B. 13.3.70
Nickname: Rodders Profession: Purchasing Manager
Single Hobbies: Weights, Swimming, Snooker

PLAYING CAREER
Honours: Lancs Youth Cup Winners 86/87 & 87/88

Club	Seasons	Transfer	Apps	Goals
Bolton Wanderers	86-88			

Priest, Jan (F)
(MEIR K. A.) Age: 22
Previous Clubs: Hanley Town Honours: None

Prime, Tony (G)
(BECKENHAM TOWN) Age: 22
Previous Clubs: Thames Polytechnic; Darenth Heathside
Honours: None

Prince, Phillip (G)
(CHEADLE TOWN) Age: 31
Previous Clubs: Thackley
Honours: North East & Northern Colleges Rep. 11's

Probert, Paul (D/M)
(OLDSWINFORD FSC) **Age:** 20

Previous Clubs: Tipton Town; Dudley Town
Honours: Dudley & Brierley Hill Schools Rep.

Pryor, Colin (D)
(STRATFORD TOWN) **Age:** 24

Previous Clubs: Wolves Youth; Mansfield Town Youth; Alveston; A. P. Leamington
Honours: 1988 Challenge Cup Winners (Stratford); Warwickshire Youth

Proctor, Keith (D)
(MARINE)

D.O.B. 2.8.70 **Nickname:** Procky
Profession: Student
Single
Hobbies: Golf, Soccer

PLAYING CAREER
Honours: Sefton & Merseyside Schoolboy Rep; Liverpool Senior Cup Winners 89/90

Club	Seasons	Transfer	Apps	Goals
No previous clubs				

Proctor, Kevin (M)
(BARROW)

D.O.B. 5.2.57 **Nickname:** Procky
Profession: Pipefitter
Married **Wife's name:** Brenda
Children: Steven & Lauren
Hobbies: Football, Socialising

PLAYING CAREER
Honours: West Lancs Lge Winners 82/83 & 83/84; Richardson Cup Winners 84/85; HFS Loans Lge Premier Div Winners 88/89; A Trophy Winners 89/90; NPL XI; Barrow P.O.Y. .gap 5 /88

Club	Seasons	Transfer	Apps	Goals
Barrow Celtic	72-77			
Barrow	77-78			
Holker OB	78-81			
Dalton United	81-85			

MICKEY PHILLIPS
(Littlehampton Town)

Prutton, Andrew (M)
(DARTFORD)

D.O.B. 21.2.69
Profession: Plumber
Single
Hobbies: Tennis, Music

PLAYING CAREER
Honours: Herts County Lge Div 1 Winners 86/87; Herts Senior Lge Cup R/U 89/90; Cheshunt P.O.Y. 88/89 & 89/90

Club	Seasons	Transfer	Apps	Goals
Wormley Rovers	85-87			
Cheshunt	87-90			

Pugh, Daral (D)
(BRIDLINGTON TOWN) **Age:** 29

Previous Clubs: Doncaster Rovers (154-15); Huddersfield Town (84-7); Rotherham United (112-6) (Cambridge United-loan-6-1); Torquay United (32)
Honours: Welsh Under-21 Int; Sherpa Van Trophy R/U; FA Vase R/U 89/90; Northern Counties East Lge Winners

Pugh, Stephen (D/M)
(WEYMOUTH)

D.O.B. 1.2.65 **Nickname:** Pughy
Profession: Carpenter
Married **Wife's name:** Helena
Children: Sophia
Hobbies: DIY, Films, Music

PLAYING CAREER
Honours: Wolverhampton & West Mids Schoolboy Rep

Club	Seasons	Transfer	Apps	Goals
Wolverhampton W	81-83			
Torquay United	83-86		120	4
Exeter City	86-87		24	1

Pullen, Michael (D)
(BOGNOR REGIS REGIS) **D.O.B.** 27.9.58

Profession: Building Estimator/Buyer
Single **Hobbies:** Golf, Fitness

PLAYING CAREER
Honours: AC Delco Cup Winners 86/87; Sussex Senior Cup Winners (6) 79/80 - 83/84 & 86/87; Vauxhall Lge Rep XI

Club	Seasons	Transfer	Apps	Goals
No previous clubs				
Bognor Regis Town			+737	+38

Pullen, Paul (M)
(BOGNOR REGIS TOWN) **D.O.B.** 27.9.58

Profession: Insurance Agent
Married **Wife's name:** Janet
Children: Sam **Hobbies:** Golf

PLAYING CAREER
Honours: AC Delco Cup Winners 86/87; Sussex Senior Cup Winners (6) 79/80 - 83/84 & 86/87

Club	Seasons	Transfer	Apps	Goals
No previous clubs				
Bognor Regis Town			+683	+75

Purdie, Jon (M)

(WORCESTER CITY)   D.O.B. 22.2.67

Honours: England Schoolboy Int

Previous Club	Seasons	Transfer	Apps	Goals
Arsenal	84-85			
Wolverhampton W	85-87		89	12
Cambridge United		loan	7	2
Oxford United	1987		11	
Brentford	87-88		6	
Shrewsbury Town	88-89		12	1
Cheltenham Town	89-90			

Purvis, Ray (D)

(DULWICH HAMLET)   Age: 31

Previous Clubs: Arsenal; Barnet; Dorking; Redhill; Croydon; Epsom & Ewell
Honours: None

RYAN PRICE (Stafford Rangers)

IAN PHILLIPS (Kettering Town)

LANCE PEDLAR (Wembley)

Quarman Paul (F)

(HITCHIN TOWN)   Age: 19

Previous Clubs: Luton Town; Caddington
Honours: Beds County Youth Rep

Queenie, Dean (G)

(ALFRETON TOWN)   Age: 18

Previous Clubs: Mexborough YC   **Honours:** None

Quidley, Chris (F)

(WINGATE)   Age: 2

Previous Clubs: None   **Honours:** None

Quinn, Dave (F)

(WELWYN GARDEN CITY)   Age: 2

Previous Clubs: Welwyn Garden United   **Honours:** None

Quinn, James (M)

(FISHER ATHLETIC)   D.O.B. 14.4.6
Profession: Self-Employed   **Married**
Wife's name: Janine   **Hobbies:** Scuba Diving

PLAYING CAREER

Honours: Vauxhall-Opel Lge Premier Winners

Club	Seasons	Transfer	Apps	Goals
Queens Park	82-84			
Clyde	84-86			
Maidstone United	86-87			
Bognor Regis Town	1987			
Yeovil Town	87-90			
Enfield	1990			

Quinnell, Robbie (D)

(BILLERICAY TOWN)   Age: 2

Previous Clubs: Enfield; Leyton Orient; Chelmsford City
Honours: F.A. Vase Q-Final 1990

KEVIN PROCTER (BARROW)

NIGEL RANSOM (WELLING UNITED)

Rains, Tony (D)

(SUTTON UNITED)

D.O.B. 16.1.61 **Nickname:** Rainsey
Profession: Not working
Single
Hobbies: Golf, Water Skiing

PLAYING CAREER

Honours: Fulham Schoolboy Rep; Surrey County Schoolboy Rep; Isthmian Lge Premier Div Winners (2); FA Trophy R/U; Surrey Senior Cup Winners (8); Hitachi Cup Winners (2); London Senior Cup Winners; Sutton P.O.Y. (2)

Club	Seasons	Transfer	Apps	Goals
Fulham	76-78			

TONY RAINS (Sutton United)

Rake, Barry (M)

(SLOUGH TOWN) **D.O.B.** 9.4.69

Profession: Not working
Single **Hobbies:** Sport

PLAYING CAREER

Honours: Berks District & County Schoolboy Rep

Club	Seasons	Transfer	Apps	Goals
Millwall	86-87			

Ramsey, David (G)

(WALTHAMSTOW PENNANT) **Age:** 21

Previous Clubs: Ford United; West Ham United; Leyton Orient; Barking; Hornchurch; Leytonstone-Ilford

Honours: Essex Schools honours; Spartan League Cup Winners Medal 1988-89

Randall, Paul (F)

(BATH CITY)

D.O.B. 16.2.58 **Nickname:** Punky
Profession: Bar Manager
Married **Wife's name:** Filomena
Children: Mark & Kelly-Marie
Hobbies: Sport

PLAYING CAREER

Honours: FA XI; Vauxhall-Opel Lge Premier Div Winners 86/87; AC Delco Cup Winners 86/87; Somerset Premier Cup Winners (2); Promotion to Football Lge Div 2; Gloucester County Cup Winners

Club	Seasons	Transfer	Apps	Goals
Frome Town	76-77			
Bristol Rovers	77-78	£200,000	52	35
Stoke City	78-80	£55,000	46	8
Bristol Rovers	80-86	£5,000	184	70
Yeovil Town	86-89			

Ransom, Nigel (D)

(WELLING UNITED)

D.O.B. 12.3.59
Profession: Bank Manager
Single
Hobbies: Golf, Sport

PLAYING CAREER

Honours: London Youth Rep; Southern Lge Premier Div Winners; Kent Senior Cup Winners; London Senior Cup Winners; Middx Wanderer; Welling P.O.Y. (5)

Club	Seasons	Transfer	Apps	Goals
No previous clubs				

Ratcliffe, Darren (M)

(WESTHOUGHTON TOWN) **Age:** 23

Previous Clubs: Wolverhampton Wanderers; Wigan Athletic; Wigan Rovers; Wigan College; Poolstock L.C.

Honours: West Lancs Division 1 Runners-Up; West Lancs Division 2 Winners; S.W.L. Cup Winners; L.G.A. Inter-League Winners

Ratcliffe, Terry (M)

(GENERAL CHEMICALS) **Age:** 33

Previous Clubs:

Honours: Cheshire U-19; Pyke Cup; Runcorn Cup; Cheshire Amateur Cup

Rawcliffe, Andrew (G)

(PEGASUS)   Age: 24

Previous Clubs: HFD Lads Club; Putson
Honours: None

Rawlings, Ian (D)

(BROMLEY)   Age: 20

Previous Clubs: Leyton Orient; Leyton Wingate
Honours: None

Rawlings, Ian (M)

(THE 61 F.C.)   Age: 26

Previous Clubs:
Honours: None

Rayson, Kevin (M)

(CORNARD UNITED)   Age: 29

Previous Clubs: Bury Town; Sudbury Town; Long Melford
Honours: None

Ray, Martin (D)

(WINGATE)   Age: 24

Previous Clubs: Wimbledon (Res.); Walton & Hersham
Honours: None

SIMON READ

Read, Andy (F)

(BOGNOR REGIS TOWN)

D.O.B. 9.9.67   Nickname: Reedy
Profession: Accountant
Single
Hobbies: Golf

PLAYING CAREER

Honours: Sussex Schoolboy & Youth Rep; South East Counties Lge Winners 89/90; Sussex County Rep

Club	Seasons	Transfer	Apps	Goals
Brighton & Hove A.	83-85			
Steyning Town	85-87			
Wick	87-90			

Read Duane (F)

(HORSHAM)   Age: 21

Previous Clubs: Youth team product   Honours: None

Read, Simon (F)

(FARNBOROUGH TOWN)   Age: 30

Previous Clubs: Staines Town; Wycombe Wanderers

Honours: FA XI, Vauxhall League Rep, Vauxhall-Opel Lge R/U 88/89, Hitachi Cup Winners

Read, Tim (G)

(WOKING)

D.O.B. 23.6.71
Profession: Bank Clerk
Single
Hobbies: Sport, Listening To Music

PLAYING CAREER

Honours: Sussex Schoolboy & Youth Rep; Sussex County Rep

Club	Seasons	Transfer	Apps	Goals
Worthing	85-90	£7,500		

Reaney, Darren (M)

(MEIR K. A.)   Age: 22

Previous Clubs: None

Honours: Staffs Senior League Champions 1988-89; Walsall Senior Cup Winners 1989-90

Redikin, Terry (M)

(LANGNEY SPORTS)   Age: 30

Previous Clubs: Eastbourne United; Hailsham Town; Eastbourne Town   Honours: None

Reed, Jason (M)

(HITCHIN TOWN)   Age: 19

Previous Clubs: Kempston Rov   Honours: Beds County Rep

Reed, Melvin (F)

(MELTON TOWN)   Age: 29

Previous Clubs: Coleby; Clayton   Honours: None

Reeves, Jon (D)
(CALNE TOWN) Age: 19
Previous Clubs: Supermarine; Calne
Honours: None

Regan, John (F)
(MARLOW)

D.O.B. 17.1.62 **Nickname:** Rego
Profession: Design Engineer
Married **Wife's name:** Lisa
Hobbies: Golf, Swimming

PLAYING CAREER
Honours: Middx Schoolboy & Youth Rep; Vauxhall-Opel Lge Div 2 Winners; Southall P.O.Y.; Chalfont P.O.Y.

Club	Seasons	Transfer	Apps	Goals
Chelsea	76-77			
Brentford	77-79			
Burnham	79-81			
Kingstonian	81-83			
Southall	83-85			
Hayes	85-86			
Chalfont St.Peter	86-88			
Wycombe Wanderers	88-89			
Hounslow	1989			

Reeves-Jones, Adrian (M)
(CONGLETON TOWN)

D.O.B. 18.10.66 **Nickname:** Aide
Profession: Works For British Coal
Married

PLAYING CAREER
Honours: None

Club	Seasons	Transfer	Apps	Goals
Port Vale	83-85		1	
Leek Town	85-87			

ANDY REID

Reid, Andy (D/M)
(ALTRINCHAM)

D.O.B. 4.7.62 **Nickname:** Hagar
Profession: Studio Manager
Single
Hobbies: Football

PLAYING CAREER
Honours: Cheshire Senior Cup Winners

Club	Seasons	Transfer	Apps	Goals
Witton Albion	82-83			
Southport	83-88			
Runcorn	88-89			

Relish, John (D)
(NEWPORT A.F.C.) Age: 36
Previous Clubs: Chester City; Newport County
Honours: Welsh Cup Winners; Hellenic League Champions

Reyner, Durk (F)
(HERTFORD TOWN) Age: 29
Previous Clubs: Mowlems; Bishop Stortford Res.; London Colney; Welwyn Garden City
Honours: None

Reynolds, (M)
(NEWTOWN) Age: 22
Previous Clubs: Newtown; Carno
Honours: Central Wales Youth XI

Reynolds, Darren (M)
(MORETON TOWN) Age: 23
Previous Clubs: Bambury United
Honours: None

Reynolds, Tony (M)
(WELLING UNITED)

D.O.B. 25.4.63 **Nickname:** Rams
Profession: Manager at coach & wheelwright firm
Married **Wife's name:** Tina
Children: Natalie & Leanne
Hobbies: Motorcycle Racing, Golf, Fishing

PLAYING CAREER
Honours: Kent Senior Cup Winners; London Senior Cup Winners

Club	Seasons	Transfer	Apps	Goals
Folkestone	83-84			
Ashford Town	84-85	£1,000		
Maidstone United	85-86			

Rich, Andy (D)
(BRIDGNORTH TOWN) Age: 27
Previous Clubs: Wolves Youth; Shrewsbury Youth; Downington Wood; GKN Sankey's
Honours: Walsall County Champions; West Midlands League Cup Winners

Rich, Paul (D)

(BRIDGWATER TOWN (1984)) Age: 25

Previous Clubs: Nether Stowey
Honours: Somerset Senior League Champions & Cup Winners

Richards, Dean (M)

(NEWPORT AFC) Age: 24

Previous Clubs: Newport Corries
Honours: Hellenic League Champions

Richards, Gary (M)

(CARSHALTON ATHLETIC)

D.O.B. 24.5.61
Profession: Not working
Single
Hobbies: Golf

PLAYING CAREER

Honours: Southern Lge Southern Div R/U 84/85; Surrey Senior Cup Winners 89/90; Leatherhead P.O.Y. 87/88 & 88/89

Club	Seasons	Transfer	Apps	Goals
Crawley Town	84-87			
Leatherhead	87-89			

Richards, Martin (D)

(CHASETOWN) Age: 28

Previous Clubs: Wolverhampton United; Hednesford Town; Shifnal Town; Willenhall Town
Honours: Banks's Premier League Cup Winners 1989-90

Richards, Nigel (D)

(SUTTON COLDFIELD TOWN) Age: 23

Previous Clubs: Paget Rangers
Honours: None

Richardson, Ian (F)

(STAINES TOWN)

D.O.B. 9.5.64

PLAYING CAREER

Honours: None

Club	Seasons	Transfer	Apps	Goals
Watford	82-84		8	2
	(Blackpool - loan 5-2;			
	Rotherham United - loan 5-2)			
Chester City	84-86		35	10
Scunthorpe United	86-88		27	9

Richardson, James (D)

(DORKING) Age: 29

Previous Clubs: Glasgow Rangers; Fulham; Lynn Oslo (Nor); Wimbledon; Wealdstone; Hendon; Leatherhead; Epsom & Ewell; Walton & Hersham; Epsom & Ewell
Honours: Middx Wanderer; Glasgow Lge XI; Vauxhall-Opel Lge Div 2 South Winners; Surrey Senior Cup R/U

Richardson, John (M)

(MARLOW)

D.O.B. 9.8.56 **Nickname:** Richo
Profession: Commissioning Engineer
Single
Hobbies: Playing Guitar, Singing

PLAYING CAREER

Honours: Athenian Lge Winners; Vauxhall-Opel Lge Div 2 Winners; FA Vase R/U; Addlestone P.O.Y.

Club	Seasons	Transfer	Apps	Goals
Queens Park Rangers	71-72			
Brentford	72-75			
Southall	75-76			
Windsor & Eton	76-78			
Addlestone & W.	78-81			
Aylesbury United	81-82			
Wycombe Wanderers	82-86			
Hayes	86-87			
Farnborough Town	87-88			
Woking	88-89			
Yeading	1989			

Richardson, Mark (F)

(EASTWOOD TOWN) Age: 30

Previous Clubs: Eastwood Town; Derby County; Boston United; Stafford Rangers; Worksop Town
Honours: Central Lge Div 1 Winners; Notts Senior Cup Winners

Richardson, Mark (M)

(BRIGG TOWN) Age: 21

Previous Clubs: Hull City; Bridlington Town; Guiseley; Bridlington Town.
Honours: None

Richardson, Mark (D)

(OAKWOOD) Age: 30

Previous Clubs: West Hoathly; Oakwood; Southwick
Honours: Mid Sussex League Rep. XI; Sussex County Intermediate Rep. XI; Southern Combination Rep. XI

Richardson, Paul (M)

(BARNET)

D.O.B. 7.11.62 **Nickname:** Tigger or Spider
Profession: Fitter
Single
Hobbies: Golf, Cricket, Snooker

PLAYING CAREER

Honours: South Notts Schoolboy Rep; England Semi-Pro Int; Middx Wanderer; GMVC R/U 88/89

Club	Seasons	Transfer	Apps	Goals
Nottingham Forest	77-79			
Eastwood Town	80-82			
Nuneaton Borough	82-84	£15,000		
Derby County	84-85		14	
Kettering Town	86-90	£12,000		

Richardson, Phil　　　　　　(F)
(OAKWOOD)　　　　　　　　　　Age: 29
Previous Clubs: West Hoathley; Oakwood; Horsham; Three Bridges
Honours: Sussex Intermediate County Winners

Richardson, Steven　　　　(M/F)
(WARMINSTER TOWN)　　　　　　Age: 23
Previous Clubs:
Honours: None

TONY RICKETTS

Ricketts, Tony　　　　　　　(D)
(BATH CITY)

D.O.B. 21.6.59　　　　　**Nickname:** Ricko
Profession: Engineer
Single
Hobbies: Golf

PLAYING CAREER
Honours: Vauxhall-Opel Lge Premier Winners 87/88 & R/U 86/87; Beazer Homes Lge Premier Div R/U 89/90; Somerset Professional Cup Winners (7)

Club	Seasons	Transfer	Apps	Goals
Clandown	76-78			
Bath City	78-85	£7,500		
Yeovil Town	85-88	£10,000		

Ridley, John　　　　　　　(D)
(NEWCASTLE TOWN)　　　　　　Age: 38
Previous Clubs: Matlock Town; Stafford Rangers; Port Vale; Chesterfield; Leicester City; Fort Lauderdale Strikers (USA, N.A.S.L.)
Honours: Bob Lord Trophy Winners; Anglo Scottish Cup Winners; Staffs Senior Cup Winners; Northern Premier Shield Winners; Vauxhall Conference Shield Winners; N.A.S.L Play-Offs Semi-Finalists; Derbyshire Senior Cup Runners-Up

Rigby, Paul　　　　　　　　(M)
(GREAT HARWOOD TOWN)　　　　Age: 26
Previous Clubs: Glossop; Chorley; Radcliffe Borough; Accrington Stanley; Radcliffe Borough　　**Honours:** None

Rigg, Malcolm　　　　　　　(M)
(PENRITH)　　　　　　　　　　Age: 26
Previous Clubs: Keswick　　　**Honours:** None

Riley, Andrew　　　　　　　(D)
(CARSHALTON ATHLETIC)

D.O.B. 28.10.62　　　　　**Nickname:** Riles
Profession: Self-Employed Decorator
Married　　　　　　**Wife's name:** Jeanette
Children: Nicky
Hobbies: Football Tours

PLAYING CAREER
Honours: Vauxhall Lge Rep; Whyteleafe P.O.Y.; Carshalton P.O.Y. (2)

Club	Seasons	Transfer	Apps	Goals
Malden Vale	84-85			
Whyteleafe	85-86			
Leatherhead	86-87			

Riley, Anthony　　　　　　(D/M)
(V S RUGBY)

D.O.B. 1.2.60
Profession: Local Government Officer
Married

Children: Liam, Joseph & Callum

PLAYING CAREER
Honours: Isthmian Lge Premier Div Winners; Southern Lge Midland Div Winners; U.A.U. Winners 1981; Birmingham Senior Cup Winners; Westgate Insurance Cup Winners; Midland Floodlit Cup Winners; VS Rugby P.O.Y. 88/89

Club	Seasons	Transfer	Apps	Goals
Alnwick Town	83-84			
E.P.A.FC (Cyprus)	82-83			
Wycombe Wanderers	84-87			

Riley, Garry　　　　　　　(D)
(MOSSLEY)

D.O.B. 23.3.59　　　　　**Nickname:** Tooly
Profession: Post Press Operative
Married　　　　　　**Wife's name:** Julie
Children: Stephen & Natalie
Hobbies: Football

PLAYING CAREER
Honours: Cheshire Senior Cup Winners

Club	Seasons	Transfer	Apps	Goals
Oldham Athletic	74-77			
Droylsden	77-78			
Salford Amateurs	78-79			
Hyde United	79-81			
Stalybridge Celtic	81-83			
Hyde United	83-84			

Rimmer, Paul (D)
(WESTHOUGHTON TOWN)   Age: 22
Previous Clubs: Marus Bridge; Wigan Rovers
Honours: West Lancs Div 2 Winners

Rinkcavage, Peter (M)
(WORKSOP TOWN)   Age: 20
Previous Clubs: Sheffield Wednesday; Rotherham United; Princess Royal (Sheffield)
Honours: None

Rishman, Barry (M)
(SELSEY)   Age: 23
Previous Clubs: None
Honours: Sussex County Five-a-Side Championship 1988-89

Ritchie, Gary (F)
(A.F.C. LYMINGTON)   Age: 31
Previous Clubs: Lymington Town; Milford; Wellworthy Athletic
Honours: Wessex League Cup Winners

Ritchie, Paul (D)
(A.F.C. LYMINGTON)   Age: 33
Previous Clubs: Lymington Town; Brockenhurst; Wellworthy Athletic
Honours: Hants Senior Rep.; Hants Senior Cup Runners-Up; Bournemouth Senior Cup Winners (x 2); Wessex League Cup Winners

TONY REYNOLDS (WELLING)

Robbins, Kevin (G)
(OAKWOOD)   Age: 20
Previous Clubs: Epsom & Ewell; Monotype
Honours: None

Robbins, Terry (F)
(WELLING UNITED)

D.O.B. 14.1.65   **Nickname:** Inchy
Profession: Bank Clerk
Married   **Wife's name:** Lorraine
Children: Samantha & Grant
Hobbies: Golf, Tennis, Cricket

PLAYING CAREER
Honours: Kent Youth Rep; Gola Lge Winners 83/84; Crawley P.O.Y. 84/85 & 85/86; Welling P.O.Y. 87/88 & 89/90

Club	Seasons	Transfer	Apps	Goals
Tottenham Hotspur	81-83			
Gillingham	1983			
Maidstone United	83-84			
Crawley Town	84-86	£8,000		

Robert, Steve (M)
(WELWYN GARDEN CITY)   Age: 28
Previous Clubs:
Honours: None

Roberts Barry (F)
(BRAINTREE TOWN)   Age: 19
Previous Clubs: Chelmsford City
Honours: None

Roberts Billy (M)
(RHYL)   Age: 29
Previous Clubs: Blackburn Rovers; Wrexham; South Liverpool; Bootle
Honours: None

Roberts, Mark (M)
(NEWTOWN)   Age: 20
Previous Clubs: Welshpool Youth; Shrewsbury Town
Honours: Centre Wales Youth Rep. XI

Roberts, Nicky (D)
(WALTHAMSTOW PENNANT)   Age: 27
Previous Clubs: Dagenham; Enfield; Woodford Town; Leytonstone-Ilford
Honours: None

Roberts, Stephen (D)
(GUISBOROUGH TOWN)   Age: 31
Previous Clubs: Marske United; Stockton Town
Honours: None

TIM READ (WOKING)

Roberts, Steve (G)
(ALTRINCHAM)

D.O.B. 10.2.66 **Nickname:** Robbo
Profession: Self-Employed Painter & Decorator
Single
Hobbies: Golf
No previous clubs

Roberts, Stuart (M:F)
(FARSLEY CELTIC) Age: 21

Previous Clubs: Farsley Celtic; Bridlington Town
Honours: None

ANDY ROBINSON

Robinson, Andy (M)
(WYCOMBE WANDERERS)

D.O.B. 10.3.66

PLAYING CAREER

Honours: England Schoolboy Int

Club	Seasons	Transfer	Apps	Goals
Manchester United	83-85			
	(Burnley - loan 5-1)			
Bury	85-86		19	
Carlisle United	86-88		46	3

Robinson, Frederick (F)
(SANDWELL BOROUGH) Age: 33

Previous Clubs: Rowley Regis; Oldbury United;
Smethwick Highfield; Ashtree Highfield **Honours:** None

Robinson, Ian (D)
(GUISBOROUGH TOWN) Age: 29

Previous Clubs: Middle Beck **Honours:** G.T.F.C. Honours

Robinson, Martin (F)
(ENFIELD)

D.O.B. 17.7.57 **Nickname:** Robbo
Profession: Chef
Married **Wife's name:** Sue
Hobbies: Tennis, Golf

PLAYING CAREER

Honours: None

Club	Seasons	Transfer	Apps	Goals
Tottenham Hotspur	74-78	£15,000	6	2
Charlton Athletic (Reading - loan 6-2)	78-85	£25,000	228	58
Gillingham	85-87	£25,000	96	24
Southend United	87-89		56	14
Cambridge United	89-90		16	1

Robinson, Stephen (D)
(HENDON)

D.O.B. 4.12.56 **Nickname:** Robbo
Profession: Not working
Married **Wife's name:** Paula **Hobbies:** Golf

PLAYING CAREER

Honours: Vauxhall-Opel Lge Div 1 R/U 86/87 & Div 2 North R/U
85/86; Boreham Wood P.O.Y. 82/83; Leyton-Wingate P.O.Y.
86/87

Club	Seasons	Transfer	Apps	Goals
Barnet	79-82			
Boreham Wood	82-84			
Finchley	84-86			
Leyton-Wingate	86-89			

Robinson, Steve (D/M)
(WELLING UNITED)

D.O.B. 7.9.63 **Nickname:** Robbo
Profession: Bank Clerk
Married **Wife's name:** Carol
Hobbies: Golf, DIY

PLAYING CAREER

Honours: Kent Schoolboy & Youth Rep; London Youth Rep;
Southern Lge Premier Div Winners (2); Southern Lge Southern
Div Winners; Southern Lge Cup Winners (2); Kent Senior Cup
Winners (2); Dartford P.O.Y. 84/85

Club	Seasons	Transfer	Apps	Goals
Arsenal	77-80			
Dartford	80-85	£3,500		
Leytonstone & Ilford	1985	£3,500		
Dartford	85-90			

DARREN ROBSON

Robson, Darren   (M)
(GOSPORT BOROUGH)

D.O.B. 18.11.68   **Nickname:** Robbo
Profession: Accounts Technician
Single
Hobbies: Tennis,Snooker,Music

PLAYING CAREER

Honours: Hants Youth Rep; Vauxhall-Opel Lge Div 1 R/U 88/89

Club	Seasons	Transfer	Apps	Goals
Petersfield United	87-88			
Andover	1988			
Waterlooville	88-89			
Basingstoke Town	88-90	£3,250		

Robson Neil   (M)
(DORKING)   **Age:** 24

Previous Clubs: Sutton United; Epsom & Ewell; Sutton United
Honours: Surrey County Rep

Roche, Noel   (G)
(WELLINGBOROUGH TOWN)   **Age:** 18

Previous Clubs: Whitworths; Wellingborough Town; Barnsley
Honours: None

Rogers, Andy   (M)
(FARNBOROUGH TOWN)   **Age:** 35

PLAYING CAREER

Honours: Surrey Senior Cup winners

Club	Seasons	Transfer	Apps	Goals
Chatteris Town				
Peterborough Utd	75-77		29	1
Kettering Town	77-78			
Hampton	78-79			
Southampton	79-81		5	
Plymouth Argyle	81-84		163	14
Reading	84-86		44	5
Southend Utd	86-87		45	2
Carshalton Ath	87-89			
Farnborough				

Rogers, Graham   (D)
(NEWPORT A.F.C.)   **Age:** 35

Previous Clubs: Newport County; Minehead; Barry Town; Newport County; Forest Green Rovers
Honours: Welsh Schools, Youth & Non-League Caps

Rogers, Kevin   (M)
(MERTHYR TYDFIL)

D.O.B. 23.9.63

PLAYING CAREER

Honours: Welsh Schoolboy & Youth Int; Welsh Semi-Pro Int; Welsh Cup Winners 86/87; Beazer Homes Premier Div Winners 88/89

Club	Seasons	Transfer	Apps	Goals
Aston Villa	81-83			
Birmingham City	83-84		9	1
Wrexham	84-85		35	3
Rhyl	85-86			

Rogers, Paul   (D/M)
(DULWICH HAMLET)   **Age:** 20

Previous Clubs: Fulham; Welling United; Bromley
Honours: None

Rogers, Paul   (M)
(SUTTON UNITED)

D.O.B. 21.3.65   **Nickname:** Curly
Profession: Commodity Broker
Single
Hobbies: Golf

PLAYING CAREER

Honours: Surrey Youth Rep.; England Semi-Pro Int; Vauxhall-Opel Lge Premier Div Winners (2); Surrey Senior Cup Winners (5); Sutton P.O.Y.

Club	Seasons	Transfer	Apps	Goals
Chipstead	81-83			

Roll, Chris   (F)
(CLACTON TOWN)   **Age:** 19

Previous Clubs: Colchester United, Wivenhoe Town
Honours: None

Rooney, Andy   (D)
(ALTRINCHAM)

D.O.B. 7.8.68   **Nickname:** Micky
Profession: Fruit Wholesaler
Married   **Wife's name:** Paula
Children: Chelsey
Hobbies: Sport

PLAYING CAREER

Honours: Cheshire Senior Cup Winners 87/88 & 88/89

Club	Seasons	Transfer	Apps	Goals
Everton	84-86			
Crewe Alexandra	86-87			
Runcorn	87-89			

ANDY ROONEY

Rooney, Neal (M)

(CALNE TOWN)   Age: 30

Previous Clubs: None

Honours: Wilts Senior Cup 1985; Wilts Ghia Cup 1980-81, 1985-86

Root, David (G)

(HENDON)

D.O.B. 21.4.61
Profession: Driver
Married   **Wife's name:** Debbie
Children: Aaron & Adam
Hobbies: Sport

PLAYING CAREER

Honours: Redbridge Schoolboy Rep.; Middx Wanderer; London Senior Cup Winners 85/86; Essex Thameside Cup Winners 85/86; Middx Charity Cup Winners 87/88; GMAC Cup R/U 86/87; AC Delco Cup R/U 86/87; P.O.Y. at Launceston 80/81, Barking 83/84, Hendon 87/88 & 89/90.

Club	Seasons	Transfer	Apps	Goals
Launceston Town	80-82			
Barking	82-85			
Walthamstow Avenue	85-86			
Hendon	86-88			
Eton Manor	1988			

Roper, Andy (M)

(WALSALL WOOD)   Age: 29

Previous Clubs: Boney Hay; Bloxwich A.F.C (Town); Lichfield; Bloxwich Town

Honours: Walsall Senior Cup Finalist (Bloxwich); Last player to score a hat-trick at Fellows Park

Ropke, Terry (M)

(CRAWLEY TOWN)   Age: 22

Previous Clubs: Burgess Hill Town; Wisbech Town; Horsham
Honours: None

Rose, Jon (M)

(CHASETOWN)   Age: 27

Previous Clubs:

Honours: Walsall Challenge Cup; Banks's Brewery League Cup

Rosegreen, Mark (F)

(V.S.RUGBY)

D.O.B. 6.12.65   **Nickname:** Rosie
Profession: Electronic Engineer
Single
Hobbies: Sport

PLAYING CAREER

Honours: West Mids Schoolboy Rep; England Schoolboy Int; Southern Lge Premier Div Winners; Westgate Insurance Cup Winners; Birmingham Senior Cup Winners; Midland Floodlit Cup Winners; Welsh FA Cup R/U; Birmingham County Rep.

Club	Seasons	Transfer	Apps	Goals
AP Leamington	82-83			
Kidderminster Harriers	83-87			
Redditch United	87-88			
Bromsgrove Rovers	88-89			
Alvechurch	1989			

Roshe, Fergus (D/M)

(SPALDING UNITED)   Age: 2

Previous Clubs: Newry Town; Brighton & Hove Albion; Hendon; Newry Town

Honours: N. Ireland Youth International; British Polytechnics

Ross, Steve (M/F)

(V.S.RUGBY)

D.O.B. 22.2.60   **Nickname:** Roscoe
Profession: Fork Lift Truck Driver
Single
Hobbies: Watching Boxing and Rugby League

PLAYING CAREER

Honours: Southern Lge Midland Div Winners; Birmingham Senior Cup Winners; Westgate Insurance Cup Winners; Midland Floodlit Cup Winners; FA XI

Club	Seasons	Transfer	Apps	Goals
Long Buckby	80-82			
AP Leamington	82-84			
Bedworth United	84-87			

Rossati, Jerry (F)

(DORKING)   Age: 2

Previous Clubs: Middlesbrough; Charlton Athletic; Welling United; Croydon

Honours: None

Rothel, Clive (D)

(CHEADLE TOWN) **Age:** 34

Previous Clubs: Ruislip Town; Bexley; Erith & Belvedere; Slade Green

Honours: A.F.A. Rep. XI; Kent League Cup Winner

Rowbotham, Neil (D)

(HORWICH RMI)

D.O.B. 23.8.61   **Nickname:** Rowy
Profession: Not working
Married   **Wife's name:** Shelagh
Children: Jac
Hobbies: Golf, Horse Racing

PLAYING CAREER

Honours: None

Club	Seasons	Transfer	Apps	Goals
Haslingden	76-80			
Accrington Stanley	80-88			
Morecambe	88-90			

Rowbotham, Rob (F)

(GAINSBOROUGH TOWN) **Age:** 29

Previous Clubs: Grimsby Pelham; Louth United

Honours:

Roux, Ian (D)

(BIDEFORD) **Age:** 19

Previous Clubs: Holsworthy
Honours: Only Youth Football

Rowberry, Steve (F)

(NEWPORT A.F.C.) **Age:** 29

Previous Clubs: Llanwern; Caerleon
Honours: Hellenic League Champions

Rowlands, Gary (G)

(BOOTLE) **Age:** 25

Previous Clubs: Bootle; St. Dominics; Prescot Cables; St. Dominics

Honours: Lancashire Amateur Cup Winners; Premier Cup Winners (Sunday)

Rowlands, Neil (M)

(BURNHAM RAMBLERS) **Age:** 19

Previous Clubs: None
Honours: None

Rowlands, Paul (D)

(ALTRINCHAM)

D.O.B. 10.1.61   **Nickname:** Rolo
Profession: Sales Executive
Married   **Wife's name:** Lynn
Children: Laura & Erin
Hobbies: Relaxing, Golf

PLAYING CAREER

Honours: Birkenhead Schoolboy Rep.; Cheshire Senior Cup Winners 85/86, 86/87 & 87/88

Club	Seasons	Transfer	Apps	Goals
Tranmere Rovers	77-80			
West Kirby	80-83			
Heswall	83-85			
Runcorn	84-88			
Bangor City	88-89			
Mount Manganui (N.Z.)	1989			

Rowley, Ian (D)

(WESTFIELDS) **Age:** 26

Previous Clubs: Brymbow Steel Works; Wrexham
Honours: HFA Senior Challenge Cup Medal (2)

Rowley, Wayne (M)

(MOOR GREEN)

D.O.B. 11.5.71
Profession: Refuse Collector
Single
Hobbies: Swimming, Weight Training

PLAYING CAREER

Honours: Birmingham Schoolboy Rep

Club	Seasons	Transfer	Apps	Goals
Shrewsbury Town	84-85			
Torquay United	85-86			
Kidderminster Harriers	86-89			

Rowntree, Geoff (G)

(SELBY TOWN) **Age:** 29

Previous Clubs:
Honours: N.C.E. Div 2 Runners-Up

Rudcen, Roger (F)

(BIGGLESWADE TOWN) **Age:** 18

Previous Clubs: None   **Honours:** None

Rudd, Jason (M)

(WESTHOUGHTON TOWN) **Age:** 17

Previous Clubs: Ince P.C.; Horwich R.M.I. (Youth)

Honours: W.A.L. Premier Runners-Up; L.F.A. U-18's Inter League Winners & Runners-Up; Bolton Boys Fed Winners; Lancs Youth Team member

Rudge, Simon (M)

(RUNCORN)

D.O.B. 30.12.64

PLAYING CAREER

Honours: None

Club	Seasons	Transfer	Apps	Goals
Bolton Wanderers	82-85		91	14
Hyde United	85-89			

Ruiz-Pombo, Callos (F)

(OAKWOOD) **Age:** 26

Previous Clubs: Malden Vale; Redhill
Honours: S.C. League Div 2 Runners-Up

Rush, Steph (F)

(COLWYN BAY) **Age:** 32

Previous Clubs: Flint Town; Rhyl
Honours: Bass North-West Counties Lge Cup Winners; Welsh Lge & Cup Winners

Russell, Andrew (D)

(WOKING)

D.O.B. 23.3.65 **Nickname:** Russ
Profession: Quantity Surveyor
Single **Hobbies:** Golf

PLAYING CAREER

Honours: Vauxhall-Opel Lge Div 1 R/U 89/90; Vauxhall-Opel Lge Div 2 R/U 87-88; Bracknell P.O.Y. 88/89

Club	Seasons	Transfer	Apps	Goals
Bracknell Town	84-89			
Wycombe Wanderers	1989			

Russell, Andy (F)

(ROMSEY) **Age:** 28

Previous Clubs: Hedge End; Eastleigh; Colden Common; B.A.T.
Honours: Soton Senior Cup; Hants League Div 1 Winner

Russell, Andy (G)

(RACING CLUB WARWICK) **Age:** 27

Previous Clubs: Wolverhampton Wanderers; Coventry Sporting; Long Buckby; Coventry Sporting
Honours: Warks County Youth Rep; Midland Combination Premier Div R/U

Russell, David (M)

(MARLOW - Player/Manager)

D.O.B. 15.1.56
Profession: Bricklayer
Married **Wife's name:** Ann
Children: Dawn, Natilie & Sophie
Hobbies: Golf

PLAYING CAREER

Honours: Bucks Schoolboy Rep.; FA XI; Vauxhall-Opel Lge Premier, Div 1 & 2 Winners; Berks & Bucks Senior Cup Winners (2); Hitachi Cup Winners

Club	Seasons	Transfer	Apps	Goals
Arsenal	72-74			
Slough Town				
Burnham				
Marlow				
Maidenhead United				
Marlow				
Slough Town				
Wycombe Wanderers				
Chesham United				

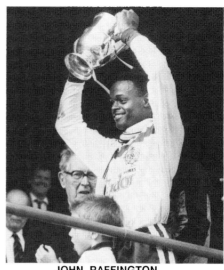

JOHN RAFFINGTON

Russell, Daz (F)

(HINCKLEY) **Age:** 21

Previous Clubs: KRR WMC; Leeds United (YTS); Manchester United (App); Real Madrid
Honours: None

Russell, Glen (F)

(ST ALBANS CITY)

D.O.B. 2.9.62
Profession: Delivery Office Manager For Royal Mail
Married **Wife's name:** Annette
Children: Samantha
Hobbies: Golf, Tennis

PLAYING CAREER

Honours: None

Club	Seasons	Transfer	Apps	Goals
Willesden	79-80			
Barnet	1980			
Finchley	80-84			
Hampton	84-85			
Finchley	85-86			
Boreham Wood	1986			
Billericay Town	86-88			
Finchley	88-90			

Russell, Guy (F)

(MOOR GREEN)

D.O.B. 28.9.67
Profession: Finance Clerk
Single
Hobbies: Golf, Cricket

PLAYING CAREER

Honours: West Mids Schoolboy Rep.; Midlands Youth Cup Winners 84/85

Club	Seasons	Transfer	Apps	Goals
Birmingham City	84-89		12	
(Carlisle United - loan - 12-2)				
Keps FC (Finland)	1989			

Russell Ian (F)

(BUCKINGHAM TOWN)   Age: 30

Previous Clubs: Buckingham Town; Aylesbury United; Buckingham Town; Brackley Town
Honours: None

Russell, Steve (D/M)

(WOLVERTON)   Age: 32

Previous Clubs: Luton Town; Brentford; Dunstable; Bedford; Milton Keynes City; Vauxhall Motors
Honours: F.A. XI Bedfordshire County

Ruso, Donato (M)

(BIGGLESWADE TOWN)   Age: 24

Previous Clubs: Buckingham
Honours: None

Rutter, Stephen (D)

(YEOVIL TOWN)

D.O.B. 14.10.62
Profession: YTS Supervisor (Football)
Single
Hobbies: Travel, Sport

PLAYING CAREER

Honours: England & Great Britain Police Rep; Vauxhall-Opel Lge Premier Div Winners; AC Delco Cup Winners; Bob Lord Trophy Winners; Wellingborough P.O.Y.; Yeovil P.O.Y. (2)

Club	Seasons	Transfer	Apps	Goals
Kettering Town	78-79			
Rushden Town	79-83			
Wellingborough Town	83-86			
Wealdstone	86-87			

Ryan, Declam (D)

(NEWPORT A.F.C.)   Age: 19

Previous Clubs: Holme Farm
Honours: None

Ryan, Keith (F)

(WYCOMBE WANDERERS)

D.O.B. 25.6.70

PLAYING CAREER

Honours: None

Club	Seasons	Transfer	Apps	Goals
Berkhamsted Town	87-89			

Ryder, Andrew (D)

(SPALDING UNITED)   Age: 27

Previous Clubs: Grantham Town; Sleaford Town
Honours: Lincs Youth Cup Winners; Floodlight Cup Winners

JERRY ROSSATI (DORKING)

DAVE RITCHIE (KETTERING)

PAUL RANDALL (Bath City) holding off **NEIL CLEMMENCE (Welling Utd)**

Saddington, James (D)

(NEWMARKET TOWN)   Age: 17

Previous Clubs: None

Honours: Cambs County Youth Rep.; East Mids Youth Comb. Winners 1990

Sadler, Stuart (M)

(REDDITCH UNITED)   D.O.B. 15.9.70

Nickname: Sag   Profession: Not working
Single   Hobbies: Sport, Music, Socialising

PLAYING CAREER

Honours: Birmingham Schoolboy Rep; West Mids County Schoolboy Rep; West Mids Intermediate Lge Cup Winners 87/88; West Mids Senior Lge R/U 89/90

Club	Seasons	Transfer	Apps	Goals
Walsall	87-90			
Stafford Rangers	90-91			

Salathiel, Dave (F)

(WELWYN GARDEN CITY)   Age: 37

Previous Clubs: Tokyington (Wembley); Hillingdon B.L.; Sudbury Court; Willsden

Honours: None

Salmon, Austin (F)

(LEEK TOWN)   Age: 31

Previous Clubs: Witton Albion; Winsford United; Witton Albion; Caernarfon Town; Northwich Victoria; Stafford Rangers; Stalybridge Celtic; Winsford United

Honours: None

Salt, Craig (F)

(PICKERING TOWN)   Age: 30

Previous Clubs: Eastfield; Bridlington Town; Scarborough; Scarborough Celtic

Honours: Not known

Samm, Garvan (M/F)

(CHIPPENHAM TOWN)   Age: 25

Previous Clubs: Moredon YC   Honours: None

Sammons, Phil (M)

(GRAYS ATHLETIC)   D.O.B. 2.8.57

Profession: Teacher   Married
Wife's name: Gina   Children: Bradley & Ryan

PLAYING CAREER

Honours: FA XI; Isthmian Lge Div 2 R/U 80/81; Athenian Lge R/U 82/83; Isthmian Lge Div 2 South Winners 84/85; Vauxhall-Opel Lge Div 1 R/U 87/88; Essex Senior Cup Winners 87/88 & R/U 88/89

Club	Seasons	Transfer	Apps	Goals
Dagenham	74-76			
Tilbury	76-77			
Walthamstow Avenue	77-78			
Hornchurch	78-82			

Sanders, Paul (M)

(ST. DOMINICS)   Age: 24

Previous Clubs: None   Honours: None

Sanders, Sean (M)

(SALISBURY)   Age: 26

Previous Clubs: Andover   Honours: None

Sanderson, Chris (M)

(WESTHOUGHTON TOWN)   Age: 28

Previous Clubs: None   Honours: None

Sanderson, Michael (D)

(SHOTTON COMRADES)   Age: 23

Previous Clubs: Hartlepool Utd; Darlington; Guisborough; Seaham Red Star; Ferry Hill

Honours: None

Sandiford, Eric (M)

(CHELMSLEY TOWN)   Age: 27

Previous Clubs: Coleshill Town; Paget Rangers

Honours: Promotion to the Beazer League

Sandrey, Gavin (D)

(WEYMOUTH)   D.O.B. 6.9.70

Nickname: Crazy Legs   Profession: Not working
Single   Hobbies: Golf, Sport

PLAYING CAREER

Honours: Wilts Schoolboy & Youth Rep; South-West England Rep; England FA Youth Rep; Midland Youth Cup R/U 87/88 & 88/89

Club	Seasons	Transfer	Apps	Goals
Weymouth	85-87			
Swindon Town	87-89			

Saunders, Kenny (F)

(KNOWSLEY UNITED)   Age: 26

Previous Clubs: Tranmere Rovers; Burnley; St Helens Town; Marine; Mossley

Honours: Bass 1st, 2nd, 3rd Winners; Senior Cup Winners (twice)

Saunt, Wayne (D)

(HINCKLEY)   Age: 21

Previous Clubs: Ellistown Colliery; Ashby United; YMCA; Ibstock Youth; Hinckley Athletic U-18

Honours: County Schools U-19's; Leicester & Rutland County U-18's

Savage, Dave (D)

(OAKWOOD)   Age: 24

Previous Clubs: Redhill

Honours: Sussex County Runners-Up & Cup Winners 1989-90

Savage, David (M)
(PENRITH) Age: 22
Previous Clubs: Greystoke Honours: None

Savage, Simon (M)
(PENRITH) Age: 22
Previous Clubs: Carlisle United Res.; Netherfield
Honours: None

Savory, Alan (F)
(PEGASUS JNRS) Age: 24
Previous Clubs: None
Honours: None

Scally, Wayne (M)
(V.S. RUGBY)

D.O.B. 1.6.68
Profession: Roofer
Single
Hobbies: Squash

PLAYING CAREER

Honours: Walsall Schoolboy Rep.; Coleshill P.O.Y.87/88

Club	Seasons	Transfer	Apps	Goals
Coleshill Town	87-88			
Paget Rangers	88-90			
Faroe Islands	1990			
Gresley Rovers	1990			

Scawthorn, Tony (F)
(WALTHAMSTOW PENNANT) Age: 24
Previous Clubs: Aveley; Clapton; Hornchurch
Honours: Spartan League Cup Winners Medal 1988-89

Schneider, Jarrod (M)
(WALTHAMSTOW PENNANT) Age: 22
Previous Clubs: Hale End Athletic
Honours: None

Schofield, Darren (F)
(DROYLESDEN) Age: 25
Previous Clubs: Horwich RMI; Curzon Ashton
Hobbies: Manchester Premier Cup Winners 89/90

Sconce, Haydn (D)
(WINSFORD UNITED) Age: 19
Previous Clubs: Chester City; Wrexham; Christleton
Honours: Cheshire Youth Rep

Scotcher, Gary (F)
(MIRLEES BLACKSTONE) Age: 33
Previous Clubs: Baker Perkins; Ramsey; St. Ives; Parson Drove; Bourne, March
Honours: U.C.L. First Div Champions

Scott, Kevin (D)
(KEYNSHAM TOWN) Age: 21
Previous Clubs: Parkway; Aidian Rangers; Mangotsfield United
Honours: None

Scott, Lloyd (G)
(PURFLEET) D.O.B. 13.10.61
Previous Clubs: Leyton Orient (79-82); Blackpool (82-83) [2 Apps]; Dagenham (83-85); Maldon Town (85-86); Dagenham (86-90); Aveley (90-91).
Honours: Essex Senior Cup Winners 86/87.

LLOYD SCOTT

Scott, Mark (M)
(SOMERSHAM TOWN) Age: 21
Previous Clubs: Warboys Town
Honours: None

Scott, Steve (M/F)
(EYNESBURY ROVERS) Age: 26
Previous Clubs: Barton Rovers; Baldock Town; Arlesey Town; Vauxhall Motors
Honours: U.C.L. Knock-Out Cup

Scrivens, Ken (G)
(RADSTOCK TOWN) Age: 19
Previous Clubs: Welton Rovers; Clutton
Honours: None

Scrivner, Michael (D)
(CHEADLE TOWN) Age: 25
Previous Clubs: Abbey Hey
Honours: None

Seagroatt, Robin (F)
(SUTTON UNITED)

D.O.B. 25.10.70   **Nickname:** Groatty
Profession: Electrician
Single
Hobbies: Golf, Tennis

PLAYING CAREER

Honours: None

Club	Seasons	Transfer	Apps	Goals
Redhill	86-87			

Searle, Curwen (G)
(CONGLETON TOWN)

D.O.B. 24.7.56
Profession: Gas Service Engineer
Divoreced
Children: Gemma
Hobbies: Sport, Music

PLAYING CAREER

Honours: Mid-Cheshire Lge & Cup Winners 79/80; Kidsgrove P.O.Y. (2); Congleton P.O.Y. (2).

Club	Seasons	Transfer	Apps	Goals
Lion FC	79-81			
Kidsgrove Athletic	81-85			
Alsagar Town	85-86			

Seasman, John (M)
(ACCRINGTON STANLEY)

D.O.B. 21.2.55

PLAYING CAREER

Honours: Football League Div 3 & 4 Winners

Club	Seasons	Transfer	Apps	Goals
Tranmere Rovers	72-74		17	
Luton Town	74-75		8	2
Millwall	75-79		158	35
Rotherham United	79-83		100	25
Cardiff City	1984		12	2
Rochdale		loan	8	
Chesterfield	84-85		10	1
Rochdale	85-87		87	4
Northwich Victoria	87-88			
Aylesbury United	88-89			
Runcorn	90-91			

Seddon, Alan (F)
(CWMBRAN TOWN)   **Age:** 27

Previous Clubs: Panteg
Honours: None

Seddon, Duncan (D)
(GREAT HARWOOD TOWN)   **Age:** 26

Previous Clubs: Accrington Stanley
Honours: Lamot Pils Cup 1990

Sedgwick, Alan (D)
(GENERAL CHEMICALS)   **Age:** 27

Previous Clubs: Dista F.C.; Arncliffe F.C.
Honours: None

Seekings, Ray (F)
(HITCHIN TOWN)   **Age:** 30

Previous Clubs: Eynesbury Rovers; Baldock Town; Potton United
Honours: United Counties Lge Winners 86/87 & 88/89

Selway, Mark (G)
(KEYNSHAM TOWN)   **Age:** 18

Previous Clubs: Bristol Rovers; Imperial Bristol; Frys Club; Clevedon Town

Honours: Somerset Floodlight Youth Champions, (Keynsham) 1989-90

Senior, Jon (M)
(HORWICH RMI)

D.O.B. 8.3.69
Profession: Office Clerk
Single

PLAYING CAREER

Honours: Bolton Schoolboy Rep; Lancs Youth Cup Winners 86/87; GMAC Cup Winners 87/88

Club	Seasons	Transfer	Apps	Goals
Bolton Wanderers	85-87			
Horwich RMI	87-90			
Northwich Victoria	1990			

Seymour, Ian (D)
(CHIPPENHAM TOWN)   **Age:** 31

Previous Clubs: Lutterworth Town; Gateshead; Whitley Bay; Alnwick Town; Fareham Town; Bashley
Honours: Leics Senior League Div 2

Sexton, Paul (M)
(A.F.C. LYMINGTON)   **Age:** 30

Previous Clubs: Brockenhurst; A.F.C. Totton; Lymington Town; Blackfield & Langley
Honours: Hants Senior Rep.

Shackleton, Paul (F)
(HINCKLEY ATHLETIC)   **Age:** 30

Previous Clubs: Witherley United; P.D.K. Denhaag; Nuneaton Boro'; Bolehall Swifts
Honours: None

Shanahan, Nigel (M)
(RACING CLUB WARWICK)   **Age:** 24

Previous Clubs: AP Leamington
Honours: Warks County Rep; British Universities Rep; Midland Combination Premier Div Winners & R/U

Shaw, Albert (M/F)

(SANDWELL BOROUGH)   **Age:** 27

Previous Clubs: Boldmere St Michaels; Smethick Highfield; Coventry Sporting; Oldbury; Blakenhall; Princess End

Honours: Walsall Senior Cup Winners; League Cup Runners-Up; Challenge Cup Runners-Up; League Winners (all Boldmere)

Shaw, Christopher (M)

(SALISBURY)   **Age:** 25

Previous Clubs: AFC Bournemouth (25-2); Bath City
Honours: None

Shaw, Jason (M)

(DARTFORD)

D.O.B. 4.12.70
Profession: Telephone Engineer
Single
Hobbies: Sport

PLAYING CAREER

Honours: None

Club	Seasons	Transfer	Apps	Goals
Redbridge Forest	88-90			

Shaw, Martin (F)

(CHIPPENHAM TOWN)   **Age:** 29

Previous Clubs: Bristol Rovers; Bath City; Witney Town; Forest Green; Banbury

Honours: Wilts Prof. Shield Winner

Shaw, Nigel (M)

(ALTRINCHAM)

D.O.B. 13.2.63
Profession: Electrician
Married   **Wife's name:** Diane
Children: Laura
Hobbies: Golf

PLAYING CAREER

Honours: HFS Loans Lge & Cup Winners; HFS Loans Presidents Cup Winners; Macclesfield P.O.Y.

Club	Seasons	Transfer	Apps	Goals
Stoke City	78-81			
Nantwich Town	81-82			
Congleton Town	82-83			
Macclesfield Town	83-89			

Shaw, Steve (M)

(TOOTING & MITCHAM UNITED)   **Age:** 24

Previous Clubs: Local football
Honours: None

Sheen, Scott (M)

(CLACTON TOWN)   **Age:** 22

Previous Clubs: Clacton Town; Brightlingsea United
Honours: None

Shelton, David (D)

(CHASETOWN)   **Age:** 25

Previous Clubs: Dudley Town; Stourbridge; Tamworth

Honours: Southern (Midland) League Champions; Birmingham Senior Cup Winners; Worcs Senior Cup Runners-Up; Banks's Premier League Cup Winners

Shepherd, David (M)

(DULWICH HAMLET)   **Age:** 24

Previous Clubs: Whyteleafe; Bromley
Honours: None

Shepherd, Ewan (M)

(WARMINSTER TOWN)   **Age:** 29

Previous Clubs: Crewe Alexandra; Henley Town
Honours: None

Shepherd, George (D)

(MACCLESFIELD TOWN)

D.O.B. 25.2.67   **Nickname:** Jud
Profession: Builder
Single
Hobbies: Sport

PLAYING CAREER

Honours: FA Youth Cup Winners

Club	Seasons	Transfer	Apps	Goals
Manchester City	83-84			
Bolton Wanderers	84-86		1	
Hyde United	87-89	£6,000		

JIMMY SHEPHERD
(Bashley)

Shepherd, Glen (D)
(HALESOWEN HARRIERS)

D.O.B. 4.1.71   **Nickname:** Shep
Profession: Sales Rep
Single
Hobbies: Snooker, Sports

PLAYING CAREER

Honours: None

Club	Seasons	Transfer	Apps	Goals
Port Vale	87-90			
Stafford Rangers	90-91			

Shepherd, John (D)
(SELSEY)   **Age:** 29
Previous Clubs: None
Honours: County League Div 2 Runners-Up; Div 2 Cup Winners

Shepherd, J. A. (F)
(TUNBRIDGE WELLS)   **Age:** 28
Previous Clubs: Tunbridge Wells; Tonbridge
Honours: Kent Champions; K.L.C. Champions

Shergold, Jeremy (M)
(SELSEY)   **Age:** 27
Previous Clubs: None   **Honours:** None

Sheridan, Frank (D)
(TOOTING & MITCHAM UNITED)   **Age:** 29
Previous Clubs: Derby County (43-5); Torquay United (27-3); Rio Ave (Portugal); Leytonstone & Ilford; Carshalton Athletic; Whyteleafe; Chipstead
Honours: None

Sheringham, Jim (M)
(DARTFORD)   **D.O.B.** 5.6.63
Profession: Bank Official
Married   **Wife's name:** Donna
Children: Annie
Hobbies: Most sport, Seeing new baby develop

PLAYING CAREER

Honours: None

Club	Seasons	Transfer	Apps	Goals
Dagenham	82-83			
Billericay Town	1983			
Barking	1983			
Walthamstow Avenue	83-84			
Barking	1985			
Grays Athletic	85-91			

Sherlock, Mark (D)
(BUCKINGHAM TOWN)   **Age:** 25
Previous Clubs: Highgate United; Banbury United; Brackley Town
Honours: None

Sherwood, Jeffrey (D)
(GLOUCESTER CITY)   **D.O.B.** 5.10.59
Profession: Electrical Engineer
Married   **Wife's name:** Angela
Children: Harry & Ivy   **Hobbies:** Squash, Volleyball

PLAYING CAREER

Honours: Avon County Schoolboy Rep; Gloucs Youth Rep; FA XI; Southern Lge Rep; Vauxhall-Opel Lge Winners; AC Delco Cup Winners; Bob Lord Trophy Winners; Taunton P.O.Y.; Bath P.O.Y. (2); Yeovil P.O.Y.

Club	Seasons	Transfer	Apps	Goals
Taunton Town	78-81	£1,500		
Bath City	81-82			
Bristol Rovers	82-83		18	
Bath City	83-87	£5,000		
Yeovil Town	87-90	£10,000		

Shields, Paul (D)
(WEMBLEY)   **Age:** 29
Previous Clubs: Willesden; Edgware Town; Kingsbury Town; Slough Town; Hendon; Wembley; Hendon; Kingsbury Town; Leytonstone & Ilford; Kingsbury Town
Honours: Middx Youth & Senior Rep; Suburban Lge Winners; Middx Senior & Charity Cup Winners

Shilvock, Robert (M)
(HALESOWEN TOWN)

D.O.B. 26.10.61   **Nickname:** Shilvs or Shink
Profession: Sales Executive
Married   **Wife's name:** Cheryl
Children: Lauren & Matthew
Hobbies: Keeping Fit, Cooking, Sport

PLAYING CAREER

Honours: Halesowen & Stourbridge Schoolboy Rep; West Midland Lge & Cup Winners 80/81, 81/82 & 82/83; Birmingham Senior Cup Winners 82/83; FA Vase R/U 82/83; Southern Lge Midland Div & Cup Winners 85/86; Bromsgrove P.O.Y. 87/88

Club	Seasons	Transfer	Apps	Goals
Halesowen Town	76-84			
Bromsgrove Rovers	85-88			
Kidderminster Harriers	88-91			

Shipp, Dean (G)
(EYNESBURY ROVERS)   **Age:** 21
Previous Clubs: Hitchin Town
Honours: Scott Gatty Cup 1990

Shirt, Paul (D)
(HENDON)   **D.O.B.** 23.9.64

Nickname: Shirty   **Profession:** Carpet Fitter
Married   **Wife's name:** Kim
Children: Gemma   **Hobbies:** Golf

PLAYING CAREER

Honours: None

Club	Seasons	Transfer	Apps	Goals
Barking	81-83			

Shirtliff, Paul (D)

(BOSTON UNITED)   D.O.B. 3.11.62

Nickname: Shirts   **Profession:** Bank Clerk
Married   **Wife's name:** Jayne
Hobbies: Fishing, Golf

PLAYING CAREER

Honours: England Semi-Pro Int; Frickley P.O.Y. 86/87 & 87/88; Boston P.O.Y. 88/89

Club	Seasons	Transfer	Apps	Goals
Sheffield Wednesday	79-84		10	
Northampton Town	84-85		32	
Frickley Athletic	85-88	£12,500		

PAUL SHIRTLIFF

Shodeinde, Peter (M/F)

(DORKING)   Age: 31

Previous Clubs: Willesden; Edgware Town; Hendon; Woking; Hampton; Leatherhead; Wembley
Honours: Vauxhall-Opel Lge Div 2 South Winners; Middx Senior Cup Winners; Middx Charity Cup Winners; Southern Combination Cup Winners; Surrey Senior Cup R/U

Shoemake, Kevin (G)

(KETTERING TOWN)   D.O.B. 28.1.65

Nickname: Shoey   **Profession:** Sales Co-ordinator
Single   **Hobbies:** Sport

PLAYING CAREER

Honours: FA XI; Southern Lge Premier Div Winners 85/86; GMVC R/U 88/89

Club	Seasons	Transfer	Apps	Goals
Leyton Orient	81-84		5	
Dartford	1984			
Harlow Town	84-85			
Chelmsford City	85-86	£3,000		
Welling United	1986	£10,000		
Peterborough United	86-88		48	

Short, Mark (D)

(SHOTTON COMRADES)   Age: 24

Previous Clubs: None
Honours: None

Short, Paul (M)

(OAKWOOD)   Age: 26

Previous Clubs: Malden Town; Redhill
Honours: S.C. League Div 2 Runners-Up & Cup Winners

Short, Rashid (F)

(TUNBRIDGE WELLS)   Age: 25

Previous Clubs: Danson
Honours: None

Showler, Paul (F)

(ALTRINCHAM)

D.O.B. 10.10.66
Profession: Police Officer
Single
Hobbies: Golf, Sport

PLAYING CAREER

Honours: FA XI; HFS Loans Lge Premier Div & Cup Winners; Goole P.O.Y.

Club	Seasons	Transfer	Apps	Goals
Sheffield Wednesday	81-84			
Sunderland	1984			
Bentley Victoria	84-85			
Goole Town	85-89			
Colne Dynamoes	89-90			

Shrieves, Terry (F)

(BUCKINGHAM TOWN)   Age: 31

Previous Clubs: Millwall; Milton Keynes City; Buckingham Town; Kettering Town; Aylesbury United; MK Wolverton Town; Buckingham Town; Boreham Wood; Rushden Town
Honours: None

Shurmer, Kevin (D)

(MORETON TOWN)   Age: 28

Previous Clubs: Banbury
Honours: Gloucester Junior & Senior County Cups; Reserve Section Hellenic League & Cup double

Shuttlewood, Justin (G)

(WARMINSTER TOWN)   Age: 19

Previous Clubs: Heytesbury
Honours: None

Siddell, Dave (F)

(KNOWSLEY UNITED)   Age: 20

Previous Clubs: None
Honours: None

MARK SHAIL (YEOVIL TOWN)

Silcock, Steve (M)

(WESTHOUGHTON TOWN)   **Age:** 27

Previous Clubs: Wigan Athletic; Chorley; Ince P.C.; Wigan Youth; Wigan College

Honours: Wigan Cup Winners; West Lancs League Div 1 Runners-Up; Wigan A.L. Premier Winners

Silver, Gary (M/F)

(GATESHEAD)

D.O.B. 8.8.67   **Nickname:** Hi-Ho
Profession: Not working
Single
Hobbies: Music, Beer

PLAYING CAREER

Honours: Oxon Schoolboy Rep; South-West England Schoolboy Rep; HFS Loans Lge Premier Div R/U 89/90; HFS Loans Lge Cup R/U 89/90.

Club	Seasons	Transfer	Apps	Goals
Oxford United	82-85			

Simmonds, Michael (G)

(DULWICH HAMLET)   **Age:** 26

Previous Clubs: Ruislip Manor
Honours:

Simmonds, Nigel (D)

(RADCLIFFE BOROUGH)   **Age:** 25

Previous Clubs: Leyland Motors
Honours:

Simmonds, Steve (D)

(BURNHAM RAMBLERS)   **Age:** 21

Previous Clubs: None
Honours: None

Simmonite, Gordon (D)

(MATLOCK TOWN)

D.O.B. 25.4.57

PLAYING CAREER

Honours: England Semi-Pro Int; NPL Winners

Club	Seasons	Transfer	Apps	Goals
Rotherham United	73-75			
Sheffield Wednesday	75-76		1	
Boston United	76-80	£15,000		
Blackpool	80-82		63	1
Lincoln City	82-87		72	
Gainsborough Trinity	88-90			

Simpson, David (M)

(SHOTTON COMRADES)   **Age:** 27

Previous Clubs: N.E.I. Parson
Honours: Benevolent Bowl Winner

Simpson, Gary (M)

(ALTRINCHAM)   **D.O.B.** 11.4.61

Nickname: Simmo   **Profession:** Assembler
Single   **Hobbies:** Golf

PLAYING CAREER

Honours: Sheffield & Yorks Schoolboy Rep.; England Semi-Pro Int.

Club	Seasons	Transfer	Apps	Goals
Stoke City	77-80			
Boston United	80-85			
Stafford Rangers	85-86			
Weymouth	86-87			
Stafford Rangers	87-89			
Boston United	89-90	£10,000		

Simpson, Wayne (D)

(STAFFORD RANGERS)   **D.O.B.** 19.9.68

Nickname: Simmo   **Profession:** Pie Maker
Married   **Wife's name:** Julie
Hobbies: Golf

PLAYING CAREER

Honours: Staffs Schoolboy Rep.; England Semi-Pro Int

Club	Seasons	Transfer	Apps	Goals
Port Vale	84-89			

Sinclair, Jade (M)

(BILLINGHAM SYNTHONIA)   **Age:** 18

Previous Clubs: Middlesbrough; Hartlepool United

Honours: None

Singh, Peter (M)

(BILLINGHAM SYNTHONIA)   **Age:** 25

Previous Clubs: None

Honours: Northern League 2nd Div Trophy 1986-87; Northern League Championship Trophy 1989-90; Northern League Cup Trophy 1989-90

Singleton, David (F)

(BATH CITY)   **D.O.B.** 20.11.56

Nickname: Loonie   **Profession:** Regional Sales Manager
Single   **Hobbies:** Flying

PLAYING CAREER

Honours: FA XI; Somerset Senior Cup Winners (8); Bath P.O.Y. 82/83

Club	Seasons	Transfer	Apps	Goals
Taunton Town	73-79	£7,500		
Weymouth	79-81	£4,500		

Sinnott, Paul (F)

(RACING CLUB WARWICK)   **Age:** 28

Previous Clubs: AP Leamington; Stratford Town
Honours: Midland Combination Premier Div Winners

Skeegs, Gary (D)

(CORNARD UNITED) Age: 27

Previous Clubs: Tiptree United; Halstead Town; Witham Town; Stanbridge

Honours: None

Skinner, Andy (M)

(BILLERICAY TOWN) Age: 25

Previous Clubs: Basildon United; Billericay Town; Aveley; Billericay Town; West Ham Utd (App.)

Honours: East Anglian Cup Runners-Up

Slack, Trevor (D)

(KETTERING TOWN)

D.O.B. 26.9.62
Profession: Not working
Married **Wife's name:** Denise
Children: Steven
Hobbies: Golf

PLAYING CAREER

Honours: England Youth Int.; Peterborough P.O.Y. 82/83

Club	Seasons	Transfer	Apps	Goals
Peterborough United	79-85	£15,000	202	18
Rotherham United	85-86	£10,000	15	1
Grimsby Town	86-87	£10,000	21	
Northampton Town	87-88		13	1
Chesterfield	88-90		21	

Slocombe, Steve (D)

(KEYNSHAM TOWN) Age: 22

Previous Clubs: Eagle House Boys; St Phillips Mas; Keynsham Town; Hungerford Ferrets (Sundays)

Honours: F.A. Colts XI; Somerset Youth & Senior

ROY SIDDERLEY
(Droylesden)

Small, Dougie (D)

(WARMINSTER TOWN) Age: 21

Previous Clubs: None

Honours: None

Smaller, Paul (M)

(BRIDLINGTON TOWN) Age: 23

Previous Clubs: Grimsby Town(2)
Honours:

Smart, Gary (M)

(BATH CITY)

D.O.B. 8.12.63 **Nickname:** Smurty
Profession: Maintenance Engineer
Single
Hobbies: Sport

PLAYING CAREER

Honours: None

Club	Seasons	Transfer	Apps	Goals
Bristol St.Georges	80-83			
Mangotsfield United	83-84			
Bristol Rovers	84-86		19	4
Cheltenham Town	86-88			
Wokingham Town	1988			

Smiles, Andrew (F)

(CORNARD UNITED) Age: 24

Previous Clubs: None **Honours:** None

Smith, Adrian (F)

(TUNBRIDGE WELLS) Age: 20

Previous Clubs: Crowborough

Honours: None

Smith, Alan (M)

(WINGATE) Age: 31

Previous Clubs: Walthamstow Avenue; Selby; Wingate

Honours: None

Smith, Barry (D)

(BECKENHAM TOWN) Age: 40

Previous Clubs: Crystal Palace; Tooting & Mitcham United

Honours: None

Smith, Bill (D)

(PEGASUS JNRS) Age: 37

Previous Clubs: Army/Combined Services; Chelmsford City

Honours: None

Smith, Carl (M)

(CLEATOR MOOR CELTIC) Age: 18

Previous Clubs: Mirehouse
Honours: None

Smith, Chris (M)

(GLOUCESTER CITY) D.O.B. 28.3.66

Nickname: Cyril **Profession:** Stone Maker
Married **Wife's name:** Sara
Children: Kayleigh **Hobbies:** Sport

PLAYING CAREER

Honours: None

Club	Seasons	Transfer	Apps	Goals
Cirencester	80-81			
Cheltenham Town	81-82			
Bristol Rovers	82-85		2	
Mangotsfield United	86-88			
Bath City	88-91			

Smith, Derek (M)

(GAINSBOROUGH TOWN) Age: 27

Previous Clubs: Louth United)
Honours: None

Smith, Gary (M)

(BANBURY UNITED) Age: 21

Previous Clubs: Walsall; Tamworth; Gillingham
Honours: None

Smith, Gary (F)

(SUTTON COLDFIELD TOWN) Age: 24

Previous Clubs: Paget Rangers
Honours:

Smith, Gary (M)

(WYCOMBE WANDERERS)

D.O.B. 3.12.68 **Nickname:** Smudger

PLAYING CAREER

Honours: None

Club	Seasons	Transfer	Apps	Goals
Fulham	84-86		1	
Colchester United	86-88		11	
Enfield	88-89			

Smith, Ian (M)

(SEATON DELAVAL AMATEURS) Age: 22

Previous Clubs: Gosforth Bohemians
Honours: None

Smith, Jimmy (F)

(SALISBURY) Age: 20

Previous Clubs: Torquay United (45-5)
Honours: None

Smith, Keith (F)

(ALFRETON TOWN) D.O.B. 17.10.63

Previous Clubs: Matlock Town; Alfreton Town; Exeter City
Honours: None

Smith, Kevin (F)

(WEYMOUTH) D.O.B. 20.4.65

Nickname: Smudge **Profession:** Postman
Single **Hobbies:** Gambling

PLAYING CAREER

Honours: None

Club	Seasons	Transfer	Apps	Goals
Cambridge United	82-84		38	4
Exeter City	84-85		25	2
Torquay United	85-86		23	1
Exmouth Town	86-89			

Smith, Kieron (F)

(GRESLEY ROVERS) Age: 30

Previous Clubs: Huthwaite; Sutton Town

Honours: Notts Senior Cup; Derbys Senior Cup; Central Midland League Cup & League

Smith, Leon (D)

(VALE RECREATION) Age: 33

Previous Clubs: Warsash F.C.; Sholing Sports; Jersey Wanderers; Guernsey Rangers; Northerners A.C.

Honours: 4 Guernsey Caps (1985-90)

Smith, Mark (D)

(DULWICH HAMLET) Age: 19

Previous Clubs: Erith & Belvedere
Honours: Kent Schoolboy Rep

Smith, Mark (M:F)

(HITCHIN TOWN) Age: 22

Previous Clubs: Hitchin Town; Letchworth Garden City
Honours: Herts County Rep

Smith, Martin (F)

(HINCKLEY ATHLETIC) Age: 25

Previous Clubs: Enderby Town (Leicester Utd); Bedworth United; Nuneaton Borough
Honours: None

Smith, Nic (M/F)

(SHOTTON COMRADES) Age: 27

Previous Clubs: Wingate **Honours:** None

Smith, Pat (D)

(WALTHAMSTOW PENNANT) Age: 27

Previous Clubs: None **Honours:** None

Smith, Peter (F)

(GREAT HARWOOD TOWN) Age: 25

Previous Clubs: Barrow; B.A.C. Preston

Honours: Lancaster Amateur Shield (3); West Lancs League (2); Lamot Pils Cup 1990

Smith, Peter (D)

(BANBURY UNITED) Age: 20
Previous Clubs: Tamworth
Honours: None

Smith, Richard (F)

(NEWPORT A.F.C.) Age: 22
Previous Clubs: Wolverhampton Wanderers; Mansfield; Stroud
Honours: Hellenic League Champions

Smith, Robert (M)

(V.S.RUGBY)

D.O.B. 24.11.67 **Nickname:** Smudge
Profession: Salesman
Single
Hobbies: Watching Films

PLAYING CAREER

Honours: Leics Schoolboy Rep

Club	Seasons	Transfer	Apps	Goals
Hillcroft	87-89			
Aylesbury United	89-90			

Smith, Sean (F)

(OAKWOOD) Age: 21
Previous Clubs: Sutton United; Charlwood
Honours: Surburban League Cup Winners; Sussex County Div 2 Runners-Up

CHRIS SMITH (Gloucester City)

Smith, Simon (G)

(GATESHEAD)

D.O.B. 16.9.62 **Nickname:** Reg
Profession: Not working
Married **Wife's name:** Lucy
Children: William & Ben
Hobbies: Golf, Tennis

PLAYING CAREER

Honours: Multipart Lge Winners; Northern Lge Winners; HFS Loans Lge Premier Div R/U 89/90; HFS Loans Lge Cup R/U 89/90; FA XI; Gateshead P.O.Y. 88/89

Club	Seasons	Transfer	Apps	Goals
Newcastle United	78-82			
Whitley Bay	82-86			
Gateshead	86-88			
Blyth Spartans	88-89			

Smith, Trevor (D/M)

(GUISBOROUGH TOWN) Age: 31
Previous Clubs: Wolves; Hartlepool United; Dartford; Scarborough; Whitby Town; Guisborough; Bishop Auckland
Honours: None

Smith, Trevor (M)

(RACING CLUB WARWICK) Age: 36
Previous Clubs: Evesham United; AP Leamington; Bromsgrove Rovers
Honours: Southern Lge Premier Div Winners

Smithers, Timothy (D/M)

(BEDWORTH UNITED)

D.O.B. 22.1.56
Profession: Production Supervisor
Married **Wife's name:** Carole
Children: Alan
Hobbies: Golf, Listening To Music

PLAYING CAREER

Honours: England Semi-Pro Int.; Birmingham Senior Cup Winners 77/78 & 79/80; Alliance Premier Lge R/U 83/84 & 84/85; Nuneaton P.O.Y. 78/79, 79/80 & 85/86; Atherstone P.O.Y. 89/90

Club	Seasons	Transfer	Apps	Goals
Nuneaton Borough	76-80	£20,000		
Oxford United	80-83		99	6
Nuneaton Borough	83-87			
Atherstone United	87-90			

Soanes, Chris (D)

(CORNARD UNITED) Age: 29
Previous Clubs: Sudbury Town; Braintree
Honours: None

Sones, Gary (G)

(WELWYN GARDEN CITY) Age: 27
Previous Clubs: Hertford Town; Stevenage Borough
Honours: Herts County U-19

Sowerby, Colin (F)
(DARTFORD)

D.O.B. 1.7.66   Nickname: Sowers
Profession: Decorator
Single
Hobbies: Golf, Badminton

PLAYING CAREER

Honours: East London & London Schoolboy Rep.; Beazer Homes Lge Premier Div R/U 87/88 & 88/89, & League Cup Winners 87/88 & 88/89 & R/U 89/90; Kent Senior Cup Winners 87/88

Club	Seasons	Transfer	Apps	Goals
Tilbury	80-82			
Aveley	82-84			
Hendon	84-85			
Southend United	85-86			
Leyton Orient	86-87			
Rainham Town	1987			

Sparrow, Brian (D)
(CRAWLEY TOWN)

D.O.B. 24.6.62

PLAYING CAREER

Honours: FA Trophy Winners 87/88

Club	Seasons	Transfer	Apps	Goals
Arsenal	80-84		2	
Wimbledon		loan	17	1
Millwall		loan	5	2
Gillingham		loan	5	1
Crystal Palace	84-86		63	2
Enfield	87-90			

Speed, Andy (F)
(BRIDGWATER TOWN 1984)   Age: 27

Previous Clubs: None

Honours: Somerset Senior League Champions & Cup Winners; County Senior Cup Finalist

Spinks, Gary (D)
(NEWPORT A.F.C.)   Age: 20

Previous Clubs: Albion Rovers; Caerleon; Merthyr Tydfil

Honours: Federated Homes League Winners 1989-90

Sprague, Keith (D)
(EXMOUTH TOWN)   Age:

Previous Clubs: Exmouth Town; Ottery St. Mary

Honours: Western League Championship Winner; Devon County

Springer, Carl (D)
(WALTHAMSTOW PENNANT)   Age: 32

Previous Clubs: Leyton-Wingate; Grays Athletic; Haringey Borough; Walthamstow Avenue

Honours: Vauxhall League Div 2 Winners Medal; Spartan League Cup Winners Medal 1988-89

Spriggs, Steve (M)
(CAMBRIDGE CITY)   D.O.B. 16.2.56

PLAYING CAREER

Honours: None

Club	Seasons	Transfer	Apps	Goals
Huddersfield Town	72-74		4	
Cambridge United	74-86		416	58
Middlesbrough	86-87		11	
Bury Town	87-89			

Sproson, Phil (D)
(NORTHWICH VICTORIA)   D.O.B. 13.10.59

Profession: Not working
Married   Wife's name: Jean
Children: Clare Victoria & Warren Jess
Hobbies: Golf, Fishing, Shooting

PLAYING CAREER

Honours: England Schoolboy Int.; Football League Div 4 Winners (5); Port Vale P.O.Y.

Club	Seasons	Transfer	Apps	Goals
Port Vale	78-89	£55,000	530	48
Birmingham City	89-90		16	2
Stafford Rangers	1990			

RICH SMITH (Boldmere St. Michael)
Photo: Sutton Observer

Stacey, Alan (D
(RACING CLUB WARWICK)   Age: 3

Previous Clubs: V.S.Rugby; AP Leamington; Southam Unite

Honours: Midland Combination Premier Div Winners & R/U Birmingham Senior Cup R/U

MARK STANTON (TAMWORTH)

Stagg, Andy (D)
(WELWYN GARDEN CITY) Age: 28
Previous Clubs: Welwyn Garden City; London Colney; Welwyn Garden United; Mowlems
Honours: Herts County Schools U-16; S.M.L. Rep. Side

Stafford, Andy (M)
(WESTHOUGHTON TOWN) Age: 26
Previous Clubs: None
Honours: L.F.A. Shield Winners; Bolton Comb. Premier Winners

Stafford, Phillip (F)
(DENABY UNITED) Age: 27
Previous Clubs: Gainsborough Trinity; Goole Town; Sheffield Club
Honours: N.C.E.L. 1st Div Champions (Sheffield)

Stanborough, N. D. (D)
(HINCKLEY ATHLETIC) Age: 21
Previous Clubs: Earl Shilton Albion; Hinckley
Honours: None

Standing, Shaun (D/M)
(PORTFIELD) Age: 29
Previous Clubs: Bracklesham
Honours: West Sussex Rep.

Stanley, Chris (M)
(BOGNOR REGIS TOWN) D.O.B. 21.9.70
Profession: Fruit Retailer
Single Hobbies: Sport
PLAYING CAREER
Honours: None

Club	Seasons	Transfer	Apps	Goals
Portsmouth	84-88			

Stanley, Garry (M)
(WATERLOOVILLE) D.O.B. 4.3.54
PLAYING CAREER
Honours: None

Club	Seasons	Transfer	Apps	Goals
Chelsea	71-78	£300,000	109	15
Everton	78-80	£150,000	52	1
Swansea City	80-83		72	4
Portsmouth	83-85		47	1
Wichita Wings (USA)	85-88			
Bristol City	88-90		10	

Stanley, Neal (F)
(SLOUGH TOWN) D.O.B. 30.5.61
Previous Clubs: Wokingham Town; Wycombe Wanderers.
Honours: Vauxhall Lge. Premier Div. Winners 89/90.

Stanley, Nick (D)
(MOSSLEY)
D.O.B. 8.6.64 **Nickname:** Half-Inch
Profession: Auto Electrician
Single
Hobbies: Golf, Cars
PLAYING CAREER
Honours: NPL Cup Winners; NPL Challenge Shield Winners; Manchester Premier Cup Winners; Reporter Cup Winners

Club	Seasons	Transfer	Apps	Goals
Oldham Town	82-84			
Port Vale	84-85			
Oldham Town	85-87			

Stanley, Tommy (M)
(SELBY TOWN) Age: 27
Previous Clubs: York City (18 appearances); Scarborough; Goole Town; Rowntrees
Honours: N.C.E. Div 1N Runners-Up 1984; Div 1 Runners-Up 1987, 1988, 1989; Division 1 Champions 1990; N.C.E. League Cup Runners-Up 1988; North Riding Senior Cup Runners-Up; N Intermediate League Cup

Stanton, Chris (D)
(NEWPORT A.F.C.) Age: 25
Previous Clubs: Caerlgon; Bath City; Mangotsfield
Honours: Hellenic League Champions

Stapleton, Lol (F)
(SAWBRIDGEWORTH TOWN) Age: 30
Previous Clubs: Sawbridgeworth Town; Ware; Billericay; Ware
Honours: Essex Thameside Trophy (Billericay); Herts Charity Cup (Ware)

NEAL STANLEY (Slough Town)

Stapleton, Simon (M)
(WYCOMBE WANDERERS)

D.O.B. 10.12.68

PLAYING CAREER

Honours: None

Club	Seasons	Transfer	Apps	Goals
Portsmouth	85-88			
Bristol Rovers	88-89		5	

Statham, Gary (D)
(HINCKLEY) Age: 20

Previous Clubs: Barwell; Barlestone
Honours: Player of the Year 1989-90

Staunton, Chris (F)
(MARINE)

D.O.B. 19.10.63 Nickname: Storto
Profession: Clothing Merchant
Single
Hobbies: Sport

PLAYING CAREER

Honours: None

Club	Seasons	Transfer	Apps	Goals
Prescot Cables	89-90			
Altrincham	1990			

Steadman, Darren (G)
(KIDDERMINSTER HARRIERS)

D.O.B. 26.1.70
Profession: Managing Director
Single
Hobbies: Sport

PLAYING CAREER

Honours: Hereford & Worcs Schoolboy Rep; Worcs County Youth Rep; England Schoolboy Int.

Club	Seasons	Transfer	Apps	Goals
No previous clubs				

Stedman, Karl (F)
(HORSHAM) Age: 24

Previous Clubs: Steyning Town; Worthing
Honours: Sussex Senior Cup Winners 88/89

Stedman, Steve (D)
(WINGATE) Age: 21

Previous Clubs: Leicester University)
Honours: None

Stedman, Tony (D)
(HORSHAM) Age: 23

Previous Clubs: Steyning Town
Honours: None

Steel, Greg (D)
(STROUD)

D.O.B. 11.3.59
Profession: Transport Manager
Married Wife's name: Sandy
Hobbies: Sport

PLAYING CAREER

Honours: Avon Schoolboy Rep; Somerset Youth Rep; Beazer Homes Midland Div Winners 88/89

Club	Seasons	Transfer	Apps	Goals
Clevedon Town	74-78			
Newport County	78-79		3	
Gloucester City	79-80			
Clevedon Town	80-87			
Forest Green Rovers	87-88			
Gloucester City	88-91			

Steele, Nigel (D/M)
(STAPENHILL) Age: 28

Previous Clubs: Derby County; Gresley Rovers; Stapenhill; Mickleover R.B.L. Thringstone

Honours: Leics Senior League Winners & Leics Senior Cup 1986-87 (Stapenhill)

Stein, Edwin (M)
(BARNET)

D.O.B. 28.9.55
Profession: Not working
Single
Hobbies: Golf, Tennis
Harrow P.O.Y. 80/81; Barnet P.O.Y. 88/89

PLAYING CAREER

Honours: None

Club	Seasons	Transfer	Apps	Goals
Edgware Town	77-78			
Luton Town	78-79			
Harrow Borough	79-81			
Dagenham	81-82	£20,000		

Stephens, Archie (F)
(GUISBOROUGH TOWN) Age: 36

Previous Clubs: Bristol Rovers; Middlesbrough; Carlisle United; Darlington

Honours: Runners-Up Division 2 Football League (Midd'boro); Winners GM Conference (Darlington)

Stephens, Freddie (F)
(KINTBURY RANGERS) Age: 25

Previous Clubs: Thatcham; Newbury; Hungerford; Basingstoke
Honours: Selected for Hampshire (1989-90)

Stephens, Micky (M)
(TOOTING & MITCHAM UNITED) Age: 30

Previous Clubs: Sutton United
Honours: England Semi-pro Int; FA XI; Vauxhall-Opel Lge Winners; FA Trophy R/U; Surrey Senior Cup Winners

197

Stephens, Neil (M)

(WARMINSTER TOWN) Age: 26

Previous Clubs: Warminster Town; Calne Town
Honours: None

Stephenson, Dave (D)

(CROYDON) Age: 21

Previous Clubs: London Boys
Honours: None

Stephenson, Geoff (D)

(BOSTON UNITED)

D.O.B. 28.4.70
Profession: Not working
Single
Hobbies: Golf, Snooker

PLAYING CAREER

Honours: None

Club	Seasons	Transfer	Apps	Goals
Grimsby Town	88-90		32	

Stepney, Mark (M)

(HORSHAM) Age: 25

Previous Clubs: Youth team product
Honours: None

MARK STEPNEY

Stevens, Andrew (M)

(BIDEFORD) Age: 20

Previous Clubs: Torrington
Honours: None

Stevens, Paul (D)

(BATH CITY) D.O.B. 4.4.60

Nickname: Stets **Profession:** Salesman
Married **Children:** Danny & Kelly
Hobbies: Sport, Eating

PLAYING CAREER

Honours: None

Club	Seasons	Transfer	Apps	Goals
Bristol City	76-85		147	3

Stevenson, Dave (D)

(WALTHAMSTOW PENNANT) Age: 34

Previous Clubs: Haringey Boro; Leyton-Wingate; Hoddesdon Town; Cheshunt; Southgate Athletic
Honours: F.A. Vase Winners Medal 1975

Stevenson, Nigel (D)

(YEOVIL TOWN)

D.O.B. 2.11.58

PLAYING CAREER

Honours: Welsh Schoolboy & Youth Int; Welsh U-21 & Full Int; Welsh Semi-Pro Int

Club	Seasons	Transfer	Apps	Goals
Swansea City	75-86		295	15
Cardiff City		loan	14	
Reading		loan	3	
Cardiff City	86-87		36	1
Newport County	87-88			
Merthyr Tydfil	88-91			

Stevenson, Ronnie (F)

(BECKENHAM TOWN) Age: 2

Previous Clubs: Southwark Sports; Beckenham Town; Dulwich Hamlet; Croydon
Honours: None

Stevenson, Terrence (G)

(YATE TOWN) Age: 2

Previous Clubs: Berkeley Town
Honours: None

Stewart, Malcolm (M

(REDBRIDGE FOREST)

D.O.B. 31.7.60

PLAYING CAREER

Honours: Vauxhall-Opel Lge Premier Winners 88/89

Club	Seasons	Transfer	Apps	Goals
Hoddesdon Town	77-81			
Dagenham	81-83			
Maidstone United	83-85			
Dartford	85-86			
Maidstone United	86-88			

Stewart, Mickey (M

(BRIDLINGTON TOWN) Age: 2

Previous Clubs: North Ferriby United; Denaby United; Sheffie FC
Honours: None

Stimson, Barry (D

(SOMERSHAM TOWN) Age: 2

Previous Clubs: Houghton & Wyton; Offord; Warboys
Honours: None

Stockley, Bob (D)

(ATHERSTONE UNITED)   D.O.B. 12.12.52

Nickname: Piggy   **Profession:** Production Supervisor
Married   **Wife's name:** Gill
Children: Robert   **Hobbies:** Fishing, Horse Racing

PLAYING CAREER

Honours: Coventry & Warwicks Schoolboy Rep; Southern Lge Premier Div Winners 74/75 ,81/82; West Midland Lge Winners 83/84; Banbury P.O.Y. 83/84; England Semi-Pro Int.

Club	Seasons	Transfer	Apps	Goals
Coventry City	68-71			
Poole Town	71-72			
Wimbledon	72-75	£300		
Atherstone United	75-78	£1,500		
Nuneaton Borough	78-82			
Banbury United	82-84			
Coventry Sporting	1984			
AP Leamington	1984			
Bedworth United	84-85			

Stokes, Stuart (M)

(GRESLEY ROVERS)   Age: 21

Previous Clubs: Derby County; Willenhall Town
Honours: None

Stone, Barry (F)

(DULWICH HAMLET)   Age: 26

Previous Clubs: Chipstead; Molesey; Croydon; Molesey; Whyteleafe
Honours: None

Stone, Kevin (D/M)

(MARLOW)   D.O.B. 26.12.62

Nickname: Stoney   **Profession:** Chairmaker
Married   **Wife's name:** Jane
Children: Amanda   **Hobbies:** Golf, Racing, Cricket

PLAYING CAREER

Honours: Bucks County Schoolboy Rep; Vauxhall-Opel Lge Div 1 & 2 Winners

Previous Clubs: Wycombe Wanderers (82-84); Maidenhead United (84-85); Beaconsfield United (85-86).

Stones, Anthony (F)

(CLEATOR MOOR CELTIC)   Age: 31

Previous Clubs: Cleator Moor Celtic; Barrow; Workington
Honours: None

Storey, John (F)

(ALFRETON TOWN)   Age: 20

Previous Clubs: Worksop Town   **Honours:** None

Stratton, Michael (M)

(CORNARD UNITED)   Age: 28

Previous Clubs: None   **Honours:** None

Stringer, David (M)

(BANBURY UNITED)   Age: 24

Previous Clubs: Nuneaton; Bedworth
Honours: None

Stringer, John (F)

(NORTHWICH VICTORIA)   D.O.B. 15.6.64

PLAYING CAREER

Honours: FA Trophy Winners 88/89 & R/U 87/88; Shropshire Senior Cup Winners

Club	Seasons	Transfer	Apps	Goals
Barnton	83-84			
Runcorn	84-86			
Telford United	86-90			

Strobl, John (F)

(VALE RECREATION)   Age: 32

Previous Clubs: Northerners; Guernsey Rangers; Sylvans; St Martin's

Honours: 1 Guernsey Priaulx Championship Medal 1979-80 (Guernsey Rangers)

Stuart, Tony (D)

(EXMOUTH TOWN)   Age:

Previous Clubs: Barnstaple Town; Exmouth Town; Saltash United

Honours: Western League Championship Winner; Devon County

Stubbs, Terry (M)

(MOSSLEY)   D.O.B. 20.6.67

Nickname: Trent   **Profession:** Sandblaster
Single   **Hobbies:** Snooker, Pool

PLAYING CAREER

Honours: None

Club	Seasons	Transfer	Apps	Goals
Winsford United	87-88			
ICI Blackley	88-90			

TERRY STUBBS

Sturgeon, Rob (D)
(SUTTON COLDFIELD TOWN) **Age:** 26
Previous Clubs: Liverpool; Coventry City; Formby; Southport
Honours: Southport P.O.Y.

Sugar, Chris (F)
(KEYNSHAM TOWN) **Age:** 22
Previous Clubs: Imperial Bristol; Shepton Mallet; Welton Rovers; Frys

Honours: Somerset Senior Champions (Frys)

Sugrue, Paul (F)
(NUNEATON BOROUGH) **D.O.B.** 6.11.60
PLAYING CAREER
Honours: None

Club	Seasons	Transfer	Apps	Goals
Nuneaton Borough	78-80			
Manchester City	80-81		6	
Cardiff City	1981		5	
Kansas City (USA)	81-82			
Middlesbrough	82-84		69	6
Portsmouth	84-85		4	
Northampton Town	85-86		8	2
Newport County	86-87		2	
Kidderminster H.	88-90			
Barnet	1990			

PAUL SUGRUE

Sullivan, Kieran (D)
(BUCKINGHAM TOWN) **Age:** 21
Previous Clubs: Banbury United **Honours:** None

Sullivan, Michael (G)
(TOOTING & MITCHAM UNITED) **Age:** 17
Previous Clubs: Crystal Palace
Honours: None

Sullivan, Nicholas (G)
(SUTTON UNITED)

D.O.B. 4.1.61 **Nickname:** Sully
Profession: Accountant
Single
Hobbies: Sport

PLAYING CAREER
Honours: England Youth Int.; FA XI; Vauxhall-Opel Lge Rep; Vauxhall-Opel Lge Premier & Div 1 R/U; London Senior Cup R/U; Tooting P.O.Y. (2); Bromley P.O.Y. (2).

Club	Seasons	Transfer	Apps	Goals
Arsenal	77-80			
Tooting & Mitcham U.	80-84			
Bromley	84-88	£1,000		
Sutton United	88-89			
Dulwich Hamlet	1989			

Sullivan, Robert (D)
(KETTERING TOWN)

D.O.B. 25.1.71 **Nickname:** Sully
Profession: Electricians Mate
Single
Hobbies: Sport

PLAYING CAREER
Honours: None

Club	Seasons	Transfer	Apps	Goals
Peterborough United	86-89			
Ramsey Town	89-90			

Sullivan, Terry (M/F)
(REDBRIDGE FOREST)

D.O.B. 11.7.55 **Nickname:** Sully
Profession: Engineer
Married **Wife's name:** Glyniss
Children: Paul & Lindsey

PLAYING CAREER
Honours: Vauxhall-Opel Lge Premier Winners; Isthmian Lge Di 1 Winners; Southern Lge Premier Div Winners; FA Troph Winners 80/81; Herts County Cup Winners; Southern Lge Cu R/U.

Club	Seasons	Transfer	Apps	Goals
West Ham United	73-77			
Bishop's Stortford	78-82			
Dartford	82-84			
Dagenham	84-85			
Maidstone United	85-86			

Sutton, Dave (F
(LEEK TOWN) **D.O.B.** 15.12.6
PLAYING CAREER
Honours: HFS Loans Lge Div. One Winners 89/90; F.A. Troph R/U 89/90.

Club	Seasons	Transfer	Apps	Goals
Stoke City	83-85			
Crewe Alexandra	86-87		1	1

Swain, Glen (M)

(BALDOCK TOWN) Age: 22

Previous Clubs: Sutton United; Clapton
Honours: None

Swallow, Gary (G)

(CALNE TOWN) Age: 25

Previous Clubs: Corsham Town; Chippenham Town
Honours: Winners Wilts Premier Shield (Chippenham); Never missed a game for Calne Town

Swann, Andrew (D)

(BANBURY UNITED) Age: 24

Previous Clubs: Brackley Town; Chipping Norton Town
Honours: None

Sweeney, Terry (D)

(GENERAL CHEMICALS) Age: 24

Previous Clubs: Owly Wood; Dane Wanderers; Tesco; Raven; Blue Barrel; Winsford Res.
Honours: None

Sykes, Bob (D)

(HEANOR TOWN) Age: 41

Previous Clubs: Derby County; Port Vale; Burton Albion; Heanor Town; Redditch; Tamworth
Honours: None

Sylvester, Ali (M)

(WALTHAMSTOW PENNANT) Age: 31

Previous Clubs: Walthamstow Avenue; Wealdstone; Hendon
Honours: Spartan Cup Winners Medal 1988-89

DAVE SUTTON
(Leek Town)

TREVOR BOOKER

(WELLING UNITED)

This photograph was just too good to leave out, but since it was an awkward size/shape for the book, we had to wait until we found a suitable position - and this is it. Looking at the photograph you might think that the stadium is a bit empty, but that is because they don't use that side of the ground at the International Stadium, Gateshead for football matches.
T.W.

EDDIE STEIN (BARNET)

Tabb, Mark (F)

(WESTFIELDS) Age: 29

Previous Clubs: Hereford United; Lads Club
Honours: None

Tafft, Darren (F)

(MOOR GREEN)

D.O.B. 12.10.73   **Nickname:** Taffty
Profession: Assistant Chef
Single
Hobbies: Football, Cooking, Dancing

PLAYING CAREER

Honours: Birmingham Schoolboy Rep; South-West England Schoolboy Rep; Hereford & Worcs Schoolboy Rep.

No previous clubs

Talboys, Steve (F)

(GLOUCESTER CITY)

D.O.B. 18.9.66   **Nickname:** Sticksy
Profession: Haulage Contractor
Single
Hobbies: Golf

PLAYING CAREER

Honours: FA XI; Beazer Homes Midland Div Winners 88/89

Club	Seasons	Transfer	Apps	Goals
Mangotsfield United	83-85			
Bath City	85-86			
Trowbridge Town	86-88			

Tanner Russell (D:M)

(BRAINTREE TOWN) Age: 18

Previous Clubs: Chelmsford City
Honours: Essex Youth Rep

Tapp, Daryl (D)

(VALE RECREATION) Age: 25

Previous Clubs: None
Honours: 4 Guernsey Caps (1984-90); Five Guernsey Priaulx Championship Medals 1982-83, 1983-84, 1985-86, 1987-88, 1988-89; 1 Channel Islands Championship Medal (Upton Park Trophy) 1988

Tapp, Gary (F)

(VALE RECREATION) Age: 26

Previous Clubs: Vale Recreation (Youth); Northerners
Honours: Six Guernsey Priaulx Championship Medals 1980-81, 1981-82, 1982-83, 1985-86, 1987-88, 1988-89; 1 Channel Islands Championship Medal (Upton Park Trophy) 1988

Tate, Colin (F)

(HENDON)

D.O.B. 2.2.60   **Nickname:** Geezer
Profession: Legal Executive
Married   **Wife's name:** Chrissie
Hobbies: Football, Golf

PLAYING CAREER

Honours: Herts & Middx County Schoolboy Rep; South-East Counties Lge Winners 79/80; FA XI; Middx Senior Cup Winners 88/89; Oxford Senior Cup Winners 83/84; GMAC Cup R/U 87/88; AC Delco Cup R/U 87/88; Hendon P.O.Y. 85/86

Club	Seasons	Transfer	Apps	Goals
Queens Park Rangers	79-80			
Oxford City	80-83			
Wycombe Wanderers	83-84			
Slough Town	84-85			
Hendon	85-87			
Harrow Borough	87-88			

Tattersall, David (D)

(GREAT HARWOOD TOWN) Age: 25

Previous Clubs: Accrington Stanley; Clitheroe
Honours: Lamot Pils Cup 1990

Taylor, Andrew (D)

(STAPENHILL) Age: 23

Previous Clubs: Walsall Wood
Honours: None

Taylor, Andrew D (D/M)

(GREAT HARWOOD TOWN) Age: 19

Previous Clubs: Burnley
Honours: None

Taylor, Andrew J (F)

(GREAT HARWOOD TOWN) Age: 19

Previous Clubs: Cutwood Rangers
Honours: Lamot Pils Cup 1990

Taylor, Andrew (M)

(BRIDGNORTH TOWN) Age: 25

Previous Clubs: Nags Head; Welshpool Town
Honours: None

ANDY TAYLOR

Taylor, Andy (M/F)

(LEATHERHEAD) Age: 20

Previous Clubs: Walton & Hersham; Dorking
Honours: None

DEREK TALLY

Taylor David   (D)

(TOOTING & MITCHAM UNITED)   Age: 26

Previous Clubs: Epsom & Ewell; Hayes; Dulwich Hamlet; Croydon
Honours: British Colleges Rep & Winners 83; 84 & 85

Taylor, Elliott   (M)

(CROYDON)   Age: 18

Previous Clubs: Youth team product
Honours: None

Taylor, Gordon   (M)

(A.F.C. LYMINGTON)   Age: 29

Previous Clubs: Everton; Partick Thistle; Grays Athletic; Ringwood Town; Lymington Town
Honours: Hants Senior Rep.; Wessex League Cup Winners; Hants Senior Cup Runners-Up

Taylor, Mark   (D)

(OLDSWINFORD)   Age: 23

Previous Clubs: Halesowen Harriers
Honours: None

Taylor, Paul   (D)

(BILLERICAY TOWN)   Age: 24

Previous Clubs: Hornchurch
Honours: None

Taylor, Paul   (M)

(BROMLEY)   Age: 29

Previous Clubs: Leytonstone-Ilford; Dagenham; Enfield; Barking; Leyton Orient; Arsenal (J); Leyton Wingate
Honours: F.A. Trophy Winner (Enfield)

Taylor, Paul   (M)

(BECKENHAM TOWN)   Age: 20

Previous Clubs: Charlton Athletic; Middlesbrough; Queens Park Rangers; Beckenham Town; Sheppey United; Dulwich Hamlet; Bromley
Honours: None

Taylor, Peter   (F)

(ENFIELD)

D.O.B. 3.1.53   **Nickname:** Spud
Profession: Insurance Consultant
Married   **Wife's name:** Jenny
Children: Chloe & Lauren
Hobbies: Squash, Tennis, Jogging

PLAYING CAREER

Honours: England Under-23 Int; England Full Int

Club	Seasons	Transfer	Apps	Goals
Southend United	70-73	£120,000	75	12
Crystal Palace	73-76	£200,000	122	33
Tottenham Hotspur	76-80	£150,000	123	31
Leyton Orient	80-82		56	11
		(Oldham Athletic - loan 4)		
Maidstone United	82-83			
Exeter City	1983		8	
Maidstone United	83-84			
Chelmsford City	84-85			
Heybridge Swifts	85-86			
Dartford	86-90			

Taylor, Robbie   (F)

(DORCHESTER TOWN)

D.O.B. 3.12.67

PLAYING CAREER

Honours: None

Club	Seasons	Transfer	Apps	Goals
Portsmouth	84-86			
Newport County	86-87		44	7
Weymouth	87-89			
Torquay United	89-90		18	1

GEOFF THOMAS (DORKING)

Templeton, John (M)
(BALDOCK TOWN) Age: 22
Previous Clubs: Stevenage Borough; Hitchin Town
Honours: None

Terrell, John (D)
(SEATON DELAVAL AMATEURS) Age: 25
Previous Clubs: Marsden C.W.
Honours: Northumberland Senior Benevolent Bowl Winners Medal; McEwans Northern Alliance Premier Division Championship Winners Medal

Thomas Geoff (D)
(DORKING) Age: 21
Previous Clubs: Charlton Athletic
Honours: England Youth Int, FA Youth Cup R/U, Vauxhall-Opel Lge Div 2 South Winners

Thomas, Kevin (M)
(CWMBRAN TOWN) Age: 27
Previous Clubs: Sully
Honours: Cardiff Schools

Thomas Mark (D:M)
(RADCLIFFE BOROUGH) Age: 29
Previous Clubs: Maine Road; Prestwich Heys; Stalybridge Celtic
Honours: England & Great Britain Fire Service Rep

Thomas, Nigel (M)
(NEWTOWN) Age: 22
Previous Clubs: Abermule; Newtown
Honours: None

Thomas Paul (M)
(BEDWORTH UNITED) Age: 27
Previous Clubs: Bedworth United; Nuneaton Borough; Bedworth United; Aylesbury United £500
Honours: Beazer Homes Lge Premier Div Winners

Thomas, Tony (F)
(NORTHWOOD) Age: 26
Previous Clubs: North Greenford; Harrow Borough; Hamwell Town; Finchley Town
Honours: None

Thompson, Andy (M)
(WALTHAMSTOW PENNANT) Age: 24
Previous Clubs: Amelia Sports **Honours:** None

Thompson, Ian (D)
(KNOWSLEY UNITED) Age: 30
Previous Clubs: Kirkby Town; Skelmersdale United; Prescot Cables; Ellesmere Port
Honours: None

Thompson, Ian (F)
(MERTHYR TYDFIL)

D.O.B. 8.6.58
PLAYING CAREER
Honours: Beazer Homes Premier Div Winners

Club	Seasons	Transfer	Apps	Goals
Salisbury	78-83			
AFC Bournemouth	83-85		121	30
Salisbury	85-87			
Newport County	87-88			

Thompson, Nigel (F)
(ALFRETON TOWN) Age: 23
Previous Clubs: Chesterfield; Leeds United; Colne Dynamoes; Gainsborough Trinity
Honours: None

Thompson, Peter (M)
(STAPENHILL) Age: 21
Previous Clubs: None
Honours: Scoreline Combination Div 1 Winners 1989

Thompson Philip (D)
(FARSLEY CELTIC) Age: 21
Previous Clubs: None
Honours: None

Thomson, Robert (F)
(FLEETWOOD TOWN)

D.O.B. 21.3.55 **Nickname:** Tommo
Profession: Not working
Married **Wife's name:** Carole
Children: Ryan & Hollis
Hobbies: Darts, Snooker, Golf
PLAYING CAREER
Honours: Strathclyde & Glasgow Schoolboy Rep; Scotland Schoolboy & Youth Int; Scotland Under-23 Int; Scottish Lge Rep; Scottish First Div Winners 77/78 & 87/88; St.Johnstone Y.P.O.Y 71/72; Morton P.O.Y. 79/80

Club	Seasons	Transfer	Apps	Goals
St.Johnstone	70-77	£70,000		
Morton	77-80	£350,000		
Middlesbrough	80-82	£20,000	20	2
Hibernian	82-85			
Blackpool	85-87		52	6
Hamilton Academical	87-89			
Colne Dynamoes	89-90			

Thorne, Nigel (D)
(KINTBURY RANGERS) Age: 26
Previous Clubs: Lambourn
Honours: Berks & Bucks Sunday Junior Winners

Thornley, Mark (G)
(FLEETWOOD TOWN)

D.O.B. 26.7.65   **Nickname:** Wolf
Profession: Wood Machinist
Married   **Wife's name:** Samantha
Children: David   **Hobbies:** Sport

PLAYING CAREER

Honours:

Club	Seasons	Transfer	Apps	Goals
Belper Town	82-85			
Sutton Town	85-86			
Alfreton Town	86-87			
Stafford Rangers	1987			
Matlock Town	87-88			

Thornton, Andrew (F)
(PICKERING TOWN)   Age: 27

Previous Clubs: Norton; Old Malton; Westlers
Honours: Too many to name

Thoroughgood, Terry (G)
(CROYDON)   Age: 21

Previous Clubs: Sutton United; Crystal Palace; Frinton Rovers; Whyteleafe
Honours: Surrey Premier Lge Winners 87/88; Surrey Premier Cup Winners 87/88 & 88/89

Thorpe, Robert (F)
(WYCOMBE WANDERERS)

PLAYING CAREER

Honours: None

Club	Seasons	Transfer	Apps	Goals
Bracknell Town	87-89			

Thorpe, Tony (D)
(GAINSBOROUGH TOWN)   Age: 25

Previous Clubs: Brigg Town; North Ferriby United; Winterton Rangers; Ross Sports; Barton Town; Clee Borough
Honours: None

Thrift, Philip (F)
(CHELMSFORD CITY)

D.O.B. 28.1.62
Profession: Electrician
Married   **Wife's name:** Sandra
Children: Chloe

PLAYING CAREER

Honours: Southern Lge Southern Div R/U 85/86; Essex Senior Cup Winners 85/86

Club	Seasons	Transfer	Apps	Goals
Writtle	79-80			
Chelmsford City	80-87			
Dagenham	87-88			
Heybridge Swifts	88-89			
Stambridge	89-90			

IAN THOMPSON (MERTHYR T.)

Thrower, Nigel (M)
(HEANOR TOWN)   Age: 28

Previous Clubs: Nottingham Forest; Shepshed Charterhouse; Kettering Town; Eastwood Town; Worksop Town; Priory Celtic
Honours: None

Thurlow, Stephen (D)
(SUTTON UNITED)

D.O.B. 26.2.70   **Nickname:** Thurls
Profession: Bank Clerk
Single
Hobbies: Cricket, Tennis, Reading, Buying Records

PLAYING CAREER

Honours: FA Youth Cup R/U 87/88

Club	Seasons	Transfer	Apps	Goals
Charlton Athletic	86-89			
Croydon	89-90			

Tilley Darren (M)
(YATE TOWN)   Age: 23

Previous Clubs: Bath City; Trowbridge Town; Mangotsfield United; Bath City
Honours: None

Tilley, Warren (M)
(HORSHAM)   Age: 19

Previous Clubs: Youth team product   **Honours:** None

Tinson Darren (D)
(COLWYN BAY)   Age: 20

Previous Clubs: Connah's Quay Nomads   **Honours:** None

Tobin, Graham (D)
(MACCLESFIELD TOWN)

D.O.B. 3.1.55   **Nickname:** Tobe
Profession: Teacher

PLAYING CAREER

Honours: Alliance Premier LgE Winners (2); NPL & Cup Winners 86/87; FA Trophy R/U 88/89; NPL Rep.; Macclesfield P.O.Y. 83/84

Club	Seasons	Transfer	Apps	Goals
Burscough	74-76			
Altrincham	76-80			

STUART TODHUNTER

Todhunter, Stuart (D)

(BARROW) Age: 31

Previous Clubs: Workington 86-87; Preston North End 87-89; Barrow

Honours: None

Tomlin, Steve (M)

(CARSHALTON ATHLETIC)

D.O.B. 23.4.57
Profession: Electrician
Married Wife's name: Sharron
Profession: Modelling

PLAYING CAREER

Honours: Surrey Senior Cup Winners 88/89 & 89/90

Club	Seasons	Transfer	Apps	Goals
Bromley	76-80			
Dulwich Hamlet	80-82			
Leatherhead	82-84			
Carshalton Athletic	84-86			
Croydon	86-88			

Tomlinson, David (F)

(BARNET)

D.O.B. 13.12.68 Nickname: Tomo
Profession: Galverniser
Married Wife's name: Deborah
Hobbies: Music, DIY, Walking

PLAYING CAREER

Honours: England Schoolboy Int

Club	Seasons	Transfer	Apps	Goals
Sheffield Wednesday	85-87			
Rotherham United	87-89		17	
Gainsborough Trinity	89-90			
Boston United	90-91			

Tomlinson Mark (M)

(RHYL) Age: 25

Previous Clubs: Hartford College Honours: None

Toone, Richard (D)

(BOSTON UNITED)

D.O.B. 31.3.69 Nickname: Ticker
Profession: Local Government Officer
Single
Hobbies: Golf

PLAYING CAREER

Honours: Lincs Schoolboy Rep.; Lincoln United P.O.Y. 89/90

Club	Seasons	Transfer	Apps	Goals
Leicester City	84-87			
Lincoln United	87-90	£1,500		

Topliss, Kevin (F)

(SPALDING) Age: 23

Previous Clubs: Grimsby Town; Scunthorpe United; Crewe Alexandra; Brigg Town; North Ferriby

Honours: None

Torrance, Dave (F)

(DESBOROUGH TOWN) Age: 25

Previous Clubs: Danesholme Albion; Stamford Town

Honours: No major honours

Toth, Zoltan (F)

(CONGLETON TOWN)

D.O.B. 2.12.64 Nickname: Zoe
Profession: Roofer
Married Wife's name: Angela
Children: Claire & Zoltan
Hobbies: Football, Snooker

PLAYING CAREER

Honours: Staffs Vase Winners

Club	Seasons	Transfer	Apps	Goals
Stoke City	81-85			
Knypersley Victoria	85-88			
Rists United	89-90			

Towell, Paul (D)
(PICKERING TOWN) Age: 18
Previous Clubs: Wykeham
Honours: None

TONY TOWNER

Towner, Tony (F)
(CRAWLEY TOWN) Age: 36
PLAYING CAREER
Honours: Football Lge Div 3 Winners 80/81

Club	Seasons	Transfer	Apps	Goals
Brighton & H A	72-78		162	24
Millwall	78-80		68	13
Rotherham Utd	80-83		108	12
Sheffield Utd (Loan)			10	1
Wolves	83-84		31	2
Charlton Ath	84-85		27	2
Rochdale	85-86		5	
Cambridge Utd	86-87		8	
Gravesend	87-88			
Fisher Ath	88-89			
Crawley Town	89-90			
Gravesend	90-91			
Crawley Town				

Townsend, Chris (F)
(BATH CITY)

D.O.B. 30.3.66
PLAYING CAREER
Honours: Welsh Schoolboy & Youth Int; Beazer Homes Midland Div Winners 88/89

Club	Seasons	Transfer	Apps	Goals
Cardiff City	83-84		5	
Newport County	84-85			
Forest Green Rovers	85-86			
Cheltenham Town	86-88			
Gloucester City	88-90	£10,000		
Dorchester Town	90-91			

Tracey, Shaun (D)
(BURNHAM RAMBLERS) Age: 21
Previous Clubs: None Honours: None

Travis, David (M)
(GOOLE TOWN)

D.O.B. 4.7.64 Nickname: Trav
Profession: JCB Operator
Married Wife's name: Karen Hobbies: Spor
PLAYING CAREER
Honours: Doncaster Schoolboy Rep; South Yorks Schoolboy Rep

Club	Seasons	Transfer	Apps	Goals
Hatfield Main	81-82			
Doncaster Rovers	82-84		12	
Scunthorpe United	84-85		13	1
Chesterfield	86-87		11	2
Gainsborough Trinity	87-88			
Bridlington Town	1989			

Tredgold, Kevin (D)
(WALTHAMSTOW PENNANT) Age: 2
Previous Clubs: Southend United (Youth) Honours: Non

Treharve, Jason (F)
(BRIDGNORTH TOWN) Age: 1
Previous Clubs: Oakengate Town; Stafford Rangers
Honours: None

Trinder, Jason (G
(OADBY TOWN) Age: 2
Previous Clubs: Oadby Town; Leicester United
Honours: Player of the Season 1989-90

Tripp, Nigel (D
(CHIPPENHAM TOWN) Age: 2
Previous Clubs: Corsham Town; Melksham Town; Chippenhar Town; Trowbridge Town Honours: Wilts Premier Shiel

Tripp, Peter (M)

(CHIPPENHAM TOWN) Age: 28

Previous Clubs: Devizes Town; Melksham Town

Honours: County Player

Trow, Robert (D)

(STAPENHILL) Age: 24

Previous Clubs: Brereton Social; Armitage; Rocester

Honours: Scoreline Combination Division 1 Championship Medal 1989-90

Truran, Gary (G)

(PICKERING TOWN) Age: 22

Previous Clubs: Pickering Town; Scarborough; Guiseley; Kiveton Park

Honours: None

Tucker, Craig (G)

(DARTFORD)

D.O.B. 7.10.62
Profession: Project Manager
Single
Hobbies: Golf, The Arts, Gardening, Walking

PLAYING CAREER

Honours: None

Club	Seasons	Transfer	Apps	Goals
Haringey Borough	79-81			
Leyton-Wingate	81-88			
Boreham Wood	88-89			
Leyton-Wingate	89-90			

Tucker, Mark (D)

(MERTHYR TYDFIL)

D.O.B. 10.2.63

PLAYING CAREER

Honours: Welsh Schoolboy & Youth Int

Club	Seasons	Transfer	Apps	Goals
Abergavenny	83-89			

Tucker, Neal (M)

(BRIDGWATER TOWN 1984) Age: 28

Previous Clubs: Bridgwater Town; Frome Town; Minehead; Taunton Town; Minehead

Honours: Somerset County Side; Somerset Senior League Winners

Tucker, Stuart (D)

(SUTTON COLDFIELD TOWN) Age: 25

Previous Clubs: Paget Rangers Honours: None

Tucknott, Darren (F)

(BECKENHAM TOWN) Age: 26

Previous Clubs: Greenwich Borough Honours: None

Tudor, Kevin (D)

(BRIDGNORTH TOWN) Age: 35

Previous Clubs: Shrewsbury Town; Telford United; Newtown; Worcester City; Redditch United; Stourbridge; Malvern Town

Honours: Welsh Cup Semi-Final; 3rd Rnd F.A. Cup; Southern Midlands Div 1 Winners 1978; S/Premier Winners 1980; Worcester Senior Cup Winner (4 times); Staffs Senior Cup

Turkington, Mark (D/M)

(SLOUGH TOWN) Age: 27

Previous Clubs: Chelsea; Charlton Ath; Woking; Maidenhead Utd; Farnborough; Leatherhead; Farnborough; Woking; Slough

Honours: Vauxhall-Opel Lge Rep, Vauxhall Lge R/U 88/89, Hants Senior Cup Winners & R/U

Turley Roy (F)

(COLWYN BAY) Age: 23

Previous Clubs: Rhyl Honours: Bass NWCL Cup Winners

Turley, Russell (D/M)

(STAFFORD RANGERS)

D.O.B. 20.8.67 Profession: Warehouseman
Married Wife's name: Claire
Hobbies: Golf, Gardening

PLAYING CAREER

Honours: None

Club	Seasons	Transfer	Apps	Goals
Nottingham Forest	83-86			
Wolverhampton W.	86-88			

Turner, Lee (M)

(HORSHAM) Age: 17

Previous Clubs: Crystal Palace Honours: None

Turner, Mike (M)

(EXMOUTH TOWN) Age: 27

Previous Clubs: Shildon, Grimsby Town; Shildon

Honours: Durham County Cup Winner

Turner, Paul (M)

(ENFIELD)

D.O.B. 13.11.68 Profession: Planer
Single Hobbies: Golf

PLAYING CAREER

Honours: None

Club	Seasons	Transfer	Apps	Goals
Arsenal	86-88			
Cambridge United	88-89		37	
Farnborough Town	89-90			

Turner, Phil (F)

(BECKENHAM TOWN) Age: 19

Previous Clubs: Greenwich Borough Honours: None

PETER SHOEINDE (DORKING)

Ullathorne, Simon (D)

(CLEATOR MOOR CELTIC) Age: 19
Previous Clubs: Workington Reds Honours: None

Underwood, Denis (G)

(GREAT HARWOOD TOWN) Age: 33
Previous Clubs: Clitheroe
Honours: B.N.W.C.L. Div 1 Champions 1985-86; Div 2 1984-85; Div 3 1983-84; Cup Runners-Up 1985-86; Lancs Junior Cup Winner 1984-85

Upton, Paul (D)

(ATHERSTONE UNITED) D.O.B. 23.3.60
Previous Clubs: Coventry Sporting (78-81); Bedworth Utd.(81-83); Stafford Rangers (83-90).
Honours: NPL Winners 84/85; Bob Lord Trophy Winners 85/86; Staffs Senior Cup Winners 86/87

Usher, Ray (F)

(STRATFORD TOWN) Age: 30+
Previous Clubs: Atherstone Town; Sutton Town; Bedworth United; Oldbury United; Oxford United (youth)
Honours: Warwickshire County Player

Vale, Dick (F)

(BIGGLESWADE TOWN) Age: 33
Previous Clubs: None Honours: None

Vangelder, Paul (M)

(WINGATE) Age: 31
Previous Clubs: Tottenham (Youth)
Honours: F.A. Youth Cup Winners Medal 1972-73; Herts Senior Trophy Winner 1988

Vassallo, Barrie (M)

(NEWPORT A.F.C.) Age: 33
Previous Clubs: Arsenal; Plymouth Argyle; Torquay; Bridgend; Merthyr Tydfil; Kidderminster Harriers; Gloucester City
Honours: Hellenic Lge Champions; Welsh Youth & S/Boy Int.

Vassell Errol (M)

(TOOTING & MITCHAM UNITED) Age: 25
Previous Clubs: None Honours: None

Vaughan, David (D)

(BOSTON UNITED) D.O.B. 16.7.56
Nickname: Norm Profession: Toolmaker
Married Wife's name: Sharon
Children: Carl & Tom Hobbies: Golf, Squash
Previous Clubs: Boston (74-77); Mossley (77-82); Burton Albion (82-86)
Honours: Midland Lge Winners 75/76; NPL Winners 78/79 & 79/80; NPL R/U 80/81; NPL Cup Winners 78/79 & 83/84; NPL Cup R/U 79/80; FA Trophy R/U 79/80 & 86/87

Veale, Garry (D)

(CHIPPENHAM TOWN) Age: 30
Previous Clubs: Merthyr Tydfil; Grays Athletic; Harlow Town; Harringey; Tooting & Mitcham; Hertford
Honours: British Colleges; Isthmian Lge Winner 83-84 (Grays)

Vessey, Tony (D)

(CRAWLEY TOWN) D.O.B. 28.11.61
Previous Clubs: Brighton & H.A.(78-80) 1 App.; Vasalund [Swe](80-82); Steyning Town (82-83); Worthing (83-86).
Honours: None

TONY VESSEY

Vincent Alan (M)

(WITHAM TOWN) Age: 25
Previous Clubs: Witham Town; Bramston CML; Braintree Town
Honours: Essex Senior Lge Winners 85/86; Jewson Lge R/U 87/88

Vincent, Tim (M)

(NORTHWOOD) Age: 30
Previous Clubs: Southall; Harrow Borough; Maidenhead United; Uxbridge; Chalfont St. Peter; Ruislip Manor
Honours: Spartan Lge & Cup Winner 89-90; Vauxhall Opel Div 2 S. R/U (Chalfont); AC Delco Cup R/U (Uxbridge); Surburban Lge Champions 81,82,83

Vines, Francis (F)

(KINGSTONIAN)
Previous Clubs: Carshalton Ath.; Thames Poly.; Molesey
Honours: None

Vircavs, Anton (D)

(CHELTENHAM TOWN) D.O.B. 28.3.61
Profession: Heating Engineer
Single Hobbies: Golf
Previous Clubs: Pressed Steel (78-80); Wycombe Wdrs (£5,000)
Honours: FA XI; Middx Wanderer

Voller, Nicholas (D)

(THATCHAM) Age: 23
Previous Clubs: Southampton; Oxford; Newbury; Thatcham; Lambourn Sports
Honours: Wessex League Cup Runners-Up

ANDY WALLACE (YEOVIL TOWN)

Wade, Cliff (M/F)

(CHIPSTEAD) Age: 32

Previous Clubs: Chipstead; Banstead; Whyteleafe
Honours: Surrey Intermediate Cup Winners Medal; Dan Air League Cup Winners

Wade, Shaun (F)

(NEWCASTLE TOWN) Age: 21

Previous Clubs: Foley; Parkway Clayton
Honours: County Youth Winner; Staffs U-19, Sentinal Shield Winner; B.N.W.C. Player of the Month April 1990

Wager, Gary (G)

(MERTHYR TYDFIL)

D.O.B. 21.5.62

PLAYING CAREER

Honours: Welsh Semi-Pro Int; Welsh Cup Winners 86/87; Beazer Homes Premier Div Winners 88/89; Middx Wanderer

Club	Seasons	Transfer	Apps	Goals
Bridgend Town	79-85			

Waite, Murana (F)

(CWMBRAN TOWN) Age: 30

Previous Clubs: Gloucester City; Ebbw Vale
Honours: National Division Winners Medal 1987-88 (Ebbw Vale)

Wakenshaw, Robert (F)

(FLEETWOOD TOWN)

D.O.B. 22.12.65 **Nickname:** Wacky or Robbo
Profession: Welder
Married **Wife's name:** Jacqueline
Children: Stephen & Simon
Hobbies: Golf, Watching Movies, Relaxing with family

PLAYING CAREER

Honours: Northumberland Schoolboy & Youth Rep; England Youth Int; FA Youth Cup Winners 83/84; England Under-21 Int; New Zealand Lge Winners 84/85; HFS Loans Lge Presidents Cup Winners 89/90

Club	Seasons	Transfer	Apps	Goals
Everton	80-85	£25,000	3	1
Hamilton Zelos (N.Z.- Loan]				
Carlisle United	85-86	£2,000	8	2
(Doncaster Rovers-loan 8-3)				
Rochdale	86-87	£2,000	29	5
Crewe Alexandra	87-89		22	1
Southport	1989			

Walbank, David (M)

(MARINE)

D.O.B. 22.11.62 **Nickname:** Warlly
Profession: Not working
Single
Hobbies: Golf

PLAYING CAREER

Honours: Lancs Youth Rep.; English County Winner 80/81; Northern County Winner 80/81; Burscough P.O.Y.88/89

Club	Seasons	Transfer	Apps	Goals
Hull City	79-81			
Skelmersdale United	81-83			
Maghull	83-85			
Burscough	87-89			

MATTHEW WHITEHEAD (TAMWORTH)

Walford, Steve (D)

(WYCOMBE WANDERERS) **D.O.B.** 5.1.58

PLAYING CAREER

Honours: England Youth Int, FA Cup Winners 79/80

Club	Seasons	Transfer	Apps	Goals
Tottenham Hotspur	74-77			2
Arsenal	77-80		77	3
Norwich City	80-83		93	2
West Ham United	83-89		115	2
(Huddersfield Town - loan 12; Gillingham - loan 4; West Bromwich Albion - loan 4)				
Hong Kong	89-90			
Turkey	1990			

Walker, Glenn (F)

(HORWICH RMI)

D.O.B. 15.3.67 **Nickname:** Dotty
Profession: Reprographic Operator
Married **Wife's name:** Lorraine
Hobbies: Watching Rugby League, Boxing

PLAYING CAREER

Honours: Warrington & Cheshire Schoolboy Rep., HFS Loans Lge Premier R/U 85/86; GMAC Cup Winners 87/88; HFS Loans Lge Challenge Cup R/U 85/86

Club	Seasons	Transfer	Apps	Goals
Burnley	83-85			
Crewe Alexandra	1985			2
Horwich RMI	85-86			
Marine	86-87			
Horwich RMI	87-88			
Warrington Town	1988			

Walker Paul (M)
(HORSHAM) Age: 27
Previous Clubs: Wokingham Town; Steyning Town; University of Surrey; Leatherhead
Honours: English Universities Rep; Sussex Senior Cup Winners 88/89

Walker, Paul (M)
(BISHOP AUCKLAND)

D.O.B. 26.2.58

PLAYING CAREER
Honours: England Semi-Pro Int; HFS Loans Div 1 Cup Winners 88/89

Club	Seasons	Transfer	Apps	Goals
Hull City	74-76			
Doncaster Rovers	76-77			4
Horden CW	77-79			
Scarborough	79-81			
Blyth Spartans	81-84			
Newcastle Blue Star	84-85			
Horden CW	85-86			
Blyth Spartans	86-87			
Whitley Bay	87-90			

Walker, Stuart (D)
(GENERAL CHEMICALS) Age: 29
Previous Clubs: Runcorn; Telford United
Honours: Pike Cup Winners & Runners-Up Medals; Cheshire Amateur Cup Winners Medal, Runcorn Cup

Walker, Trevor (M)
(THATCHAM) Age: 29
Previous Clubs: None **Honours:** None

Wallace, Brian (D)
(FARLEIGH ROVERS) Age: 25
Previous Clubs: None **Honours:** None

Wallace, Stephen (F)
(ST ALBANS CITY)

D.O.B. 29.3.61 **Nickname:** Wally
Profession: Site Manager
Married **Wife's name:** Jane
Children: Zaca
Hobbies: D.I.Y.

PLAYING CAREER
Honours: South-East Counties Cup R/U 78/79; Herts Senior Cup Winners; Herts Charity Cup Winners; Boreham Wood P.O.Y. (3)

Club	Seasons	Transfer	Apps	Goals
Watford	77-79			
Boreham Wood	79-85			
St.Albans City	85-86			
Boreham Wood	86-88			
Chesham United	88-89			
Hendon	89-90			

Wallduck, Steve (G)
(HARLOW TOWN) Age: 28
Previous Clubs: Hoddesdon Town, Cheshunt, Boreham Wood, Walthamstow Avenue.
Honours: Vauxhall-Opel Lge Div 2 North Winners; East Anglian Cup Winners; Herts Charity Cup Winners; Knight Floodlit Cup R/U; Essex County Rep.

Wallis, Kevin (D)
(DARTFORD)

D.O.B. 22.11.59
Profession: Company Director
Married **Wife's name:** Elaine
Children: Danielle & Jonathan
Hobbies: Sport

PLAYING CAREER
Honours: None

Club	Seasons	Transfer	Apps	Goals
Gravesend & Northfleet	77-81			
Hastings United	81-84	£1,000		
Gravesend & Northfleet	84-86			
Corinthian	86-87			
Dartford	87-88			
Worthing	88-89			
Gravesend & Northfleet	89-90			

Walmersley, Chris (M
(HORWICH RMI)

D.O.B. 21.7.66 **Nickname:** Dicky
Profession: Not working
Single
Hobbies: Boxing, Rugby League

PLAYING CAREER
Honours: Wigan Schoolboy Rep; England Colts Rep; GMAC Cup Winners 87/88

Club	Seasons	Transfer	Apps	Goals
Daisy Hill	84-86			
Horwich RMI	86-88			
Atherton LR	1988			

Walsh, Martin (M
(WOLVERTON) Age:
Previous Clubs: Wolverton Town; Hemel Hempstead Town; Milton Keynes Borough; Shenley & Loughton
Honours: None

Walsh, Paul (F
(SELSEY) Age:
Previous Clubs: Arundle; Littlehampton **Honours:** None

Walshaw, Mark (F
(GAINSBOROUGH TRINITY)

D.O.B. 11.11.66 **Nickname:** Wally
Profession: Not working
Single
Hobbies: Music, Concerts, Clubbing

PLAYING CAREER

Honours: FA Colts Rep; NECL Div 1 Winners 88/89

Club	Seasons	Transfer	Apps	Goals
AFC Bournemouth	84-88		2	
Frickley Athletic	87-88			
Sheffield FC	88-90			

Walters, Jimmy (M)
(CHIPPENHAM TOWN) Age: 29

Previous Clubs: Hungerford Town; Oxford City; Banbury; Witney; Fairford Town

Honours: Wilts Senior Cup; Oxford Senior Cup; Gloucester Senior Cup

Walton, Chris (M)
(HAYES)

D.O.B. 12.2.63   Nickname: Walts
Profession: Engineer
Single
Hobbies: Snooker, Golf

PLAYING CAREER

Honours: Vauxhall Lge Rep; AC Delco Cup R/U; Middx Senior Cup R/U; Hayes P.O.Y. 88/89 & 89/90

Club	Seasons	Transfer	Apps	Goals
Kingstonian	78-80			
Feltham	80-81			
Wimbledon	81-83			
Hanwell Town	83-84			

Walton, David (F)
(SEATON DELAVAL AMATEURS) Age: 27

Previous Clubs: Benwell Blues; Washington

Honours: Northumberland Minor Cup Winners Medal; Northumberland Senior Benevolent Bowl Winners Medal; McEwans Northern Alliance Premier Division Championship Winners Medal

Walton, Graeme (F)
(SEATON DELAVAL AMATEURS) Age: 22

Previous Clubs: Westerhope Juniors

Honours: Northumberland Senior Benevolent Bowl Winners Medal; McEwans Northern Alliance Premier Division Championship Winners Medal

Walwyn, Keith (F)
(KETTERING TOWN) Age: 35

PLAYING CAREER

Honours: Football Lge Div Four winners 83/84

Club	Seasons	Transfer	Apps	Goals
Winterton Rangers	77-79			
Chesterfield	79-81	£4,000	3	2
York City	81-87	£35,000	245	119
Blackpool	87-89		69	16
Carlisle Utd	89-91		45	13

Ward, Ian (D)
(CHEADLE TOWN) Age: 29

Previous Clubs: Droylsden; Curzon Ashton; Winsford United

Honours: North West Counties Championship

Ward, Mick (F)
(CHASETOWN) Age: 27

Previous Clubs: None

Honours: None

Ward, Warren (F)
(SPALDING UNITED) Age: 28

Previous Clubs: York City; Lincoln City; Exeter City; Boston United; Kings Lynn

Honours: None

Wardle, Stephen (G)
(SALTASH UNITED) Age: 25

Previous Clubs: Shakespeare United 1980-88; Saltash Res.

Honours: Plymouth & District League Winners Div 5, 4, 3, 2, 1, Premier and Cups

Warmington, Curtis (D)
(ENFIELD)

D.O.B. 30.11.64
Profession: Architectual Technician
Married   Wife's name: Sandie
Hobbies: Swimming, Golf

PLAYING CAREER

Honours: Blackheath & Inner-London Schoolboy Rep; South-East Counties Lge & Cup Winners; Surrey Senior Cup Winners

Club	Seasons	Transfer	Apps	Goals
West Ham United	79-83			
Thames Poly	83-85			
Dulwich Hamlet	85-87	£1,000		
Yeovil Town	1987	£2,000		
Carshalton Athletic	87-90	£1,500		

Warner, Roger (M)
(DULWICH HAMLET) Age: 18

Previous Clubs: Charlton Athletic
Honours: None

Warren, Jeffery (D)
(MEIR K. A.) Age: 28

Previous Clubs: Miners (Sandford Hill)

Honours: Staffs Senior League Champions 1988-89; Walsall Senior Cup Winners 1989-90

Warwick, Peter (F)
(GODALMING TOWN) Age: 23

Previous Clubs: None

Honours: None

Washington, Darren (M)
(CONGLETON TOWN)

D.O.B. 6.2.69   **Nickname:** Tommy
Profession: EDM Technician
Single
Hobbies: Cricket, Golf

PLAYING CAREER

Honours: Sentinel Cup Winners

Club	Seasons	Transfer	Apps	Goals
Knypersley Victoria	84-88			
Eastwood Hanley	88-90			

Watkin, Philip (M)
(DENABY UNITED)   **Age:** 27

Previous Clubs: Barnsley; Matlock Town; Gainsborough Trinity
Honours: Sheffield Senior Cup Winners and Runners-Up

Watkins, Mark (M)
(MARLOW)

D.O.B. 28.8.63   **Nickname:** Watty
Professions: Pensions Manager
Married   **Wife's name:** Grace
Hobbies: Football

PLAYING CAREER

Honours: Herts County Rep

Club	Seasons	Transfer	Apps	Goals
Winslow United	80-81			
Aylesbury United	81-83			
St.Albans City	83-84			
Tring Town	84-85			
Harrow Borough	86-86			
Tring Town	86-88			

Watling, Tony (F)
(SELBY TOWN)   **Age:** 26

Previous Clubs: York R.I.; North Ferriby United; Selby Town; York R.I.
Honours: Northern Counties East Div 1 Champions & League Cup Winners 1988; F.A. Vase Semi-Finalist 1989

Watts, Russell (F)
(KINTBURY RANGERS)   **Age:** 22

Previous Clubs: Wantage Town
Honours: Oxfordshire

Wealands, Jeff (G)
(ALTRINCHAM)

D.O.B. 26.8.51   **Nickname:** Wealo
Profession: Property Developer
Married   **Wife's name:** Carol
Children: Shaun & Stuart
Hobbies: Golf

PLAYING CAREER

Honours: FA Trophy Winners

Club	Seasons	Transfer	Apps	Goals
Wolverhampton Wanderers	69-70			
Darlington	70-72		31	
Hull City	72-79		270	
Birmingham City	79-83		117	
Manchester United	83-85		8	
(Oldham Athletic - loan - 10)				
(Preston North End - loan - 4)				
Altrincham	85-87			
Barrow	87-88			

Weale, David John (G)
(CHASETOWN)   **Age:** 2

Previous Clubs: Bridgnorth
Honours: None

Webb, Ashley (D)
(MEIR K. A.)   **Age:** 2

Previous Clubs:
Honours: None

Webb, David (M)
(GLOUCESTER CITY)

D.O.B. 12.8.66   **Nickname:** Webby
Profession: Sales Executive
Single   **Hobbies:** Spo

PLAYING CAREER

Honours: Swindon Schoolboy Rep; Wilts County Youth Rep; Wilts Senior Cup Winners

Club	Seasons	Transfer	Apps	Goals
Supermarine	82-87			
Wantage Town	87-88			
Devizes Town	88-89			
Stroud	89-90			

JEFF WEALANDS (ALTRINCHAM)

Webb, Robin (M)

(RACING CLUB WARWICK) **Age:** 26

Previous Clubs: Manchester City; Trollhaten IF (Swe); AP Leamington; Stockport County; V.S.Rugby; Coventry Sporting; V.S.Rugby

Honours: FA Youth Cup Winners; Southern Lge Cup Winners; Birmingham Senior Cup Winners

DAVE WEBLEY

Webley, David (F)

(MERTHYR TYDFIL)

D.O.B. 25.2.64

PLAYING CAREER

Honours: Welsh Semi-Pro Int; Welsh Cup Winners 86/87; Beazer Homes Premier Div Winners 88/89

Club	Seasons	Transfer	Apps	Goals
Pontllanfraith	82-84			
Abertillary Town	84-85			

Webster, Andy (D/M)

(OAKWOOD) **Age:** 26

Previous Clubs: Whyteleaf; Banstead Athletic; Whyteleaf; Redhill

Honours: S.C. League Div 2 Runners-Up & Cup Winners

Webster, Ian (D)

(GAINSBOROUGH TRINITY)

D.O.B. 30.12.65 **Nickname:** Webbo
Profession: Not working
Single
Hobbies: Sport

PLAYING CAREER

Honours: West Yorks Youth Rep; HFS Loans Lge Cup Winners 87/88

Club	Seasons	Transfer	Apps	Goals
Scunthorpe United	82-86		18	
Mqabba FC (Malta)	86-87			
Frickley Athletic	1987			
Goole Town	87-89			

Weir, Martin (D)

(KIDDERMINSTER HARRIERS)

D.O.B. 4.7.68 **Nickname:** Weirdo
Profession: Not working
Single
Hobbies: Music, Relaxing

PLAYING CAREER

Honours: Midland Youth Cup Winners 84/85; Kidderminster P.O.Y. 88/89

Club	Seasons	Transfer	Apps	Goals
Birmingham City	84-86			

Welch, Robin (F)

(DULWICH HAMLET) **Age:** 25

Previous Clubs: Whyteleafe; Malden Vale

Honours: None

Welch Tony (M)

(TOOTING & MITCHAM UNITED) **Age:** 24

Previous Clubs: Leatherhead

Honours: None

Welford, Marcus (Utility)

(WESTBURY) **Age:** 20

Previous Clubs: Devizes Town; Trowbridge Town

Honours: Trowbridge Player of the Year

Weir, Steven (F)

(CHEADLE TOWN) **Age:** 17

Previous Clubs: Stockport County (YTS)

Honours: None

Wells, Paul (D)

(SANDWELL BOROUGH) **Age:** 24

Previous Clubs: Cheadle Town; Ashtree Highfield

Honours: England Schoolboy

West, Andrew (F)

(HORSHAM) **Age:** 23

Previous Clubs: Horley Town; Corinthian Casuals

Honours: None

West, Mark (F)

(WYCOMBE WANDERERS)

D.O.B. 12.2.66

PLAYING CAREER

Honours: England Schoolboy Int; Vauxhall-Opel Lge Premier Div Winners 86/87; Hitachi Cup Winners 84/85; Berks & Bucks Senior Cup Winners 87/88 & 89/90; Wycombe P.O.Y. 87/88

Club	Seasons	Transfer	Apps	Goals
West Ham United	82-83			
Reading	83-84			
Wycombe Wanderers	84-Date		302	135

DAVID WHITTON (ATHERSTONE UTD)

West, Michael (M)

(KINTBURY RANGERS) Age: 25

Previous Clubs: Lanbourn Sports
Honours: None

West, Paul (M)

(MARLOW)

D.O.B. 7.11.60 **Nickname:** Westy
Profession: Heating Engineer
Married **Wife's name:** Nicola
Hobbies: Football, Tennis, Boxing

PLAYING CAREER

Honours: Bucks County Youth Rep; Vauxhall-Opel Lge Premier Div & Div 1 Winners & R/U; Hitachi Cup R/U; Berks & Bucks Cup R/U

Club	Seasons	Transfer	Apps	Goals
Flackwell Heath	79-80			
Wycombe Wanderers	80-83			
Hillingdon Borough	83-84			

Westley, Graham (F)

(KINGSTONIAN)

D.O.B. 4.3.68

PLAYING CAREER

Honours: England Youth Int

Club	Seasons	Transfer	Apps	Goals
Queens Park Rangers	84-85			
Gillingham	86-87			2
Barnet	86-87	£10,000		
Wycombe Wanderers	1987			
Kingstonian	87-89			
Wealdstone	89-90			

Weston, Chris (M)

(OLDSWINFORD) Age: 25

Previous Clubs: Halesowen Town; Lye Town
Honours: F.A. Vase Finalist (Halesowen Town)

Weston, Ian (M)

(BATH CITY)

D.O.B. 6.5.68 **Nickname:** Wez
Profession: Not working
Single
Hobbies: Snooker

PLAYING CAREER

Honours: Freight Rover Trophy R/U 88/89

Club	Seasons	Transfer	Apps	Goals
Bristol Rovers	84-88		16	
Torquay United	88-90		62	2

Westwood, Gary (G)

(WOKINGHAM TOWN)

PLAYING CAREER

Honours: England Youth Int

Club	Seasons	Transfer	Apps	Goals
Ipswich Town (Reading-loan-5)	81-83			
Reading	83-88		123	

Wetherell, Simon (G)

(HARROGATE TOWN) Age: 19

Previous Clubs: Knaresborough Town; Chelsea; Halifax Town
Honours: North Yorkshire County Rep.; County Rep. at E.S.F.A. selection

Whalley, David (M)

(WEYMOUTH)

D.O.B. 29.4.72
Profession: Not working
Single **Hobbies:** Sport

PLAYING CAREER

Honours: Dorset Schoolboy Rep

Club	Seasons	Transfer	Apps	Goals
West Bromwich Albion	87-89			

Whalley, Paul (M)

(GREAT HARWOOD TOWN) Age: 24

Previous Clubs: Clitheroe; Accrington Stanley
Honours: None

Wharton, David (M)

(BOSTON UNITED)

D.O.B. 13.4.60

PLAYING CAREER

Honours: None

Club	Seasons	Transfer	Apps	Goals
Eastwood Town	79-82			
Shepshed Charterh.	82-84			
Kettering Town	84-87			
Stafford Rangers	87-89	£500		

Wheatley, Paul (D)

(LANGNEY SPORTS) Age: 22

Previous Clubs: Eastbourne Town; Brighton & Hove Albion (Youth); Eastbourne United

Honours: Sussex County League Challenge Cup Winner 1989-90; Eastbourne Charity Cup Winner 1989-1990

Wheeler, Sean ( )

(NEWMARKET TOWN) Age: 17

Previous Clubs: None   **Honours:** Suffolk Schools Rep.

Whelan, Sean (M)

(CHELTENHAM TOWN)

D.O.B. 7.12.67   **Nickname:** Whelo
Profession: Storeman
Single
Hobbies: Hurling, Gaelic Football

PLAYING CAREER

Honours: Glos County Youth Rep; South West Youth Rep

Club	Seasons	Transfer	Apps	Goals
No Previous clubs				

Whellans, Robert (F)

(HARROGATE TOWN) Age: 21

Previous Clubs: Leicester City (Schoolboy); Bradford City; Rochdale

Honours: West Yorkshire Young Player of the Year (Bradford City)

Whitby, Steve (D)

(WYCOMBE WANDERERS)

D.O.B. 27.8.70

PLAYING CAREER

Honours: None

Club	Seasons	Transfer	Apps	Goals
Berkhamsted Town	87-89			

ARTHUR WILLIAMS

White, Dale (D)

(MALDEN VALE) Age: 17

Previous Clubs: Youth team product
Honours: Youth team P.O.Y. 89/90

White, Darrell (F)

(RACING CLUB WARWICK) Age: 28

Previous Clubs: Birmingham City; Banbury United; V.S.Rugby
Honours: Midland Combination Premier Div Winners & R/U

White, Darren (D)

(ST ALBANS CITY)

D.O.B. 3.3.68
Profession: Diamond Setter
Single
Hobbies: Golf, Going out for Chinese meals

PLAYING CAREER

Honours: Brent & Middx Schoolboy Rep; FA Youth Cup R/U 85/86; Suburban Lge Rep; Finchley P.O.Y. 88/89

Club	Seasons	Transfer	Apps	Goals
Watford	84-86			
Hendon	86-87			
Harrow Borough	1987			
Finchley	87-90			
Hendon	1990			

White, Stuart (M)

(WELLING UNITED)

D.O.B. 30.11.63   **Nickname:** Whitey
Profession: Not working
Married   **Wife's name:** Carolyn
Children: Stephanie
Hobbies: Golf

PLAYING CAREER

Honours: Southern League Premier Div Winners; Kent Senior Cup Winners; London Senior Cup Winners

Club	Seasons	Transfer	Apps	Goals
Charlton Athletic	80-81			
Gillingham	81-82			

White, Tony (D)

(DORCHESTER TOWN)

D.O.B. 3.11.66

PLAYING CAREER

Honours: Northern Ireland Under-21 Int

Club	Seasons	Transfer	Apps	Goals
Dorchester Town	83-85			
AFC Bournemouth	85-87			1

Whitehead, Keith (M/F)

(GUISBOROUGH TOWN) Age: 25

Previous Clubs: Middleback (Local)
Honours: G.T.F.C. honours

Whitehead, Linden (D)

(ALFRETON TOWN) Age: 18.6.69

Previous Clubs: None
Honours: None

Whitehead, Steve (D)

(NORTHWOOD) Age: 25

Previous Clubs: Hillingdon Boro; Uxbridge; Harrow Boro
Honours: Spartan League Cup Winners & League Runners-Up 1989-90

Whitehouse, Mark (F)

(KIDDERMINSTER HARRIERS)

D.O.B. 27.9.61
Profession: Building Inspector
Married
Hobbies: Sport

PLAYING CAREER

Honours: FA XI

Club	Seasons	Transfer	Apps	Goals
Moor Green	80-82			
Oldbury United	82-83			
Tamworth	83-85			
Redditch United	85-87			
Worcester City	87-88			
Burton Albion	88-89	£10,000		

Whiteside, Nigel (D)

(CLITHEROE) Age: 30

Previous Clubs: Clitheroe; Radcliffe Borough
Honours: Lancs Comb. Champions; Bass N.W. Counties 1st & 3rd Div Champions

Whitfield, Nicholas (G)

(PENRITH) Age: 20

Previous Clubs: Carlisle City
Honours: None

Whitham, Darren (M)

(DENABY UNITED) Age: 24

Previous Clubs: Ecclesfield Red Rose; Sheffield; Armthorpe; Belper Town
Honours: None

Whitney, John (D/M)

(WINSFORD UNITED) Age: 19

Previous Clubs: Wigan Athletic; Skelmersdale United
Honours: None

Whittingham, Bob (D)

(SUTTON COLDFIELD TOWN) Age: 23

Previous Clubs: Northfield Town
Honours: Birmingham County F.A.Rep; Sutton P.O.Y.88/89; Sutton Coldfield Sports Personality of the Year 1988

Whoolley, Tim (D/F)

(BRIDGWATER TOWN (1984)) Age: 23

Previous Clubs: Bridgwater Town 1984; Minehead
Honours: Somerset Senior League Champions & Cup Winners; County Senior Cup Finalist

Whorriskey, Hugh (Utility)

(THATCHAM TOWN) Age: 19

Previous Clubs: Reading (Youth)
Honours: Wessex League Cup Runners-Up

Wick, Jason (D)

(SPALDING UNITED) Age: 18

Previous Clubs: Cambridge United; Peterborough United
Honours: None

HARRY WIGGINS

Wiggins, Harry (D)

(ALTRINCHAM)

D.O.B. 21.11.59
Profession: Sheet Metal Worker
Single
Hobbies: Golf, Tennis, Badminton

PLAYING CAREER

Honours: FA Trophy Winners 88/89 & R/U 87/88; Shropshire Senior Cup Winners; Telford P.O.Y. (4)

Club	Seasons	Transfer	Apps	Goals
Telford United	84-90			

Wilcox, Brett (M)

(BRIDGNORTH TOWN)

Previous Clubs: GKN Sankey   Age: 21   Honours: None

Wilcox, Peter (D)

(CONGLETON TOWN)

D.O.B. 29.4.65   Nickname: Wilky
Profession: Industrial Engineer
Married   Wife's name: Helen
Hobbies: Golf, Music, Reading

PLAYING CAREER

Honours: Staffs & North-West England Schoolboy Rep

Club	Seasons	Transfer	Apps	Goals
Kidsgrove Athletic	82-84			
Warwickshire Police	84-86			
Newcastle Town	86-89			

Wilding, Brian (M/Asst. Man)

(MEIR K. A.)   Age: 36

Previous Clubs: Honours: Too many to list

Wilkin, Tony (M)

(BURNHAM RAMBLERS)   Age: 32

Previous Clubs: Burnham Ramblers; Wivenhoe

Honours: F.A. Vase Q-Final; Essex Senior League Cup Runners-Up (twice)

Wilkins Peter (D)

(BEDWORTH UNITED)

Previous Clubs: Bulkington   Age: 23   Honours: None

Wilkinson, Mark (M)

(TUNBRIDGE WELLS)   Age: 23

Previous Clubs: Danson

Honours: None

Wilkinson, W (F)

(SHOTTON COMRADES)   Age: 19

Previous Clubs: Peterlee U-19

Honours: None

Willetts, Kevin (D)

(CHELTENHAM TOWN)

D.O.B. 15.8.62   Nickname: Wilbur
Profession: Plasterer
Married   Wife's name: Julie
Children: Charlotte & Emma
Hobbies: Golf

PLAYING CAREER

Honours: Middx Wanderer; Glos County Rep; Cheltenham P.O.Y. 85/86

Club	Seasons	Transfer	Apps	Goals
Longlevens	77-79			
Sharpness	79-84			

Williams, Alan (D)

(THATCHAM TOWN)   Age: 22

Previous Clubs: Wokingham Town

Honours: Player of the Year 1987-88 & 1989-90 (Wokingham)

Williams, Alan (M)

(ROMSEY TOWN)   Age: 33

Previous Clubs: New Milton; A.F.C. Totton; Road Sea

Honours: Hants F.A. Rep. XI (27 caps & Capt); Captain Wessex League Red XI; Winner South West Counties (2); Winners Hants League Div 1 (2); Winners Wessex League; Winners Russell Cotes Cup; Winners Southampton Senior Cup (2)

Williams, Andy (M)

(KEYNSHAM TOWN)   Age: 28

Previous Clubs: St Phillips Adult School; Keynsham Town; Welton Rovers

Honours:

Williams, David (F)

(CWMBRAN TOWN)   Age: 35

Previous Clubs: Barry Town; Merthyr Tydfil; Ton Pentre; Cardiff Corinthians

Honours: Welsh Amateur Cup Winners Medal 1984-85 (Cardiff Corin.); Cardiff & South Glamorgan Schools

Williams, Darren (M)

(WORCESTER CITY)

D.O.B. 15.12.68
Profession: Warehouseman
Single
Hobbies: Weight training, squash, sleeping and attending church

PLAYING CAREER

Honours: None

Club	Seasons	Transfer	Apps	Goals
Leicester City	87-90		14	2
		Licoln City (loan) 9		

Williams, David (D)

(SAWBRIDGEWORTH TOWN)   Age: 36

Previous Clubs: Epping Town; Bishops Stortford; Stansted; Ware Town

Honours: F.A. Vase Winners 1984-85; E.S.L. Cup Winners; East Anglia Cup Winners; Courage Floodlight Cup Winners; Herts Charity Cup Winners; Herts Charity Shield Winners; Herts County Honours (4)

Williams, Ian (D)

(RHYL)   Age: 21

Previous Clubs: Brymbo Steelworks
Honours: Welsh Schoolboy Int

Williams, Ian (M)

(FARLEIGH ROVERS)   Age: 27

Previous Clubs: Sutton United; Banstead Athletic; Whyteleafe;
Honours: F.A. XI v Combined Services 1981

Williams, Ian (F)

(SPALDING UNITED) Age: 19

Previous Clubs: Leicester City (Trainee); Holbeach United; Spalding United

Honours: Midland Inter Cup Winners & Youth Cup Winners (Leicester); United Counties League & Cup Double (Holbeach)

KEVIN WILLIAMS

Williams, Kevin (M)

(DROYLESDEN) Age: 27

Previous Clubs: Kidsgrove Athletic
Honours: HFS Loans Lge Div 1 R/U 89/90

Williams, Lee (G)

(COLWYN BAY) Age: 22

Previous Clubs: Bolton Wanderers; Birmingham City; Bethesda United **Honours:** Bass NWCL Cup Winners

Williams, Mark (D)

(NEWTOWN) Age: 19

Previous Clubs: Manchester City; Crewe Alexandra **Honours:** None

Williams, Mark (M)

(WESTFIELDS) Age: 32

Previous Clubs: Arsenal; Newport County; Yeovil; Telford United; Gloucester; Trowbridge

Honours: Herefordshire Senior County Challenge Cup Winners (2); Banks's Brewery Div 1 Champions (all Westfields)

Williams, Martyn (D/M)

(GLOUCESTER CITY)

D.O.B. 16.6.65 **Nickname:** Maz
Profession: Electrician
Wife's name: Sally **Married**
Hobbies: Squash

PLAYING CAREER

Honours: Glos & Avon Schoolboy & Youth Rep; Beazer Homes Midland Div Winners 88/89; Hellenic Lge Winners.

Club	Seasons	Transfer	Apps	Goals
Bristol Rovers	79-80			
Sharpness	80-84			
Forest Green Rovers	84-88			

Williams, Pat (M)

(KEYNSHAM TOWN) Age: 22

Previous Clubs: Bristol Manor Farm
Honours: None

Williams, Paul (F)

(CWMBRAN TOWN) Age: 29

Previous Clubs: Tonyrefail
Honours: None

Williams, Paul (D)

(CWMBRAN TOWN) Age: 28

Previous Clubs: Cardiff Corinthians; Ebbw Vale

Honours: Welsh Amateur Cup Winners Medal 1984-85 (Cardiff Corin.); National Division Winners Medal 1987-88 (Ebbe Vale); Welsh Schools International; Brother of David Williams, Assistant Manager at Norwich City

Williams, Paul (M)

(NORTHWICH VICTORIA)

D.O.B. 10.10.71
Profession: Not working
Single
Hobbies: Sport

PLAYING CAREER

Honours: England Schoolboy Int; FA School of Excellence

Club	Seasons	Transfer	Apps	Goals
Manchester City	88-90			

Williams, Phil (F)

(GODALMING TOWN)

Age: 28

Previous Clubs: Cranleigh

Honours: None

Williams, Phillip (M)

(CHELTENHAM TOWN)

D.O.B. 24.11.66
Profession: Not working
Single
Hobbies: Snooker, Cricket

PLAYING CAREER

Honours: Welsh Schoolboy Int; Welsh Youth Int; Wales Semi-Pro Int.

Club	Seasons	Transfer	Apps	Goals
Swansea City	82-87		59	5
Newport County	87-88			

Williams, Timmy (M)

(COLWYN BAY) Age: 28

Previous Clubs: Flint Town
Honours: Rhyl Welsh Semi-pro Int; Bass NWCL Cup Winners

Williamson, Paul (D)

(HARROGATE TOWN) Age: 26

Previous Clubs: Middlesbrough (Schoolboy); Leeds United (Youth); Bradford City (Res.); Harrogate Railway

Honours: H.F.S. First Division League Cup Winners 1989-90

Willis, Ritchie (D)

(NEWPORT A.F.C.) Age: 30

Previous Clubs: Caerleon; Mangotsfield; Trowbridge; Brecon

Honours: Hellenic League Champions

Willis, Roger (F)

(BARNET)

D.O.B. 17.6.67 **Nickname:** Harry
Profession: Not working
Single
Hobbies: Tennis

PLAYING CAREER

Honours: None

Club	Seasons	Transfer	Apps	Goals
Birmingham City	1984			
Notts County	86-87			
Grimsby Town	87-90			9

Williscroft Mark (F)

(COLWYN BAY) Age: 23

Previous Clubs: Brymbo Steelworks **Honours:** None

Wills, Shaun (M/F)

(RUSHDEN TOWN)

D.O.B. 26.1.71
Profession: Sprayer
Single **Hobbies:** Sport

PLAYING CAREER

Honours: Kettering & Corby Schoolboy Rep

Club	Seasons	Transfer	Apps	Goals
Burton Park Wanderers	86-87			
Peterborough United	87-89			
Burton Park Wanderers	89-90			

Wills, Simon (D)

(FARLEIGH ROVERS) Age: 27

Previous Clubs: Bromley; Warlingham **Honours:** None

Wilson, Adam (F)

(RADCLIFFE BOROUGH) Age: 18

Previous Clubs: Wigan Athletic

Honours: None

Wilson, Alistair (D)

(RACING CLUB WARWICK) Age: 24

Previous Clubs: Bedworth U.; Nuneaton B. **Honours:** None

Wilson, Carl (M)

(CHELMSLEY TOWN) Age: 22

Previous Clubs: Mile Oak Rovers; Paget Rangers; Coleshill Town **Honours:** None

Wilson, David (F)

(A.F.C. LYMINGTON) Age: 28

Previous Clubs: Testwood; Hythe & Dibden; Ordnance Survey
Honours: None

Wilson, Ian (D)

(MORETON TOWN) Age: 23

Previous Clubs: Alcester Town; Evesham United; West Heath
Honours: None

Wilson, Lee (D)

(CORNARD UNITED) Age: 21

Previous Clubs: None **Honours:** None

Wilson, Michael (M/F)

(CHESTER-LE-STREET) Age: 19

Previous Clubs: None **Honours:** None

Wilson, Paul (D)

(BARNET)

D.O.B. 26.9.64 **Nickname:** Wils
Profession: Pipe Fitter **Single**
Hobbies: Golf, Chess

PLAYING CAREER

Honours: Essex Youth Rep; FA Youth Cup Winners; South Eastern Counties Lge & Cup Winners; Barking & Billericay P.O.Y.

Club	Seasons	Transfer	Apps	Goals
West Ham United	81-83			
Billericay Town	84-86			
Darking	86-88			

Wilson, Paul (F)

(YEOVIL TOWN)

D.O.B. 16.11.60
Profession: Blacksmith **Nickname:** Willow
Married **Wife's name:** Marie
Children: James **Hobbies:** Sport

PLAYING CAREER

Honours: England Semi-Pro Int; Bob Lord Trophy Winners 89/90; Gola Lge R/U 85/86, Frickley P.O.Y. (2)

Club	Seasons	Transfer	Apps	Goals
Frickley Athletic	82-86			
Heidelburg Alex.(Aust.)	86-87			
Boston United	87-89	£13,000		

Wilson Richard (G)

(EASTWOOD TOWN) **Age:** 24

Previous Clubs: Notts County; Chesterfield; Grantham Town; Lincoln City; Spalding United
Honours: GM Vauxhall Conference Winners 87/88; Notts Senior Cup Winners

Wilson, Russell (F)

(EXMOUTH TOWN) **Age:**

Previous Clubs: Hucknall Town
Honours: None

Wingate, John (F)

(TUNBRIDGE WELLS) **Age:** 31

Previous Clubs: None
Honours: Kent League Champions; Kent League Cup Winners 1985-86, 1987-88

Winter, Steve (D)

(YATE TOWN) **Age:** 16

Previous Clubs: Soccer School of Excellence
Honours: None

Wintersgill, David (D/M)

(GUISBOROUGH TOWN) **Age:** 24

Previous Clubs: Wolves; Wimbledon; Tornavan Pallo-55 (Finland); Scarborough; Darlington; Bishop Auckland; Colne Dynamoes
Honours: Finish 2nd Div Champions; H.F.S. Div 1 Runners-Up

Winwood, Mark (F)

(BIGGLESWADE TOWN) **Age:** 17

Previous Clubs: None
Honours: None

Withey, Graham (F)

(GLOUCESTER CITY)

D.O.B. 11.6.60
Profession: Insurance Agent
Single
Hobbies: Sport

PLAYING CAREER

Honours: None

Club	Seasons	Transfer	Apps	Goals
Welton Rovers	78-80	£3,000		
Bath City	80-82	£5,000		
Bristol Rovers	82-83	£50,000	22	10
Coventry City	83-85	£20,000	22	4
Cardiff City	84-86		27	7
Bristol City	86-87			2
Bath City	1987			
Exeter City	87-88		7	2
Brisbane City (Australia)	88-89			

Wonham, Graham (G)

(GODALMING TOWN)

Age: 30

Previous Clubs: Chelsea youth; Aldershot; Westfield; Guildford & Worplesden

Honours: League Cup winners 1985/86

Wood, Brian (D)

(HINCKLEY **Age:** 28

Previous Clubs: Leicester United; St. Andrews

Honours: Leicestershire Senior League Winners; Senior Cup; Coalville Cup; T&B Cup; Challenge Cup

Wood, Clark (D)

(RADCLIFFE BOROUGH) **Age:** 19

Previous Clubs: Oldham Athletic
Honours: None

Wood, Fraser (D)

(STAFFORD RANGERS)

D.O.B. 18.12.58
Profession: HGV Driver
Married **Wife's name:** Jayne
Hobbies: Water Polo

PLAYING CAREER

Honours: West Bromwich Schoolboy Rep; Stafford P.O.Y. 89/90

Club	Seasons	Transfer	Apps	Goals
Tipton Town	78-79			
Stafford Rangers	79-84	£3,000		
Kidderminster Harriers	84-85			

Wood, John (M:F)

(MALDEN VALE) **Age:** 26

Previous Clubs: Vikings FC; Vikings P.O.Y.87/88
Honours: None

STEVE WOOD

Wood, Steve (M)
(MOSSLEY)

D.O.B. 23.6.63   **Nickname:** Woody
Profession: Plant Operator
Married   **Wife's name:** Margaret
Hobbies: Sport

PLAYING CAREER
Honours: None

Club	Seasons	Transfer	Apps	Goals
Chadderton	81-89			

Woodbridge, Simon (F)
(LEWES)   Age: 23
Previous Clubs: Wimbledon; Queens Park Rangers; Woking
Honours: Surrey Schoolboy & Youth Rep

Woods, Mark (M)
(COLWYN BAY)   Age: 25
Previous Clubs: United Services (Chester); Flint Town
Honours: None

Woods, Mark (D)
(WINDSOR & ETON)

D.O.B. 8.1.64   **Nickname:** Woodsy
Profession: Quantity Surveyor
Married   **Wife's name:** Gail
Hobbies: Eating Out, Holidays

PLAYING CAREER
Honours: Surrey Schoolboy Rep; Surrey Colleges Rep; South-East Schools Championship Winners 77/78; South-East Counties Div 1 R/U 79/80; Berks & Bucks Senior Cup Winners 87/88 & 88/89; Windsor P.O.Y. 88/89 & 89/90

Club	Seasons	Transfer	Apps	Goals
Queens Park Rangers	78-80			
Addlestone & Weybridge	80-84			
Windsor & Eton	84-86			
Tooting & Mitcham United	86-87			
Walton & Hersham	1987			

Woods, Patrick (D)
(FARSLEY CELTIC)   Age: 24
Previous Clubs: Billingham Town; Hartlepool United
Honours: None

Woodyard, Jamie (M)
(WITHAM TOWN)   Age: 23
Previous Clubs: Maldon Town; Burnham Ramblers; Tiptree United; Heybridge Swifts
Honours: None

Woolf, Garry (D/M)
(SELSEY)   Age: 28
Previous Clubs: Selsey; Portfield
Honours: None

GARY WOODALL (MACCLESFIELD)

Woolley, Andy (Utility)
(BILLERICAY TOWN)   Age: 24
Previous Clubs: Heybridge Swifts; Bowers United; Basildon
Honours: F.A. Vase Q-Final 1990

Woolley, Julian (D)
(WINSFORD UNITED)   Age: 21
Previous Clubs: Stoke City; Wolverhampton Wanderers; Leek Town; Congleton Town
Honours: Birmingham Senior Cup Winners 1987

Wooler, Paul (D)
(LEATHERHEAD)   Age: 20
Previous Clubs: Woking
Honours: None

Worrall, Rob (F)
(EYNESBURY ROVERS)   Age: 24
Previous Clubs: Alconbury
Honours: Scott Gatty Cup 1990

Worswick, John (M)

(WESTHOUGHTON TOWN) **Age:** 28

Previous Clubs: Hindley Greens Parish
Honours: Wigan A.L. 1st, 2nd, 3rd Div Championship Winners

Worthington, Clive (D)

(SPALDING UNITED) **Age:** 28

Previous Clubs: Boston United; Skegness Town
Honours: None

Wotton, Jamie (F)

(RACING CLUB WARWICK) **Age:** 23

Previous Clubs: Wellsbourne
Honours: Midland Combination Div 2 R/U; Birmingham County Vase R/U

Wragg, Kevin (D)

(EASTWOOD TOWN) **Age:** 26

Previous Clubs: Staveley Works; Matlock Town
Honours: Notts Senior Cup Winners; Evans Halshaw Cup Winners

Wragg, Tim (D)

(DENABY UNITED) **Age:** 24

Previous Clubs: Worksop Town; Goole Town; Matlock Town; Gainsborough; Belper Town
Honours: Presidents Cup Winner 1987-85

Wrench, Mark (D)

(NORTHWICH VICTORIA)

D.O.B. 27.9.69
Profession: Electrician
Single
Hobbies: Record Collecting

PLAYING CAREER

Honours: Runcorn Schoolboy Rep.; Cheshire Schoolboy Rep

Club	Seasons	Transfer	Apps	Goals
Chester City	87-88			
Wrexham	88-90		6	

Wright, Andy (M)

(AYLESBURY UNITED)

D.O.B. 14.11.62
Profession: Fireman
Married
Hobbies: Golf

PLAYING CAREER

Honours: None

Club	Seasons	Transfer	Apps	Goals
Kettering Town	79-81			
Rothwell Town	82-85			
Desborough Town	86-88			
Kettering Town	88-90	£8,000		

Wright, Steve (D)

(WIVENHOE TOWN)

D.O.B. 16.6.59

PLAYING CAREER

Honours: None

Club	Seasons	Transfer	Apps	Goals
Colchester United	76-81		117	2
HJK Helsinki (Fin)	81-83			
Wrexham	83-84		76	
Torquay United	84-85		33	
Crewe Alexandra	85-87		72	3
Rhyl	87-88			
Chelmsford City	88-89			

Wright, Steve (M)

(BIGGLESWADE TOWN) **Age:** 30

Previous Clubs: Letchworth; Baldock; Arlesey; Stotfold; Potton
Honours: Hertfordshire County Cap; Beds County Cap

Wright, Tony (D:M)

(LEATHERHEAD) **Age:** 3

Previous Clubs: Burnham; Dunstable; Maidenhead United Windsor & Eton; Worthing
Honours: Berks & Bucks Senior Cup Winners; Spartan Lge Winners

Wright, Trevor (D/M)

(CHIPSTEAD) **Age:** 3

Previous Clubs: Arsenal; Orient; Chipstead; Three Bridges
Honours: Dan Air Champions; Getting a pass from Phil Barnes o Colin Miles

Wye, Lloyd (D)

(WOKING)

D.O.B. 14.5.67
Profession: Mechanical Design Officer
Single
Hobbies: Golf, Cricket

PLAYING CAREER

Honours: Surrey Youth Rep; FA XI; Vauxhall-Opel Lge Rep Woking P.O.Y. 86/87

Club	Seasons	Transfer	Apps	Goals
Southampton	82-83			

Wylly, Andy (G)

(HINCKLEY) **Age:** 2

Previous Clubs: Earl Shilton Albion; Wigston Fields; Birsta United; Leicester United
Honours: Leicester City League Winners; Midland Combinatio Reserve League Runners-Up (Leicester United)

STEVE BURR (MACCLESFIELD TOWN)

TIM BUZAGLO (WOKING)

Yates, John (M)

(ST. DOMINICS) Age: 17

Previous Clubs: None
Honours: Liverpool County F.A. Youth XI

Yeates, Daryl (D/M)

(VALE RECREATION) Age: 23

Previous Clubs: Guernsey Rangers (Youth)
Honours: Guernsey Priaulx Championship 86-87, 87-88, 88-89

Yeates, Paul (D)

(WESTHOUGHTON TOWN) Age: 31

Previous Clubs: Ashton Athletic; Ashton Town; Wigan College
Honours: West Lancs Lge Div 1 R/U; Wigan Cup Winners

York, Paul (M)

(RUSHDEN TOWN) D.O.B. 13.2.64
Nickname: Yorky **Profession:** Contracts Engineer
Married **Wife's name:** Mary
Children: Hannah & Elliot **Hobbies:** Sport

PLAYING CAREER

Honours: FA XI; Beazer Homes Midland Div R/U 89/90;
Rothlingborough P.O.Y. 84/85

Club	Seasons	Transfer	Apps	Goals
Rothlingborough D's	83-86			
Kettering Town	86-87			
Aylesbury United	1987			
Baldock Town	87-88			

Yorke, Richard (M)

(DORKING) Age: 28

Previous Clubs: Banstead Athletic
Honours: FA Colts Rep; Athenian Lge Winners; Vauxhall-Opel
Lge Div 2 South Winners

RICHARD YORKE

Young, Colin (D)

(BIGGLESWADE TOWN) Age: 20

Previous Clubs: Biggleswade Tn (Yth) **Honours:** None

Young, David (D)

(STRATFORD TOWN) Age: 27

Previous Clubs: Alveston; Racing Club Warwick
Honours: Midland Football Combination - Division 2 Champions
85-86; Premier Division Champions 86-87

Young, David (D)

(NORTHWICH VICTORIA) D.O.B. 27.4.62

PLAYING CAREER

Honours: Staffs Senior Cup Winners; Mid-Cheshire Senior Cup
Winners (3); Cheshire Senior Cup R/U

Club	Seasons	Transfer	Apps	Goals
Wrexham	79-81			
Mossley	81-82			
Wigan Athletic	82-83		3	
Tranmere Rovers	83-84			

Young, David (D)

(CONGLETON TOWN) D.O.B. 17.3.62

Profession: Works For British Coal **Married**
Wife's name: Joanne **Hobbies:** Golf

PLAYING CAREER

Honours: Knypersley P.O.Y

Club	Seasons	Transfer	Apps	Goals
Congleton Town	82-85			
Knypersley Victoria	85-88			

Young, Gary J. (D)

(SEATON DELAVAL AMATEURS) Age: 21

Previous Clubs: Westherhope Hillheads
Honours: Northumberland Senior Benevolent Bowl Winner;
McEwans Northern Alliance Prem. Div. Champions

Young, Geoffrey (F)

(CLITHEROE) Age: 30

Previous Clubs: None
Honours: N.W.C. Div 1 Champions 85-86; N.W.C. P.o Y. 89-90

Young, Neil (F)

(ALTRINCHAM) D.O.B. 2.11.71

Nickname: Youngy **Profession:** Marine Insurance
Single **Hobbies:** Tennis, Mountain Climbing
Honours: None
Previous Clubs: Tranmere Rovers (88-90)

Young, Stuart (D)

(HENDON) D.O.B. 16.8.70

Nickname: Youngy **Profession:** Civil Servant
Single **Hobbies:** Cricket, Music
Honours: None
Previous Clubs: None

Zelem, Alan (G)

(MACCLESFIELD TOWN) D.O.B. 13.2.62

Nickname: Zel **Profession:** Window Cleaner
Single **Hobbies:** Snooker, Tennis

PLAYING CAREER

Honours: None

Club	Seasons	Transfer	Apps	Goals
Stalybridge Celtic	80-82			
Bolton Wanderers	83-84			

NEAL STANLEY
(SLOUGH TOWN)

STEVE KERLEY
(FARNBOROUGH TOWN)

THE 'OLD BOYS'

Many players move on from pyramid league clubs to try their luck as full time professionals in the Barclays League, and this next section gives details of them.

Alan Platt has kindly drawn up a list of these Non-League 'Old Boys', which is shown overleaf, and we have then also included the entries for many of them as they appeared in the Barclays League Club Directory 1991, published last September, interspersed with some photographs.

In some cases the player's early clubs were not originally known but it is interesting to trace the progress of many Non-League favourites and to see how some have become household names.

TIM CLARKE,
joined Coventry City from Halesowen Town.

STEVE BUTLER, stayed with Maidstone,
when they moved into the Football League.

The Old Boys

PLAYER	FROM (Non-Lge)	CURRENT CLUB	PLAYER	FROM (Non-Lge)	CURRENT CLUB
Steve Adams	Workshop Tn	Doncaster Rov	David Crown	Walthamstow Ave.	Gillingham
Tony Agana	Weymouth	Sheffield Utd	Paul Culpin	Nuneaton Boro'	Peterborough Utd
John Aldridge	South Liverpool	Real Sociedad (Sp.)	Tony Cunningham	Stourbridge	Bury
Keith Alexander	Barnet	Lincoln City	Nicky Cusack	Alvechurch	Motherwell
Brett Angell	Cheltenham Tn	Southend Utd	Paul Dalton	Brandon United	Hartlepool Utd
Andrew Ansah	Dorking	Southend Utd	Simon Darlaston	Shortwood Utd	Bristol City
Robert Atkins	Enderby Town	Preston N. E.	Peter Davenport	Cammell Laird	Sunderland
Dennis Bailey	Farnborough Tn	Birmingham City	Aidan Davison	Billingham Syn.	Bury
Danny Bailey	Wealdstone	Reading	Bobby Davison	Seaham Red Star	Leeds United
Paul Baker	Bishop Auckland	Hartlepool Utd	Keith Day	Aveley	Leyton Orient
Phil Barber	Aylesbury	Crystal Palace	Alan Devonshire	Southall	Watford
Andy Barnsley	Denaby Utd	Rotherham Utd	Kerry Dixon	Dunstable	Chelsea
Tony Barratt	Billingham Tn	York City	Ian Dowie	Hendon	Luton Town
Graham Barrow	Altrincham	Chester City	Keith Downing	Mile Oak Rovers	Wolverhampton W.
Kevin Bartlett	Fareham Town	Notts County	John Dreyer	Wallingford Tn	Luton Town
Warren Barton	Leytonstone & Ilford	Wimbledon	Dean Edwards	Telford United	Torquay United
Dave Beasant	Edgware Town	Chelsea	Paul R. Edwards	Altrincham	Coventry City
Chris Beaumont	Denaby United	Stockport County	Matthew Elliott	Epsom & Ewell	Torquay
Paul Beesley	Marine	Sheffield Utd	Tony Ellis	Horwich R.M.I.	Stoke City
Gary E. Bennett	Ashton United	Sunderland	Karl Elsey	Pembroke Boro'	Maidstone Utd
Gary M. Bennett	Kirkby Town	Chester City	Paul Emson	Brigg Town	Darlington
Ian Bennyworth	Nuneaton Boro'	Hartlepool Utd	Stewart Evans	Gainsborough T.	Rotherham United
Keith Bertschin	Barnet	Chester City	Andy Feeley	Trowbridge Tn	Bury
Wayne Biggins	Matlock Town	Stoke City	Alan Finley	Marine	Stockport County
Peter Billing	South Liverpool	Coventry City	Tony Finnigan	Corinthian Cas.	Hull City
Garry Birtles	Long Eaton Utd	Grimsby Town	John Flower	Corby Town	Aldershot
Ernie Bishop	Runcorn	Chester City	Darren Foreman	Fareham Town	Crewe Alexandra
Nicky Bissett	Barnet	Brighton & H. A.	Gerry Forrest	South Bank	Rotherham Utd
Ian Blackstone	Harrogate Town	York City	David Frain	Dronfield Utd	Stockport Co
Kevin Blackwell	Barnet	Notts County	John Francis	Emley	Burnley
Noel Blake	Sutton Coldfield	Stoke City	Tony Fyfe	Penrith	Carlisle Utd
Gary Blissett	Altrincham	Brentford	Steve Galliers	Chorley	Maidstone Utd
Paul Bodin	Bath City	Swindon Town	Tony Galvin	Goole Town	Swindon Town
Bob Bolder	Dover Town	Charlton Athletic	Steve Gaughan	Hatfield Main	Sunderland
John Bramhall	Stockton Heath	Scunthorpe Utd	Pat Gavin	Hanwell Town	Leicester City
Mark Bright	Leek Town	Crystal Palace	Brian Gayle	Tooting & Mitcham	Ipswich Town
Ian Brightwell	Congleton Town	Manchester City	John Gayle	Burton Albion	Birmingham City
Gary Brook	Frickley Athletic	Blackpool	Dave Gilbert	Boston United	Grimsby Town
Tony Brown	Thackley	Rochdale	Jon Gittens	Paget Rangers	Swindon Town
David Brown	Horden C. W.	Halifax Town	Nigel Gleghorn	Seaham Red Star	Birmingham City
Richard Brown	Kettering Town	Blackburn Rovers	Craig Goldsmith	Mirrlees Blackstone	Carlisle United
Steve Bull	Tipton Town	Wolverhampton W.	Mick Gooding	Bishop Auckland	Reading
John Butler	Prescot Cables	Stoke City	Clive Goodyear	Lincoln United	Wimbledon
Lee Butler	Harworth C. I.	Aston Villa	Colin Gordon	Oldbury United	Birmingham City
Steve Butler	Wokingham Town	Maidstone United	Andy Gray	Dulwich Hamlet	Crystal Palace
David Byrne	Kingstonian	Watford	Gareth Gray	Darwen	Rochdale
Richard Cadette	Wembley	Brentford	Ron Green	Alvechurch	Walsall
Danny Carter	Billericay Tn	Leyton Orient	Phil Gridelet	Barnet	Barnsley
Tony Cascarino	Crockenhill	Aston Villa	Paul Groves	Burton Albion	Blackpool
Jimmy Case	South Liverpool	Southampton	Peter Guthrie	Barnet	AFC Bournemouth
Peter Cawley	Chertsey Town	Exeter City	Gary Hackett	Bromsgrove Rov.	West Bromwich A.
Martyn Chalk	Louth Utd	Derby County	Paul Hardyman	Waterlooville	Sunderland
Alec Chamberlain	Ramsey Town	Luton Town	Mark Harris	Wokingham Town	Swansea City
Gary Chapman	Ossett Albion	Notts County	Michael Heathcote	Spennymoor Utd	Shrewsbury Town
Vincent Chapman	Tow Law Town	Rochdale	Ian Hedges	Gloucester City	AFC Bournemouth
Micky Cheetham	Basingstoke Tn	Cambridge Utd	Liburd Henry	Leytonstone & Ilford	Maidstone Utd
Steve Claridge	Weymouth	Cambridge Utd	Martin Hicks	Stratford	Reading
Tim Clarke	Halesowen Town	Coventry City	Stuart Hicks	Wisbech Town	Scunthorpe Utd
Gary Clayton	Burton Albion	Cambridge Utd	Richard Hill	Nuneaton Boro'	Oxford Utd
Glenn Cockerill	Louth United	Southampton	Mark Hine	Whitby Town	Peterborough Utd
Robert Codner	Barnet	Brighton	Joe Hinnigan	South Liverpool	Chester City
Stan Collymore	Stafford Rangers	Crystal Palace	Kevin Hitchcock	Barking	Chelsea
Graham Cooper	Emley	Wrexham	David Hockaday	Billingham Syn	Hull City
Steve Cooper	Moor Green	Tranmere Rovers	Andy Holden	Rhyl	Oldham Athletic
Tony Coton	Mile Oak Rov.	Manchester City	Mike Hooper	Mangotsfield	Liverpool
Barry Cowdrill	Sutton Coldfield	Bolton Wanderers	Barry Horne	Rhyl	Southampton

232

PLAYER	FROM (Non-Lge)	CURRENT CLUB
Andy Hunt	Kettering Town	Newcastle Utd
Terry Hurlock	Leytonstone & Ilford	Glasgow Rangers
Chris Hutchings	Harrow Borough	Walsall
Tony James	Gainsborough T	Leicester City
Richard Jobson	Burton Albion	Oldham Athletic
Nicky Johns	Minehead	Maidstone Utd
Andy Jones	Rhyl	AFC Bournemouth
Murray Jones	Carshalton Ath.	Bristol City
Vinny Jones	Wealdstone	Sheffield Utd
Roger Joseph	Southall	Wimbledon
Mark Kearney	Marine	Mansfield Tn
John Keeley	Chelmsford City	Oldham Athletic
Tony Kelly	Prescot Cables	Shrewsbury Tn
David Kelly	Alvechurch	Leicester City
John Kelly	Cammell Laird	Walsall
Alan Kennedy	Colne Dynamoes	Wrexham
Andy Leaning	Rowntree Mack	Bristol City
Mark Leonard	Witton Albion	Bradford City
Mike Leonard	Epsom & Ewell	Chesterfield
Matthew Le Tissier	Vale Recreation	Southampton
David Leworthy	Fareham Town	Reading
Peter Litchfield	Droylsden	Scunthorpe Utd
David Logan	Whitby Town	Scarborough
Tony Lowery	Ashington	Mansfield Tn
Sean McCarthy	Bridgend Town	Bradford City
John McClelland	Bangor City	Leeds United
Rodney McDonald	Colne Dynamoes	Walsall
Andy McFarlane	Cradley Town	Portsmouth
Eddie McGoldrick	Nuneaton Boro'	Crystal Palace
Ian McInerney	Newcastle Blue S	Stockport Co.
Les McJannet	Matlock Town	Darlington
David McKearney	Prescot Cables	Crewe Alexandra
Chris Marples	Goole Town	York City
Nigel Martyn	St Blazey	Crystal Palace
David Miller	Colne Dynamoes	Carlisle United
Andrew Milner	Netherfield	Rochdale
Trevor Morgan	Leytonstone	Exeter City
Trevor Morley	Nuneaton Boro'	West Ham Utd
Grant Morrow	Rowntree Mack	Doncaster Rov.
Neil Morton	Northwich Vic	Chester City
Andy Mutch	Southport	Wimbledon
Mark Newson	Maidstone Utd	Fulham
Eric Nixon	Curzon Ashton	Tranmere Rovers
Steve Norris	Telford United	Halifax Town
Charles Ntamark	Boreham Wood	Walsall
Sean O'Driscoll	Alvechurch	AFC Bournemouth
Vince O'Keefe	A.P. Leamington	Wrexham
George Oghani	Hyde United	Scarborough
Ian Ormondroyd	Thackley	Aston Villa
Gary Pallister	Billingham Tn	Manchester Utd
Alan Paris	Slough Town	Leicester City
Neil Parsley	Witton Albion	Huddersfield Tn
Trevor Peake	Nuneaton Boro'	Coventry City
Stuart Pearce	Wealdstone	Nottingham Forest
Nigel Pearson	Heanor Town	Sheffield Wed.
John Pemberton	Chadderton	Sheffield Utd
David Penney	Pontefract Col.	Oxford United
Gary Penrice	Mangotsfield	Watford
Gerry Peyton	Atherstone Tn	AFC Bournemouth
Chris Pike	Barry Town	Cardiff City
Nicky Platnauer	Bedford Town	Notts County
David Platt	Chadderton	Aston Villa
Trevor Putney	Brentwood & W	Middlesbrough
David Putnam	Leicester United	Lincoln City
Jimmy Quinn	Oswestry Town	West Ham Utd
Andy Rammell	Atherstone Utd	Barnsley
Alan Reeves	Heswall	Chester City
David Reeves	Heswall	Bolton Wand.
Cyrille Regis	Hayes	Coventry City
Dave Regis	Barnet	Notts County
Carl Richards	Enfield	Blackpool
Steve Richards	Gainsborough T	Scarborough
David Riley	Keyworth Utd	Peterborough Utd
Graham Roberts	Weymouth	West Bromwich A.
Colin Robinson	Mile Oak Rov.	Hereford United
Ronnie Robinson	S. C. Vaux	Rotherham Utd
Kevin Rose	Ledbury Town	Bolton Wand.
Nigel Saddington	Roker	Carlisle United
Lawrie Sanchez	Thatcham Town	Wimbledon
Morrys Scott	Colchester Utd	Southend Utd
Trevor Senior	Dorchester Tn	Reading
Craig Short	Pickering Town	Notts County
Malcolm Shotton	Nuneaton Boro'	Hull City
Carl Shutt	Spalding Utd	Leeds United
Alan Smith	Alvechurch	Arsenal
Darren Smith	Burton Albion	Wolverhampton W.
David Smith	Welling Utd	Bristol City
Kevin Smith	Stockton	Darlington
Mark Smith	Kettering Town	Huddersfield Tn
Neville Southall	Winsford Utd	Everton
Nigel Spackman	Andover	Glasgow Rangers
Dean Spink	Halesowen Tn	Shrewsbury Town
Stuart Storer	V.S. Rugby	Bolton Wand.
Mike Stowell	Leyland Motors	Wolverhampton W
Kenny Swain	Wycombe Wand.	Crewe Alexandra
Nicky Tanner	Mangotsfield	Liverpool
Bob Taylor	Horden C.W.	Bristol City
Paul Tester	Cheltenham Tn	Hereford United
Dean Thomas	Nuneaton Boro'	Notts County
Steve Thompson	Boston Utd	Lincoln City
Adrian Thorpe	Heanor Town	Northampton Tn
Andy Tillson	Grimsby Town	Queens Park R.
Andy Toman	Bishop Auckland	Darlington
Andy Townsend	Weymouth	Chelsea
Geoff Twentyman	Chorley	Bristol Rov.
Imre Varadi	Letchworth G.C.	Leeds United
Chris Waddle	Tow Law Town	Marseille
Bryan Wade	Trowbridge Tn	Brighton & H.A.
Alan Walker	Telford United	Gillingham
David Walter	Bideford	Plymouth Argyle
Keith Walwyn	Winterton Rgrs.	Carlisle Utd
Mark Ward	Northwich Vic.	Manchester City
Peter Ward	Chester le St.	Rochdale
Andy Watson	Harrogate Tn	Swansea City
Paul West	Alcester Town	Port Vale
Paul Wheeler	Aberaman	Hereford Utd
Steve White	Mangotsfield	Swindon Town
Billy Whitehurst	Mexborough Tn	Sheffield Utd
Michael Whitlow	Witton Albion	Leeds United
Guy Whittingham	Yeovil Town	Portsmouth
Steve Wigley	Curzon Ashton	Portsmouth
Russell Wilcox	Frickley Ath.	Hull City
Richard Wilkins	Haverhill Rov.	Cambridge Utd
Andy Williams	Solihull Boro'	Leeds United
Paul A. Williams	Nuneaton Boro'	Stockport Co.
Paul A. Williams	Woodford Town	Sheffield Wed.
Kevin Wilson	Banbury Utd	Chelsea
Tony Witter	Grays Athletic	Crystal Palace
Ian Wright	Greenwich Boro'	Crystal Palace
Eric Young	Slough Town	Crystal Palace

ALAN SMITH, now of Arsenal & England, seen here in his England Semi-Pro days.

PLAYERS NAME / Honours	Ht	Wt	Birthdate	Birthplace / Transfers	Contract Date	Clubs	APPEARANCES				GOALS			
							League	L/Cup	FA Cup	Other	Lg	L/C	FAC	Oth
Steve Adams	5.8	10.4	07.09.59	Sheffield		Manawatu Utd(NZ)								
						Rotherham Utd								
						Blackpool								
						Worksop Town								
					02.09.87	Scarborough	25+23	0+2	0+2	4	4			2
				£3,500	14.12.89	Doncaster Rovers	23+7			4+2	1			1
Tony Agana	5.11	12.0	02.10.63	London		Weymouth								
				£35,000	13.08.87	Watford	12+3	1+1	2		1	2		
				£45,000	19.02.88	Sheffield Utd	81+8	7	14	4+1	36	2	5	1
Keith Alexander	6.4	12.7	14.11.58	Nottingham		Barnet								
					11.07.88	Grimsby Town	64+18	4	8	4+1	26	1	1	1
Brett Angell	6.1	12.2	20.08.68	Malborough		Portsmouth								
						Cheltenham Town								
				£40,000	19.02.88	Derby County								
					20.10.88	Stockport Co	60+10	3	3	6	28		1	4
Andrew Ansah					21.03.89	Brentford	3+5				2			
				Free	29.03.90	Southend Utd	6+1				1			
Robert Atkins	6.0	12.2	16.10.62	Leicester		Leicester City								
Via Enderby Town to					23.07.82	Sheffield Utd	36+4	6+1	3	2+1	3			
				£12,500	15.02.85	Preston N.E	198+2	14	12	18	3		2	2
Dennis Bailey	5.10	11.6	13.11.65	Lambeth		Farnboroug								
				£10,000	02.12.87	Crystal Palace	0+5							
				Loan	27.02.89	Bristol Rovers	17			1+1	8			1
				£80,000	03.08.89	Birmingham City	40+3	4	4	2	18	2		
Danny Bailey	5.7	12.7	21.05.64	London		Bournemouth (A)								
				Free	01.08.89	Exeter City	46	7	6	3+1	1		1	
Paul Baker	6.1	12.10	05.01.63	Newcastle		Bishop Auckland								
				£4,000	01.07.84	Southampton								
				f	02.07.85	Carlisle Utd	66+5	4	3	2+1	11	1		
					31.07.87	Hartlepool Utd	120+2	4	10	9	40	2	3	3
Phillip Barber	5.11	12.6	10.06.65	Tring		Aylesbury								
				£7,500	14.02.84	Crystal Palace	194+21	11+4	8	18	34	3	1	2
Andy Barnsley	6.0	11.11	09.06.62	Sheffield		Denaby Utd								
Div.4'89					10.07.85	Rotherham Utd	28		3	3				
				£25,000	17.07.86	Sheffield Utd	73+4	3	5+1	7				
				£30,000	15.12.88	Rotherham Utd	58+6	4	3	3	3			1
Tony Barratt	5.7	10.3	18.10.65	Salford		Burnley (A)								
						Gillingham								
					16.08.85	Grimsby Town	20+2	3	1	2				
					04.12.86	Hartlepool Utd	70+5	4	8	5	4			
					23.03.89	York City	58	4	1	3	5			
Graham Barrow	6.2	13.7	13.06.54	Chorley		Altrincham				7				
FRT'85				£10,000	27.07.81	Wigan Ath	1+14	731+6	1	13	35	3		5
				£6,000	04.08.86	Chester City	142	6	9+2	13	13	1		2
Kevin Bartlett	5.8	11.5	12.10.62	Portsmouth	06.09.80	Portsmouth	0+3							
						Fareham								
				Free	23.09.86	Cardiff City	60+21	2+2	8	11+2	25	1	4	
				£125,000	16.02.89	West Brom A	25+12	2	3	1	10		1	
				£100,000	13.03.90	Notts County	14			2	8			
Warren Barton	6.0	11.0	19.03.69	London		Redbridge Forest								
					28.07.89	Maidstone Utd	41+1	0+2	3	6			1	
					07.06.90	Wimbledon								
Dave Beasant	9.0	12.0	20.03.59	Willesden		Edgware Town								
E: 2;B.6;Div4'83; Div2'89; FAC'88; ZDC'90				£1,000	07.08.79	Wimbledon	340	21	21	7				
				£800,000	13.06.88	Newcastle Utd	20	2	2	1				
				£725,000	14.01.89	Chelsea	60	2	3	6				
Chris Beaumont	5.11	11.7	05.12.65	Denaby		Denaby Utd								
				m	21.07.88	Rochdale	31+3	0+1	2	2	7	1	1	
				£8,000	21.07.89	Stockport Co	19+3	1		4	5			1
Paul Beesley	6.1	11.5	21.07.65	Liverpool		Maritime (Por)								
					22.09.84	Wigan Ath	153+2	13	6	5	3			
				£175,000	20.10.89	Leyton Orient	32		1	1	1			1
					10.07.90	Sheffield Utd								
Gary Bennett	6.1	12.1	04.12.61	Manchester	08.09.79	Manchester City								
Div.3.88					16.09.81	Cardiff City	85+2	6	3		11	1		
					26.07.84	Sunderland	217+3	25	5	12	18	1		
Gary Bennett	6.1	12.6	20.09.63	Liverpool	09.10.84	Wigan Ath	10+10		1	3+1	3			1
FRT'85				Free	22.08.85	Chester City	109+17	5+4	8	10	36	1	5	5
					11.11.88	Southend Utd	36+6	4	1	2+1	5	4		
				£20,000	01.03.90	Chester City	8				1			

PLAYERS NAME Honours	Ht	Wt	Birthdate	Birthplace Transfers	Contract Date	Clubs	APPEARANCES				GOALS			
							League	L/Cup	FA Cup	Other	Lg	L/C	FAC	Oth
Ian Bennyworth	6.0	12.4	15.01.62	Hull	24.01.80	Hull City (A)								
NPLC'82,GMVC'87						Gainsborough T		1						
						Nuneaton Borough	1		1					
						Scarborough	88+1	12+1	4	6	3			
				£15,000	26.12.89	Hartlepool Utd	27				2			
Keith Bertschin	6.1	11.8	25.08.56	Enfield		Barnet								
E:u21.3,Y,FAYC75					01.10.73	Ipswich Town	19+13	1			8			
				£100,000	30.07.77	Birmingham City	113+5	7+1	8+1		29	1	8	
				£200,000	27.08.81	Norwich City	112+2	11	13		29	4	5	
				£50,000	15.11.84	Stoke City	82+5	4	3+4	1	29	2		5
				£32,500	25.03.87	Sunderland	25+11	2	0+1	3+1	7			3
				£30,000	01.08.88	Walsall	40+15	1+3	3+1	5+1	9		2	4
Wayne Biggins	5.11	11.0	20.11.61	Sheffield	22.11.79	Lincoln City	8				1			
						Kings Lynn								
						Matlock T								
				£7,500	04.02.84	Burnley	78	6	3	7	29	1	1	5
				£40,000		Norwich City	66+13	6	4	6+2	16	2		3
				£150,000	15.07.88	Manchester City	29+3	4	2		9	1		
				£250,000	10.08.89	Stoke City	35		1	2	10			1
Peter Billing	6.1	13.11	24.10.64	Liverpool		South Liverpool			1					
					15.01.86	Everton	1			4				
				£12,000	23.12.86	Crewe Alexandra	83+5	2	5	9	1			
				£120,000	28.06.89	Coventry City	16+2	3	1	1				
Gary Birtles	6.0	12.0	27.07.56	Nottingham		Long Eaton Utd								
E:3,u21.2,B1,LgC'79,E.Cup'79,80				£30,000	01.12.76	Nottm. Forest	87	18	5	22	32	10	1	8
				£1,250,000	21.10.80	Manchester Utd	57+1	2	4		11		1	
				£275,000	03.09.82	Nottm. Forest	122+3	13	6	5+2	38	5	2	
				f	07.07.87	Notts County	62+1	6	4	9	9	1	1	1
				Free		Grimsby Town	36+2	1+2	3	2	8	1		
Ernie Bishop	5.11	12.0	28.11.62	Liverpool		Winsford Utd								
LDC'90						Northwich Victoria								
via Altrincham and Runcorn to					17.03.88	Tranmere Rovers	41+27	8+3	1+2	2+1	16	3		
Nicholas Bissett	6.1		05.04.64	Fulham		Barnet								
				£125,000	01.09.88	Brighton & H.A	44+1	2		2	5			
Ian Blackstone						Harrogate Railway								
						Accrington Stanley								
						Harrogate Town								
					Oct 1990	York City								
Kevin Blackwell	5.11	12.10	21.12.58	Luton		Boston Utd								
GMVC'87						Barnet								
						Scarborough	44	11	2	2				
				Loan	08.11.89	Notts County								
				£15,000	14.12.89	Notts County								
Noel Blake	6.0	13.11	12.01.62	Kingston(Jam)	01.08.79	Aston Villa	4							
				Loan	01.03.82	Shrewsbury Town	6							
				£55,000	15.09.82	Birmingham City	76	12	8		5			
				£150,000	24.08.84	Portsmouth	144	14	10	5	10	1	1	1
				Free	04.07.88	Leeds Utd	51	4	2	4	4			
				£175,000	09.02.90	Stoke City	18							
Gary Blissett	6.0	12.7	29.06.64	Manchester	23.08.83	Crewe Alexandra	112+10	9	4	6+1	8	3		4
				£60,000	26.03.87	Brentford	121+3	6	1	3+1	31	3		
Paul Bodin	5.10	10.11	13.09.64	Cardiff	01.08.82	Cardiff City								
W:u21.1,Y						Bath City								
				£15,000	27.01.88	Newport Co	6				1			
				£30,000	07.03.88	Swindon Town	56+7	8	3	6	7			
Bob Bolder	6.1	14.8	02.10.85	Dover	01.03.77	Sheffield Wed	196	16	12					
				£125,000	08.08.83	Liverpool								
					16.10.85	Sunderland	22	2	3	2				
					15.08.86	Charlton Ath	137	9	7	14				
John Bramhall	6.2	13.6	20.11.56	Warrington	01.07.76	Tranmere Rovers	164+6	16	8		7	1		
				£10,000	25.03.82	Bury	165+2	9	9	5	17	2	1	
				Loan	21.11.85	Chester City	4							
				f	11.08.86	Rochdale	86	8	2	6	13			1
					03.08.88	Halifax Town	62	6	6	6	5		1	1
				£12,500	18.01.90	Scunthorpe Utd	25							
Mark Bright	6.0	11.0	06.06.62	Stoke		Leek Town								
					04.08.82	Port Vale	18+11	1+1	0+1	2	10		1	
				£33,000	19.07.84	Leicester City	26+16	3+1	1		6			
				£75,000	26.01.87	Crystal Palace	148	9	9+1	13	63	3	2	6
Ian Brightwell	5.10	11.7	09.04.68	Lutterworth		Congleton								
				Free	07.05.86	Manchester City	82+21	3+1	4+1	1	9			

ALAN PARDEW, seen here in action for Dulwich Hamlet, is now with Crystal Palace.

PLAYERS NAME / Honours	Ht	Wt	Birthdate	Birthplace / Transfers	Contract Date	Clubs	APPEARANCES League	L/Cup	FA Cup	Other	GOALS Lg	L/C	FAC	Oth
Gary Brook	5.10	10.10	09.05.64	Dewsbury		Frickley Athletic								
				£7,500	24.12.87	Newport Co	13			0+1	2			
				£10,000	25.03.88	Scarborough	59+5	10	2	8	16	2	1	3
				£80,000	15.11.89	Blackpool	23+2		6		6		1	
Antony J Brown	6.2	12.7	17.09.58	Thackley		5								
				f	24.03.83	Leeds Utd	24				1			
				f	03.11.84	Doncaster Rovers	85+2	4	3	3	2			
				£10,000	27.07.87	Scunthorpe Utd	46+8	7+1	2+1	3	2			
				Free		Rochdale	43	2	5	2				
David Brown	6.1	12.8	28.01.57	Hartlepool	01.02.77	Middlesbrough	10							
				Loan	10.08.79	Plymouth A	5	3						
				£40,000	11.10.79	Oxford Utd	21	3						
				£5,000	12.09.81	Bury	146	7	6	5				
					03.07.86	Preston N.E	74	9	6	8				
				Loan	06.01.89	Scunthorpe Utd	5							
				Free		Halifax Town	27	2		3				
Richard Brown						Derby County								
						Ilkeston Town								
						Sheffield Wed.								
						Ilkeston Town								
						Grantham Town								
						Boston Utd								
						Kettering Town								
				£25,000	Sept 1990	Blackburn Rovers								
Steve Bull	5.11	11.8	28.03.65	Tipton	24.08.85	West Brom A. (A)	3+2	2		1+2	2	1		
E:11,u21.5,Div.4'88; Div3'89; SVT'88				£35,000	21.11.86	Wolverhampton W	161	10	4	23	109	7	4	27
John Butler	5.11	11.7	07.02.62	Liverpool		QPR								
					15.01.82	Wigan Ath	238+7	16+1	20+1	18	13		1	
				£100,000	23.12.88	Stoke City	69	2	1	2	1			
Lee Butler	6.2	13.0	30.05.66	Sheffield		Haworth Co								
					16.06.86	Lincoln City	30	1	1					
				£100,000	21.08.87	Aston Villa	4			1				
Steve Butler	6.2	13.0	27.01.62	Birmingham		Wokingham Town								
E:Semi.Pro,VMVC						Windsor								
via Brentford to					28.07.89	Maidstone Utd	44	2	3	6	21	1	1	3
David Byrne	5.8	11.0	05.03.61	Hammersmith		Kingstonia								
Div2'88					15.07.85	Gillingham	18+5	2	0+3	1+1	3			
				£5,000	04.08.86	Millwall	52+11	5+1	3	4	2	1		
				Loan	08.09.88	Cambridge Utd	4							
				Loan	23.02.89	Blackburn Rovers	4							
					16.03.89	Plymouth A	51+4	3	1	1	2			
				Loan	01.02.90	Bristol Rovers	0+2		0+1					
Richard Cadette	5.7	10.10	21.03.65	Hammersmith		Wembley								
					25.08.84	Leyton Orient	19+2	4	1	2	4		1	
				Free	15.08.85	Southend Utd	90	5+1	4	5	49	1	5	1
				£130,000	20.07.87	Sheffield Utd	26+2	1	2	2	7			
				£80,000	22.07.88	Brentford	38+10	1		3	13			1
				Loan	22.03.90	Bournemouth	4+4				1			
Danny Carter			29.06.69		04.07.88	Leyton Orient	29+4	4	1	1	5	2		
Tony Cascarino	6.2	11.10	01.09.62	St. Pauls Cray		Crockenhill								
Ei:26; Div2'88					14.01.82	Gillingham	209+10	18	15+1	9	78	11	9	4
				£200,000	23.06.87	Millwall	105+42	10+1	8+2	5	33		1	1
				£1,500,000	16.03.90	Aston Villa	10				2			
Jimmy Case	5.9	12.5	18.05.54	Liverpool		S Liverpoo								
E:u23.1,ESC'77,LC'81,Div1'76-'80,EC'77'78'81,UEFAC'76					01.05.73	Liverpool	170+16	21+1	20+1	28+3	23	3	7	13
					19.08.81	Brighton & H.A	124+3	8	13+1		10		5	
					20.03.85	Southampton	189+1	30	12	7	9	2		1
Peter Cawley	6.4	14.8	15.09.65	London	26.01.87	Wimbledon								
				Loan	26.02.87	Bristol Rovers	9+1							
				Loan	14.12.88	Fulham	4+2		1					
				Free		Bristol Rovers	1+2							
				Free	06.07.90	Southend Utd								
Martyn Chalk					23.01.90	Derby County								
Alec Chamberlain	6.2	11.11	20.06.64	Ely		Ramsey Tow								
				Free	27.07.81	Ipswich Town								
				Free	03.08.82	Colchester Utd	188	11	10	10				
				£80,000	28.07.87	Everton								
				£150,000	27.07.88	Luton Town	44	3	1	3				
(F) Gary Chapman	5.8	11.0	01.05.64	Leeds		Frickley Athletic								
					27.09.88	Bradford City	2+3	0+1						
				Loan	13.09.89	Notts County								
				£15,000	23.02.90	Notts County	13+6			2	4			

PLAYERS NAME Honours	Ht	Wt	Birthdate	Birthplace Transfers	Contract Date	Clubs	APPEARANCES League	L/Cup	FA Cup	Other	GOALS Lg	L/C	FAC	Oth
Vincent Chapman	5.9	11.0	05.12.67	Newcastle		Tow Law Town								
					29.01.88	Huddersfield Town	4+2							
				Loan	23.03.89	York City								
				Free		Rochdale	4							
Steve Claridge	5.11	11.8	10.04.66	Portsmouth		Bournemouth	3+4							
						Weymouth								
					11.10.88	Crystal Palace								
					25.11.88	Aldershot	57+4	2+1	6	5	19		1	2
				£75,000	08.02.90	Cambridge Utd								
Tim Clarke						Cradley Town								
						Halesowen Harriers								
						Halesowen Town								
					Sept 1990	Coventry City								
Gary Clayton ESP1	5.10	11.7	02.02.63	Sheffield		Rotherham Utd. (A)								
						Burton Albion								
					23.08.86	Doncaster Rovers	34+1	2	3	2	5			
				£10,000	02.07.87	Cambridge Utd	90+1	6	5	5	6	1		1
Glen Cockerill	6.0	12.4	25.08.55	Grimsby		Louth Utd								
					01.11.76	Lincoln City	65+6	2	2		10			
					06.12.79	Swindon Town	23+3	3			1			
					12.08.81	Lincoln City	114+1	16	7	1	25	1		
					23.03.84	Sheffield Utd	62	6	1		10	1		
				£225,000	17.10.85	Southampton	175+6	22	11+1	7	27	3	2	
Robert Codner E: S-P.	5.11		23.06.65	Walthamstow		Barnet								
				£125,000	08.09.88	Brighton & H.A	67+6	2	2	2	10		1	
Stan Collymore Birm'ham County Schoolboy Rep.			22.01.71		86-87	Birmingham City								
					87-88	Walsall								
					88-89	Wolverhampton W								
					1990	Stafford Rgrs.								
				£100,000	Dec 1990	Crystal Palace								
Graham Cooper	5.10	11.0	22.05.62	Huddersfield	22.03.84	Huddersfield Town								
				£5,000	03.08.88	Wrexham	45+9	3+1	2+1	4+3	15	1	1	1
Steve Cooper	6.1	11.10	22.06.64	Birmingham	10.11.83	Birmingham City								
				Loan	23.12.83	Halifax Town	7				1			
				Free	28.09.84	Newport Co	38		2	5	11			
				Free	09.08.85	Plymouth A	58+15	2+3	5+1	0+1	5	1	2	
				£100,000	28.07.88	Barnsley	54+11	2	9	1	5		3	
Tony Coton	6.2	13.7	19.05.61	Tamworth		Mile Oak Rovers								
					13.10.78	Birmingham City	94	10	10					
				£300,000	27.09.84	Watford	233	18	32	8				
					20.07.90	Manchester City								
Barry Cowdrill SVT'89	5.11	11.4	03.01.57	Birmingham		Sutton Coldfield Tn								
					07.04.79	West Brom A	127+4	9+1	6	1			1	
Loan 30.10.85 Rotherham Utd. 2 Lg Apps				Free	07.04.88	Bolton W	81+1	10	4	14	3	2		
David Crown	5.10	11.4	16.02.58	Enfield		Waltham Avenue								
					23.07.80	Brentford	44+2	4	3		8	1	1	
					27.10.81	Portsmouth	25+3		2		2			
				Loan	24.03.83	Exeter City	6+1				3			
					04.08.83	Reading	87+1	4	6	2+1	14	2	1	
					26.07.85	Cambridge Utd	106	12	3	4	45	6	2	2
					07.11.87	Southend Utd	113	8	4	7	61	1	3	3
				£50,000	27.06.90	Gillingham								
Paul Culpin	5.10	10.8	08.02.62	Kirby Muxloe		Nuneaton Borough		2					1	
				£50,000	10.06.85	Coventry City	5+4	1		1	2			
				£55,000	10.10.87	Northampton T	52+11	3	2+1	6	23	2		1
				£40,000	06.10.89	Peterborough U	9+3		2+1	1	2			
Tony Cunningham	6.1	13.2	12.11.57	Jamaica		Stourbridge								
				£20,000	11.05.79	Lincoln City	111+12	13	5+1		32	7		
				£85,000	23.09.82	Barnsley	40+2	2	1		11			
					10.11.83	Sheffield Wed	26+2		4+1		5			
					30.07.84	Manchester City	16+2	5	0+1		2	3		
					07.02.85	Newcastle Utd	37+10	2	1+1		4	2		
					04.08.87	Blackpool	71	8	5	6	18	3	2	2
				£40,000	02.08.89	Bury	25	2	2	5	8			2
Paul Dalton	5.11	12.00		Middlesborough	03.05.88	Manchester Utd								
					04.03.89	Hartlepool Utd	57+5	2	1	2	13	1		
Peter Davenport E:1,B1	5.10	11.12	24.03.64	Birkenhead		Cammel Lai								
					05.01.82	Nottm. Forest	114+4	10	7+1	10+1	54	1	1	2
				£750,000	12.03.86	Manchester Utd	73+19	7+2	2+2		22	4		
				£750,000	03.11.88	Middlesbrough	53+6	2	4	7+1	7			1
					19.07.90	Sunderland								

DAVE REGIS, showing the style for Barnet that persuaded Notts County to buy him.

PLAYERS NAME Honours	Ht	Wt	Birthdate	Birthplace Transfers	Contract Date	Clubs	APPEARANCES League	L/Cup	FA Cup	Other	GOALS Lg	L/C	FAC	Oth
Aidan Davison	6.1	13.2	11.05.68	Sedgefield		Bill								
					25.03.88	Notts County	1							
				Loan	07.09.89	Leyton Orient								
				Loan	07.10.89	Bury								
				£6,000	17.11.89	Bury								
				Loan	21.03.90	Chester City								
Bobby Davison	5.10	11.5	17.07.59	South Shields		Seaham CW								
Div.2 '87,'90				£1,000	02.07.80	Huddersfield Town	1+1							
				£20,000	28.08.81	Halifax Town	63	5	3		29	3		
				£90,000	02.12.82	Derby County	203+3	18	11	4	83	6	7	2
				£350,000	27.11.87	Leeds Utd	77+7	4	2+1	6	30	1	1	3
Keith Day	6.1	11.6	29.11.62	Grays		Aveley								
					23.08.84	Colchester Utd	113	5	6	5	12			
					21.07.87	Leyton Orient	125	10	8	11	6	1		
Alan Devonshire	5.10	11.0	13.04.56	London		Southall								
E:8,B1,FAC'80,Div2'81				£5,000	01.10.76	West Ham U	331+5	41+3	29	6	29	2	1	
				Free	25.07.90	Watford								
Kerry Dixon	6.0	13.0	24.07.61	Luton		Tottenham H. (A)								
E:8,u21.1; Div2'84'89; ZDC'90						Dunstable								
				£20,000	22.07.80	Reading	110+6	6+1	2+1		51			
				£175,000	17.08.83	Chelsea	266+1	31	14+1	17	132	20	7	12
Iain Dowie			09.01.65	Hatfield		Hendon								
				£30,000	14.12.88	Luton Town	27+10	1+1	0+1	3	8			4
				Loan	13.09.89	Fulham								
Keith Downing	5.8	11.0	23.07.65	Birmingham		Mile Oak Rovers								
Div.4'88; Div.3'89; SVT'88					16.05.84	Notts County	23				1			
				Free	06.08.87	Wolverhampton W	78+19	3+3	4	10+3	5		1	1
John Dreyer	6.0	11.6	11.06.63	Alnwick		Oxford Utd	57+3	10+1		2	2			
				Loan		Torquay Utd	5							
				Loan		Fulham	12				2			
				£140,000	27.07.88	Luton Town	54+2	8	1	2	3	1		
Dean Edwards	5.10	10.7	25.02.62	Wolverhampton	26.02.80	Shrewsbury Town (A	7+6				1			
					25.10.85	Wolverhampton W	28+3		0+1		9			
					27.03.87	Exeter City	51+3	2	1	2	17			
					12.08.88	Torquay Utd	56+14	4	6+2	6+3	11		1	3
Paul R Edwards	5.11	11.0	25.12.63	Birkenhead		Altrincham								
					12.01.88	Crewe Alexandra	82+4	6	8	7+1	6			1
				£350,000	16.03.90	Coventry City	6+2							
Tony Ellis	5.11	11.0	20.10.64	Salford		Horwich RMI								
						Northwich Victoria								
					22.08.86	Oldham Ath	3+2	1		1				
				£23,000	06.10.87	Preston N.E	80+8	3	5	11+1	27			5
				£250,000	20.12.89	Stoke City	24				6			
Karl Elsey	5.10	12.6	20.11.58	Swansea		Pembroke Borough								
					06.01.79	Q.P.R	6+1							
					16.07.80	Newport Co	114+9	8+3	7	3+2	15	1		
				P.E.	30.09.83	Cardiff City	59	4	2	5				
				Free	13.08.85	Gillingham	126+2	11	10	16	13		1	2
				£20,000+PE	26.08.88	Reading	41+3	4	7	3	3		2	
				£20,000	26.07.89	Maidstone Utd	44	2	3	6	4		1	
Paul Emson	5.11	11.3	22.10.58	Lincoln		BCit								
				£5,000	26.09.78	Derby County	112+15	4+3	1+3		13			
					15.08.83	Grimsby Town	89+7	12	3+1		15	1	1	
					15.08.86	Wrexham	42+7	3	2+1	4+2	5	2		1
					02.08.88	Darlington	27+7	2	1	1				
Stewart Evans	6.3	11.5	15.11.60	Maltby	17.11.78	Rotherham Utd. (A)								
Div.4'83,'89						Gainsbro								
				£6,000	18.11.80	Sheffield Utd								
					15.03.82	Wimbledon	165+10	13	9	1	50	13	2	
					19.08.86	West Brom A	13+1	2		1				
					27.03.87	Plymouth A	32+8	2+1	1	1	10		1	
					11.11.88	Rotherham Utd	31+12		5	7	10		1	
Andy Feeley	5.9	10.10	30.09.61	Hereford		Hereford Utd. (A)								
						Trowbridge Town								
				£10,000	08.02.84	Leicester City	74+2	4	6					
				Free	24.08.87	Brentford	57+10	2	1	2				
				Free	01.08.89	Bury	26+4	2	2	2	3			
Alan Finley	6.4	13.10				Maritime (Por)								
				Free	01.07.88	Shrewsbury Town	60+3	3	2	4	2			
Tony Finnigan	6.0	12.0	17.10.62	Wimbledon	19.03.85	Crystal Palace (A)	94+11	7+1	2+1	2	10			
				£45,000	29.07.88	Blackburn Rovers	21+14	3	5	3			1	1
					01.08.90	Hull City								

PLAYERS NAME Honours	Ht	Wt	Birthdate	Birthplace Transfers	Contract Date	Clubs	APPEARANCES				GOALS			
							League	L/Cup	FA Cup	Other	Lg	L/C	FAC	Oth
Darren Foreman	5.10	10.4	12.02.68	Southampton	03.11.86	Barnsley	33+14	2+1	2+3	1	8			
E:S				£80,000	08.03.90	Crewe Alexandra								
Gerry Forrest	5.10	10.11	21.01.57	Stockton		South Bank								
Div3'81					01.02.77	Rotherham Utd	357	36	22	3	7	2		
					05.12.85	Southampton	112+3	11	5	3			1	
				Free	01.08.90	Rotherham Utd								
David Frain	5.8	10.8	11.10.62	Sheffield	07.09.85	Sheffield Utd. (A)	35+9	3+2		2	6			
				f	18.07.88	Rochdale	42	2	2	2	12		1	
				£50,000	21.07.89	Stockport Co	25+4	1	0+2	4	2			
John Francis	5.8	11.2	21.11.63	Leeds		Emley								
E: FLg.u18					15.09.88	Sheffield Utd	14+28	0+2	0+1	3+2	6			1
				£90,000	24.01.90	Burnley	18+1				4			
Tony Fyfe	6.3	12.0	23.02.62	Carlisle	07.07.88	Carlisle Utd	28+20	0+2	1+2	1+1	12			
				Loan	28.12.89	Scarborough	6				1			
				£25,000	24.01.90	Halifax Town	10+2							
Steve Galliers	5.6	9.7	21.08.57	Fulwood		Chorley								
Div.4.83				£1,500	10.08.77	Wimbledon	148+7	17+1	13+1		10	2		
				£70,000	23.10.81	Crystal Palace	8+5							
				£15,000	18.08.82	Wimbledon	145+1	14	10	1	5	2		
				£37,500	10.09.87	Bristol City	74+3	9	6+1	12	5			
				£25,000	08.08.89	Maidstone Utd	7+1	2	2					
Tony Galvin	5.9	11.5	12.07.56	Huddersfield		Goole Town								
Ei:27,FAC'81'82,EUFA'84				£30,000	26.01.78	Tottenham H	194+7	20+3	22+1	24	21	3	2	6
				£140,000	29.08.87	Sheffield Wed	21+15	4+2		1+1	1			1
				Free	18.08.89	Swindon Town	6+5	0+1						
Stephen Gaughan			14.04.70	Doncaster	08.07.88	Doncaster Rovers (A)	42+25	2+2	4	5+1	3			
				Free	01.07.90	Sunderland								
Patrick Gavin					09.03.89	Gillingham	13				7			
					16.06.89	Leicester City								
				Loan	01.09.89	Gillingham	18+16		0+2	2+1	1			
Brian Gayle	6.1	12.7	06.03.65	London	03.06.85	Wimbledon (A)	76+7	7	4	2	3	1	1	
				£325,000	06.07.88	Manchester City	55	8	2	1	3			
				£330,000	19.01.90	Ipswich Town	20		0+1					
John Gayle	6.4	13.01	30.07.64	Birmingham		Burton Albion								
				£30,000*	01.03.89	Wimbledon	10+3	1			1			
Dave Gilbert	5.4	10.4	22.06.63	Lincoln	29.06.81	Lincoln City (A)	15+15	5	3		1			
Div.4'87				f	18.08.82	Scunthorpe Utd	1	1		1+1				
				f		Boston Utd								
					30.06.86	Northampton T	120	10	6	9	20	2	3	1
					23.03.89	Grimsby Town	56	4	3	2	13	1	1	
Jon Gittons	5.11	12.6	22.01.64	Moseley	16.10.85	Southampton	18	4	1					
				£40,000	22.07.87	Swindon Town	97+2	11+1	6	12+1	5			
Nigel Gleghorn	6.0	12.13	12.08.62	Seaham		Seaham R S								
						Ipswich Town	56+12	3+2	3+1	5+2	11			2
				£47,500	04.08.88	Manchester City	27+7	2+1		1	7	2	1	1
				£175,000	09.09.89	Birmingham City	43	2	4	2	8		3	
Craig Goldsmith	5.7	11.3	27.08.63	Peterborough	12.08.88	Peterborough U	39+7	4	4	2+1	6	1		
				£20,000	23.12.89	Carlisle Utd	21+5				1			
Mick Gooding	5.7	10.7	16.02.59	Newcastle		Bishop Auckland								
Div.3'89					18.07.79	Rotherham Utd	90+12	9	3	0+2	9	3		
					24.12.82	Chesterfield	12							
					09.09.83	Rotherham Utd	149+7	18	13	7	32	3	4	
				£18,000	13.08.87	Peterborough U	47	8	1	4	21	2	2	2
				£85,000	20.09.88	Wolverhampton W	43+1	4		5+1	3			1
				£65,000	26.12.89	Reading								
Clive Goodyear	6.0	11.4	15.01.61	Lincoln	11.10.78	Luton Town	85+5	5	4		4			
Div2'82,FAC'88				£50,000	23.08.84	Plymouth A	99+7	6+2	7	4	5	1	1	
				£50,000	29.07.87	Wimbledon	25+1	2		1				
Colin Gordon	6.1	12.12	17.01.63	Stourbridge	01.11.84	Swindon Town	70+2	6	2	3	34			
				£80,000	03.07.86	Wimbledon	2+1	2		1		1		
				Loan	15.02.87	Gillingham	4				2			
				£80,000	17.07.87	Reading	23+1	6	0+1	1	9	2		
				Loan	24.03.88	Bristol City	8			2	4			
				£90,000	07.10.88	Fulham	12+5		1		2			
				£80,000	29.06.89	Birmingham City	14+7	2+1			3			
Andy Gray	5.10	10.2	22.02.64	Brixton		Corinthian Casuals		2						
via Dulwich Hamlet to				£2,000	08.11.84	Crystal Palace	92+6	9+1	3	0+1	27	2		
E: u21.2				£150,000	25.11.87	Aston Villa	34+3	3	3+1	0+2	4	1		
				£425,000	02.02.89	Q.P.R	11				2			
				£500,000	18.08.89	Crystal Palace	35	4	7	5			2	2
Gareth Gray						Bolton W (T)								
				Transfer	30.07.90	Rochdale								

MARK WARD, now with Manchester City but seen here in his England Semi-Pro days.

PLAYERS NAME Honours	Ht	Wt	Birthdate	Birthplace Transfers	Contract Date	Clubs	APPEARANCES				GOALS			
							League	L/Cup	FA Cup	Other	Lg	L/C	FAC	Oth
Ron Green	6.2	14.0	13.10.56	Birmingham		Alvechurch								
					11.06.77	Walsall	163	10	11	2				
				Free	02.07.84	Shrewsbury Town	19							
				£10,000	01.03.85	Bristol Rovers	56	4	4	3				
					21.08.86	Scunthorpe Utd	68	7	5	4				
				Free	09.09.88	Wimbledon	4	1						
				Loan	30.09.88	Shrewsbury Town	17			1				
				Loan	16.02.89	Manchester City								
				£20,000	23.03.89	Walsall	23	1	2	2				
Phil Gridelet			30.04.67	Hendon		Watford								
England Semi-Pro Int.						Hendon								
						Barnet								
				£170,000	Sept 1990	Barnsley								
Paul Groves	5.11	11.5	28.02.66	Derby	01.10.86	Burton Albion								
				£12,000	18.04.88	Leicester City	7+9	1	0+1	0+1	1	1		
				Loan	20.08.89	Lincoln City	8	2			1			
				£60,000	25.01.90	Blackpool	18+1		4		1		1	
Peter Guthrie	6.1	12.12	10.10.61	Newcastle		Blyth Spar								
						Weymouth								
				£100,000	04.01.88	Tottenham H								
				Loan	26.02.88	Swansea City	14			4				
				Loan	23.12.88	Charlton Ath								
				£60,000	01.08.89	Barnet								
				£15,000	01.08.90	Bournemouth								
Gary Hackett	5.8	10.1	11.10.62	Stourbridge		Bromsgrove								
				£5,000	21.07.83	Shrewsbury Town	142+8	15	6	2+1	17	2	1	
				£80,000	16.07.87	Aberdeen	14	4						
				£110,000	11.03.88	Stoke City	64+9	3+1	3+1	3	7			
				£70,000	01.03.90	West Brom A	9+5				2			
Paul Hardyman	5.8	11.4	15.09.65	Manchester		Waterloovi								
E:u21.2						Fareham T								
					17.05.84	Portsmouth	113+4	5	6	8	1			1
				£130,000	25.07.89	Sunderland	42	7			7	2		
Mark Harris	6.1	13.0	15.07.63	Reading		Workingham								
					18.05.88	Crystal Palace	0+2							
				Loan	07.08.89	Burnley	4	2						
				£22,500	22.09.89	Swansea City	41		4	2	2			
Michael Heathcote	6.1	12.7	10.09.65	Kelloe		Spennymoor								
					19.08.87	Sunderland	6+3							
				Loan	17.12.87	Halifax Town	7		3	3	1			
				Loan	04.01.90	York City	3							
					12.07.90	Shrewsbury Town								
Ian Hedges			05.02.69		84-85	Bristol M Farm								
					85-86	Newport County								
					86-88	Bristol M Farm								
						Gloucester City								
					Nov 1990	AFC Bournemouth								
Liburd Henry	5.11	11.0	29.08.67	Dominica		Colchester Utd								
				£20,000	20.11.87	Watford	8+2	1	3	1	1			
Loan 1.9.88 Halifax T 1+4 Lg Apps					01.07.90	Maidstone Utd								
Martin Hicks	6.3	13.6	27.02.57	Strafford-on-Avon		Stranraer								
Div.49,Div.3'86,SC'88				N.C		Reading								
				f	01.02.77	Charlton Ath								
				£3,000	15.02.78	Reading	411+1	31	28	12+1	21	1		
Stuart Hicks	6.1	12.6	30.05.67	Peterborough	10.08.84	Peterborough U								
						Wisbech								
					24.03.88	Colchester Utd	41+3		5	4			1	
				Monthly	01.08.90	Scunthorpe Utd								
Richard Hill	6.0	12.1	20.09.63	Hinckley	14.11.81	Leicester City								
						Grankulla								
						Nuneaton								
				Free	21.06.85	Northampton T	86	6	5	6	46		3	3
				£258,000	03.07.87	Watford	2+2							
				£250,000	18.09.87	Oxford Utd	48+9	5+2	4+1	1+1	14		3	1
Mark Hine	5.8	9.11	18.05.64	Middlesbrough	06.10.83	Grimsby Town	20+2	1	1		1			
				f	03.07.86	Darlington	126+2	10	3	9	8	2		
				£50,000	05.01.90	Peterborough U	22			1	4			

PLAYERS NAME Honours	Ht	Wt	Birthdate	Birthplace Transfers	Contract Date	Clubs	APPEARANCES League	L/Cup	FA Cup	Other	GOALS Lg	L/C	FAC	Oth
Joe Hinnigan	6.1	12.7	03.12.55	Liverpool		South Liverpool								
				£1,000		Wigan Ath	66	4	7		10			
				£80,000	20.02.80	Sunderland	63	1	1		4			
				£15,000	24.12.82	Preston N.E	51+1	3	1	3	8	2		
				Free	17.08.84	Gillingham	99+4	8	8	8	7	1	1	
				Free	05.08.87	Wrexham	28+1	1	2	2	1		1	
					13.08.88	Chester City	52+2	4	2	3	2			1
Kevin Hitchcock FRT'87	6.1	12.2	05.10.62	Custom House		Barking			3					
					04.08.83	Nottm. Forest								
					01.02.84	Mansfield Town	182	12	10	20				
					25.03.88	Chelsea	11			4				
David Hockaday Div.4.86	5.10	10.9	09.11.57	Billingham	01.06.75	Blackpool	131+16	18+1	10+2		23		2	
					02.08.83	Swindon Town	226+15	20	18+2	22	5		2	1
Andy Holden W:1,u21.1	6.1	13.2	14.09.62	Flint		Rhyl								
					18.08.83	Chester City	100	8	2	3	16	2		2
				£45,000	30.10.86	Wigan Ath	48+1	3	7	7	5			
				£130,000	12.01.89	Oldham Ath	13				4			
Mike Hooper CS'86	6.3	13.0	10.02.64	Bristol	08.11.83	Bristol City	1		1	1				
				Free	08.02.85	Wrexham	34	4						
				£40,000	25.10.85	Liverpool	30	6	3	2+1				
Barry Horne WC86	5.10	12.3	18.05.63	St.Asaph		Liverpool								
					26.06.84	Wrexham	136	10	7	15	16	1	2	3
				£60,000	17.07.87	Portsmouth	86+4	3	6		7			
					22.03.89	Southampton	39+1	4+1	3		4	1	1	
Andrew Hunt			09.06.70		89-90	Kings Lynn								
					1990	Kettering Town								
				£150,000	Jan 1991	Newcastle Utd								
Chris Hutchings	5.10	11.0	05.07.57	Winchester		Southall								
						Harrow Borough								
				£10,000	19.07.80	Chelsea	83+4	7	7		3			
				£50,000	25.11.83	Brighton & H.A	153	7	11	3+1	4	1	1	
				£25,000	04.12.87	Huddersfield Town	110	6	8	5	10			
				Free	01.08.90	Walsall								
Nicholas Johns	6.2	11.8	08.06.57	Bristol		Minehead								
					02.02.76	Millwall	50	6	5					
via Tampa Bay Rowdies to				Loan	05.09.78	Sheffield Utd	1	1						
					22.12.78	Charlton Ath	288	18	14	2				
					30.12.87	Q.P.R	10	2	3	1				
				Free	12.03.90	Maidstone Utd	13			3				
Andy Jones W:5	5.10	12.7	09.01.63	Wrexham		Rhyl								
				£5,000	03.06.85	Port Vale	87+3	9+1	3+1	8	49	6		6
				£350,000	26.09.87	Charlton Ath	46+13	3+3	4	2	15	2	2	
				Loan	02.02.89	Port Vale	8+9				3			
				Loan	30.11.89	Bristol City	2+2			1	1			1
Vinny Jones FAC'88; Div.2'90	6.0	11.12	05.01.65	Watford		Wealdstone								
				£10,000	20.11.86	Wimbledon	77	6+2	2+2	3	9		1	
				£650,000	20.06.89	Leeds Utd	43+2	2	1	4	5			
Roger Joseph	5.11	11.10	24.02.65	Paddington		Southall								
				Free	04.10.84	Brentford	48+1	1	2	5	4	1	1	
				£150,000	25.08.88	Wimbledon	45+5	8	2+1	4				
Mark Kearney FRT'87	5.10	11.0	12.06.62	Ormskirk		Maritime (Por)								
					08.10.81	Everton								
					18.03.83	Mansfield Town	228+2	16	6+3	20+1	29	2	1	5
John Keeley	6.0	12.3	27.07.61	Plaistow	13.08.79	Southend Utd. (A)	63	4	5	3				
						Chelmsford			2					
					23.08.86	Brighton & H.A	138	6	9	7				
					01.08.90	Oldham Ath								
Tony Kelly FRT85	5.10	13.2	01.10.64	Prescott	30.09.82	Liverpool (A)								
				f	04.01.84	Wigan Ath	98+3	4	10	12	15	2	1	4
					26.04.86	Stoke City	33+3	2	5	1	4			
				£60,000	13.07.87	West Brom A	26	2	1	3	1			
				Loan	22.09.88	Chester City	5	2						
				Loan	24.10.88	Colchester Utd	13		4	3	2			
				Loan	28.01.89	Shrewsbury Town								
					10.03.89	Shrewsbury Town	62+1	4	1	3	5			
David Kelly	5.11	11.3	25.11.65	Birmingham		Alvechurch								
					21.12.83	Walsall	115+32	11+1	12+2	14+3	63	4	3	10
				£600,000	01.08.88	West Ham U	29+12	11+3	6	2+1	7	5		2
				£300,000	22.03.90	Leicester City	10				7			

EFAN EKOKU, now playing for Bournemouth, seen here in action for Sutton in 1989.

PLAYERS NAME Honours	Ht	Wt	Birthdate	Birthplace Transfers	Contract Date	Clubs	APPEARANCES League	L/Cup	FA Cup	Other	GOALS Lg	L/C	FAC	Oth
John Kelly	5.10	10.9	20.10.60	Bebbington	10.09.79	Tranmere Rovers	55+9	7	1		9			
					08.10.81	Preston N.E	85+8	11	4	3	20	1	1	
					12.08.85	Chester City	85	6	8	6	17		2	1
					24.06.87	Swindon Town	3+4	1			1			
					13.11.87	Oldham Ath	10			1				
				£35,000	09.08.89	Walsall	24+2	1+1	2	3	1			2
				Loan	22.03.90	Huddersfield Town	9+1				1			
Alan Kennedy					08.03.90	Wrexham	6+1							
Andy Leaning	6.0	13.0	18.05.63	York		Rowntree Mack								
				Free	01.07.85	York City	30		7	2				
				Free	28.05.87	Sheffield Utd	21	2	2					
				£12,000	09.11.88	Bristol City	25	4	2	1				
Mark Leonard	5.11	11.10	27.09.62	St Helens		Witton Alb								
					24.02.82	Everton								
				Loan	24.03.83	Tranmere Rovers	6+1							
				Free	01.06.83	Crewe Alexandra	51+3	4	2	3+1	15	2		
				Free	13.02.85	Stockport Co	73	5	1	2	23	2		3
				£40,000	27.09.86	Bradford City	90+30	8+3	3+3	6+4	25	4	1	3
Michael Leonard	5.11	11.0	09.05.59	Carshalton		Epsom & Ewell								
					01.07.76	Halifax Town	69	6	1					
				£30,000	14.09.79	Notts County	204	15	17	15				
					03.03.89	Chesterfield	62	2	2	4				
Matthew Le Tissier E: u20.2	6.0	11.10	14.10.68	Guernsey		Vale Recreation								
					17.10.86	Southampton (A)	78+28	10+6	5+1	4+1	36	8	2	2
David Leworthy	5.9	12.0	22.10.62	Portsmouth	18.09.80	Portsmouth	0+1							
						Fareham								
				£51,000	24.08.84	Tottenham H	8+3	0+1		0+1	3	1		1
				£165,000	24.12.85	Oxford Utd	25+12	2+3	2+1	2	8			1
				Loan	01.10.88	Shrewsbury Town	6				3			
				Free		Reading								
Peter Litchfield	6.1	12.12	27.07.56	Manchester		Manchester City (A)								
						Droylesden								
				£3,000	03.01.79	Preston N.E	107	17	7	3				
				£10,000	09.07.85	Bradford City	88	10	6	6				
				Loan	03.01.79	Oldham Ath	3							
				Free		Scunthorpe Utd	17	1	4	1				
David Logan Div.4.87	5.11	10.11	05.12.63	Whitley		Whitby								
					21.06.84	Mansfield Town	67	5	3	7	1			
				£12,000	20.02.87	Northampton T	39+2	3	0+1	1				
					15.08.88	Halifax Town	3	2						
					21.11.88	Stockport Co	70	1	1	4	4			
Tony Lowery FRT'87	5.9	10.6	06.07.61	Wallsend		Ashington								
					02.03.81	West Brom A	1							
				Loan	04.02.82	Walsall	4+2				1			
					23.04.83	Mansfield Town	244+1	19	15	25+1	19		2	4
Sean McCarthy	6.1	11.7	12.09.67	Bridgend		Bridgend T								
					22.09.85	Swansea City	76+15	4+1	5+2	9+1	17	3	4	2
				£50,000	18.08.88	Plymouth A	67+3	7	3	0+1	19	5	1	1+1
				£250,000	04.07.90	Bradford City								
John McClelland NI:53,FLg,SkolC84,SLC2	6.2	13.2	07.12.55	Belfast		Portadown								
					01.02.74	Cardiff City	1+3				1			
						Bangor City								
				£10,000	18.05.78	Mansfield Town	122+3	8+1	8		8	2	1	
				£90,000	01.05.81	Glasgow Rangers	96	29	12	14	4	2	1	1
				£225,000	08.11.84	Watford	186	12	32	3+1	3			
				£100,000	16.06.89	Leeds Utd	3+1							
				Loan	10.01.90	Watford	1							
Andy McFarlane						Moxley Rangers								
						Cradley Town								
				£20,000	Nov 1990	Portsmouth								
Eddie McGoldrick via Nuneaton Boro'(1 FAC App) Div.4'87	5.10	11.7	30.04.65	London to		Kettering Town			2					
				£10,000	23.08.86	Northampton T	97	9	6+1	7	9		1	1
				£200,000	10.01.89	Crystal Palace	40+3	3		8+1				1
Ian McInerney					21.09.88	Huddersfield Town	5+5			0+1	2			
				Free		Stockport Co	30+4	2+1	2	2+1	8	1		
Les McJannett NPL,PC'83		10.4	02.08.61	Cumnock	01.08.79	Mansfield Town (A)	73+1							
						Ashi								
						Matlock Town								
						Burton Albion								
					05.08.87	Scarborough	29+5	2+1	1	2				
					29.12.88	Darlington	26				1			

PLAYERS NAME Honours	Ht	Wt	Birthdate	Birthplace Transfers	Contract Date	Clubs	League	L/Cup	FA Cup	Other	Lg	L/C	FAC	Oth
							APPEARANCES				**GOALS**			
David McKearney	5.10	11.2	20.06.68	Liverpool	23.11.87	Bolton W								
				Free	13.10.89	Crewe Alexandra	14+3			0+1	1			
Chris Marples	5.11	12.0	03.08.64	Chesterfield	21.03.84	Chesterfield	84		5	5				
Div.4'85					25.03.87	Stockport Co	57	2	4	2				
					12.07.88	York City	91	6	2	6				
Nigel Martyn	6.2	13.10	11.08.66	St. Austell		St.Blazey								
E: u21.12; Div.3'90					06.08.87	Bristol Rovers	101	6	6	10				
				£1,000,000	21.11.89	Crystal Palace	25		7	5				
David Miller	5.11	11.2	08.01.64	Burnley	11.01.82	Burnley (A)	27+5	1	2	2+1	3			
				Loan	18.03.83	Crewe Alexandra	3							
					16.07.85	Tranmere Rovers	25+4	4	1	2	1			
						Colne Dynamoes								
					18.12.86	Preston N.E	49+8	6	0+2	7+4	2			
				Loan	16.02.89	Burnley	4							
				£30,000	14.09.89	Carlisle Utd	42		2	3	3			
Andrew Milner	6.0	11.12	10.02.67	Kendal		Netherfield								
					24.01.89	Manchester City								
				£20,000	18.01.90	Rochdale	14+2		2		4			
Trevor Morley	5.11	12.1	20.03.62	Nottingham		Derby County								
ESP:6; Div.4'87						Corby Town								
						Nuneaton B			3					
				£20,000	21.06.85	Northampton T	107	16	6	7	39	4	2	
				£175,000	22.01.88	Manchester City	69+3	7	1	2	14	3		
				£500,000	28.12.89	West Ham U	18+1		1		10			
Grant Morrow						Rowntree Mack								
						Doncaster Rovers	1+6				2			
Neil Morton						Crewe Alex.								
						Northwich Vic.								
					Oct 1990	Chester City								
Mark Newson	5.11	12.0	07.12.60	Stepney	15.12.78	Charlton Ath								
E:SP5,Div3'87						Maidstone Utd			12+3					
				Free	24.05.85	Bournemouth	172+5	12	11	4+1	23	2	2	
				£125,000	28.02.90	Fulham	16							
Eric Nixon	6.4	14.3	04.10.62	Manchester		Curzon Aston								
LDC'90				£1,000	10.12.83	Manchester Utd	58	8	10	8				
				Loan	29.08.86	Wolverhampton W	16							
				Loan	28.11.86	Bradford City	3							
				Loan	23.12.86	Southampton	4							
				Loan	23.01.87	Carlisle Utd	16							
				£60,000	26.07.88	Tranmere Rovers	99	13	6	17				
Steve Norris	5.10	10.10	22.09.61	Coventry		V S Rugby								
E: SP						Telford								
					25.07.88	Scarborough	35+10	9	2	3+2	13	2		1
				Loan	08.11.89	Notts County	0+1		1					
				Loan	28.12.89	Carlisle Utd								
				£40,000	19.01.90	Carlisle Utd	19+5				3			
Sean O'Driscoll	5.8	11.3	01.07.57	Wolverhampton		Abam								
Ei:3,AMC'84,Div3'87						Alvechurch								
					26.11.79	Fulham	141+7	12+1	11+1		14			
					16.02.84	Bournemouth	269+5	18+1	9	19	16	1	1	2
Vince O'Keefe	6.1	12.10	02.04.57	Birmingham	01.07.75	Birmingham City (A)								
FMC'87					01.07.76	Walsall								
						A P Leamin			4					
					01.06.78	Exeter City	53	11	3					
					29.02.80	Torquay Utd	108	4	6	3				
				£15,000	18.08.82	Blackburn Rovers	68	7	1	5				
				Loan	27.10.83	Bury	2							
				Loan	26.12.86	Blackpool	1							
				Loan	17.02.89	Blackpool	6			1				
				Free	20.07.89	Wrexham	43	2		2				
George Oghani	5.10	12.3	02.09.60	Manchester	01.02.78	Bury								
						Hyde United								
					16.10.83	Bolton W	86+13	9+2	2+4	13+1	27	3	1	7
				Loan	12.03.87	Wrexham	6+1							
					24.06.87	Burnley	73+1	8	2	9	21	3		3
				Free	01.06.89	Stockport Co	5+3	1+1			2			
				Monthly	12.10.89	Hereford Utd	7+1		1	0+1	2			
					15.02.90	Scarborough	13+1				4			
Ian Ormondroyd	6.4	13.7	22.09.64	Bradford		Thackley								
					06.09.85	Bradford City	72+15	12+2	7	6+2	20	4	2	1
				Loan	27.03.87	Oldham Ath	8+2							
				£600,000	02.02.89	Aston Villa	28+9	1+1	4	5	5		2	

PHIL GRIDELET, another ex Barnet player, now with Barnsley.

PLAYERS NAME / Honours / Transfers	Ht	Wt	Birthdate	Birthplace	Contract Date	Clubs	League	L/Cup	FA Cup	Other	Lg	L/C	FAC	Oth
Gary Pallister E:2; FAC'90	6.4	13.0	30.06.65	Ramsgate		Bilkingham								
					02.04.85	Middlesbrough	156	10	10	13	5		1	
Loan					18.10.85	Darlington	7							
£2,300,000					29.08.89	Manchester Utd	35	3	8		3			
Alan Paris	5.11	10.12	15.08.64	Slough		Slough								
					03.11.82	Watford								
					09.09.85	Peterborough U	135+2	12	10	8	2			
					29.07.88	Leicester City	70+5	5+2	2	2	3	1	1	
(D) Neil Parsley	5.9	10.12	25.04.66	Liverpool		Witton Albion								
£20,000					08.11.88	Leeds Utd								
Loan					13.12.89	Chester City	6							
Free					25.07.90	Huddersfield Town								
Trevor Peake ES.P2,FAC'87	6.0	12.9	10.02.57	Nuneaton		Nuneaton B								
£27,750					15.06.79	Lincoln City	171	16	7		7	2		
£100,000					06.07.83	Coventry City	239+1	25	15	8	5		1	
Stuart Pearce E: 5;U21.1; LC'89'90; SC'89	5.10	11.2	24.04.62	London		Wealdstone								
£25,000					20.10.83	Coventry City	51		2		4			
£					03.06.85	Nottm. Forest	173	30	11	8	22	5	1	5
Nigel Pearson	6.1	12.6	21.08.63	Nottingham		Heanor Tow								
£5,000					12.11.81	Shrewsbury Town	153+3		19	6	5			
£250,000					16.10.87	Sheffield Wed	89	3	4	5	5			
John Pemberton	5.11	11.9	18.11.64	Oldham		Chadderton								
Free					26.09.84	Rochdale	1							
Free					03.07.85	Crewe Alexandra	116+5	7	3	7	1	1		
					24.03.88	Crystal Palace	76+2	6+1	8	12	2			
					27.07.90	Sheffield Utd								
David Penney	5.8	10.7	17.08.64	Wakefield		Pontefract								
£1,500					26.09.85	Derby County	6+13	2+3	1	1+3		1	1	1
£175,000					23.06.89	Oxford Utd	20+9	2	1		2			
Gary Penrice	5.8	10.8	23.03.64	Bristol		Mangotsfield								
					06.11.84	Bristol Rovers	186+2	11	11	12+2	54	1	7	2
£500,000					14.11.89	Watford	29		3	1	12			1
Gerry Peyton Ei:23,Div3'87	6.2	13.11	20.05.56	Birmingham		Atherstone								
					01.05.75	Burnley	30	1	1					
£40,000					01.12.76	Fulham	345	26	20	2				
Loan					16.09.83	Southend Utd	10							
					22.07.86	Bournemouth	166	14	9	6				
Chris Pike	6.2	12.7	19.10.61	Cardiff		Barr								
					14.03.85	Fulham	32+10	3+1		3	4	2		1
Loan					12.12.86	Cardiff City	6		3		2		1	
Free						Cardiff City	41	2	4	1	18	1	1	
Nicky Platnauer	5.11	12.10	10.06.61	Leicester		Bedford Town								
Free					04.08.82	Bristol Rovers	21+3	1	0+1		7	1		
£50,000					26.08.83	Coventry City	38+5	5	4		6			
£60,000					14.12.84	Birmingham City	23+5	3	5		2			
Loan					30.01.86	Reading	6			1				
Free					26.09.86	Cardiff City	110+5	6	9	14	7	2		
£50,000					01.08.89	Notts County	44	2	1	4				
David Platt E: 11;B.3;u21.4	5.11	11.7	10.06.66	Oldham		Chadderton								
					24.07.84	Manchester Utd. (A)								
Free					23.02.85	Crewe Alexandra	134	8	3	7	56	4	1	
£200,000					02.02.88	Aston Villa	86	9	2	2	31	7	2	4
Trevor Putney	5.7	10.11	11.02.61	Harold Hill		Brentwood								
					19.09.80	Ipswich Town	94+9	15	9		8	1		
					13.06.86	Norwich City	76+6	6	6	6	8	1	1	
£300,000					14.08.89	Middlesbrough	25	4		3				
David Puttnam	5.10	11.9	03.02.67	Leicester										
					09.02.89	Leicester City (T)	4+3	0+1						
Loan					11.01.90	Lincoln City								
£35,000					21.03.90	Lincoln City	23				1			
Jimmy Quinn NI:27	6.0	11.6	18.11.59	Belfast		Oswestry								
£10,000					31.12.81	Swindon Town	34+15	1+1	5+3	1	10		6	2
£32,000					15.08.84	Blackburn Rovers	58+13	6+1	4	2	17	2	3	1
£50,000					19.12.86	Swindon Town	61+3	6	5	10+1	30	8		5
£210,000					20.06.88	Leicester City	13+18	2+1			6			
					17.03.89	Bradford City	35	2		1	13	1		
Loan					30.12.89	West Ham U								
£320,000					08.01.90	West Ham U	18+3		1		13			
Alan Reeves					20.09.88	Norwich City								
Loan					09.02.89	Gillingham	18							
£10,000					18.08.89	Chester City	28+2	1	1	2	2			

PLAYERS NAME Honours	Ht	Wt	Birthdate	Birthplace Transfers	Contract Date	Clubs	APPEARANCES League	L/Cup	FA Cup	Other	GOALS Lg	L/C	FAC	Oth
David Reeves	6.0	11.7	19.11.67	Birkenhead		Heswall								
				Free	06.08.86	Sheffield Wed	8 + 9	1 + 1	1		2	1		
				Loan	17.12.86	Scunthorpe Utd	3 + 1				2			
				Loan	20.11.87	Burnley	16			2	8			1
				£80,000	17.08.89	Bolton W	41	7	1	5	10	1		2
Cyrille Regis E:5,B3,U21.6,FAC'87	6.0	13.4	09.02.58	French Guyana		Moseley								
						Hayes								
				£5,000	01.05.77	West Brom A	233 + 4	27 + 1	25	10	82	16	10	4
				£300,000	11.10.84	Coventry City	200 + 4	19	11 + 1	3	42	9	3	
Carl Richards E:SP1,Div3'87	6.1	13.6	12.01.60	St Marys (Jam)		Dulwich Hamlet								
						Enfield			3					
				£10,000	08.07.86	Bournemouth	57 + 14	7 + 3	2	3	16		2	
				£70,000	13.10.88	Birmingham City	18 + 1				2			
				£37,000	14.07.89	Peterborough U	16 + 4	2	2 + 1	2	5	2		
				£60,000	25.01.90	Blackpool	16				4			
Steve Richards GMVC'87	6.0	12.0	24.10.61	Dundee	26.10.79	Hull City	55 + 3	3	4		2			
						Glentoran								
				N.C	22.12.84	York City	6 + 1			3				
						Goole Town								
					16.08.85	Lincoln City	21	2	1	1			1	
				f	28.03.86	Cambridge Utd	4				2			
				f		Scarborough	119	13	4	10	10	3		2
David Riley	5.7	10.10	08.12.60	Northampton		Keyworth Utd								
					04.01.84	Nottm. Forest	7 + 5	1			2			
				Loan	27.02.87	Darlington	6				2			
				Loan	28.07.87	Peterborough U	12	4			2	1		
				£20,000	19.10.87	Port Vale	41 + 1	2 + 1	4	3 + 1	3		1	
					01.03.90	Peterborough U	15				5			
Colin Robinson WC'84	5.10	11.0	15.05.60	Birmingham		Mile Oak R								
					09.11.82	Shrewsbury Town	176 + 18	19	5 + 2	2 + 1	41	8	2	
					22.01.88	Birmingham City	34 + 3	4	1		6			
					18.08.89	Hereford Utd	25 + 4	4	3	3 + 1	4	1	1	
Ronald Robinson	5.9	11.0	22.10.66	Sunderland	06.11.84	Ipswich Town								
					22.11.85	Leeds Utd	27							
					25.02.87	Doncaster Rovers	27 + 2	2	3	1	5			
					22.03.89	West Brom A	1							
					18.08.89	Rotherham Utd	43	4	3	4	1			1
Kevin Rose	6.1	13.6	23.11.60	Evesham		Ledbury Town								
				£10,000	25.08.79	Lincoln City								
via Ledbury Town to					16.03.83	Hereford Utd	268	16	13	19				
				£25,000	07.07.89	Bolton W	6	2						
				Loan	22.03.90	Carlisle Utd	11							
Nigel Saddington	6.1	12.0	09.12.65	Sunderland	28.09.84	Doncaster Rovers (A)	6							
				Free	17.01.86	Sunderland	3		1	1				
					19.02.88	Carlisle Utd	97	4	6	5	5		1	1
Lawrie Sanchez NI:1,Div4'79,FAC'88	5.11	12.0	22.10.59	Lambeth		Thatcham T								
				Free	22.09.78	Reading	249 + 13	20 + 1	14	1	28		1	
				£29,000	10.12.84	Wimbledon	179 + 4	16	14	5	24		2	
Trevor Senior Div3'86	6.1	12.8	28.11.61	Dorchester		Dorchester			4 + 3	1				
				£25,000	31.12.81	Portsmouth	11	0 + 2			2			
				Loan	24.03.83	Aldershot	10				7			
				£30,000	25.08.83	Reading	164	10	12	4	102	11	10	
				£325,000	28.07.87	Watford	22 + 2	3 + 1	3 + 1	1	1	1	2	1
				£200,000	24.03.88	Middlesbrough	9	1		4	2			2
				£150,000	14.10.88	Reading	37		7	3	15		4	4
J. Craig Short E:S	6.0	11.4	25.06.68	Bridlington		Pickering Town								
					15.10.87	Scarborough	61 + 2	6	2	7	7			1
				£100,000	27.07.89	Notts County	44	1	1	3	2		1	
Malcolm Shotton Div.3.84,Div.2.85,LgC'86	6.3	13.12	16.02.57	Newcastle	01.02.75	Leicester City (A)								
						Nuneaton Borough								
				£15,000	19.05.80	Oxford Utd	262	41 + 1	21	6	12	2	1	
				£70,000	28.08.87	Portsmouth	10	2						
				£20,000	16.02.88	Huddersfield Town	16	2			1			
					09.09.88	Barnsley	64 + 2	2	3 + 1	2	6			
				£35,000	28.02.90	Hull City	16				2			
Carl Shutt Div.2'90	5.10	11.13	10.10.61	Sheffield		Spalding U								
					13.05.85	Sheffield Wed	36 + 4	3	4 + 1		16	1	4	
				£55,000	30.10.87	Bristol City	39 + 7	5 + 2	7 + 1	10 + 1	11	4	4	4
					23.03.89	Leeds Utd	9 + 14		1	0 + 2	6			2
Alan Smith E: 4;B.1;S-P.3; F.Lg.1; Div1'89	6.3	12.0	02.11.62	Bromsgrove		Alvechurch								
					14.06.82	Leicester City	190 + 10	8 + 1	8		76	4	4	
				£800,000	26.03.87	Arsenal	109 + 4	16 + 1	7	3	44	9	1	

ANDY ANSAH, moved from Dorking to Southend United.

EDDIE McGOLDRICK, another Crystal Palace player with non-league roots.

PLAYERS NAME Honours	Ht	Wt	Birthdate	Birthplace Transfers	Contract Date	Clubs	APPEARANCES League	L/Cup	FA Cup	Other	GOALS Lg	L/C	FAC	Oth
Darren Smith						Burton Albion								
					Sept 1990	Wolverhampton W.								
David Smith	5.11	11.12	25.06.61	Sidcup		Welling								
				£3,000	23.08.86	Gillingham	90+14	7	4+1	11+4	10		1	3
					03.08.89	Bristol City	45	2	7	2+1	4	1		
Kevan Smith	6.3	12.6	13.12.59	Eaglescliff		Stockton								
				f	28.09.79	Darlington	242+3	10+1	18	4	11		1	
				f	31.07.85	Rotherham Utd	59	6	5	2	4		1	
				£60,000	04.12.86	Coventry City	5+1		1					
				£40,000	11.05.88	York City	31+1			2	5			
				(V.C.)	09.06.89	Darlington	39		5	5	3			1
Mark Smith	5.9	12.2	19.12.61	Sheffield		Sheffield Utd								
Via Worksop Town, Gainsborough T, Kettering Town to					15.07.88	Rochdale	26+1	2	2	2	7			
					10.02.89	Huddersfield Town	56+8	3	4	2	9		1	1
Neville Southall	6.1	12.2	16.09.58	Llandudno		Bangor								
W:44;Div1'85'87;FAC'84;CS'84'85;ECWC'85						Winsford U								
				£6,000	14.06.80	Bury	39		5					
				Loan	27.01.83	Port Vale	9							
				£150,000	13.07.81	Everton	291	41	47	24				
Dean Spink	6.1	13.6	22.01.67	Birmingham		Halesowen Town								
					01.07.89	Aston Villa								
				Loan	20.11.89	Scarborough	3			1	2			
				Loan	01.02.90	Bury	6				1			
				£75,000	15.03.90	Shrewsbury Town	13				5			
Stuart Storer	5.11	11.8	16.01.67	Harborough	23.08.83	Mansfield Town (T)	0+1							
SVT'89				Free	10.01.85	Birmingham City	5+3	1						
				P.E	06.03.87	Everton								
				Loan	23.07.87	Wigan Ath	9+2	2		1				
					24.12.87	Bolton W	60+16	4	2+2	9+3	7		1	1
Michael Stowell	6.2	12.6	19.04.65	Portsmouth		Leyland Mo								
				NC	14.02.85	Preston N.E								
					12.12.85	Everton								
				Loan	03.09.87	Cfld	14			3				
				Loan	24.12.87	York City	6							
				Loan		Port Vale	7			1				
				Loan	17.03.89	Wolverhampton W	7			1				
				Loan	08.02.90	Preston N.E	2							
					28.06.90	Wolverhampton W								
Ken Swain					06.09.88	Crewe Alexandra	83+1	4	9	6	1			
(D) Nick Tanner	6.2	13.7	24.05.65	Bristol		Bristol Rovers	79+2	5	10	5	3			
				£20,000		Liverpool	2+2							
				Loan	01.03.90	Norwich City	6							
Bob Taylor	5.10	11.9	03.02.67	Horden	27.03.86	Leeds Utd	33+9	3+1	1	4+1	9	3		1
					23.03.89	Bristol City	49	2	7	1	35	2	5	
Paul Tester	5.9	10.10	10.07.59	Stroud		Cheltenham								
WC84				£10,000	21.07.83	Shrewsbury Town	86+12	7+3	1+3	2+1	12	1		
				£10,000	31.08.88	Hereford Utd	68+6	5	4	7	11	1	1	1
Dean Thomas	5.9	11.8	19.12.61	Bedworth		Nuneaton Borough								
				£7,000	20.07.81	Wimbledon	57	2		5+1	8			
						Aachen (Ger)								
						Fort								
				£50,000	04.08.88	Northampton T	74	6	6	5	12		1	
				£175,000	21.03.90	Notts County	10				1			
Steve Thompson	5.10	12.0	28.07.55	Sheffield		Boston Utd								
				£15,000	01.04.80	Lincoln City	153+1	17	9	3	8		1	1
				£25,000	15.08.85	Charlton Ath	95	6+1	3	8				
				£40,000	14.07.88	Leicester City								
				£20,000	15.11.88	Sheffield Utd	20		2	1	1			
				Free	17.08.89	Lincoln City	27	1	2					
Adrian Thorpe	5.7	10.10	25.11.63	Chesterfield	24.08.82	Mansfield Town	0+2				1			
						Heanor Town								
					06.08.85	Bradford City	9+8	3+1	1	1				
				Loan	04.11.86	Tranmere Rovers								
				£50,000	06.11.87	Notts County	48+11	3	1	1+1	9	1	1	2
				£75,000	15.08.89	Walsall	24+3	2	2	2+1				
				£50,000	23.03.90	Northampton T	13				3			
Andrew Tillson	6.2	12.7	30.06.68	Huntingdon		Kettering Town								
				f	14.07.88	Grimsby Town	86+1	6	9	3	5			
Andy Toman	5.10	11.7	07.03.62	Northallerton		Bishop Auckland								
				£10,000	16.08.85	Lincoln City	21+3	2		0+1	4			
					23.01.87	Hartlepool Utd	112	4	9	7	28		4	
				£40,000	01.08.89	Darlington	39+1	1	4	5	7		1	

PLAYERS NAME Honours	Ht	Wt	Birthdate	Birthplace Transfers	Contract Date	Clubs	APPEARANCES				GOALS			
							League	L/Cup	FA Cup	Other	Lg	L/C	FAC	Oth
Andy Townsend	5.10	12.7	27.07.63	London		Weymouth			1					
Ei: 17					15.01.85	Southampton	77+6	7+1	2+3	3+2	5			
				£300,000	31.08.88	Norwich City	66+5	3+1	7	3	8		2	
				£1,200,000	05.07.90	Chelsea								
Geoff Twentyman	601	13.2	10.03.59	Liverpool		Chorley								
Div.3'90					25.08.83	Preston N.E	95+3	11	3+1	4+1	4	4		
					22.11.86	Bristol Rovers	170+3	7	11	13	5			
Imre Varadi	5.8	11.2	08.07.59	Paddington		Letchworth								
Div.2'90				Free	01.03.78	Sheffield Utd	6+4		2		4			
				£80,000	01.03.79	Everton	81	4	5		39	1	2	
				£100,000	27.08.81	Newcastle Utd	81	4	5		39	1	2	
				£150,000	26.08.83	Sheffield Wed.	72+4	12	7		33	2	5	
				£285,000	19.07.85	West Brom A	30+2	5	2	2	9	4		
					17.10.86	Manchester City	56+9	4	6	2	9			2
				P.E.	30.09.88	Sheffield Wed.	14+8	1+1	2	1	3	1	2	
				£50,000	27.08.81	Leeds Utd	12+1				2			
Alan Walker	6.1	12.2	17.12.59	Ashton-U-Lyme	23.08.78	Stockport Co								
FAT'83						Telford								
					14.10.83	Lincoln City	32+1	2	5	4	4		1	2
				£32,500	30.07.85	Millwall	92	7	9	6	8	3	1	1
				£50,000	25.03.88	Gillingham	67	4	2	3	3	1		1
David Walter	6.3	13.3				Bideford								
Div.4'90					02.12.88	Exeter City	44	7	2	2				
				Loan	08.03.90	Plymouth A								
					25.07.90	Plymouth A								
Keith Walwyn	6.1	13.2	17.02.56	Jamaica	02.11.79	Chesterfield	3	0+1	1+1	0+1	2			
Div.4.84				£4,000	28.07.81	York City	245	18	24	4	117	9	11	1
				£35,000	03.07.87	Blackpool	51+18	6+1	4	6	17		1	1
				Free	03.07.89	Carlisle Utd	39+1	2	1	2+1	11	1		
Mark Ward	5.5	10.0	10.10.62	Hutton	05.09.80	Everton (A)								
ESP1				Free		Northwich Victoria			3				2	
				£10,000	19.07.83	Oldham Ath	84	5	3		12			
				£250,000	15.08.85	West Ham U	163+2	20+1	17	6	11	2		
				£1,000,000	29.12.89	Manchester City	19		3		3			
Peter Ward	5.10	11.7	15.10.64	Durham		Chester le St								
					07.01.87	Huddersfield Town	24+13	1+1	2	1	2			
				Free		Rochdale	39+1	2	5	2	5		1	
Andrew Watson					12.09.88	Halifax Town	75+8	5+1	6	6	15	2	1	1
					31.07.90	Swansea City								
Paul West			Aged 20			Washford Mill FC								
						Alcester Lord Nelson								
						Alcester Town								
					1991	Port Vale								
Paul Wheeler	5.7	11.2	03.01.65	Caerphilly	05.01.83	Bristol Rovers (A)								
E: S				f		Aberaman Ath								
				f	29.08.85	Cardiff City	72+29	5+2	3+1	5+3	9	2	1	2
				N.C	16.10.89	Hull City								
				f	01.02.90	Hereford Utd	21			1	8			
Steve White	5.10	11.4	02.01.59	Chipping Sodbury		Mangotsfield								
Div.2.82					11.07.77	Bristol Rovers	46+4	2	3		20	1	3	
				£200,000	24.12.79	Luton Town	63+9	3+1	2		25	1		
					30.07.82	Charlton Ath	29	2			12			
				Loan	28.01.83	Lincoln City	2+1							
				Loan	24.03.83	Luton Town	4							
					26.08.83	Bristol Rovers	89+12	8	7+1	5+2	24	2	2	1
				Free	08.02.86	Swindon Town	129+16	11+3	5+3	19+1	57	6		13
Billy Whitehurst	6.0	13.0	10.06.59	Thurnscoe		Mexborough Town								
					25.10.80	Hull City	176+17	13+1	10	7	47	5	3	1
				£230,000	06.12.85	Newcastle Utd	29	1+1	1		7			
				£175,000	16.10.86	Oxford Utd	36+4	3+2	1+1	2	4			2
				£120,000	12.02.88	Reading	17	2			8			
				£100,000	16.09.88	Sunderland	17			1	3			
				P.E	29.12.88	Hull City	36		3+1		5		2	
				£35,000	07.02.90	Sheffield Utd	9+5		2					
Michael Whitlow	6.1	11.6	13.01.68	Liverpool		Witton Albion								
Div.2'90				£10,000	11.11.88	Leeds Utd	45+4	2		6	2			
Guy Whittingham					09.06.89	Portsmouth	39+3	2	1	1	23		1	
Steven Wigley	5.9	10.12	15.10.61	Ashton-under-Lyme		Curzon Ash								
					24.03.81	Nottm. Forest	69+13	8+1	5	10	2	1		
					25.10.85	Sheffield Utd	21+7	1+1	1	1	1			
				PE	20.03.87	Birmingham City	87	6	4	2	4		1	
					23.03.89	Portsmouth	100	8	2	2	4			

PLAYERS NAME Honours	Ht	Wt	Birthdate	Birthplace Transfers	Contract Date	Clubs	APPEARANCES				GOALS			
							League	L/Cup	FA Cup	Other	Lg	L/C	FAC	Oth
Russell Wilcox	6.0	11.10	25.03.64	Hemsworth	28.05.80	Doncaster Rovers (A)	1							
E: S-P,Div.4'87						Frickley Athletic			7				1	
				£15,000	30.06.86	Northampton T	137+4	6	10	8	9			1
					01.08.90	Hull City								
Richard Wilkins	6.0	11.6	28.05.65	Haverhill		Haverhill Rov								
					20.11.86	Colchester Utd	107+2	4	5+3	8+2	19		4	3
				Free	25.07.90	Cambridge Utd								
Andy Williams	6.0	11.10	29.07.62	Birmingham		Sutton Coldfield Tn								
Div.2'90				£20,000	24.07.85	Coventry City	3+6			0+1				
				P	16.10.86	Rotherham Utd	87	8	6	5	13			2
				£175,000	11.11.88	Leeds Utd	7+11		1					
Paul Williams	5.7	10.3	16.08.65	West Ham		Woodford T			1					
					23.02.87	Charlton Ath	74+8	6	6+1		23	3	3	
				Loan	20.10.87	Brentford	7			1	3			3
				£		Sheffield Wed								
Kevin McAllister	5.6	10.0	08.11.68	Falkirk		Falkirk	59+5	2+1	2		18			
Div2'89; FMC'86; ZDC'90				£34,000	23.06.85	Chelsea	69+19	9+2	2+2	10+7	7	1	1	3
				Loan	01.03.88	Falkirk								
Tony Witter						Yeading								
						Uxbridge								
						Grays Athletic								
					Sept 1989	Crystal Palace								
Ian Wright	5.10	11.0	03.11.63	Woolwich		GreenwichB								
				Free	02.08.85	Crystal Palace	150+19	14	6+2	13+2	70	6	2	10
Eric Young	6.3	12.6	25.03.60	Singapore		St Annes								
via Slough Town to				£10,000	01.11.82	Brighton & H.A	126	8	11	2	10		1	
FAC'88				£70,000	29.07.87	Wimbledon	96+3	12	5	5	9		1	
						Crystal Palace								

COHEN GRIFFITH, seen here nearly scoring for Kettering against Darlington, is now with Cardiff City.

Thank you very much

Once again you have responded to our plea for the photos needed for this book and I hope I have credited you all in the list below, if your name does not appear to be mentioned, my sincere apologies, maybe your name was not on the back of the photo.
So once again thank you for all your efforts they have been appreciated.

Paul Barber
Bill Beminster
Richard Birch
Peter Burrin
Alan Casse
Alan Cave
Mick Cheney
M Close
Paul Collins
Tony Colliver
Duncan Cook
Jo Corkett
Malcolm Couzens
Steve Daniels
John Denton
Andrew Eggleton
Keith Gillard
Peter Haynes
David Hewitson
David Hills
Colin Horne
J W Hutton
Kappa Sports Pictures
Derrick Kinsey

Tim Lancaster
W Leigh
Eric Marsh
Messenger Newspaper
Dennis Nicholson
Northamptonshire E. Tel
Bob Patie
Jeff Pitt
Portsmouth News
Roger Price
Neil Pugh
E F Roffey
John Rooney
Shropshire Star Ltd
Keith Slater
Somerset Gazzett
Sutton Observer
Bob Thomas
John Vass
Mark Ward
Dave West
Bob Whitaker
Willenshaw Times & News

PAUL CULPIN, now with Peterborough Utd., seen here scoring for the England Semi-Pro team.